Official Microsoft FrontPage 98 Book

Kerry A. Lehto and
W. Brett Polonsky

Microsoft

PUBLISHED BY
Microsoft Press
A Division of Microsoft Corporation
One Microsoft Way
Redmond, Washington 98052-6399

Library of Congress Cataloging-in-Publication Data
Lehto, Kerry A., 1966-
Official Microsoft FrontPage 98 Book / Kerry A. Lehto and W. Brett Polonsky.
p. cm.
Includes index.
ISBN 1-57231-629-2
1. Microsoft FrontPage. 2. Web sites--Design. 3. Web publishing.
I. Polonsky, W. Brett, 1965- . II. Title.
TK5105.8885.F76L44 1997
005.7'2--dc21 97-33679
CIP

Printed and bound in the United States of America.

2 3 4 5 6 7 8 9 QMQM 2 1 0 9 8

Distributed to the book trade in Canada by Macmillan of Canada, a division of Canada Publishing Corporation.

A CIP catalogue record for this book is available from the British Library.

Microsoft Press books are available through booksellers and distributors worldwide. For further information about international editions, contact your local Microsoft Corporation office. Or contact Microsoft Press International directly at fax (425) 936-7329. Visit our Web site at mspress.microsoft.com.

Acquisitions Editor: Casey D. Doyle
Project Editor: Maureen Williams Zimmerman

For Janell, Gage & Emma,
who lived through six long
weeks with a crazy man,
and didn't even complain
that much.
I love you!
—WBP

To my ultra-sensational family
and friends, everyone who loves
Jeep CJs as much as I do, and
Kaline, my faithful Siamese kitty.
Sleep tight, Kaline, you'll get more
wet food in the morning.
—KAL

Table of Contents

Foreword .... *xv*
Introduction .... *xxi*

PART I

The Beginning Stages

1 FrontPage and the Internet 3
- It's Here, It's Now 3
- Coming Up 11

2 The Web Site Development Process 13
- Planning the Information Flow 13
- Planning an Intranet Site 17
- Coming Up 21

PART II

Creating and Managing Your Site

3 Inside the FrontPage Explorer 25
- Your Site, from See to Shining See 25
- Starting the Explorer 26
- Creating a Site from Scratch 28
- Opening an Existing Site 31
- The Explorer Point of View 32
- One Button Publishing 60
- Performing Other Functions of the Explorer 62
- Coming Up 71

4 Templates and Wizards 73
Life in the Fast Lane 73
Templates 74
Wizards 81
Coming Up 101

5 Managing Your Web Site 103
The Explorer Makes It Easy 103
Security 104
Testing Your Site 112
Going Live with Your Site 113
Updating Your Site 114
Coming Up 116

PART III Building Your Pages

6 Creating Your Pages 121
HTML Got You Down? 121
The Editor in Brief: WYSIWYG 122
Let the Construction Begin 125
Working with Page Files 134
Making Tables 143
WYSIWYG Frames 160
Coming Up 170

7 Fine-Tuning Your Pages 173
I Wonder What This Would Look Like… 173
Fonts 173
Paragraph-Level Formatting 178
Further Enhancements 184
Active Elements 200
Page Properties 210
The Editor View Tabs 214
Utilities and Useful Commands 217
Coming Up 227

8 Getting into Graphics 229
Images: A Balancing Act 229
Graphic Formats 230
Color Management 231
Bringing in Those Images 235
The Images Are In—Now What? 238
Cool Stuff You Can Do to an Image 245
Coming Up 255

9 FrontPage Components and Forms 257
We All Need a Break 257
What Are Components? 257
Creating and Using Forms 273
Coming Up 307

PART IV
Finishing Touches

10 Advanced Features 311
Getting Interactive 311
The Advanced Toolbar 312
Inserting HTML 312
Inserting an ActiveX Control 312
Inserting a Java Applet 316
Inserting a Plug-In 318
Inserting VBScript or JavaScript 320
Cascading Stylesheets (CSS) 321
Dynamic HTML—What the Heck Is It? 331
Database Integration 333
Give Me a PUSH 336
Accessibility 339
Other Advanced Features 339
Coming Up 340

11 Web Servers 343
FrontPage Knows Servers 343
Server Administration 347

APPENDIX A

Installing FrontPage

Index 366

Acknowledgments

This is the third version of this book in under two years, and I've learned one important thing. You have to find something that keeps you going, keeps the motivation level up, and helps get you through the long hours of writing. For me it was constant music, a steady diet of Neil Diamond, *In My Lifetime,* with a little Steel Pulse and Beck thrown in for variety. Besides that motivating factor, in order to produce a book like this, you need to be associated with great people, and on that I've been very lucky:

Randy Forgaard, for his fabulous foreword and his FrontPage vision.

To everyone at Microsoft Press: Casey Doyle, for helping to put the project together and giving me the chance to do this one myself; Maureen Zimmerman, for managing the project and for putting out the fires; and to all of the others at Press who had a hand in this book.

Robert Akimoto, my Skywards business partner, and his wife Susan.

Last, but certainly not least, to Kerry Lehto, a great writer, a true friend, and a generous collaborator. I missed you on this one, it wasn't quite the same.

The sound that the keyboard makes when you type in that last word, is a beautiful noise, if you know what I mean.

Foreword

On the afternoon of Thursday, April 7, 1994, my wife took an urgent phone call from a man on a carphone. He had gotten my name from my MIT master's thesis adviser, and was calling to offer me a job. Thinking he was a headhunter, my wife declined to give him my work phone number, but said he could phone back that evening. He was worried about the delay, but nonetheless called back at 7:00 P.M. and we chatted. The man was Charles H. Ferguson, a well-known computer industry consultant and author on technology policy and corporate strategy. We met and talked several times over that weekend. Four days after the first phone call, I quit my job and became cofounder of Vermeer Technologies, Inc., named after Charles's favorite 17th century Dutch painter. As it turns out, Charles's general sense of urgency was extraordinarily justified.

In the beginning, Charles was the idea and business person, and I was the technical person charged with transforming the ideas into concrete product features that could be implemented by a small group of talented engineers within a reasonable timeframe. When we began, we actually had not heard of the Web. Charles's original notion was that it was wasteful for companies like CompuServe, Dow Jones, Bloomberg, and Apple to have each spent millions of dollars building proprietary online services with incompatible client software and based on outmoded mainframe server technology. Our goal was to build inexpensive, standardized, and interoperable client, server, and authoring software that any company could buy to set up a dial-up online service for information dissemination and commerce. End-users could run the same client software to access all online services built using our technology.

This idea changed dramatically a month after the company was formed. In May 1994, we got wind that the Internet was starting to be adopted by businesses, and that a new infrastructure called the World Wide Web provided online service functionality on top of Internet protocols. Mosaic, the first graphical user interface for the Web, had been released five months earlier by the National Center for Supercomputing Applications (NCSA). Netscape Communications Corp. (then called Mosaic Communications) had been founded in April (the same time as Vermeer), and would release their famous commercial Web browser toward the end of that year.

It occurred to us that the Web provided much of what we were trying to achieve: standardized protocols (HTTP), server software that supported those protocols (various Web servers), universal client software that supported those protocols (various Web browsers), and even a communications infrastructure (the Internet) that was more robust and convenient than we were planning (dial-up to each online service). The major missing piece, with respect to our original plans, was a complete, visual authoring tool for nonprogrammers to create, maintain, and administer whole Web sites (online services), including the individual pages that comprise such sites. The creation of such a Web authoring tool became the focus of Vermeer.

We were extraordinarily fortunate to attract the most talented group of individuals I have ever met, despite the fact that we had no funding yet (except for direct expenses, paid for by Charles), and asked everyone to take no salary for many months. Andy Schulert and Peter Amstein, both seasoned professionals, were our first two engineering hires and became our two technical team leaders. We were joined by many other first-rate engineers, plus excellent marketing, sales, quality assurance, documentation, technical support, administrative, and executive personnel. Every one of them was a consummate professional, driven and focused on the task at hand.

The name "Vermeer" turned out to be an interesting choice. Many thought we were a Dutch company, and we got e-mail from strangers in Holland. Early on, we were contacted by Vermeer Manufacturing Co., a maker of construction equipment in Iowa, asking if we were interested in giving them our registered Internet domain name, *vermeer.com*. (We weren't.) During the big exhibition of Vermeer paintings in Washington, D.C., art lovers visited our Web site expecting...well...art. But the nontraditional company name also helped us stand out a bit from the sea of other high-tech companies.

For the first eight months, everyone at Vermeer worked out of their homes, with e-mail and fax machines keeping all of us in touch. We had weekly get-togethers at the Cambridge, Massachusetts, offices of Andy Kerr, our part-time CFO. Charles, Andy Kerr, and I shopped around for venture capital financing, toting a Visual Basic mock-up of our software written by Peter, while the engineers worked hard on a functional prototype. At that time, it was still not completely clear that the Web would be an unqualified success. Our business plan forecasted sales of 500 units of our product in the first year, and it went on to explain how our software could be ported to Lotus Notes or our own infrastructure if the Internet failed to catch on.

Vermeer closed its first round of $4 million funding in January 1995, with Sigma Partners and Matrix Partners as lead investors, and Atlas Venture as an additional investor. This cash let us lease some office space in Cambridge, start paying modest salaries, purchase needed computer equipment, move beyond the prototype, and start writing the actual software in earnest.

While Vermeer was building its first product, the Web became an unprecedented success. There were only an estimated 10,000 Web sites in existence when Vermeer was formed, but one year later there were approximately 500,000 such sites, including both external sites on the Internet and intranet sites within organizations. By just about any measure—communications traffic, new Web sites going up, downloads of Web browsers, new Internet accounts—the Web was growing at twenty percent per month, the fastest-growing phenomenon in economic history.

Vermeer shipped version 1.0 of its product in October 1995, just one week behind schedule. The name of the product, FrontPage, was suggested by Mitch Kapor, the founder of Lotus. On one hand, FrontPage was a great success, winning industry awards and praises from customers. On the other hand, during the brief life of Vermeer, Web authoring had advanced from a curious backwater to a major focus of some of the largest players in the software industry. Tiny Vermeer, with just 35 employees, suddenly found itself in the hot seat.

At around this time, Microsoft Corporation became interested in Web authoring tools. Steven Sinofsky, group program manager for the Microsoft Office product line, discovered the 30-day evaluation version of FrontPage 1.0 posted on the Vermeer Web site. Steven showed it to Mike Mathieu, program manager for Microsoft Word, who wrote up a 10-page review. Mike showed it to Chris Peters, vice president of the Microsoft Office and a 14-year veteran of Microsoft. Chris gave FrontPage to Bill Gates to try out during Bill's annual "think week." At Vermeer, we watched our Web server logs as 25 different Microsoft people downloaded FrontPage 1.0 over a two-week period.

So, on November 8, 1995, Chris Peters called us up. They really liked the product. They felt we had just the right idea—focusing on building a whole Web site, not just creating individual pages. They appreciated the fact that FrontPage looked just like a Microsoft Office application. They were impressed that we seemed to be 9 to 12 months ahead of the industry. They wanted to know if we were interested in some sort of relationship, anywhere from co-marketing, to technology licensing, to the "full meal deal" as Chris called it—being acquired by Microsoft.

We took a hard look at Microsoft and were extremely impressed. They had recently transformed themselves into a highly Internet-focused company. They were extraordinarily good at shipping products. Chris Peters himself would resign from his highly visible role in charge of the Microsoft Office product unit to personally take command of tiny FrontPage. And we realized that our efforts would be multiplied a thousandfold by joining Microsoft. So, on January 12, 1996, we did.

I got my first taste of Life in Redmond when I visited Microsoft headquarters together with Vermeer's President, John Mandile, to participate in the announcement of the acquisition. We found a huge, professionally designed vinyl banner hanging in Building 18, welcoming Vermeer to Microsoft. The Associated Press leaked the story of the acquisition a day early, keeping busy a small army from Microsoft's public relations firm. Literally overnight, Microsoft graphic artists created a complete mock-up of a new Microsoft FrontPage box (wrapped around a box of Excel—who's to know?) for Bill Gates to hold during the photo session later that day. Microsoft Studios zipped around campus, shooting 20 minutes of "B-roll" video segments (Gates being interviewed about the acquisition, Sinofsky using FrontPage, Peters/Mandile/Forgaard pretending to talk earnestly about something, Microsoft flag waving in the breeze) to be shown behind newscasters nationwide as they reported the story. Microsoft webmasters moved Vermeer's Web site to Redmond by the next morning. John and I participated with Microsoft officials in a giant conference call announcing the deal to 350 journalists. I did FrontPage demos for hundreds of Microsoft employees. Using a Redmond-to-Atlanta satellite linkup, Chris Peters was interviewed live on CNN. The acquisition was reported by local television affiliates around the country and seen by 50 million viewers. The Wall Street Journal was the first national paper to break the story, on the first page of the business section. The Microsoft machine in action was an awesome sight indeed.

Virtually the entire Vermeer engineering, quality assurance, and documentation teams moved to Microsoft headquarters in Redmond, Washington. Twenty-five families said good-bye to everything in Boston, and hello to the trees and lattes and grunge bands of the Pacific Northwest. You could almost see the yanked roots dangling from beneath the airplane. FrontPage 1.1 was released to manufacturing on April 24, 1996, just a few days after everyone arrived in Seattle.

None of us were really prepared for the magnitude of what happened next. In June 1996, the first month of availability, FrontPage 1.1 hit PC

Week's list of best-selling retail software in the #22 slot. By July, we were #7. In August, FrontPage was the third best-selling software package in retail stores across the country, outselling even Microsoft Office itself. Whereas Vermeer had sold a total of 275 copies of FrontPage in the company's short life, Microsoft sold 150,000 copies of FrontPage in the first three months. FrontPage 97, released to manufacturing on November 13, 1996, was the first Microsoft product to be released simultaneously in six languages. It easily broke the sales thresholds of FrontPage 1.1 and became the leading Web authoring software worldwide.

As I write this, the Beta version of FrontPage 98 will be posted to the Microsoft Web site in just two days. It is the fourth release of FrontPage in less than two years. It is the most significant release yet, adding site-wide themes, automatic navigation bars, WYSIWYG frames editing, mouse-drawn tables, and many other new capabilities and ease-of-use features. The goal for this release of FrontPage is, as always, to take the best of the latest Web technologies and make them accessible to everyone. We hope you will enjoy using it as much as the FrontPage team has enjoyed creating it.

W. Brett Polonsky and Kerry Lehto, the authors of this book, share our vision for FrontPage. They had access to some of the earliest builds of FrontPage 98, and it shows in the depth and insight of their coverage here, with clear descriptions, tips, and advice on all of the new and existing FrontPage features. I found this book to be thoroughly accessible, informative, and fun, and I believe you will, too.

With time comes change. Today, if you visit www.vermeer.com, you'll find out about construction equipment rather than Web authoring. Our large photographic reproduction of Jan Vermeer's *The Concert* now hangs in Redmond instead of Cambridge. But as the months pass and the future of the Web unfolds before us, I know that there will always be a spark of tiny Vermeer at Microsoft...and in FrontPage.

Randy Forgaard
Co-founder of Vermeer Technologies, Inc.
August 9, 1997

Introduction

Welcome to FrontPage

The Internet, the World Wide Web, intranets, extranets—all of these things have become as common as the telephone, for businesses as well as for the home enthusiast. The vast array of technologies that have taken hold alongside them have become a part of our everyday lives, and will continue to change the way we live and work. Intranets, which use Internet technologies within a business or across an enterprise, once the latest trend, have spawned a new one. The newest type of "net" has businesses sharing information by linking intranets together to form the new "buzz," extranets. One can only guess what will be next.

Similar to other booms the computing world has witnessed, thousands of companies have formed to search for a piece of the Internet pie. Scores of good Internet-related products are available, but most of us don't have the time or the expertise required to sort through them, learn their pros and cons, and put them to use, whether at work or at home.

Microsoft FrontPage makes it easy for you to establish a presence on the World Wide Web or create a Web site for your organization's intranet. Designed to fit seamlessly into the Microsoft Office suite of applications, FrontPage is the first easy-to-use Internet client *and* server product that allows you to develop an entire Web site and connect it to many kinds of servers. If you want to set up a Web site but you're not a programming whiz, don't worry—FrontPage can do the programming for you. But FrontPage is also robust enough for amateur and professional developers who do want to toy with the code.

FrontPage comes with several additional elements, collectively called the FrontPage Bonus Pack:

- **Microsoft Image Composer**, which allows you to create and manipulate images for your Web site, and comes with image effects and more than 200 MB of sample photos that you can use.
- **Microsoft Personal Web Server**, a version of Microsoft's Internet Information Server (IIS) that runs on Windows 95 and Windows NT Workstation. The Microsoft Personal Web Server has improved performance and additional features over the FrontPage Personal Web Server, which is included as a part of FrontPage.
- **Web Publishing Wizard**, which allows you to publish your FrontPage Web sites to any Internet service provider that you have an account for, or to online services such as America Online and CompuServe. You typically use this wizard for servers that are not running the FrontPage Server Extensions.
- **Microsoft Internet Explorer**, which is Microsoft's Web browser.

Talk About Easy!

The Official Microsoft FrontPage 98 Book is your in-depth, one-stop shop for learning the ins and outs of FrontPage. You'll learn how to develop and maintain a Web site with the FrontPage Explorer, develop high-quality Web pages with the FrontPage Editor, and run your Web site with one of the Personal Web Servers for Windows 95 or another server of your choice. You'll also learn how to incorporate material from Microsoft Office files into your site, and link to, from, and within those files. You'll learn about some exciting new additions in FrontPage 98, such as adding graphic Themes to your site, WYSIWYG frames, dynamic HTML support, improved Explorer views, cascading stylesheet support, and a completely new image toolbar, which is like having a mini image-editing suite right in the Editor.

Because some of you like to lift the hood and tinker with the controls, this book also includes information about more advanced topics, such as Secure Sockets Layer (SSL) security, connecting to ODBC-compliant databases using the Database Region Wizard, editing the source code of your Web pages, and FrontPage's server administration tools and Server Extensions.

A Look at the Book

Part 1, "The Beginning Stages," introduces you to FrontPage; talks about the birth of the Internet, the World Wide Web, and intranets; and explains how FrontPage fits into all three scenes. You'll learn some great tips on producing sites for the Web and for your organization's intranet, and you'll learn about the exciting new ways that FrontPage works in conjunction with Microsoft Office.

Part 2, "Creating and Managing Your Site," tells you everything you need to know about creating and administering Web sites in the FrontPage Explorer. In the Explorer you can view your site in different ways—including the exciting new Navigation view, which lets you create a site map and translate it to navigation on your pages. In Part 2 you'll also learn how to use the FrontPage templates and wizards. FrontPage has designed dozens of new Web, page and frames templates—just pick one and you're on your way. Web site management, including changing passwords, access privileges, and much more, is also explained in detail in this part.

Part 3, "Building Your Pages," looks into the FrontPage Editor, which you'll use to create and edit your Web pages. Here, you'll find in-depth instructions for creating terrific-looking Web pages that can include video, audio, marquees, colored text, tables, frames, character formatting, font styles, and much more. You'll find the Editor as easy to use as a word processor. Part 3 also contains some hearty content on Web site graphics, how FrontPage uses them, and ways to make them appear faster in a browser. A detailed look at the FrontPage components and forms is also presented in this part.

Part 4, "The Finishing Touches," introduces you to the many advanced features of FrontPage, like cascading stylesheets, dynamic HTML, push technology using the Channel Definition Wizard, the Database Region Wizard, ActiveX, VB and JavaScript, as well as some accessibility tips. The final chapter talks about using servers with FrontPage. Here, you'll learn about the Microsoft Personal Web Server and the FrontPage Personal Web Server, which allow you to test Web pages and set up an intranet on your local computer or network. You'll also learn about the FrontPage Server Extensions, which extend a server's capability to take advantage of features available in FrontPage. These extensions are available for a wide variety of servers that use platforms such as Microsoft Windows 95, Microsoft Windows NT, and various flavors of UNIX.

The appendix shows you how to install FrontPage on a computer with Windows 95 or Windows NT.

Tips, Shortcuts, Notes, and Warnings

The book also includes Shortcuts, Tips, Notes, and Warnings that provide more details about the subject at hand. Shortcuts show you ways to save time, such as clicking a toolbar button or using a keyboard shortcut instead of using a menu command. Just as there's more than one way to get from

Cairo to Cooperstown, Tips offer alternative ways to carry out tasks, and they give you additional information on a topic. Notes give you a little something extra to think about, and Warnings caution you against performing actions that can lead to trouble.

Who Should Read This Book?

The Official Microsoft FrontPage 98 Book is designed for both beginning and advanced FrontPage users. Just as FrontPage is designed for nonprogrammers, so is this book. It's ideal for those who want to learn how to use FrontPage to create a World Wide Web site or an intranet site.

This book picks up where the product's online help leaves off; within these pages, you'll find in-depth descriptions and scenarios about possible uses of FrontPage that draw on our experience in Web site creation, design, and management. We hope this book will help you fill in the holes and answer your questions as you make your FrontPage sites "sights to see."

PART I

1 FrontPage and the Internet

2 The Web Site Development Process

The Beginning Stages

CHAPTER 1

FrontPage and the Internet

It's Here, It's Now

There's no escaping the *Internet;* it's become almost as essential as the fax machine. Businesses large and small are using it to tap information sources world-wide, communicate via e-mail, and post *World Wide Web* sites; millions of individuals "surf" the Web from their homes. The sites filling today's Internet differ considerably from those populating it just a year ago. Web sites have become increasingly interactive, from enabling visitors to buy and sell via secure transactions, to incorporating streaming audio and video. You're as likely to come across a site for a large corporation advertising its wares as you are of finding a site where someone is showing off pictures of his kids or sharing an old family recipe.

This chapter provides some background on the Internet, the World Wide Web, and intranets. It describes how FrontPage fits into this scene, explains how easily it integrates with Microsoft Office, and shows how *you* might fit into the latest wave of this technology.

The Net, the Web: What's the Difference?

The Internet is older than you might think—it's been around for almost 30 years. Considering that the first electrical computer was built just over half a century ago, the Internet is quite the veteran in the computing world. It started out in the late 1960s as a U.S. government communications network (called *ARPAnet*), and was used mainly by the government, universities, and other research institutions until the mid-1980s, when it expanded and took on the name *Internet*.

So How Does It Work?

Computers interoperating with other computers within a group constitutes a *network*. The Internet is one huge network of computers that consists of thousands of smaller networks world-wide. You might think of a computer as a leaf on a tree: many similar leafs comprise the branches, and you could think of each of these branches as a network of leafs. All of these networks together form the entire tree, and there you have it—in computing terms, the Internet. The diagram in Figure 1-1 illustrates the basic organizational makeup of the Internet.

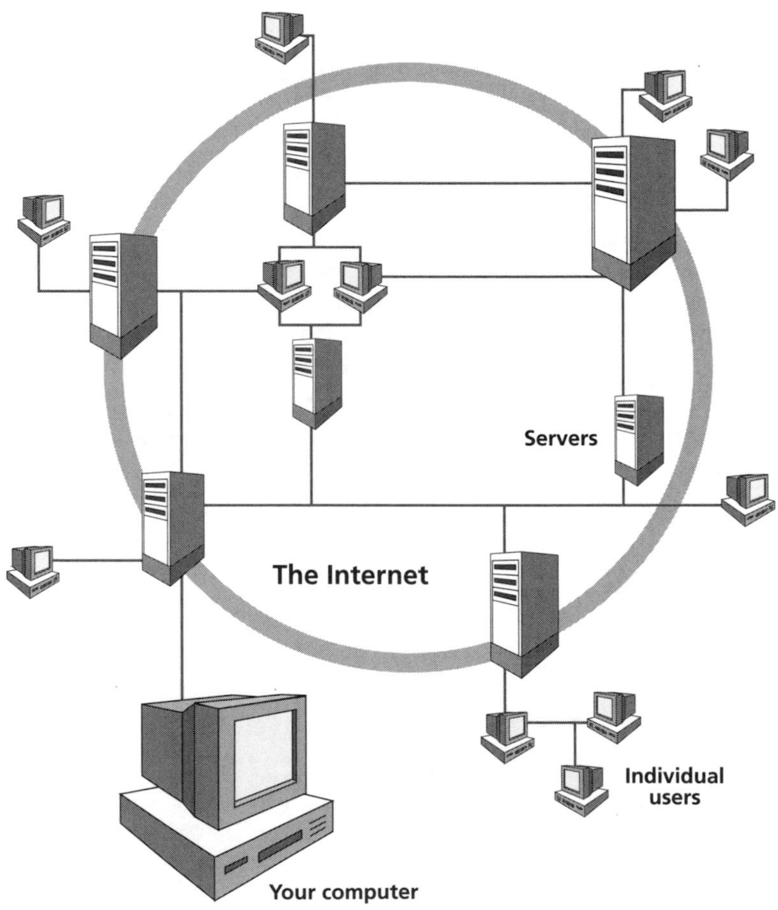

Figure 1-1

The computers on the Internet share a common language, and that language is stated in *protocols*—a protocol is a set of agreed-upon rules governing how they interact. The standard protocols used for exchanging data on the Internet are Transmission Control Protocol and Internet Protocol; the combination of the two is known as *TCP/IP*. TCP/IP organizes information into tidy little packages before shipping it across the network. Each package contains a portion of the information being sent, along with a description of what the information is, where it's coming from, and where it's heading. Sending data across the Internet is like disassembling a jigsaw puzzle in one room and reassembling it in another room. To put it together again quickly, you have to identify the pieces in relation to each other and put them back together in sequence.

How About the Web?

In the late 1980s, when the Internet was growing gradually with the addition of a few major networks here and there, a scientist named Tim Berners-Lee began seeking a better way for his colleagues at the European Laboratory for Particle Physics (known by its French acronym, CERN) to communicate by computer. At the time, the only information that could be transmitted across the Internet appeared as simple text on computer screens. Berners-Lee and his associates created an interface for linking information from various sources. The eventual result was the defining of the *URL*, *HTTP*, and *HTML* specifications on which the World Wide Web is based. Today, Web technology allows users to create a formatted page of information that they can then "link" to other pages of information and access across a network.

In simple terms, the *Web* is a collection of information that is accessible via *Web browsers*. The first significant Web browser was Mosaic, developed by the National Center for Supercomputing Applications (NCSA) at the University of Illinois at Urbana-Champaign. The market now offers more than two dozen Web browsers, and that number continues to grow. Currently, Netscape Navigator and Microsoft Internet Explorer (see Figure 1-2) hold the lion's share of the Web-browser market. A *Web browser* consists of a window that displays Web pages, and, typically, also includes toolbars and menu commands that let users explore pages and sites and adjust the browser's settings. Because of the proliferation of Web browsers and the variety of different ways in which you can configure them to display information, a Web page viewed in one browser can, in theory, look significantly different in another browser. However, this problem has lessened as Netscape and Microsoft have come to dominate the browser market, since their browsers display pages similarly.

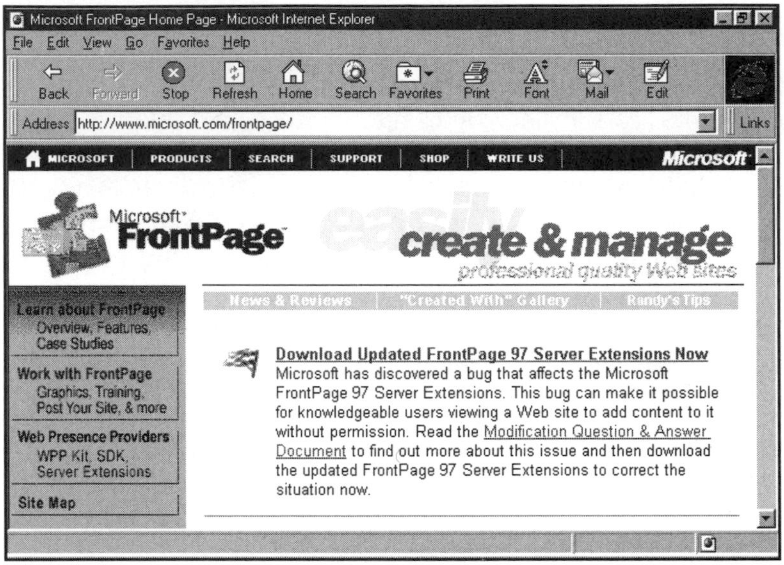

Figure 1-2

A Web page from the FrontPage area of Microsoft's World Wide Web site, as viewed in Internet Explorer 3.0.

In addition to text, Web pages can include graphics, sounds, animation, and other special effects. Individual pages can be linked to other pages to provide access to additional information. All of this information is transmitted using the physical medium and the protocols of the Internet. That's why many people think of the Web as synonymous with the Internet.

The Web has grown at an incredible rate. Thousands of people have their own Web sites, and numerous businesses have put their names up in Web lights. (The term *home page* is often used to refer to a Web site; actually, a home page is the opening page of a Web site—its default page—and it usually has links to other pages.) The Internet and the Web have dramatically changed people's business habits in the last few years; have you noticed that it's now standard to include your e-mail and Web addresses on your business card?

When you develop a Web site (or Web sites), you want to streamline it so that it downloads quickly, but at the same time, you want it to have a good, professional-looking design and you also want to be able to update it frequently. FrontPage makes all these requirements, and more, possible—even easy! The next chapter gives you some pointers on how to create a successful Web site *now*.

Where Do Intranets Fit In?

Now that you know what the Internet and the World Wide Web are, you might be wondering what an *intranet* is. The key lies in the prefixes: *inter* (between or among) and *intra* (within). The Internet connects computers from a variety of different organizations; an intranet (sometimes called an *internal Web*) connects computers networked within a single organization. The term *intranet* also implies that the network supports Web technology. So, basically an intranet is just like the Internet, except that an intranet's content is accessible only to the organization's users and not to users across the world-wide Internet. Intranets can also be linked to the Internet, but they don't have to be.

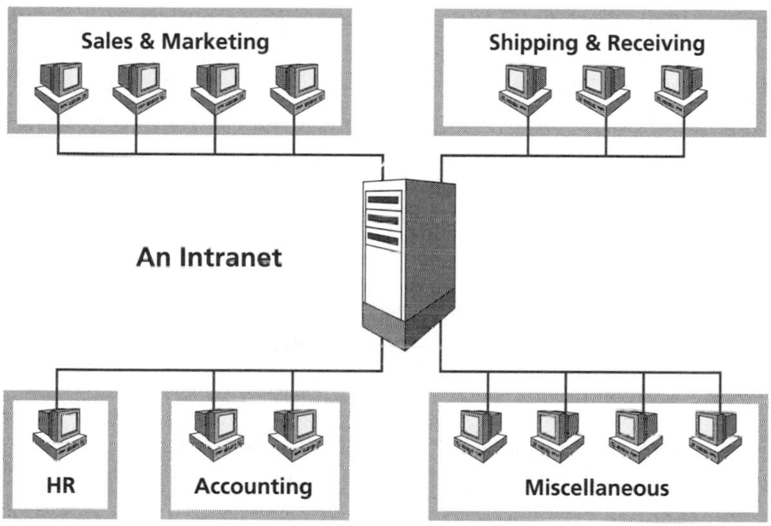

Figure 1-3

Large corporations are already realizing the potential of intranets, and smaller businesses are not far behind. Intranets are an effective and efficient method of communicating within an organization. In the coming years, intranets should do for businesses what e-mail has done in the past few years—make communication easier.

Frequently, the networked computers on an intranet are at one location (such as a single office); sometimes they can span several departments within an organization. An intranet can encompass remote locations as well. Suppose Cascade Coffee Roasters has branches in Washington, Wyoming, and Wisconsin, and all the company's computers are networked together. The company can set up an intranet so that its employees can communicate and share information via computer. Sounds like a typical network, right? Well, it's an intranet because it's a network that supports TCP/IP and has servers with content that employees can access by using a Web browser. Figure 1-3 shows a possible setup for a company's intranet.

FrontPage in the Spotlight

Web site developers have a "cast of thousands" when it comes to choosing a Web authoring tool, and competition between products is driving up the quality of these tools. The choices include HTML editors that require HTML mastery; graphical Web authoring applications that require some HTML expertise; and the star performer, FrontPage, which requires little to no HTML knowledge. FrontPage has become the premier Web authoring tool by offering a powerful product that makes developing professional-looking Web sites for the Internet or intranets extraordinarily easy. FrontPage is unique in that it exploits client-server computing, which makes it easy to integrate into many computing systems. Let's dig into that a little deeper.

Client-Server Computing—It's Hip, It's Hot

In a client-server system, a *server* is a computer or application that supplies data or resources that users can access across a network. A *client* is a computer or application that takes advantage of the data or resources. In many cases, the server is a powerful computer and the client is a typical desktop system. For example, suppose that the invoices received at Cascade Coffee Roasters are all stored in a database on the server. In a client-server invoice system, you input the information on a client computer and store the information centrally on the server when you complete the invoice. That way, you can hook up an unlimited number of client computers to the server, and each can have access to the same data.

FrontPage works in a similar way; in fact, it contains both a client and a server. Its client software consists of the FrontPage Explorer and Editor. The Explorer allows you to view and administer your site in several different ways. You create new pages and edit existing pages in the Editor. Later chapters will describe these features in more detail, along with other client-side features, such as templates and wizards.

For the server side of FrontPage, you can use the FrontPage Personal Web Server or the Microsoft Personal Web Server on Windows 95 or Windows NT Workstation. On Windows NT Server, which ships with Microsoft Internet Information Server (IIS), FrontPage automatically detects and uses the IIS Web server. You can install the Personal Web Servers on a computer on a local area network (LAN) or on a wide area network (WAN) running

TCP/IP and instantly transform that network into an intranet. You can even house the Personal Web Servers on the same computer that you're using for the client software. If you need to create or edit new pages in your site, you can do so on any client computer that's linked to the server—even if your client-server setup spans halfway around the world.

The Personal Web Servers are best used as low-volume servers, and are ideal for developing and testing your sites internally. They are not recommended for use as World Wide Web servers, however—if you expect high volume for an intranet or Internet server, or you need tighter security than the Personal Web Server allows, you probably want a more powerful solution, such as any of the leading Web servers on the market today. The Microsoft Personal Web Server and IIS are both excellent production Web servers. Note that the license for Windows NT Workstation (commonly used with the Microsoft Personal Web Server) permits only ten simultaneous Web connections. If you want to support heavier traffic, you can move up to Windows NT Server and IIS, or use a UNIX-based Web server and one of the many FrontPage-supported Web servers for UNIX. For more information on servers, see Chapter 11. Figure 1-4 illustrates the client-server relationship.

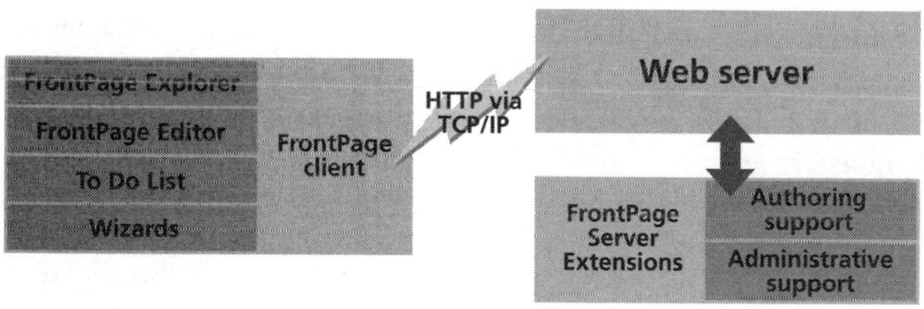

Figure 1-4

FrontPage also provides *FrontPage Server Extensions* to enable any of the leading Web servers to communicate with FrontPage. If your organization already uses a high-end Web server, you can drop in the Server Extensions to achieve seamless communication between FrontPage and the server. Chapter 11 offers more details on the Server Extensions.

The Perfect Partnership: FrontPage 98 and Microsoft Office

The Microsoft Office suite of applications includes Microsoft Word, Excel, PowerPoint, and Access. Office is the best selling suite of office applications on the market. The content creation capabilities of Office combined with the Web site management and Web page creation features of FrontPage provide an ideal way to create Web sites. Here are some ways in which the two make a seamless partnership:

- In the FrontPage Explorer's Folders, All Files, Navigation, and Hyperlinks views, Office documents appear with the same icons as in the Windows Explorer.
- FrontPage's capability for verifying and repairing links extends to any Office documents within your site that contain links.
- You can easily copy material from Office files onto your FrontPage Web pages. For example, you can copy part or all of an Excel spreadsheet onto a page in the Editor, using either the Clipboard or drag-and-drop, and FrontPage automatically converts it into an HTML table.
- You can drag Office documents from the Windows Explorer into the FrontPage Explorer, and those documents will be automatically imported into your site.

As Expensive as It Gets

If you don't have Office running on your machine but still want to view an Office document that's in a FrontPage Web site, you can use an Office viewer. *Office viewers* are separate applications that users can download (free) at Microsoft's Web site (www.microsoft.com). Viewers are available for Word, Excel, and PowerPoint. If you have a viewer installed, you can click on a link to a Word, Excel, or PowerPoint document in any Web site, and the document appears as a read-only file in the viewer. You can configure a viewer in various ways; for example, to show or hide various toolbars, bookmarks, and format marks. You can also print the file that appears in a viewer. The README file that you receive when you download and set up the viewer from Microsoft includes more specific information on using the viewers.

To download the viewers, connect to Microsoft's Web site. Select Products and find the appropriate application: Word, Excel, or PowerPoint. Click the link to the application's home page. The application's home page has instructions on how to locate and download the viewer.

Ready for Launch!

When you build or update your Web site, you can open Office files in their native application from within the FrontPage Explorer; that way, you don't have to concern yourself with opening the Office application separately. When you double-click from the Explorer on a document created in Word,

Excel, or PowerPoint, FrontPage automatically launches the appropriate application so that you can edit the document in its native environment.

Office look and feel. FrontPage sports the look and feel of Office. Toolbar buttons, menu commands, dialog boxes, and keyboard shortcuts are designed to be instantly recognizable by Office users.

Office thesaurus. Just in case you're at a loss for words, the Editor includes the thesaurus used in Office.

Office spell checker. The Editor allows you to check the spelling of the current page, and the Explorer allows you to check the spelling of selected pages or the entire site, both using the same spell checker used in Office.

None of us has ever won a national spelling contest. (If you have, you can leave the room.) But have you ever noticed the number of misspellings on Web pages? They can be thigh-slapping funny, but it's also very sad when you consider that the information on the Web is presented for all the world to see. A misspelling in a site on an intranet can be even more embarrassing. Suppose you misspell your boss's name or title in a corporate bio. That could get you fired—or worse, your boss could force you to make the next two weeks' worth of bagel runs.

FrontPage could save you a bunch of bagel bucks if you use the dictionary and suggestion routines available in Word, but no spell checker can substitute for good spelling knowledge. Of course, you might as well use the best if you're going to rely on one!

Coming Up

Now that you have a better idea of how FrontPage fits into the Internet and intranet scenes, and how it works with Microsoft Office, it's time to plan your first Web site. You'll learn how to do this in Chapter 2, and you'll also learn how to make your sites ones that viewers won't want to leave.

CHAPTER 2

The Web Site Development Process

Planning the Information Flow

Surf on the World Wide Web today, and you'll find some very good sites—ones that download quickly, are pleasing to the eye, organize the flow of information into well-defined areas, allow for discoverable and easy-to-use navigation, and are well written. These sites simply *invite* you to come in, take off your shoes, stay awhile, have some fun, and learn something new.

If you stay a long time at a site without realizing it, you've probably found a well-thought-out site. Take a step back and try to see the big picture here. Can you see the structure, the organization? Does the information flow easily? Understanding how information flows through a site is the first step in creating a functional, easy-to-use site. If you can understand how that concept works, and implement it in your site, you'll already be miles ahead of most other Web site developers.

Many site developers don't take the time to understand the *flow;* they're only concerned with putting words and pictures on a page. Although many sites proudly boast that they receive many more hits (connections) than their competitors, the number of visitors really isn't a good indication of how good a site is. How long a viewer stays at a site is a much better indicator. If users stay at your site long enough to go through the various levels and areas within it, then you know you've done the job right. That means that they can find what they need, get around, and get back, without having to think too much about it.

To create an effective Web site, you need to visualize the flow of information and the various paths that a user can take through it. In other words, you need to see your site from the user's point of view. Planning a site can involve a substantial amount of work, but it certainly doesn't have to be *all* work—if you have fun in the planning stages, you'll probably end up with a better site.

When you use FrontPage, you don't have to be a Webmaster to create a site that visitors will return to time and time again. The kind of site you create, and the kinds of information you include in it, both depend on your target audience. This chapter discusses sites targeted toward an Internet audience as well as sites intended for an intranet within your business or organization.

Guidelines for a Good Site

The best Web sites are ones that look appealing, get the message across succinctly, and don't make users wait too long for information to appear on their screens. The following are some guidelines for creating a successful site:

- **Have a clear purpose.** What are your goals? Just to get on the Web? If so, you're like many others, and you shouldn't be surprised if your site ends up like most others. Make your goals as specific as possible. Perhaps you want your site to show off your company's products. That's all fine and dandy, but consider *how* you want to show off those products. How do you want your products positioned in the Web market? Asking these deeper-level questions will result in a clearly defined goal. Without a well-defined goal, your site is doomed for a trip to the Internet graveyard.
- **Always keep your audience in mind.** Who is the primary (and secondary) audience for your site? How old are they? What do they do for a living? How much time do they have to look at your site? For every piece of information, every graphic, and every content decision you make, ask yourself, "How will the audience react to this?"
- **Use items that download quickly.** The number one reason that people leave a site quickly—or don't visit a site at all—is that it takes too long for the information to appear on their screens. Large file-size graphics cause users to twiddle their thumbs, and it's all too easy for them to click a Stop button in their browser to stop downloading your site. For more ideas on how to streamline graphic size, see Chapter 8.

- **Make your site visually appealing.** You've undoubtedly seen some plain, boring sites on the Web. What makes them plain? Lack of color and lack of variation in text and heading sizes, perhaps. You've probably seen some cluttered and chaotic sites as well; ones that use too many fonts in too many sizes or too many colors. As you build your site, remember that a well-laid-out page brings you one step closer to a well-done site.

- **Don't try to put everything on one page.** Be careful not to clutter your pages with too much information. We know that writers like to write and graphic designers love to create cool images. As the developer of the site, it's up to you to create that delicate harmony between these two very different groups of people.

  Try to strike that balance between text and art: Think about who's going to be reading those pages. Think about how difficult reading a lot of text on a computer screen can be, and write the content for your pages accordingly. Try adding white space by increasing the page margins, or by using tables creatively. To learn more about using tables, see Chapter 6. Think about your graphics in terms of what value they add to the page. Are they serving a purpose, or do they just look good? But remember that good-looking graphics sometimes serve the purpose by themselves. What all Web site developers are striving toward are pages that look good, contain useful information, and allow the user to easily explore the site.

TIP

We often think our sites are right on target with our intended audiences, but it's easy to miss the mark. To avoid this, be humble and try to have your site plan and content reviewed by as many people as possible, especially potential members of your audience. This step is critical but often overlooked.

- **Organize your content in intelligent ways.** Maybe you've heard the saying that "content is king." It's true. How many times have you visited a site and thought, "There's nothing here"? Perhaps some good content is buried deep within the site, but the only viewers who will "dig it up" are those who randomly come across it. If you have some information that you feel your viewers *must* see, don't bury it in hidden pages. Make your important information as obvious and easy to find as possible.

Don't forget that your site will likely be more than one level deep. Organize secondary material into groups of related information. For example, suppose you're setting up an online catalog for a music store. Would you list your jazz CDs and rock CDs in the same section? Of course not. It's admittedly a glaringly simple example, but the point is, when you look at all your information in terms of appropriate categories, you end up with a much better organized site than most of the ones out there.

- **Include appropriate buttons for exploring the site.** Most site developers use linked buttons to represent the various areas within the site. These buttons are usually found on all pages within a site, and are usually grouped together in the same place on the page. Keeping them together and in the same place increases their discoverability and usefulness. The user can simply click a navigation button to move to another section of the site.

  Here are some things to keep in mind while creating your navigation buttons:

  - Include a button that takes the user back to the home page. If your viewers are buried five levels deep into a site, they should, in the event that they want to start over, be able to click a button to return to the first page. If they're stuck using the Back button in their browser, chances are that they'll get frustrated and leave your site. In other words, don't rely on the user's browser to do the navigation for you; be sure to design it into the site yourself.
  - Be prepared for people to come to your site with graphics turned off in their browsers. It's a good idea to have a linked text version to go along with the linked graphical buttons. That way, the user can use either version to explore your site. Most of the time you'll see a text version right next to the graphical buttons.

  The bottom line is: Make it easy for viewers to move through your site. When you design a site, ask yourself whether you'd want to move between certain points. Answer that question, and you're bound to come up with good ways to make your viewers happy little surfers.

- **Take advantage of the Navigation view in the FrontPage Explorer.** Navigation view can prove particularly helpful if you have a difficult time visualizing information. Start with your home page and work down. This visual representation can help you "see" your content, organize it more clearly, and avoid major reorganizing phases as you build your site. It also helps you see your site's structure more clearly, and can lead to new ideas for improving the structure and flow. For more information on Navigation view in the Explorer, see Chapter 3.

- **Test your site thoroughly.** The Web audience can use a number of different browsers, each of which can present your site quite differently. Test your site using as many different browsers as possible, on different platforms (such as Windows 95, Windows NT, UNIX, and Macintosh), and at different modem speeds. It's not unusual to find a navigation button properly appearing in a corner of a page in one browser but in the middle of a page in another browser; it happens all the time. Wise owls test every page and every link in their sites using several different browsers. You can easily verify all of the links within your site by using the Verify Hyperlinks command, as well as by using the Hyperlink Status view in the Explorer. See Chapter 3 for more information on these features.

  Another great way to test your site is to use the Preview In Browser command in the Editor. It lets you preview your page using any browser installed on your machine. It also lets you preview the page at different window sizes. If you normally run your screen resolution at 1024 x 768, for example, you can find out how your Web page will look at a window size of 640 x 480. For more information, see Chapter 7.

TIP Another good way to treat your audience kindly is to provide a searching mechanism so that they can find information in your site quickly. Using the FrontPage Search Component, you can add a complete search engine to your site in just a few seconds. To find out how, see Chapter 9.

Planning an Intranet Site

If you're in charge of developing an intranet site at a business or other organization, you have no small task ahead of you. You have many of the same things to think about as when you develop a public site for the World Wide Web, with a few interesting exceptions. Because you usually know the exact audience for the site, you have the luxury of being more focused and specific. You should have a good idea about such points as what types of computers are being used, how fast they are, which browser is most commonly used, and how the site is being accessed (via modem or via direct connection). Knowing these details can greatly affect how you develop the site. As when you develop a World Wide Web site, up-front planning is the key to developing a successful site.

Depending on the size of your company, the site can be large and can involve many people in charge of different sections. FrontPage makes managing intranets easy; see Chapter 5 for details.

Does your organization need an intranet? Traditionally, you see companies using the old-fashioned printed method for generating internal information such as corporate policies, training information, phone listings, and company news. After printing the information, it has to be distributed, often across various geographical regions. With every update or change, reprinting and redistributing the information is necessary. Generating, maintaining, and distributing information in this manner not only is costly for the company, but it *wastes* resources.

When you have an intranet in place, you can easily and quickly update company information, and you can make it available to everyone (or to those who have the correct access rights). Different departments can be in charge of maintaining their area on the site and keeping the company abreast of changes as they occur. This process is seamless and painless.

Questions to Ask

When you create an intranet site, pay attention to the same issues of design, organization, and navigation that you need to address when you build a site for the World Wide Web. In addition, if you can address the following intranet-specific issues up-front, you can save a great deal of trouble.

- **Audience.** What members of the company or organization will have access to the site? What kinds of information will the site include? Will all of the information in the site be accessible to everyone?
- **Work in progress.** Who will update the site? Who will be in charge of which sections and which tasks? Spell this out as clearly as possible before you create the site, because as you go along you'll probably discover more tasks that need to be performed regularly by *someone*. FrontPage makes assigning tasks easy, in the Tasks view of the Explorer (explained in detail in Chapter 3).
- **Keeping it under control.** How will you keep the site from getting out of control? The key to controlling the size of a site is in controlling who can add material to it. If everyone in your company can add pages, change information, add links, and so on, your site will quickly seem like a runaway freight train bound for the bottom of Whiskey Gulch.

You can control these privileges by setting browse, author, and administrative permissions. You'll find more details on this in Chapter 5.

Perhaps your business or organization already has a network in place, and routing files and viewing others' documents and presentations is easy, but the process really is cumbersome; you have to connect to a network location, move the files to your computer or open them on another computer, launch the appropriate application to help you view and manipulate the files, and so on. Plus, when you're looking at a network location, all you see is a list of files. There's little presentation involved. And unless you know where to look for a specific file, it can be difficult to find a file on a network, especially if you don't know the exact file name.

Intranets allow this sharing of information in a visual forum. Suppose you want to find out your company's sales information for the previous quarter and that a Microsoft Excel file contains that information. In a typical network setting, you have to find the appropriate file, open it, and then view the information in Excel on your own computer.

Using an intranet site enables company personnel to access information without having to memorize a network location. All they have to do is find the company sales information page on the intranet and then click a link to open the file from the network. Or you could choose to have that information displayed directly on a page in the site. If they can't find the sales information page easily (which would be indicative of a bad design), they can find it in a few seconds by using a Web search engine.

Servers

If you set up an intranet site, you need a Web server to run it on. Just as with traditional network servers, you often must dedicate a single computer for use as a Web server. The faster and more powerful the computer, the better your site will run.

The Web server that you want to use will depend on the amount of traffic you expect to see. If you have a relatively small company, you might be able to use the FrontPage Personal Web Server or the Microsoft Personal Web Server as your sole Web server. These servers aren't designed to handle a high amount of traffic, so you might need to choose a server that can handle higher volumes. For more information on servers, see Chapter 11.

Security

You can use your network security features to protect many of the files used on your intranet. After all, these files are stored on the actual network. If you want only certain personnel to be able to change information in files used on an intranet, for example, you can restrict access at the network level.

In addition to network security, FrontPage allows three levels of access to a Web site. The Web server you use for your intranet also might interact with these security features.

- Browsing (end-user access)
- Author access (accessing, updating, and maintaining the site using FrontPage)
- Administrative access (updating security permissions); administrators also have all author access rights

With FrontPage, you have many options for configuring the security on your site. For more information, see Chapter 5.

Content

A company or organization can harness the power of an intranet in many ways:

- **Make documents and other corporate information widely available.** Companies can use an intranet site to house policy manuals, training manuals, company schedules, product data, and the like. This can save tremendous amounts of time, effort, and money.

  Suppose Linda works in the Bed & Bath department at a department store, and she needs specifics on what kind of perfume the store sells so that she can propose a bundling of towels and perfume for a holiday promotion. Instead of calling the head of the Perfume department, who would pass the request to an assistant, who would then direct Linda to a file on the network containing pricing, availability, and sales information, Linda can simply go to the appropriate intranet site and access that information herself.
- **Update your employees on company news.** An intranet site is an ideal forum for placing a news bulletin about your company. If you want to provide employees with information about the annual picnic, you can put it in one place for all to see. An intranet site also is an ideal place for gathering your company's press releases for employees to read.
- **Use the intranet site for in-house promotions.** Even though the primary purpose of an intranet site is to streamline information flow within a company or organization, that doesn't mean it can't be fun to use.

- **Connect your intranet site with the Internet.** Through the use of security measures such as *firewalls* and *proxy servers*, you can link your intranet site to the Internet and still keep the intranet secure. You can provide links to your competitors' Web sites to keep your employees up-to-date on their goings-on, or to other useful and timely information your employees might need to know. If information about your company appears on others' Web sites, you can link to those locations so that your company's personnel can see what all the hoopla is about.

Coming Up

Now that you have an idea of what you can do with a Web site, it's time to learn some specifics concerning how to use FrontPage to create your site. Chapter 3 starts you out on that journey by taking a detailed look at the FrontPage Explorer.

PART II

3 Inside the FrontPage Explorer

4 Templates and Wizards

5 Managing Your Web Site

Creating and Managing Your Site

CHAPTER 3

Inside the FrontPage Explorer

Your Site, from See to Shining See

Okay, you've been designing Web sites for a while now, and you're pretty good at it—but you know all too well that it can be a managerial nightmare, with dozens of HTML pages linked every which way, and little buttons and graphics here and there. You have to deal with writers and graphic designers, not to mention your boss, and every one of them looking to you for answers. Somewhere, in the midst of all this mayhem, you still need to map out your site. You know that you need the time, and place, to be able to visualize your site. How many times have you tried to pencil your site out on paper, drawing links this way and that? And, of course, you have to be able to get your boss, or your client, to "see" what you're trying to do.

And as for you beginning Web site developers, you may be wondering whether you haven't gotten in over your heads with all this Web stuff. When you put your ideas down on paper and chart out a few pages, it seems pretty straightforward, right? But when you begin drawing links between all your pages, it can feel like you're climbing Mt. Everest with a day pack, one bandage, and a bag of BBQ chips.

Several good software flowchart programs enable you to build a map of your site and manipulate it as you please. Even if you use one of these programs, though, you still need to use a Web authoring tool to create your site, which means that you have to input the data in two separate programs. Wouldn't it be easier if you could input the data only once?

If you want to organize your site in a single program, you've come to the right place, because that's what the FrontPage Explorer does for you. The FrontPage Explorer gives you many different ways to view your site, allowing you to view and manipulate it as a whole. And there's no need to worry about making separate, manual changes to these views; the FrontPage Explorer updates each view as you make changes to your site, so that you can see the changes instantly in any view. This greatly simplifies site creation and maintenance, and it'll no doubt save you hours and hours of time for every site you work on. And if you work with particularly large sites, it might just save your sanity in a big way, as well.

You can maintain consistency, maintain links, and perform operations across the entire site. For example, just as you don't want to spell check a word processing document one paragraph at a time, you don't want to spell check a Web site one page at a time, so the FrontPage Explorer allows you to spell check an entire site. FrontPage pioneered this notion of a Web site as a single unit, and the FrontPage Explorer is the means by which you manipulate this new Web type.

This chapter presents the FrontPage Explorer in detail. The FrontPage Explorer forms the framework of the FrontPage client software, giving you direct or indirect access to the FrontPage Editor, as well as the FrontPage templates and wizards. These tools are explained in greater detail in later chapters; this chapter simply focuses on how to access them through the FrontPage Explorer itself.

Now, don't confuse the FrontPage Explorer with the Windows 95 Explorer—although it was designed to have the same look and feel and similar operations. Nor should you confuse the FrontPage Explorer with Microsoft Internet Explorer, which is Microsoft's Web browser. The FrontPage Explorer gives you an overview of your Web site. In the rest of this chapter, and indeed, throughout the entire book, the term Explorer refers to the FrontPage Explorer; the Windows 95 Explorer is referred to as the Windows Explorer.

Starting the Explorer

When you launch the Explorer for the first time, you'll see the Getting Started dialog box, which gives you a couple options concerning how to proceed. If you want to skip this dialog box the next time you start FrontPage, click in the Always Open Last Web check box, at the bottom of the dialog box. Thereafter, FrontPage remembers the last Web site you worked on and automatically starts the Explorer using that site. During installation, FrontPage automatically checks to see if you currently have a Root Web; if not, FrontPage will create a root Web for you automatically. This cuts down on the hassle of having to learn how to open or create a new Web site using the Explorer's menu commands. Figure 3-1 shows the Getting Started dialog box:

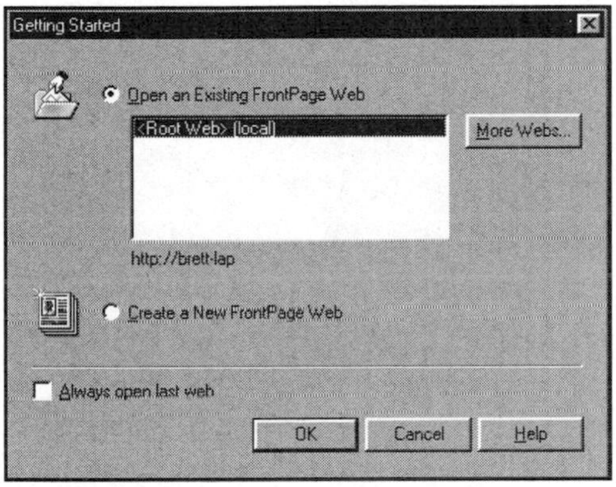

Figure 3-1

FrontPage will also check to see if you've opened any Web sites before, and lists the most recently accessed sites in the dialog box. Notice that the address for the selected site appears under the list box. If the currently selected Web site requires SSL, the address will begin with *https//*. For more information on SSL, see the section "Making Use of SSL," in Chapter 5. Later in this chapter, the section "Opening an Existing Site" discusses how to open sites when you're in the Explorer. But for now, here's how to proceed:

Open an Existing FrontPage Web. In this section, you have two options: You can open one of the Web sites listed, or you can select the More Webs button. If you opt to open one of the listed sites, FrontPage opens the site in the Explorer. If you select the More Webs button, the Open FrontPage Web dialog box appears. See the section, "Opening Sites Authored in FrontPage" later in this chapter, for a description of the Open FrontPage Web dialog box.

Create a New FrontPage Web. You can also create a new FrontPage Web site from the Getting Started dialog box. To create a new site, select the Create A New FrontPage Web radio button, and then click OK. The New FrontPage Web dialog box appears. You use this same dialog box to create a new site from the Getting Started dialog box, or from within the Explorer. The next section details this process.

Creating a Site from Scratch

When you launch the Explorer, you'll see the Getting Started dialog box (unless you have enabled the Always Open Last Web check box). If you're already in the Explorer, just use FrontPage's menu commands to create or open your sites. If you're creating a site from scratch, and you want to take advantage of FrontPage's site management features, it's wise to first construct the framework for the site in the Explorer. The site's framework can consist of simply a name and a preconstructed page or two that you can work on later. FrontPage saves this framework on your Web server (or, if you want to create a site for only your own use, it saves the framework on your hard disk), and from that point forward, you can work on it in the Explorer or the Editor, depending on what tasks you're completing.

In the Explorer, choose New from the File menu, and then choose FrontPage Web from the New submenu, to open the New FrontPage Web dialog box (see Figure 3-2).

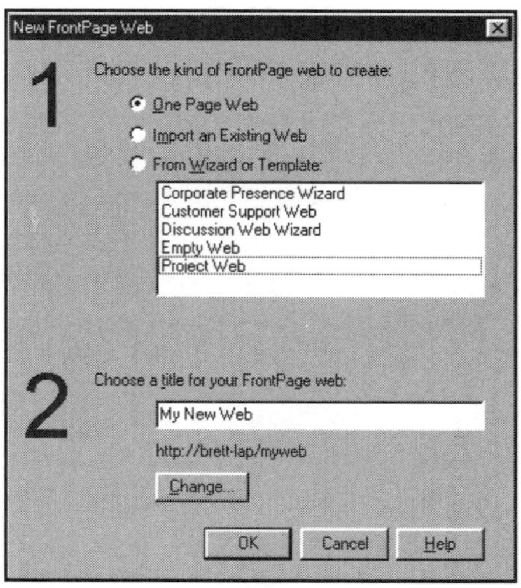

Figure 3-2

The New FrontPage Web dialog box shows you the two steps that you must perform to create a new Web site.

1. Choose the type of FrontPage web site that you want to create. The first step gives you three options for creating your site:

   One Page Web. Choose this option if you want to create a site that consists of one blank page. When you choose this option, FrontPage will create a one page site and open the site in the Explorer.

Import an Existing Web. If you have a non-FrontPage site, or individual Web files that you want to import into FrontPage, you can do so by using the Import Web Wizard. Choosing the Import an Existing Web option and clicking OK opens the Import Web Wizard dialog box. In this dialog box, you can specify the destination server or file location on which to house the site, as well as the new site name. You'll find a complete description of the Import Web Wizard in Chapter 4.

From Wizard or Template. Listed in the New FrontPage Web dialog box are your wizard and template choices. One of the easiest ways to create a site is to use one of these templates or wizards, which can eliminate many preliminary design hassles. Templates and wizards are explained in detail in the next chapter, but for now, if you're creating your first site, here's a brief outline of what each of these templates and wizards can do for you:

- **Corporate Presence Wizard.** This wizard is an excellent place to start if you're creating a business site. It asks you a series of questions and offers numerous kinds of pages to highlight your business.
- **Customer Support Web.** This template sets up a customer support site for a business.
- **Discussion Web Wizard.** This wizard creates a discussion group with threads, a table of contents, and full-text searching.
- **Empty Web.** This template creates a new site with nothing in it. Generally, you'll want to begin with the Normal Web template.
- **Personal Web.** This template creates a personal Web site that you can fill in with information such as employee data, biographical information, your interests, and more.
- **Project Web.** This template creates a new site to help you manage a project. It includes a list of participants, project status, project schedule, and more.

2. Name your new Web site, and if necessary, change its location. The default name is My New Web. It's always a good idea to change the name of the Web site here to a name more specific to your site. Notice that the address, including the new Web name, appears under the text box. When you click the OK button, FrontPage creates your Web, using the new name, on your local server. FrontPage, by default, uses the local server location. Alternatively, you can change its location: just click the Change button to bring up the Change Location dialog box (see Figure 3-3), and then make the appropriate changes.

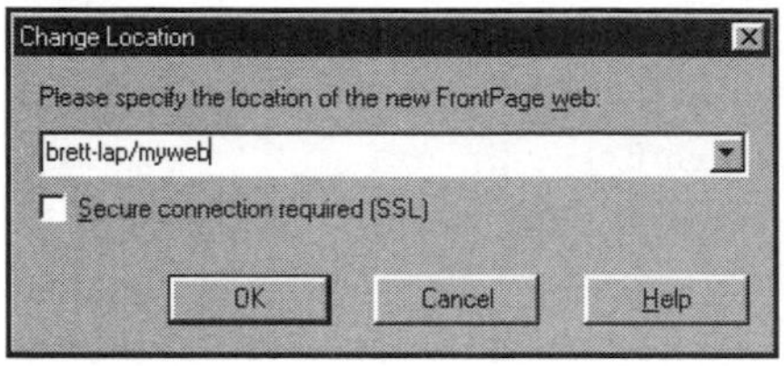

Figure 3-3

If you're not happy with the server location suggested by FrontPage, don't worry; FrontPage will remember its most recently used servers, so you don't have to. Use the drop-down list box to choose from any of the servers listed. But wait, what if the server I want isn't listed? Again, no need to worry: All you have to do is type the name of the desired server in the list box. For example, if the current location is *server1/myweb* and you want FrontPage to create *myweb* on *server2,* which isn't on the list, just change the location to read *server2/myweb,* and FrontPage creates the Web appropriately.

NOTE If you want to add your new site to an existing FrontPage Web, make sure that the existing Web site is open in the Explorer before you begin the process, and then select the Add To Current Web option.

If you're creating the site on a secure area on the server, and that server supports SSL (Secure Sockets Layer), select the Secure Connection Required (SSL) check box. For more information on SSL, see Chapter 5.

When you've finished making your selections, click the OK button. FrontPage then sets up your new site. This might take a few minutes, depending on the speed of your computer and your Web server, and on the type of site you've chosen to create. FrontPage creates a folder for the site on the server that you have designated. It gives the folder the same name that you gave your site. If you use a template to create your site, FrontPage adds files to this folder for each of the pages in the template. If you use a wizard, you get a series of screens in which you can customize your site before the pages are created by FrontPage. For more information on using wizards, see Chapter 4.

When the process is complete, FrontPage displays the site in the Explorer.

Opening an Existing Site

You can open any Web site in FrontPage, regardless of the Web authoring application it was created with.

Opening Sites Authored in FrontPage

If you've already created a site in FrontPage and want to open it in the Explorer, here's how to do it:

1. In the Explorer, choose Open FrontPage Web from the File menu, which opens the Getting Started dialog box, described earlier in this chapter. If the site you want to open is not listed, select the More Webs button which opens the Open FrontPage Web dialog box, shown in Figure 3-4, presenting you with several options.

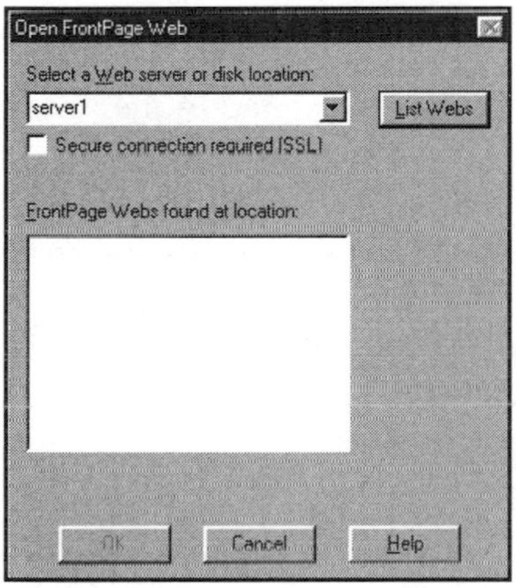

Figure 3-4

2. In the Select a Web Server Or Disk Location text box, enter the name of the Web server on which you want to put the Web site, enter a pathname if you want to put the site on a hard disk or a LAN, or select a location from the drop-down list. If you want to communicate with your site using Secure Sockets Layer (SSL) security, select the Connect Using SSL check box.
3. Click the List Webs button. FrontPage searches the server or file location you specified and displays a list of sites in the FrontPage Webs list box.
4. Double-click a title or select a title from the FrontPage list box, and then click OK.

SHORTCUT To quickly open a site, you can click the Open FrontPage Web toolbar button, which is the standard Open button that you find in many Windows 95-based applications. Alternatively, you can choose a site from the recently opened sites listed at the bottom of the File menu.

Opening Sites Authored in Other Applications

If you want to open a site authored in another application, the best-case scenario is when the site is on a Web server on which the appropriate FrontPage Server Extensions are installed. The Server Extensions gather the additional information that FrontPage needs and make the site's content available for editing. So, if the right FrontPage Server Extensions are installed, you might not have to change a site's format in order to work with the site in the Explorer.

To open such a site, follow the procedure outlined in the above section, "Opening Sites Authored in FrontPage." For more information on the FrontPage Server Extensions, see Chapter 11.

If you want to open a site from a server that does not have the FrontPage Server Extensions installed, however, doing so is still pretty easy. You use the Import Web Wizard, which is described in Chapter 4.

The Explorer Point of View

When you think of a Web site, do you see it spatially, as a bunch of interconnected pages, or do you think of it linearly, as a bunch of collected pages in a row? Either way is fine, of course—it all depends on how each person thinks. FrontPage has adopted the popular Outlook style user interface, and gives you seven different ways to view and manipulate your site. Perhaps the single most powerful feature of the Explorer is that it enables you to view your site in these different ways, as seen in Figure 3-5 on the next page.

The next several sections present each of the views in turn, to show you the unique ways in which they enable you to look at a Web site. Then I show you some of the features that are common throughout all of the views.

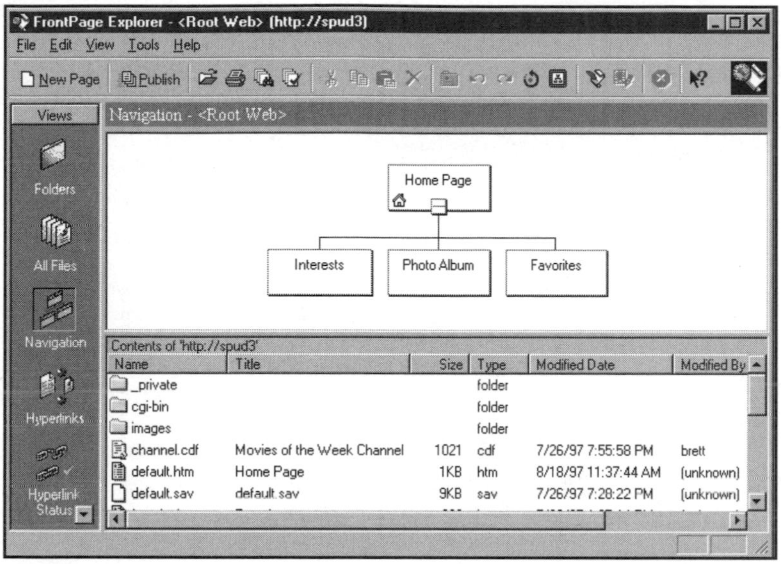

Figure 3-5

This is a screen of a typical site in the Explorer. A unique icon represents each view, listed vertically to the left side of the window, under the heading Views.

Folders View

If you use Windows 95, you should find Folders view easy to grasp. Folders view is similar to that of the Windows Explorer. It presents the folder structure of your Web site, on whatever drive or server it's on. It also presents the contents of those folders for you, so you don't need to be concerned with keeping track of your site's files.

To look at a site in Folders view, click the Folders icon on the Views toolbar, or choose Folders from the View menu.

For a look at Folders view, see Figure 3-6, on the next page. The figure shows a site called Project One, which was created using the Project Web template. For instructions on creating a site, see "Creating a Site from Scratch," earlier in this chapter.

Folders view divides the screen into two vertical windows to the right of the Views bar. The left pane contains the folder structure of the site. The top-level folder contains files and subfolders. FrontPage creates all sites with specific folders according to the type of site. A site created using the Project Web template, for example, may have different subfolders than a site created using the Corporate Presence Wizard.

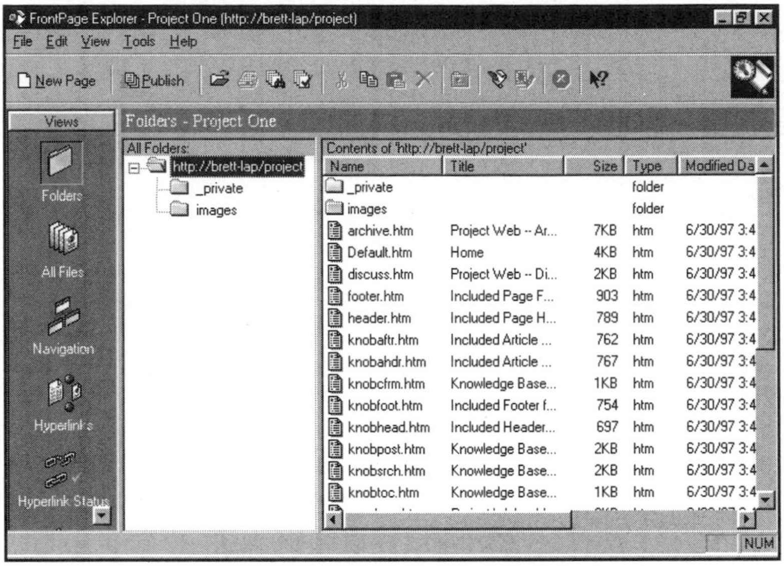

Figure 3-6

Notice in the preceding graphic that *http://brett-lap/project* is highlighted: it's the URL for the site, *brett-lap* being the server name, and *project* being the directory in which the site is located on the server. Just above the URL, you see Folders – Project One. That's the site's friendly name, the name that appears in the title bar of most browsers. All of the site's files are collected in the subfolders underneath this top-level location. The number of folders for a given site is not static, however; you can create your own folders to organize your files. To learn how, see the next section, "Creating Your Own Folders."

The right pane contains a list of the contents of whatever is highlighted in the left pane. You might recognize this as the same functionality used in the Windows Explorer. The folders and files listed in the right pane are accompanied by descriptive information, such as name, title, size, type, date last modified, who modified them, and any comments about the file.

Figure 3-7, on the facing page, shows the contents of the images subfolder for the Web site, Project One.

To sort the list of files based on a column in Folders view, click the column heading. Files are sorted in ascending order, except when you specify to sort files based on the Modified Date column, in which case, they're sorted in chronological order starting with the most recent date and time.

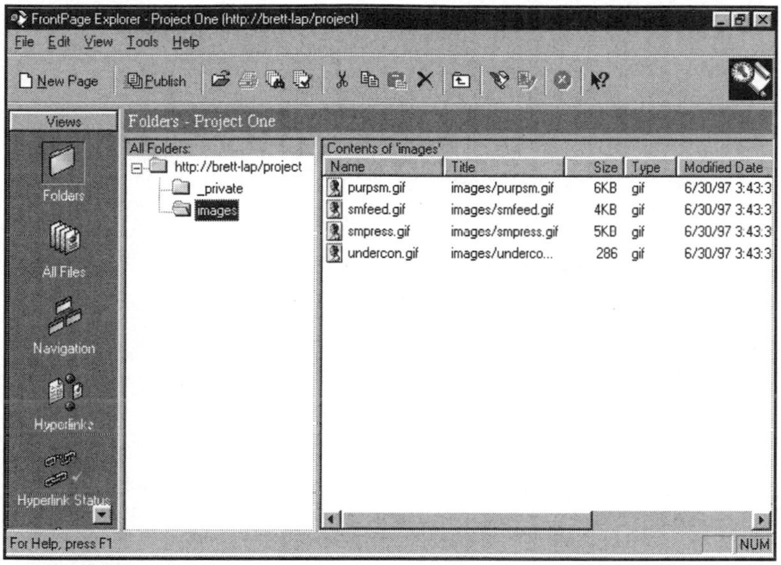

Figure 3-7

In your FrontPage journeys, you're likely to see a number of different icons in the right pane in Folders view, appearing beside the names of the files and folders. One icon is the yellow folder icon itself; that one's easy to figure out. Another icon you often see looks like a painting; it denotes image files, such as JPEG and GIF files. A third icon looks like a page with lines on it; that one indicates HTML files, and you can expect to see these quite often. You also might see a familiar-looking icon that looks like a mini-version of an icon from your favorite Microsoft Office program. When you import any Office file into a site, FrontPage uses the same icons that you're used to seeing in Office to represent the various types of files. It's just one more way in which using Microsoft Office with FrontPage is as easy as it gets. For more information, see "Importing a File into a Site" later in this chapter.

Creating Your Own Folders

Suppose you're a Webmaster in charge of maintaining a site on your company's intranet, and that the site includes numerous Office files from various contributors. One way to organize those files is to collect them in a folder structure called *Office*. Then, the *Office* folder can have a *Word* folder in which you could store Word files. Here's how to go about adding a new folder:

1. In the Explorer, with a Web site open in Folders view, highlight the folder under which you want the new folder to go by clicking the folder in the left pane.
2. Choose New from the File menu, and then choose Folder from the New submenu.
3. A new folder appears in each pane of Folders view.
4. The new folder is highlighted, ready for you to give it a name. Make the name of the new folder *Office*, and then press Enter.
5. Highlight the *Office* folder by clicking it in the left pane.
6. Repeat steps 2 and 3, naming the new folder *Word*. Figure 3-8 shows what the folder structure should look like.

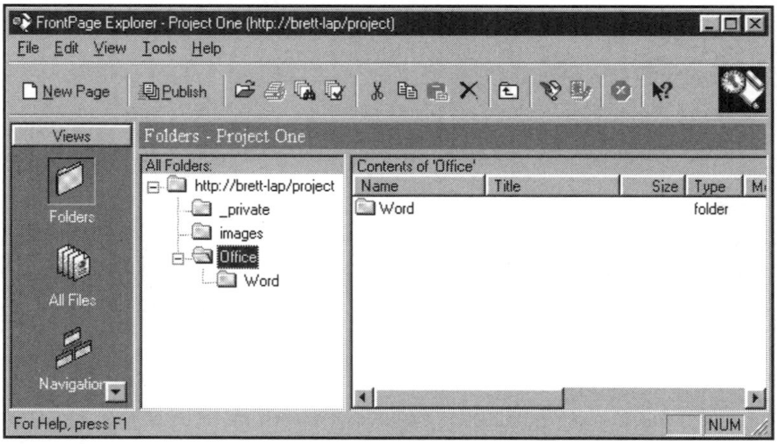

Figure 3-8

SHORTCUT To quickly add a new folder in Folders view, right-click in the right pane, and select New Folder from the pop-up menu.

Now when your coworkers send you their Word files for the site, you have a logical place to store them. Better yet, perhaps you can train them to import the files themselves! To learn how to import those files, see "Importing a File into a Site," later in this chapter.

Perhaps the most obvious use for the folders in Folders view is to collect your material in a logical, organized way. One way to do that is to create your own folders, as detailed by the steps earlier in this section.

Drag and Drop Files

As you're working in the Explorer's various views. you may want to use the drag and drop technique, to move files from one place to another. For example, you could be working in Navigation view and add a new page to your site, and you want the page to be located in a certain folder. You could drag the file from Navigation view, and drop it into Folders view, in exactly the folder you want. This is just another way you can use the views together, to create your sites. The process for doing a drag and drop is simple:

1. Select a file (or a selection of files).
2. Hold down the right mouse button. Drag the selection onto one of the icons on the Views bar. The corresponding view becomes the active view, visible in the right pane.
3. While still holding down the mouse button, move the mouse back over to the right pane and release the mouse button. The selection has been successfully dropped.

The drag and drop technique, described here, is performed the same way in all of the views in the Explorer, but the technique can produce different results depending on which view you use it in. So, drag and drop is discussed separately in the following sections for each view that uses it.

Drag and drop in Folders view. Folders view gives you two drag and drop options from which to choose:

- Drag a single file (or a selection of files) onto the Navigation icon in the Views bar, and drop and attach them to a parent page. For more information on the Navigation view and parent pages, see "Navigation View" later in this chapter.
- Drag a single file onto the Task icon in the Views bar, and drop it into the Tasks window. Thereupon, the New Task dialog box opens, and in it, you can create and assign a new task based on the file you dropped. For more information on the Tasks view, see "Tasks View" later in this chapter.

Here are some other good uses for Folders view:

- Finding all files of a specific file type in a folder, such as Office files. Group the list by type of file by clicking the Type column, and then look for the specific file type.
- Renaming a file. Rename a file in exactly the same manner as in the Windows Explorer. Just click a file, wait a moment, and click again. You can then rename the file, and FrontPage automatically updates any links to that file.
- Modifying the folder structure. Rearrange the folder structure of your Web site by dragging files from one folder to another, just as you would do in the Windows Explorer, and FrontPage automatically reconfigures the links.

Besides sorting the items in the right pane of Folders view, there's another way to change the view: You can change column widths. Place your mouse in the column heading area, near a border between the columns. When the cursor changes to a crosshair with left and right arrows, click and drag to adjust the width.

All Files View

You're having a good ol' time building your site, you've added lots of pages and cool graphics, and you've moved them all around, placing them in this folder and that one. You think to yourself, "Boy, it sure would be nice if I could somehow see all these files together in one place, maybe in a list." Well, FrontPage is way ahead of you. The All Files view is just what you need, and as you might have already guessed, it lists all the files in the site in a straight, one-column list.

To see your site in All Files view, click the All Files icon on the Views bar, or select All Files from the View menu. Figure 3-9 shows how the Project One site looks in All Files view.

To sort the list based on a column in All Files view, click the column heading. Files are sorted in ascending order, except when you sort via the Modified Date column, in which case, it sorts them in chronological order beginning with the most recent date and time.

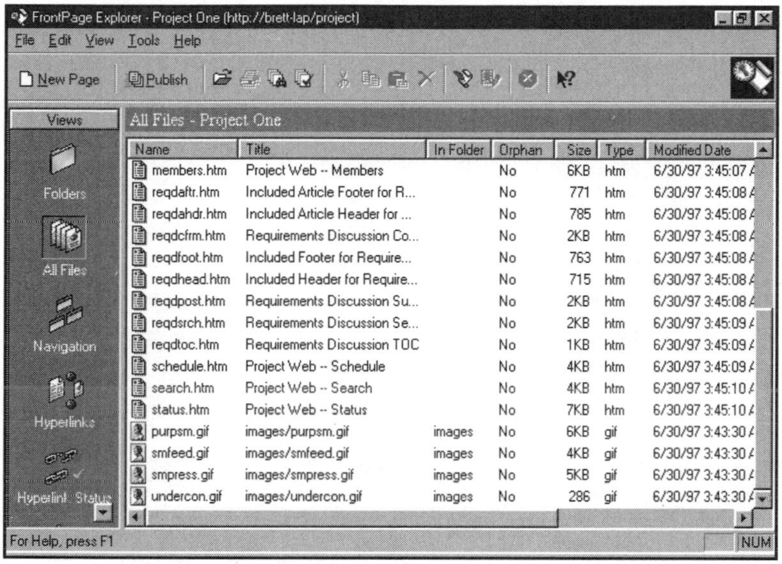

Figure 3-9

Drag and drop in All Files view. Although the All Files view just gives you a static list of the files in your site, you can use the drag and drop movement (explained in the sidebar "Drag and Drop Files" earlier in this chapter) to pull off a few useful actions beyond sorting the columns:

- Drag a single file (or a selection of files) onto the Folders icon in the Views bar, and drop them into the currently opened folder.
- Drag a single file (or a selection of files) onto the Navigation icon in the Views bar, and then drop and attach them to a parent page. For more information on the Navigation view and parent pages, see "Navigation View" later in this chapter.
- Drag a file onto the Task icon in the Views bar, and drop it into the Tasks window. The New Task dialog box opens, and in it, you can create and assign a new task, based on the file you dropped. For more information on the Tasks view, see "Task View" later in this chapter.

Navigation View

When it comes to mapping out your Web site, you can do it in many different ways. You can buy a few packs of sticky notes and plaster them all over the walls. You can use a few hundred 3x5 cards and try to keep them organized, or you can doodle little sketches all over the place. The makers of FrontPage, however, decided to save you some time and trouble—not to mention, a few trees. To that end, they included a way of mapping out your site structure directly within the FrontPage Explorer. It's called the Navigation view, and it gives you the ability to design your structure visually, and it even lets you print it out. You can also use the structure you build in the Navigation view to create *navigation bars* in the FrontPage Editor. For more information on navigation bars, see Chapter 7.

To see your site in Navigation view, select Navigation from the Views bar, or select Navigation from the View menu.

Figure 3-10 below shows the default <Root Web> as seen in the Navigation view.

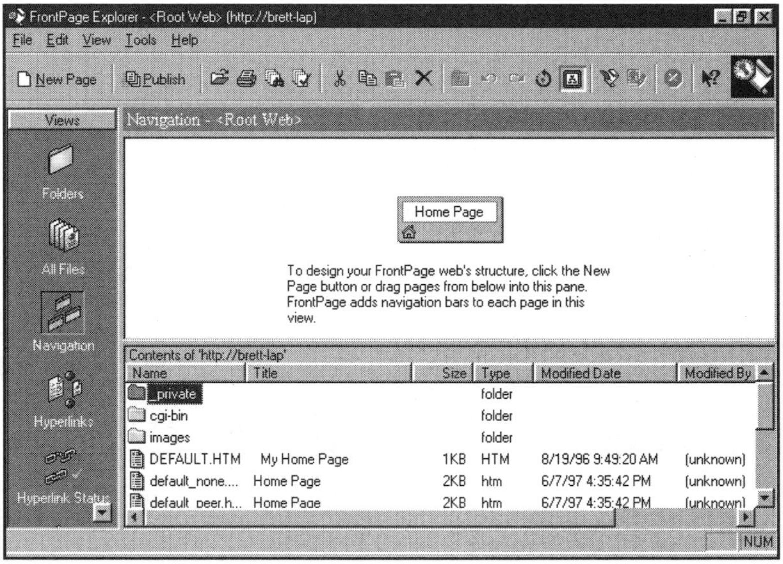

Figure 3-10

As you can see, the Navigation view presents pages visually as a rectangular box, with the title of the page in the middle. The Navigation view divides the screen into two horizontal panes. The top portion is a workspace in which you can design your structure, and the bottom portion is a simple folders view. The folders view corresponds with the contents of the Folders view, described earlier in "Folders View." These two "folder" views always match; if you move items around in the folder pane of the Navigation view, the same items are moved in the Folders view.

Editing the Page Title

You can easily edit the title of a page in Navigation view, in several different ways:

- Click the page that you want to edit and select Rename from the Edit menu.
- Click the page once to select it, and then click again, on the title. The title becomes highlighted and you can enter the new name.
- Click the page once, and press the F2 button on your keyboard.

NOTE Changing the title of a page changes only its "friendly name," the title that appears in the header of most browsers, it has no effect on the page's URL. For example, the name of your home page usually is something like *default.html* or *index.html,* but the friendly name, or title, usually is something like the name of the company or the name of a department.

After you finish changing the page name, you can click anywhere on the background or hit the Enter button on your keyboard to save the change. If you accidentally double-click a page, don't worry; you'll just end up with the page open in the FrontPage Editor. For more information on working with pages in the Editor, see Chapters 6 and 7.

Parents, Children, and Peers

When designing the structure of your site, you usually build from the top down; in another words, you create your pages at different levels. This structure forms the hierarchy of your site, and helps define the priorities of the content on the site. Most of the time, you place the more important information higher in the hierarchy to make it easier to find. You usually include related or supporting information on lower level pages, making them accessible via links from higher pages. Knowing that your site's hierarchy and link structure can get rather confusing, the makers of FrontPage have incorporated a naming system: FrontPage calls each level by a different name.

- **Parent pages.** Parents are pages that have child pages linked below them.
- **Child pages.** Child pages live directly below a parent, and usually are linked to the parent page via a graphic or text hyperlink, or a navigation bar.
- **Peer pages.** Peers are pages that share a common parent.

If you think of your pages as people—stay with me here—you can see that pages can be parents, peers, and children all at the same time, just as people can.

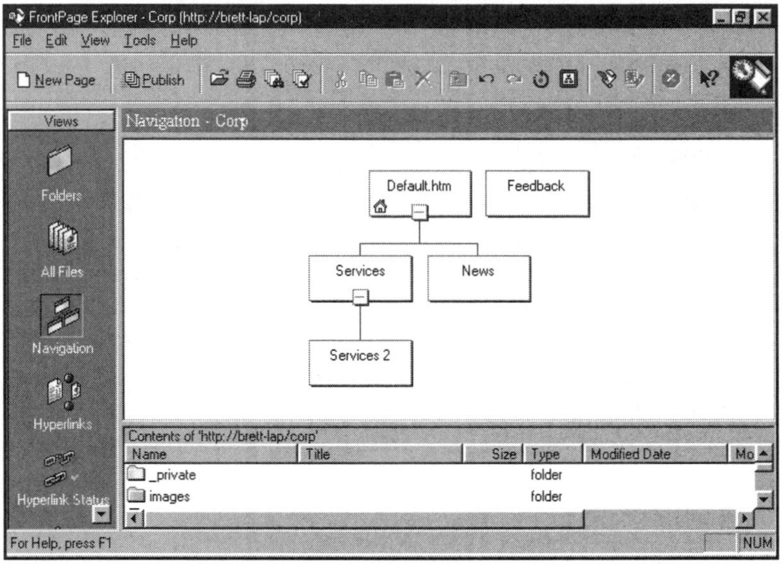

Figure 3-11

Figure 3-11 shows a typical site structure, where *default.htm* is the parent to Services and News, Services and News are peers to each other, and Services 2 is a child page of Services. You may be asking yourself, "What the heck is the Feedback page then?" Well, the Feedback page is a *global page*. A global page is a page that, when used with navigation bars, can be a link that appears on every page in the site that uses the navigation bars. Since navigation bars are created using the hierarchy designed in Navigation view, and the global page is parallel to the Home page, it's not subject to the hierarchy. Global pages appear to the left or right of the home page in Navigation view. For more information on navigation bars, see Chapter 7.

As you can see from Figure 3-12, FrontPage indicates pages that are linked together by including a line between them—this gives you an easy visual depiction of the site's hierarchy. If a page is a parent, you can collapse the child pages, including any of their child pages, by clicking the minus sign. In turn, you can expand the structure, by clicking the plus sign, one parent at a time, to see the respective child pages. Being able to collapse and expand the site's structure becomes very useful when you have a large site composed of many different levels.

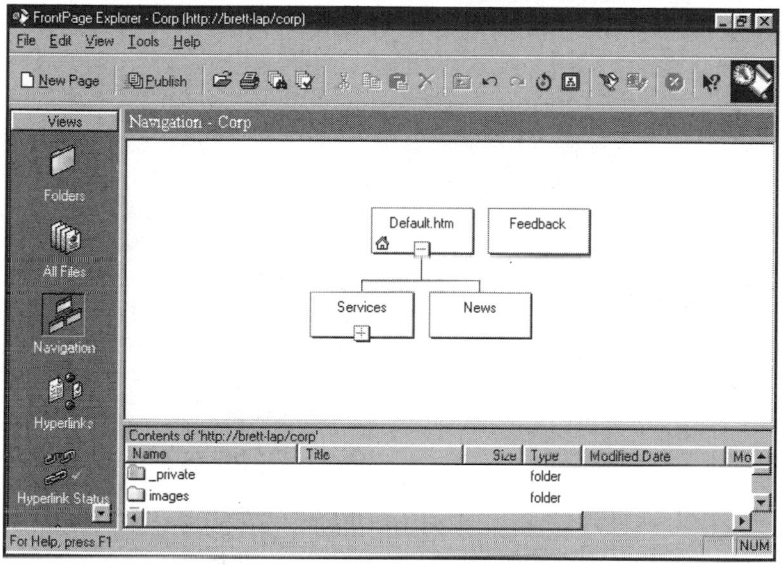

Figure 3-12

Changing the Structure

You can use the drag and drop method to move your pages around, creating your structure as you go. Unlike when you drag and drop between views, described earlier in the section "The Explorer Point of View," here you drag and drop in one or both panes of the Navigation view. You can drag a file from the lower pane, up into the structure pane, and you can move pages around within the structure pane.

To bring a page into the structure pane from the lower folder pane, do the following:

1. Right-click and hold down the mouse button on the file that you want to move from the lower pane.
2. Drag the file up into the structure pane. As you move the mouse around the upper pane, still holding down that button, you can see a dotted outline of the page you're moving.
3. Move the outline near another page in the structure view, and a dotted line appears, connecting the pages, as shown in Figure 3-13.

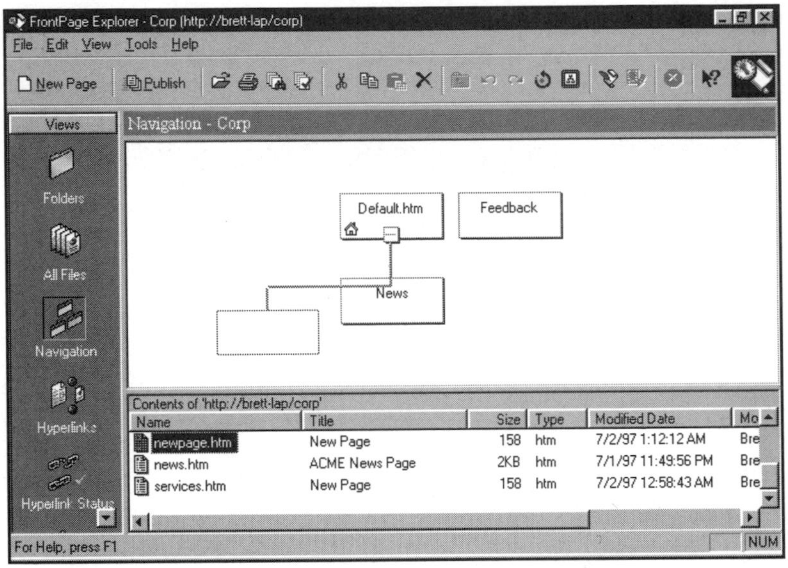

Figure 3-13

4. When you have the page positioned where you want it, release the mouse button to drop the page into place.

You can now see the page in the structure pane, its title visible, each page connected together by a blue line. Now don't worry; you have complete design control. You can move the pages in the structure pane around—and around—until you get them just the way you like. That's the heart of the Navigation view; the whole idea is to give you a view in which you can build the flow of information that forms the foundation of your site.

To add new pages to your site, see the section, "Adding a New Page to a Site," later in this chapter.

TIP If you build a large site, you'll notice that when you have many pages expanded in Navigation view, some of the pages move beyond the view that your monitor affords. You can use the scroll bars to move around, or you can use a simple sleight of hand to move the view anywhere you like. To pull off the latter feat, just click-and-hold anywhere on the background and hold down the mouse button until your mouse pointer changes into a hand. After the pointer changes, as long as you continue to hold down the mouse button, when you move the mouse, the view moves around the window.

If you've built a site that consists of many pages, you may be asking yourself, "With all these pages, what if I can't find my way home?" or "Where's my home page?" There's no need to click your ruby slippers; your home page is always located either at the top of the view or at the upper-left corner of the view. It's also easy to spot, because it's the one that has the little house icon in its lower-left corner.

Deleting a Page from Your Structure

Deleting a page from the top pane in Navigation view is easy. You can use any of the delete options described in the section "Deleting Files" later in this chapter. When you attempt to delete a page from the site structure, FrontPage asks you if you want to remove the page from the Navigation view only, or delete the page completely from the Web. Choose wisely.

Adjusting Your View

After you begin building your site, its structure can get rather lengthy, and, unless you have one of those cool 21″ monitors, finding your way around can get a bit complicated. FrontPage gives you a few ways to change and improve your view; namely, the commands Size to Fit, Rotate, and Expand All. You can access the Size to Fit, Rotate, and Expand All options by right-clicking in the top pane and selecting an option, or you can use the Size to Fit and Rotate commands by clicking their corresponding buttons on the Explorer toolbar. (The Expand All command does not have a corresponding toolbar button.) You also can select View from the Explorer menu and choose any of these options.

- **Size to Fit.** Using Size to Fit automatically collapses your site so that it fits into the top pane without scrolling.
- **Rotate.** Some people like to view the site structure from top to bottom, while others prefer to view it from left to right, so FrontPage includes the Rotate command, which enables users to toggle between both views.
- **Expand All.** In Navigation view, hidden or collapsed child pages are indicated by the plus sign. If you want to see the entire structure of a site, and you don't want to click every plus sign, you can use the Expand All command. Choosing Expand All opens all hidden or collapsed child pages, exposing the entire structure of your Web. If your structure is already completely expanded, or contains no plus signs, Expand All will have no effect.

Applying the Changes

So you've been playing around in Navigation view for a while and you have the structure just the way you want it—it's perfect, a work of art—and now you want to save it. Well, FrontPage automatically saves the structure in the Navigation view as you go, but if you want your navigation bars to recognize the new structure, you have to update your changes. For more information on navigation bars, see the section, "Automatic Navigation" in Chapter 6.

To apply the changes that you've made to the site structure, right-click in the top pane and select Apply Changes from the pop-up menu. FrontPage might take a minute or two to complete this task, depending on the size of your structure.

Refreshing the Structure

If you've been busy building away, and then all of a sudden look at what you've done and wonder what in the world you were thinking, you can always get your structure back. To "refresh" your structure, select Refresh from the View menu, or press F5 on your keyboard. Refresh sets the structure back to the position it was when you last applied changes.

Printing Your Site Map

Often times, people need to see and feel something in order to understand it, and a site structure can be a hard thing to explain. So, not only could it come in handy to have a printed copy of the structure to share with your boss, but it's also great to share with other members of the Web development team, the client, your significant other, whomever, and who knows it may even be suitable for framing.

FrontPage prints the site structure only as it appears in the Navigation view, even if you can't see it all on your monitor, so be sure to expand it to show all the levels you want to print. To save room when printing, FrontPage prints only the plus signs, to indicate unseen portions of the structure, and does not print the minus signs.

If you want to see how the structure will look when it's printed, before you actually print it, select Print Preview from the File menu. The Print Preview window gives you a few options. For more information on Print Preview, see the section "Print Preview" in Chapter 6.

When you have arranged the structure to your satisfaction, you can print it by selecting Print Navigation View from the File menu, or by pressing Ctrl+P. Either option opens the standard Print dialog box.

Adding a Navigation View to an Old Site

If you upgrade from an earlier version of FrontPage or import a site from another program, and you want to take advantage of the Navigation view to build your sites structure, you're in luck. FrontPage automatically starts you off by placing a Home Page in the top pane, ready for you to begin the building process. From this point on, the Navigation view works like it does with any other site.

Hyperlinks View

Hyperlinks view is the graphical representation of the links within a segment of your Web site. To see your site in Hyperlinks view, choose Hyperlinks view from the View menu. Another quick way to see your site in Hyperlinks view is to click the Hyperlink icon on the Views bar.

The following screen shot shows how a site looks in Hyperlinks view. The Hyperlinks view divides the screen into two panes; the left pane presents an outline of your site, and the right pane shows the files of your site as large icons, linked together by a series of lines. The file names appear directly beneath the icons. Links are shown in a left-to-right fashion; links *to the page* appear to the page's left, and links *from the page,* or, *to other pages and elements,* go to the page's right.

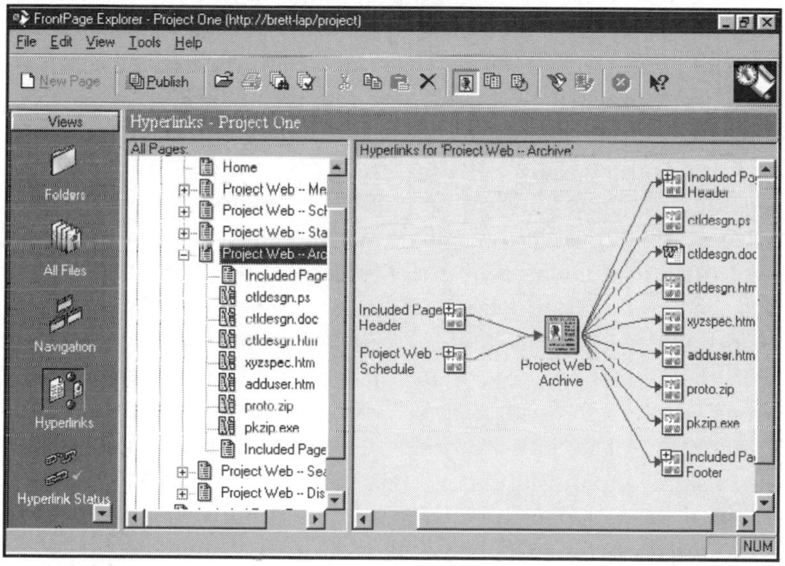

Figure 3-14

In Figure 3-14, the plus sign indicates that you can expand the view; therefore, more links either are coming to or going from the page. Clicking the plus sign expands the view. After you expand a view, the plus sign changes to a minus sign, indicating that you can collapse the view.

If you let your mouse pointer hover over an icon, a ScreenTip pops up that indicates the file name and other information.

Many different icons appear in both panes of Hyperlinks view. For example, envelope icons with a mailto: protocol indicate links that send e-mail; that is, links on pages that allow users to send e-mail directly from the page. For example, you might include such a link on your pages to give your users a convenient way to provide you (the Webmaster) with feedback. Icons of paintings indicate image files, and globe icons indicate links to the World Wide Web. As in Folders view, you also see icons for Office files when they're a part of your site.

You also need to know about two other icons, but these are not icons that you want to see on your page; namely, the icon for broken links and the icon for errors. The broken link icon looks like a page that has been split down the middle and the error icon looks like a small triangle pointing up.

The broken link icon indicates a link, either internal or external to the current Web site, that's configured incorrectly. You can fix a broken link by opening the page that contains the link in the Editor and correctly configuring the link. (See Chapter 7 for more details.) If you see an error icon after opening the page in the Editor, you know that a FrontPage component isn't configured properly and needs to be corrected. (For more information on FrontPage components, see Chapter 9.)

You may notice that some links end with an arrow. An arrow indicates that the page contains a hyperlink that jumps to another page.

The left pane of Hyperlinks view shows an outline of the site. The home page of the site appears at the top, represented by a cute house. Initially, all the material that appears in the site shows up below this icon.

Just as in Folders view, clicking an item in the left pane causes the information in the right pane to change. In Hyperlinks view, when you click something in the left pane, that item appears centered in the right pane, along with any of its links to other files or addresses. Clicking the plus and minus signs expands and contracts the outline, respectively.

Hyperlinks view is especially useful for determining just how many links come to and go from each page, as well as for seeing what other pages link to your page. Suppose you went live with a new page on your intranet a week ago, and you want to know how many others in your organization have linked to your page. You can simply look at your page in Hyperlinks view to find out.

Hyperlinks view also comes in handy if you need to verify that you've included all the links that you think you have on a particular page. Suppose you promised several departments in your organization that you'd link to their home page from your "For More Information" page, and that those links are embedded in the paragraphs on your page. Well, you can view all the links on your page in one place—Hyperlinks view—and check that against your list, instead of having to look at the page in an editor, find the links, and then check them against a master list.

Another way in which Hyperlinks view can prove useful is when you need to find all pages that point to a particular page. Also, by expanding the links (by clicking the plus signs), you can find various paths through your site. This is useful, for example, to figure out how many mouse clicks it takes to get from one particular page to another.

Modifying the View

The size of the Hyperlinks view window and the size of your monitor dictate how much of your site appears in Hyperlinks view. You'll notice, as you expand the site, more and more links drop out of view on your screen. You can view the off-the-screen material in two ways: by using the scroll bar at the bottom of the window, or by clicking any open area, holding down the mouse until the pointer changes to a hand, and then, still holding down the mouse button, dragging the material wherever you want it.

There's also a way to center any item on your screen in Hyperlinks view: Right-click the item and choose Move To Center from the pop-up menu. You'll also notice that because Hyperlinks view is a representation of links, it can seem to go on forever. Again, if you think spatially, you'll see that if page A is linked to page B, which is linked to page C, which is linked back to page A, then you're already going around in circles. And that's only a tiny example. It's best to use Hyperlinks view for viewing small portions of your site. You can get a good overall view of your site by collapsing everything; when you need to see specifics, it's time to expand those icons.

Hyperlinks Status View

Testing links is a vital component of any site-testing plan. You must make sure that your links work. Broken links not only make your site look bad, they make *you* look bad. Even for small sites, however, link testing can take a long time. Hyperlinks Status view presents a graphical list that shows the status of the hyperlinks in your Web, including both internal and external links. To see your site in Hyperlink Status view, choose Hyperlinks Status from the View menu. Another quick way to see your site in Hyperlinks Status view is to click the Hyperlinks Status icon on the Views bar. Figure 3-15, on the next page, shows a screen shot of Hyperlinks Status view.

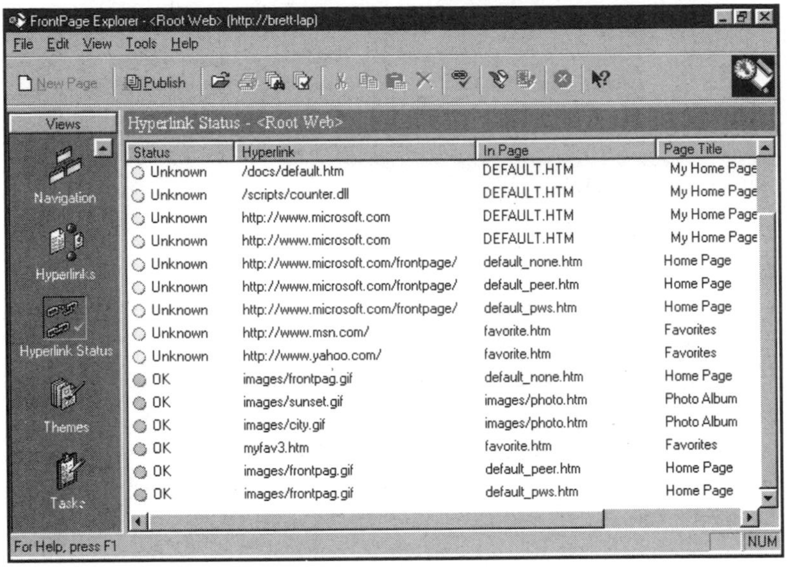

Figure 3-15

Hyperlinks Status view organizes your hyperlinks vertically, presenting information about the links in columns to the right of the links. Here you can see a link's status (Status), its hyperlink (Hyperlink), that is, where it's supposed to link *to,* which page the link is "on" (In), the page's title (Page Title), and who last modified the link (Modified By). A green, yellow, or red circle precedes each link. The yellow circles change color after you verify the links:

- **Green.** Indicates that the link is okay.
- **Yellow.** Indicates that the link is unknown or not yet verified, or that it has changed since the last verification.
- **Red.** Indicates that the link is broken.

FrontPage includes a tool, called Verify Hyperlinks, that you can use to verify the destinations of your links, which can save you oodles of time in a crunch. You can use this tool to verify links in HTML files and Office documents.

TIP *Verifying links* ensures that the targets of your links exist, and that they will work in a browser. It does not confirm that your links jump where you want them to. That, you must confirm on your own.

To use the Verify Hyperlinks tool, do the following:

1. With the site open in the Explorer, choose Verify Hyperlinks from the Tools menu. If you're not already in the Hyperlinks Status view, FrontPage switches views for you. You also can right-click in the Hyperlinks Status view pane, and then select Verify Hyperlinks from the pop-up menu. The Verify Hyperlinks dialog box appears, giving you the option of verifying all the hyperlinks in the site or only links that you select.
2. To start the process, choose Verify All, or Verify Selected, and then click the Start button. FrontPage checks all links, and then reports their status in the Status column. To verify external links, such as links to the World Wide Web, FrontPage must be able to reach those links; in other words, to verify Web links, you must be connected live to the Web. Since FrontPage has to go to each page to verify the links, verifying external World Wide Web links can take a long time.

TIP Click the Stop button on the Explorer toolbar to stop the process at any time. If you want to resume verification after you stop, select Verify Hyperlinks from the Tools menu. FrontPage remembers that you didn't finish the last verification, and automatically checks the Resume Verification button in the Verify Hyperlinks dialog box.

Once you've verified the hyperlinks in your site, you probably will need to do some link editing—if not this time, then the next time; there's no getting out of it. To fix a broken link, right-click that link, and then click Edit Hyperlink from the pop-up menu to open the Edit Hyperlink dialog box, as seen in Figure 3-16 below.

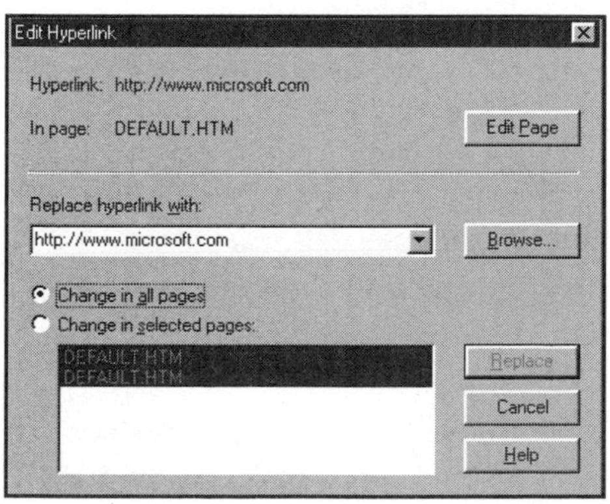

Figure 3-16

- **Hyperlink.** The first item listed on the dialog box shows the current location the link points to.
- **In page.** The second item listed on the dialog box shows the page the link is in.
- **Edit Page.** To move to the page that contains the link, click the Edit Page button. The page opens in the Editor and scrolls to the link, allowing you to edit the link or remove it. (For information on editing a link in the Editor, see Chapter 7.)
- **Replace hyperlink with.** Change the URL in the Replace hyperlink with correct address.
- **Change in all pages.** If you want the new link you just replaced, changed on every page in your site that contains the old link, select the Change In All Places radio button. FrontPage will search the entire site and change the old link to the new one you just made. It's a good idea to let FrontPage do this for you.
- **Change in selected pages.** If you want FrontPage to change the new link only on certain pages on which it appears, select Change In Selected Pages, and then choose the pages from the list.

After you make your choices in the Edit Hyperlink dialog box, select the Replace button. FrontPage will go through your site and make the appropriate changes. If you don't have time to fix the link right away, or you need some time to find the correct address, you can add the task to the Tasks view by right-clicking the link and selecting Add Task from the pop-up menu. For more information on the Tasks view, see the section "Tasks View" later in this chapter.

Themes View

How many times have you visited a Web site, only to find it just plain old ugly—no interesting colors or buttons, and the only thing consistent between the pages that they're consistently bad? Have you ever felt as if you'd like to put together a great, professional-looking site, one that looks like the pages go together, but simply didn't have the time, or didn't think you had the talent, to become a professional graphic designer? Well, FrontPage is going to make your day, because with Themes, and the Themes view, you can do all that and more. No one ever has to know that you didn't spend years in art school.

The makers of FrontPage have designed Themes with the new or business user in mind. Professional graphic designers will probably want to create their own graphics from scratch. For more information on creating graphics for the Web, see Chapter 8. When you apply a theme to your site, you get professionally designed buttons, banners, backgrounds, text, and link colors, all of them predesigned to look good and work together to form a consistent-looking site.

To see the Themes view, as shown in Figure 3-17 below, select Themes from the View menu, or select the Themes icon on the Views bar.

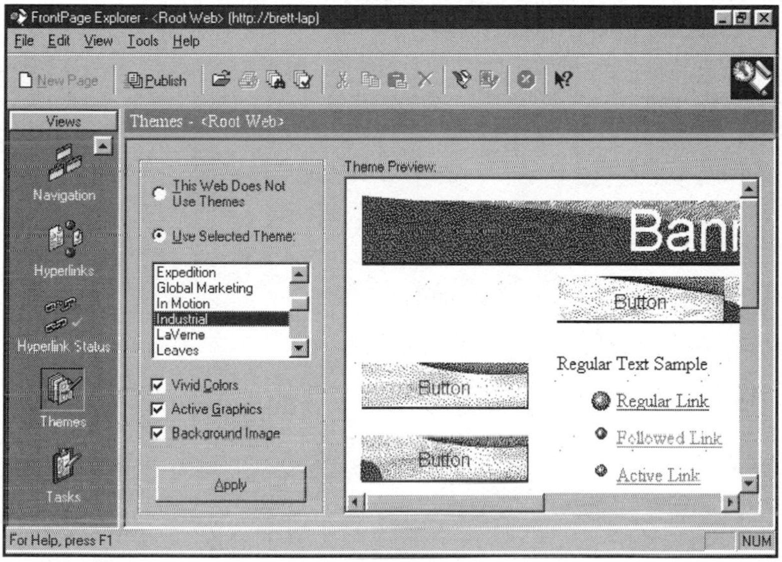

Figure 3-17

If no theme has been applied to your Web, the first option, This Web Does Not Use Themes, is selected. If a theme currently is applied to your Web, its name is highlighted in the list under Use Selected Theme.

The right portion of the Themes view contains a Theme Preview window. As you select the various themes in the list, FrontPage displays them here. You can scroll around this preview window to view all the options in the selected theme. FrontPage comes with plenty of themes to choose from, so have some fun and look around. As always, you'll want to keep in mind who you're creating the site for and how a given theme might effect the user experience.

To ensure that the themes remain consistent and work together properly, you cannot pick and choose pieces of one theme and add them to another theme. When you choose a theme, you have three options that slightly affect the way the theme is presented in the browser.

- **Vivid Colors.** Check this box to make the colors of the various elements, such as buttons and backgrounds, more obvious. If you don't check this box, most of the elements display as black and white, with color enhancing only a few pieces.
- **Active Graphics.** Check the box to populate your site with more "interactive" graphics. Some elements, like bullets, become animated. Navigation buttons change appearance as the user rolls the mouse over or clicks them. Be careful here, because too much action on a page can be a distraction to the user. If you do not check this box, the elements on the page are not interactive, they have a more subtle elegance, and they'll download faster in the user's browser.
- **Background Image.** This option acts as a toggle to switch between having a background image and having a background color. All of the themes have a tiled background designed to fit with the look and feel of the theme. If you select Vivid Colors but do not select Background Image, FrontPage chooses an appropriate background color for your theme.

After you choose a theme and decide on your theme options, click the Apply button. FrontPage will apply your new theme to all the pages in your site. If you want to apply a theme to single page, you do so in the FrontPage Editor. For more information on applying a theme to a page, see Chapter 6.

Tasks View

It's said that Albert Einstein chose not to memorize his phone number because he believed that memorizing such details took up too much space in his brain and too much energy. He preferred to reserve his brainpower and energy for his creative endeavors, and would simply write down any details that he could look up later.

Don't you wish you could do that with the small details about your site so you wouldn't have to remember them all? If you had to write down a long list of tasks, however, keeping track of them would be difficult. Luckily, FrontPage supplied a better solution: the Tasks view. The Explorer creates a Tasks view for every Web site that you create with FrontPage, and it shares this list with all authors across the site.

The Tasks view is a list of tasks that need to be completed for a given site. It records not only all those nagging details, but also allows you the luxury of not having to organize them. It lists each task, describes it, prioritizes it, indicates who's assigned to complete it, and more, freeing you up to take care of other details. Plus, the Tasks view is completely customizable, allowing you to change and rearrange the tasks to your heart's content.

To show the Tasks view for your site, as seen below in Figure 3-18, choose Tasks from the View menu in the Explorer, or click the Tasks icon on the Views bar. The following screen shot shows the Tasks view window, with a list of tasks ready to be completed.

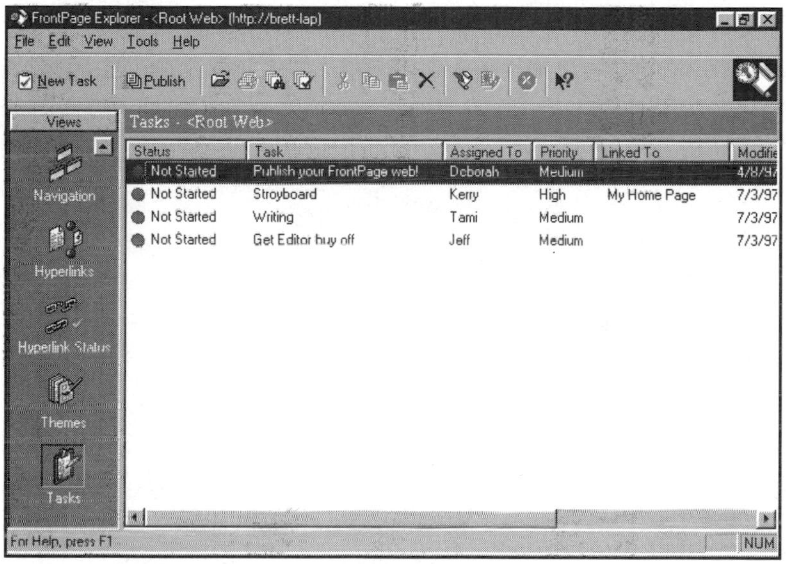

Figure 3-18

The leftmost column, the Status column, lists the status of a task. The second column, the Task column, describes the tasks. The next column, the Assigned To column, lists who's responsible for completing each task. The Priority column notes whether the task has a priority of high, medium, or low. The Linked To column indicates the page or file that requires editing for completion of the task. The Modified Date column lists the date on which the task was last modified. And, finally, the rightmost column, the Description column, provides a description of each task.

The following items describe the features of the Tasks view.

Showing history. If you want to see a list of all of the tasks ever assigned in the Web, including those marked as completed, view the Tasks History. Select Task History from the View menu, or right-click in the Tasks view pane, and select Task History from the pop-up menu. When you select Task History, FrontPage adds all of these tasks to the list, along with the date on which the task was marked as completed. When Task History is not selected, the Tasks view shows only tasks that still need to be completed.

Sorting the columns. Sorting the columns can be useful for large lists, and it's easy to do—you simply click a column heading. Suppose you want to find out how many tasks are assigned to you. Just click the Assigned To column heading, and then find your name in the column, all of the tasks assigned to you will be grouped together. In the Tasks view, as in the other views, sorted tasks are in ascending alphabetic order unless you want to sort by date, in which case, it sorts from most recent to oldest.

You also can adjust the column widths by moving your mouse pointer between the column headings until it changes to a crosshair with left and right arrows, and then clicking and dragging. This lets you expand a column to see detailed descriptions that are too long to fit into a column.

Completing a task on the spot. This is one of the most helpful features of the Tasks view. If you see a task in the list that's assigned to you or someone else and you want to complete the task right then and there, you can do so. Suppose you want to complete the "Writing" task shown in the previous figure. All you would need to do is select the task, right-click, and then choose Do Task from the pop-up menu. The Editor opens to the appropriate page for the task that you need to complete. Even better, the page opens to the very spot described in the task, so you don't have to search for it. If a task is not associated with a particular page, the Do Task button is grayed out. When you save the page containing the unfinished task, FrontPage asks you whether you want to mark the task as completed in the Tasks view. Once you mark the task as complete you can't undo that action, so make sure you're really finished before you do so.

Changing the details for a task. You can reassign a task, change the priority of a task, and change the description of a task in the Task Details dialog box. You can access the Task Details dialog box by right-clicking a selected task and choosing Edit Task from the pop-up menu, or you can, with a task selected, choose Open from the Edit menu. Either way, the Task Details dialog box opens, as shown in Figure 3-19.

To change the task name, or to assign the task to a different person, or to change the description of the task, simply replace the existing text. To change the priority, select the appropriate option button. You'll notice that not all details can be changed—only those mentioned here. For tasks created by you or other users, you also can change the task name. When you finish entering the new information, click OK to return to the Tasks view.

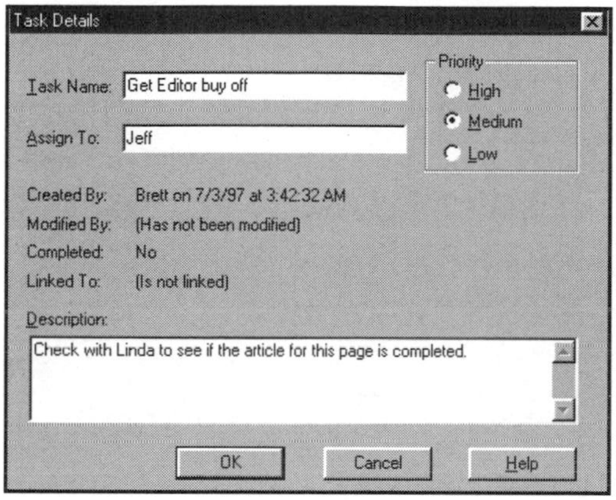

Figure 3-19

Marking a task as completed or deleting a task. If you want to mark a task as completed, or if you want to delete a task all together, right-click the task and select either Mark Complete or Delete from the pop-up menu. You also can select a task and choose either Mark Task Complete or Delete from the Edit menu. After a task has been marked completed, its status changes to reflect the change, and the colored ball changes to green. The Delete option is useful when you no longer want a task to appear in the Tasks view history.

Adding a task. If a you don't need a task to be linked to a particular page, click the New Task button on the Explorer menu bar while in the Tasks view, or right-click in the Tasks view pane and select New Task from the pop-up menu. If you want to link a new task to a page in your site, start in one of the other Explorer views, such as the All Files view, right-click the page, and then choose Add Task from the pop-up menu. With either method, the New Task dialog box opens, as seen in Figure 3-20 on the next page.

Enter the task name in the Task Name text box, and assign it to someone in the Assign To text box. Mark the priority as High, Medium, or Low in the Priority section of the dialog box. Finally, add a description of the task in the text box at the bottom, and then click OK. Be sure to use a short but specific description, because the column widths in the Tasks view often are rather narrow.

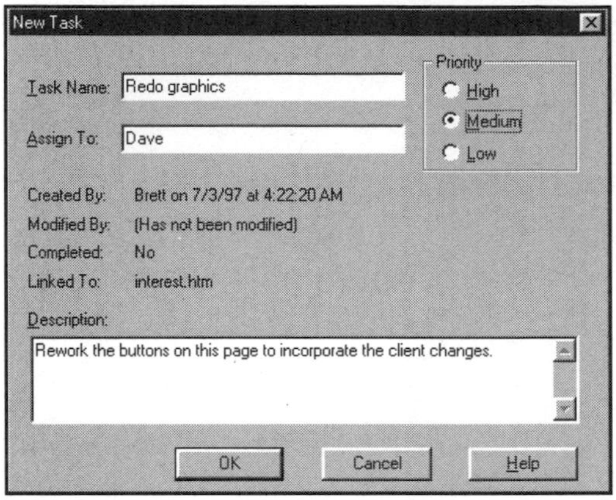

Figure 3-20

Managing with the Tasks View

The Tasks view can be a powerful management tool. It gives you the ability to assign or reassign tasks, observe what work has been completed in a site, and determine what work still needs to be done. You can perform the following team management tasks using the Tasks view:

Evening up the workload. If someone on your team has a great deal more work to perform on a site than others, you can even up the workload by reassigning some of that person's tasks.

Seeing whether a task is completed. R. U. Awake, your team's resident procrastinator, often takes a long time to get things done. To check on her progress, you can look at the Tasks view and sort the Task column to find a task. If the task doesn't appear in the list, R. U. gets a reprieve; if it's still there, it's time for R. U. to write on her whiteboard 50 times, "I will get my Tasks view tasks done on time."

Determining the state of your site. You can determine a site's condition in many ways by using the Tasks view. One way is to simply look at the number of tasks to be completed. Another way is to sort the tasks by priority: If you see many high- and medium-priority tasks remaining, you have more work to do than if most of the remaining tasks were low-priority level tasks.

Determining what pages or files need the most work. Sorting on the Linked To column can give you an indication of which pages and/or files in your site need the most work. If you have many tasks associated with a few pages, you can assign more resources to those areas.

What Do the Explorer Views Have in Common?

You can access some features from each of the Folders, All Files, Navigation, and Hyperlinks views in the Explorer. These are the views that contain file names and lists. Here's the rundown:

Adjusting the Column Widths

You can change column widths. Place your mouse in the column heading area, near a border between the columns. When the cursor changes to a crosshair with left and right arrows, click and drag to adjust the width.

Opening Files from a View

These views are not just a compilation of pages and links; they also are avenues for opening their associated files in the Editor or whatever application you want to work in to manipulate those files. For example, to manipulate a Graphics Interchange Format (GIF) file that appears in any these views, you can launch the application and edit the file with a few clicks of the mouse.

You can open files from anywhere you can see the file name listed. To open a file, right-click the title or the icon, and then choose Open from the pop-up menu. If the file is an HTML file, the page appears in the Editor, ready for you to edit. If you choose the Open With command, you can open the page with any other editor. After you choose Open With, you get a list of editors in the Open With Editor dialog box; you can select an editor and click OK.

But what if you want a different editor to open when you choose the Open command for a particular type of file, or what if your editor doesn't show up at all in the Open With Editor dialog box? You can change the editor type by choosing the Options command from the Tools menu and clicking the Configure Editors tab. (See "Configuring Editors," later in this chapter.)

SHORTCUT You can also double-click a file in one of these views to open it. The file opens with its associated editor.

Viewing File Properties

To view properties for a file, select the file and then choose the Properties command from the Edit menu. The Summary tab of the Properties dialog box provides information such as when the file was created, who created it, when it was modified, and who modified it. It also includes a text box in which you can add comments to the file.

SHORTCUT You can access the properties for an item by right-clicking the item and choosing Properties from the pop-up menu.

On the General tab, you'll find general information on the file, such as its name, title, type, size, and location. The location can be a file location or a URL. A URL indicates the address of a resource on a network and the method by which it can be accessed. URLs can use various protocols; the most common one on the World Wide Web today is HTTP. The terms *URL* and *HTTP address* refer to the same thing.

Refreshing a View

To update the views in the Explorer, choose Refresh from the View menu. The command refreshes all views for the current site in the Explorer. If more than one person is working on a site at one time, refreshing the site allows you to see all of the changes.

Changing the Size of a View

A split bar separates the panes in the Folder, Navigation, and Hyperlinks views. To move the bar and change the amount of the window devoted to each of the views, place your cursor directly over the bar until it changes to a double-line cursor with left and right arrows, and then click and drag the bar.

One Button Publishing

If you want to move your site to another server, FrontPage makes it easy. For example, suppose you've been testing your site locally on the Microsoft Personal Web Server or the FrontPage Personal Web Server, and you want to move the site to a higher-volume server that powers your intranet or to a Web server connected to the Internet. You can use the Publish button on the File menu to copy a site that is currently open in the Explorer to a server. Assuming that the appropriate FrontPage Server Extensions are installed for the server to which you're copying, and that you have administrator level access, it's an easy task—one that you can do at the push of a button. Here's how to do it:

1. With the site you want to copy currently open in the Explorer, select the Publish button from the Explorer toolbar. The Publish dialog box appears, as seen in Figure 3-21 on the facing page.
2. FrontPage remembers the server to which you last published and displays it in the Publish FrontPage Web to: list box.

3. If you only want to publish changes to the Web, select the Publish Changed Pages Only check box.

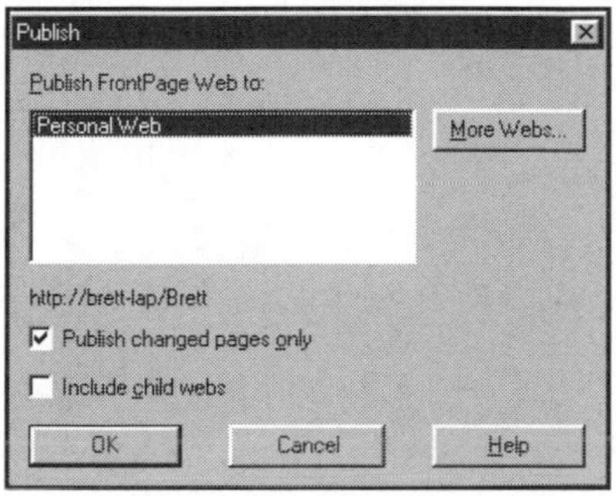

Figure 3-21

4. If you're publishing on the root Web and you want to publish all the other Webs on the same server too, check the Include Child Webs option.
5. Click OK. FrontPage locates the server and publishes the Web as directed.

If you want to publish to a different server, choose the More Webs button from the Publish dialog box. The Publish FrontPage Web dialog box opens, as shown in Figure 3-22 below.

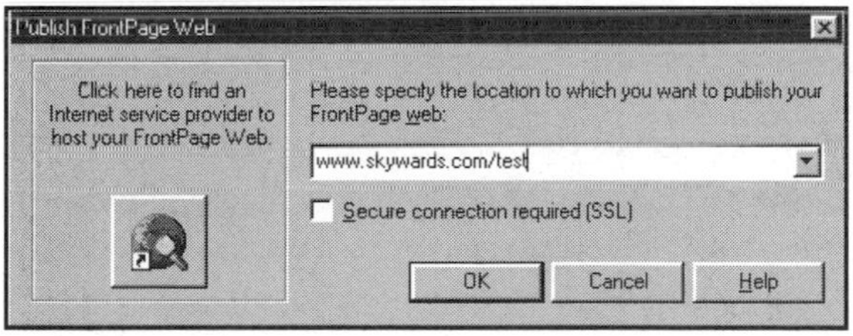

Figure 3-22

1. In the Publish FrontPage Web dialog box, select a location from the drop-down list, or enter the name of the Web server directly. You can also enter a pathname if you want to place the site on a hard disk or LAN. If you want to communicate with your site using Secure Sockets Layer (SSL) security, select the Connect Using SSL check box.
2. Click OK after you finish. FrontPage locates the server or file location and publishes the Web as directed.

You also can use either of these methods to publish to Web servers that don't have the FrontPage Server Extensions installed. In this case, FrontPage notices that the Server Extensions are not installed on the destination Web server, and automatically launches the Web Publishing Wizard (a separate component that you can install from the FrontPage CD). The wizard will publish your site to the destination server using the FTP protocol. (It does ask you for information, such as the FTP server name, user name, password, and destination folder.) The wizard also knows how to save sites to online services such as America Online, CompuServe, and others.

Performing Other Functions of the Explorer

So far in this chapter, you've learned that you can use the Explorer to create, open, and publish sites, as well as to view them in several different ways. The Explorer also sports a host of other functions that you can use in your everyday site management.

Closing a Site

Because the FrontPage Explorer can display only one site at a time, it closes the current site whenever you open another site or create a new one. To close the current site without opening another, choose Close FrontPage Web from the File menu. The Getting Started dialog box appears, asking where you want to go.

Deleting a Site

You must have administrative access with FrontPage to delete a site, and the site must be open in the Explorer before you can delete it. To delete the site that is currently open, choose Delete FrontPage Web from the File menu in the Explorer.

WARNING Be sure to delete sites by using the Delete FrontPage Web command, not by manually removing their files from a server. If you remove the files manually, FrontPage might not recognize that they've been deleted, and the Web sites would still be listed in the Open FrontPage Web and Getting Started dialog boxes. If you tried to open one, you'd get a warning that says that the directory that would hold the URL of the site does not exist on the server.

Consider this before you delete: Once you delete a site, even if you've removed it properly with the Delete FrontPage Web command, you cannot recover it––not even from the Recycle Bin in the Windows Explorer, or from any directory that FrontPage may have created for the site. FrontPage posts this reminder every time you choose this command.

Deleting Files

You must have at least author-level access before you can delete files in the Explorer. You can delete files by selecting them in the Folders, All Files, Navigation, or Hyperlinks views and then choosing Delete from the Edit menu, or by right-clicking the file and choosing Delete. FrontPage asks you to confirm the deletion before it carries out the action.

If you're building your site one page at a time, perhaps not taking advantage of one of the Web wizards, be sure to add and delete pages individually. If you do use a Web wizard, be careful when deleting any pages: you don't want to delete any links or pages that are referenced in other areas that the wizard created.

Adding a New Page to a Site

You can add a new page to a site from within the Folders, All Files, and Navigation views. You can add a new page to your site in a couple different ways:

- Select New from the File menu and choose Page from the New submenu.
- Click the New Page button on the Explorer toolbar.
- Right-click in the file list portion of the window, and choose New Page from the pop-up menu.
- Press the F2 button on your keyboard.
- Use the Copy and Paste buttons, respectively, on the Explorer toolbar.

When you create your new page, FrontPage adds it to the Web as a newpage.htm. It's a good idea to rename the page right away, so you don't end up with *newpage2.htm, newpage3.htm,* and so on, each time you add a page.

Importing a File into a Site

An application's ability to incorporate documents created in earlier versions of the program or in competing programs is one way of determining its value: "utility" versus "futility." You shouldn't have to lose the work you've already done in another Web authoring application if you're moving over to FrontPage. If you've already created pages or files (for example,

RTF or HTML files) that you'd like to include in your current site, FrontPage allows you to do it, and quite easily.

You can import Word documents, Excel spreadsheets, and more into your sites—FrontPage allows you to import non-Microsoft files into your site, as well. An intranet site can consist of dozens, hundreds, or even thousands of documents. If you're in charge of getting those documents into the site, you'll be relieved to know that you can import all those files at once if you want to.

You can import files into a site using two methods: by using a menu command or by dragging and dropping files into the Explorer from elsewhere on your computer. Here's how to use the menu command:

1. With the destination site open in the Explorer, choose Import from the File menu. The Import File To FrontPage Web dialog box appears, as seen below in Figure 3-23.

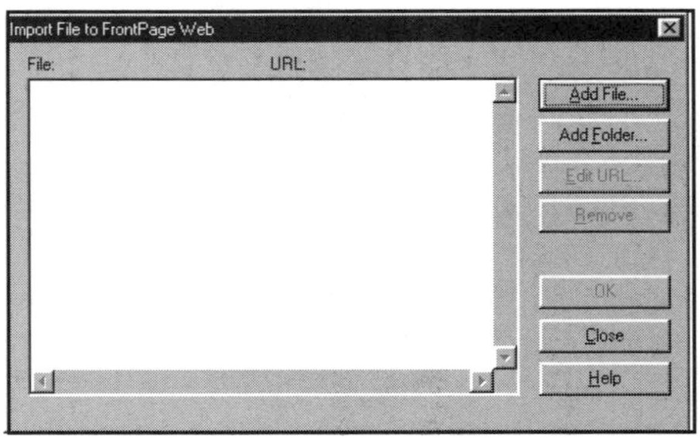

Figure 3-23

2. Click the Add File button. The Add File To Import List dialog box opens, and in it, you specify the file or files you want to import. Locate the folder that contains the file by using the folder controls at the top of the dialog box. Be sure to select the type of files to be listed by using the Files Of Type drop-down list. (If you're not sure of the type of file you're looking for, select All Files from the drop-down list.)
3. Select the file or files that you want to import. You select files here in the same way that you do in the Windows Explorer. To select a group of contiguous files, click the first file in the group, press the Shift key, and then click the last file in the group. To select multiple noncontiguous files, press the Ctrl key while clicking the files you want to

select. To remove a file from a selection, press the Ctrl key while clicking the file.

4. Click the Open button. That closes the Add File To Import List dialog box and adds the files to a list in the Import File To FrontPage Web dialog box.
5. If you need to add more files to the list, repeat steps 2, 3, and 4. To remove files from the list before you add them to your site, select them and click the Remove button.
6. If you want to change the URL of any file, select the file in the Import File To FrontPage Web dialog box and click the Edit URL button. It comes in handy when you want to save the file separately from the other material in the site; you enter the new URL (pointing the file to the folder of your choice) in the Edit URL dialog box that appears, and then click OK.
7. Click the OK button to add the files to your site. When you click the OK button, it changes to a Stop button so that you can halt the process at any time.

FrontPage closes the Import File To FrontPage Web dialog box after it finishes importing the files. The imported files are not linked to any pages in the site. If you try to close the Explorer while items are still in the Import list, the Explorer warns you.

You also can add image files to your site by using the Import command. As described in Chapter 8, you can do this in several different ways in the Editor, but if you know you're going to use certain files in your site, the Import command allows you to add them all at once.

Dragging and dropping a file into a site. There will be times when you want to import just a file or two into your site, and the process of using the Import command is too time-consuming for its own good. For those times, FrontPage supports dragging and dropping those files into the Explorer, which works similarly to dragging and dropping files onto a view, described in the sidebar "Dragging and Dropping" earlier in this chapter. The only difference is that you drag a file from a location outside of your Web, and drop it into your Web.

Exporting a File from a Site

Suppose you want to copy an item, such as a page or an image, from your site to another location. You can save any file to your hard disk, a network location, or a floppy disk by choosing the Export command from the File menu in the Explorer. First, select the file in either the Folders, All Files, Navigation, or Hyperlinks views, and then choose Export from the File menu. In the Export Selected As dialog box that appears, you can specify the location you want the file to be copied to. When you click the Save button, the file is copied to the specified location.

The Export command does not remove the file from your site. To remove a file from your site, you must delete it.

Changing Site Settings

Nightmare on Web Street, scene one: You've just completed a site for your company, which includes the company's phone and fax numbers on nearly every one of its 169 pages. After you come up for air, you read in the morning paper that your area code is about to change. After you wonder where the heck you've been for the past nine months, you're faced with editing every one of those 169 pages. You could use a utility program to search for the old area code and replace it with the new one, and there are other ways to get the job done. But how about a one-stop-shop way?

TIP You can also change information on all of the pages in your site that do not use parameters and configuration variables, by using FrontPage's Find and Replace commands. For more information, see Chapter 7.

FrontPage uses placeholders, also called *parameters* or *configuration variables*, so that it can track where this information is used in the current site. The templates and wizards in FrontPage add some parameters automatically. You can define your own and insert them using the FrontPage Substitution Component discussed in Chapter 9. By using the Web Settings command on the Tools menu in the Explorer, you can update the information wherever it occurs in your site. You can also access the FrontPage Web Settings dialog box in any view, except Themes view, by right-clicking in the view pane and selecting Web Settings from the pop-up menu. Choose the command, and you'll see the FrontPage Web Settings dialog box, which has four tabs (see Figure 3-24).

Parameters Tab

If your site was constructed using a template or wizard that contained parameters for later authors to fill in, or if you've defined your own, those parameters will show up here.

You can add parameters by clicking the Add button. The Add Name And Value dialog box appears, prompting you for the name and value of the parameter (whatever information you want to enter). Click OK to exit the dialog box and add the new parameter to your list.

To change the parameter information, such as in the scenario described above, select the parameter you want to change and click the Modify button, and then enter the new information in the Modify Name And Value dialog box that appears. Click OK to save the information and exit the dialog box. FrontPage then automatically updates the parameter in all pages of your site on which that parameter appears.

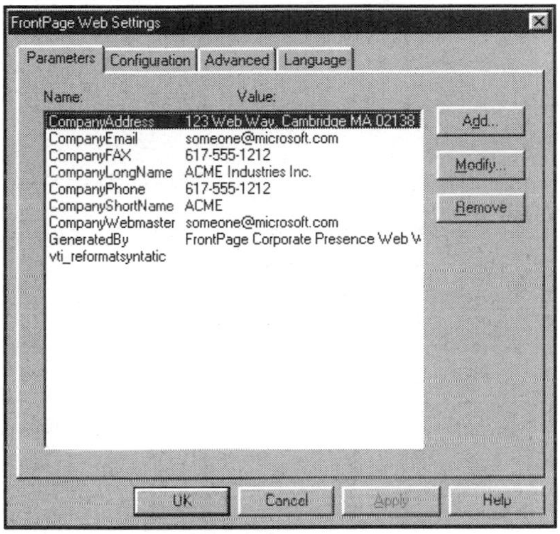

Figure 3-24

Clicking the Remove button removes the selected parameter from the list.

Configuration Tab

To change the name and title of your site, click the Configuration tab of the FrontPage Web Settings dialog box, replace the information, and then click OK. The name should not contain spaces, because the name is used as part of the site's URL, and URLs do not contain spaces. The site title, however, can contain spaces.

TIP It's important to give your site a name that you can easily recognize among a list of sites. Each time you open a site to work on it in the Explorer, you select the site from a list; if you create numerous sites on your server, that list can get long and confusing. You can save yourself future headaches by giving your site an intuitive and distinctive name at the outset.

Advanced Tab

The Advanced tab allows you to set or modify advanced settings, including the following:

- You can configure how FrontPage supports image maps in the Image Maps section. From the Style drop-down list, select the server type for the images, and then set an optional prefix if the Prefix text box is enabled. The default setting, FrontPage, allows image maps to be used no matter what Web server you use, as long as you have the FrontPage Server Extensions installed. Select the Generate Client-Side Image Maps check box if you want FrontPage to generate image maps from the client and not from the server.

  It's a good idea to select this check box. FrontPage generates client-side image maps in such a way that if a browser does not support client-side image maps, it simply ignores the client-side image map information in the HTML file. Therefore, selecting this check box can cause no harm, and in fact, often can give you gains in speed—see Chapter 8 for more details.

- In the Validation Scripts section, you can specify the validation scripting language. The options available are VBScript, JavaScript, and <None>.

  If you use the Form Field Validation feature of FrontPage, FrontPage will automatically generate JavaScript or VBScript right onto the page to perform the validation. This setting allows you to select which language to use. If you use JavaScript, it will work with both Internet Explorer and Netscape Navigator. If you choose VBScript, it will work only with Internet Explorer.

- In the Options section, select the Show Documents In Hidden Directories check box to display documents in hidden folders. Hidden folders are preceded by an underscore (_). By default, you can't view pages and files in hidden folders when you're in the Explorer. This feature allows you to act as a moderator for a discussion group; individual messages in a discussion are kept in a hidden folder.

- In the Recalculate Status section, there are two check boxes that allow you to specify when FrontPage recalculates your Web site. These options are Included Page Dependencies Are Out Of Date and Text Index Is Out Of Date.

Language Tab

The Language tab allows you to set the default language and HTML encoding for your site. The Default Web Language setting is used by the FrontPage

Server Extensions so that when error messages need to be returned back to the browser, the specified language is used. The Default HTML Encoding setting specifies the default character set for new pages.

FrontPage 98 is available in English, Baltic, Central European, Chinese, French, German, Greek, Italian, Japanese, Korean, Spanish, and Turkish editions. Even if the FrontPage user interface is not available for a particular language, you can still create sites for essentially any language, using the extensive list of HTML encodings available from this dialog box.

Changing a Password

Your officemate, Sissy LeJerk, looked over your shoulder and memorized your FrontPage administrator password as you were typing it in. What to do? Change your password when Sissy isn't looking over your shoulder. Here's how: First, tell her there's a mongo sale of her favorite perfume, Evening d'Armpit, in the mall next door. After she leaves the office, choose the Change Password command from the Tools menu in the Explorer. You'll see a dialog box asking you for your old password, which Sissy knows; for your new password, which she'll never have a clue about because you'll be watching over your shoulder from now on; and for a confirmation of that password. Enter the passwords and the confirmation, and then click OK to exit the dialog box and save your new password. Then put a small bag of used cat litter in Sissy's briefcase.

TIP The Change Password command might appear grayed out. For several of Microsoft's Web servers, access control is handled by the system instead of by FrontPage. For more information, see Chapter 5.

Configuring Editors

Have you ever opened a file from the Windows Explorer? If you have, you know that the file opens in an application that it can be viewed and/or edited in. The FrontPage Explorer offers the same feature. When you double-click a file in your Web site, such as a GIF or JPEG file, or any Office file, the FrontPage Explorer opens the file in the application specified in the Windows Explorer.

If you want to invoke a different editor than what is currently specified in the Windows Explorer, here's how: First, choose Options from the Tools menu. The Options dialog box appears (see Figure 3-25). Click the Configure Editors tab.

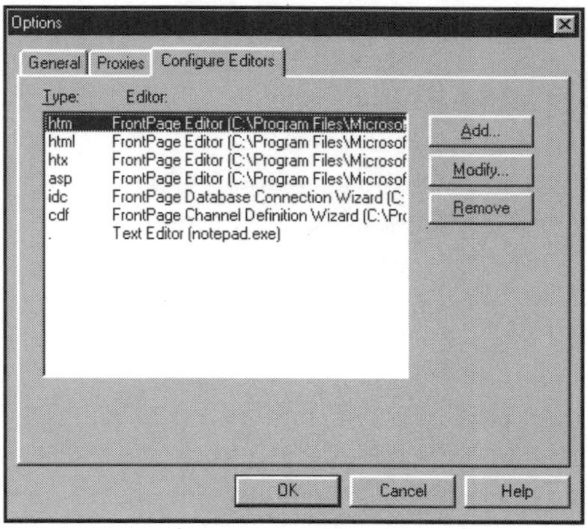

Figure 3-25

The list box on the tab has two columns, one for the extension of the file type to edit and the other for the application that's used to edit the file. As you can see, the dialog box includes default settings for some common file types and their editors.

To add a file type, click the Add button. The Add Editor Association dialog box opens. Add the extension that identifies the file type in the File Type text box and type, and enter the name you want to use for the editor in the Editor Name text box. Then enter the name and location of the executable file in the Command text box. If you don't know the exact location, click the Browse button to search your folders for the executable file. When you finish, click OK.

To modify settings for an existing entry, select the entry and click the Modify button. This takes you to the Modify Editor Association dialog box, where you can change the editor name and the command to execute the editor.

You can also remove an entry in the list by selecting the entry and clicking Remove.

FrontPage allows you to designate only one editor application per file type. Each of the editors listed on the Configure Editors tab appears in the Open With Editor dialog box under the Edit menu. If you don't specify an editor for a particular file type in the Explorer, FrontPage uses the default Windows editor for that file type.

SHORTCUT FrontPage does not ask you to confirm the removal of an entry on the Configure Editors tab when you click Remove. If you remove an entry by mistake, you must reenter it by clicking Add.

Recalculating Hyperlinks

Recalculating hyperlinks updates or "refreshes" your site. If you've made significant changes to your site, such as removing entire pages, it's wise to go through the recalculating hyperlinks operation.

This is especially true if you've added, deleted, or modified documents in your site without using FrontPage. All you need to do is choose Recalculate Hyperlinks from the Tools menu. FrontPage warns you that the process might take a long time, and asks you if you want to proceed. You can recalculate hyperlinks in any view in the Explorer.

When you use this command, FrontPage performs the following tasks:

- Updates the display for the current site in the Explorer views.
- Updates your list of links for the current site. If you delete material from your site and you want to check your links using the Verify Hyperlinks command, some of the deleted links might still be listed in the Verify Hyperlinks dialog box. Therefore, it is a good idea to use the Recalculate Links command after you have deleted material from your site.
- Updates the text index that's created by a FrontPage Search Component. When you implement searching on a page using this FrontPage component, FrontPage creates a text index for the component to use. When you add a page or save a modified page in your site, entries are added to the text index, but no entries are deleted. Thus, if you delete material from a page and then save the modified page, the text index still contains entries for the deleted material. Whenever you delete material, including entire pages, from your site, you need to use the Recalculate Links command to update the text index. (For more information on the FrontPage Search Component, see Chapter 9.)

Coming Up

As you can see, you can use the Explorer, the engine of FrontPage's client software, not only to view a Web site but to administer it. Two additional key parts of the FrontPage client, templates and wizards, are detailed in the next chapter.

CHAPTER 4

Templates and Wizards

Life in the Fast Lane

Imagine what an announcer would say if FrontPage were ever featured in a late-night infomercial: "Tired of staying up night after night memorizing *thousands* of HTML commands? Tired of taking hours and hours to create that one final page that'll make your site shine?" In a fictitious world, you'd also be real excited about the prospect of losing five pounds and getting great abs while sitting there creating your Web sites, but we're here to tell you that FrontPage can actually save you so much time with its templates and wizards that you *might* even be able to take your family on that three-week cross-country trip to Wally World that you've been dreaming about for the past 15 years.

Everyone's looking for a shortcut, and you've got a huge one in FrontPage by not having to know a lick of HTML to create professional-looking Web sites. FrontPage also provides a couple other pretty cool shortcuts in its templates and wizards. A *template*, as you might know, is a "shell" that you use as the basis for a new document. A *wizard* is a software module of one or more screens that asks you questions, offers you choices, and then generates a customized document as a result. Templates are not customizable up-front the way that wizards are. The result of both templates and wizards is a document that serves as a framework for your finished product—a framework that you can modify if you like, and add information to.

This chapter explores the FrontPage templates and wizards. It shows you how to work with them, and it gives you plenty of examples along the way. You'll find that using templates and wizards is a terrific way to get started on your Web site, and a sensational time-saver as well.

Templates

Templates are examples of sites or pages that FrontPage provides to fill a particular need. Like wizards, they give you a framework, or a great place to start, for a site or a page. *Wizards,* however, offer you choices in creating a customized site or page; when you select a template, you get an exact copy of the template itself, with dummy text that you replace with your own copy.

Web Templates

Most of the Web templates in FrontPage are based on small sites; they have few items that need customizing. You can, however, enhance these pages by adding images, text, links, and so forth—in the FrontPage Editor. You can also add your own pages to sites created using Web templates.

You can access the Web templates in the FrontPage Explorer by choosing New from the File menu, and then choosing FrontPage Web from the submenu that appears. In the New FrontPage Web dialog box (see Figure 4-1), you can select one of the following templates to use as the basis for your site or page:

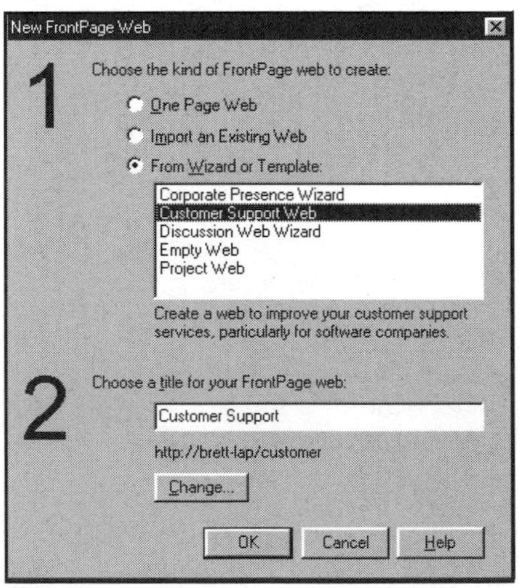

Figure 4-1

- **Customer Support Web.** This template creates a place where your customers can go to report bugs, find solutions to previously reported problems, and suggest improvements for your products and services. This is an ideal site for software companies, but it is applicable to many kinds of businesses.
- **Empty Web.** When you want to create an entire site from scratch, you can use this "template." It creates an empty site with no pages, and you do all the rest by adding content in the Explorer and Editor.
- **Project Web.** Use this template to create a site that will serve as a central informational forum for a project. This template creates a home page, a page that lists members of the project team, a schedule page, a status page, a search page, various forms and discussion pages, and a page that links to all public discussions about the project.

I talk more about the Web wizards that are listed in the New FrontPage Web dialog box, in the section, "Web Wizards," later in this chapter.

Page Templates

FrontPage offers you a wide variety of page templates, ranging from a bare-bones Normal page to a fairly complex Three Column Staggered page. Adding pages to an existing site with a page template is a fast and easy way to customize a site.

Using Page Templates

You create a page using a template in the Editor. The process is very simple:

1. In the Explorer, open the site that you want the new page to belong to. (You can skip this step if you want to; after you save the page, you can import it to any Web site.)
2. In the Editor, choose New from the File menu.
3. In the New dialog box that appears, select a template from the Page tab (see Figure 4-2), and then click OK.

NOTE This list also includes the Form Page Wizard; for more information on this wizard, see the section "The Form Page Wizard" later in this chapter. The New dialog box also contains a Frames tab; for more information on creating frames pages, see the next section, "Making Frames."

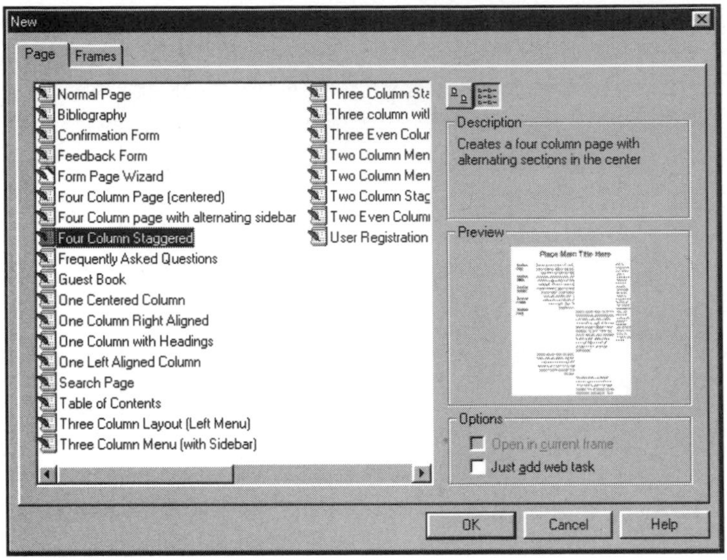

Figure 4-2

You can choose from a wide variety of different page templates to create new pages in your site. The templates are listed in the window on the left side of the New dialog box, along with a description and preview on the right side of the dialog box. You can view the templates as a list or as large icons by selecting the appropriate button, located above the description. If you have a frameset currently open in the Editor, and you want your new page to open the current frame, check the Open In Current Frame check box. If you have a site open in the Explorer and you want to add the new page to the Tasks view, to be worked on later, check the Just Add Web Task check box.

You'll find that the templates have many varied uses, and that some of them are designed to be used together in the same site. Take a look through the templates; if you know your options, you'll be better prepared to create the site you want.

When you finally decide on a template, FrontPage creates the page using the template you select, and presents it in the Editor for you to work on.

Whenever you create a new page from a page template, it includes dummy text, called lorem ipsum (or greeking), and example text, like Place Main Title Here, that you replace with your own text. The example shown in Figure 4-3, created with the Four Column Staggered page template shows the lorem ipsum text and example text.

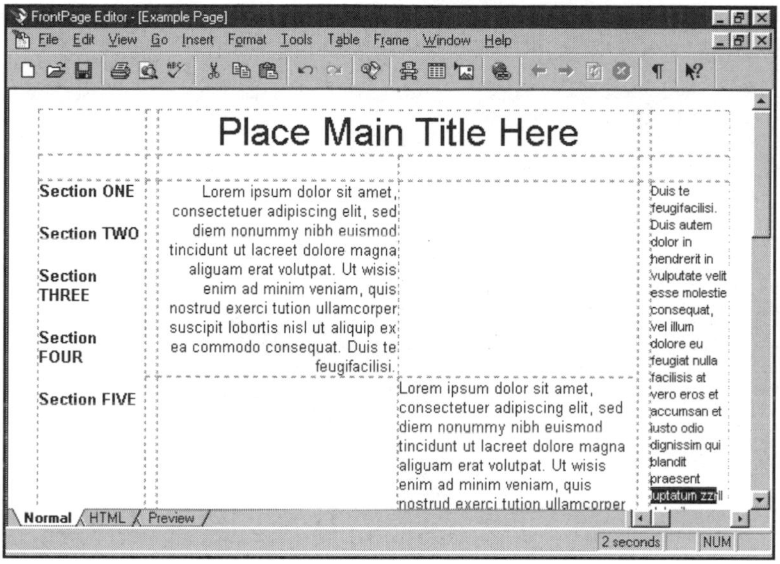

Figure 4-3

Making Frames

Frames enable you to divide a page into rectangular regions in a browser, each of which displays its own page. You can place one or more frames on a page (referred to as the frameset for that page). This means that you can create a page on which different regions have different content. Changing the content of one region doesn't necessarily change the content of another, but if you want, links in one frame can cause the page that is displayed in another frame to change.

Here's the classic example of the use of frames: Imagine a Web page divided vertically into two regions, each of which is a frame. The left frame is occupied by a Table of Contents page, containing a complete list of links to all pages in the site. The contents of the frame on the right side of the screen change, depending on what link you click on in the table of contents on the left side. If you click a link to an Issues page in the table of contents, the Issues page appears on the right side; if you click the Results link, the Results page appears, and so on. Figure 4-4 depicts this scenario.

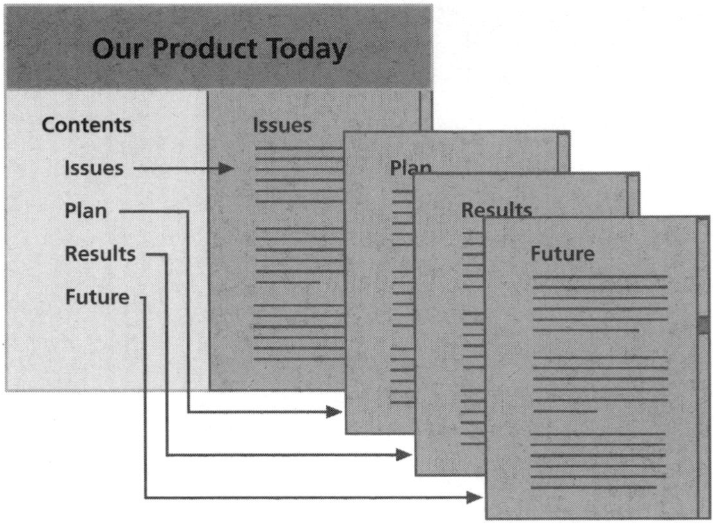

Figure 4-4

A page divided into frames. Click a link in the TOC on the left side, and that page appears on the right side.

Frames have become very popular with Web designers, and some of them have gotten a little carried away, dividing their pages into five, six, or even more frames. Since that can make the site really slow, not to mention annoying, FrontPage gives you ten frames templates, each containing no more than four frames in the frameset.

Using Frame Templates

You create a frames page using a frame template in the Editor. The process goes like this:

1. In the Explorer, open the site to which the new frameset will belong. (You can skip this step if you want to; after you save the frameset, you can import it to any Web site.)
2. In the Editor, choose New from the File menu.
3. In the New dialog box that appears, select a template from the Frames tab (see Figure 4-5), and then click OK.

You can preview how your frameset will look in the New dialog box. It works in exactly the same way as the New dialog box, described earlier. After you decide on a frameset, FrontPage builds the pages and displays them in the Editor. For more information on working with frames in the Editor, see Chapter 6.

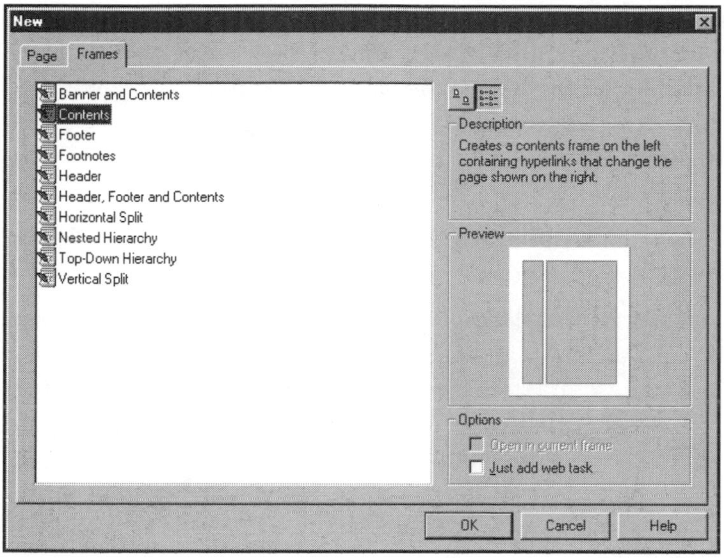

Figure 4-5

Custom Templates

Because everyone has a different style, and because you might have specific needs that the templates don't address, FrontPage allows you to create and save your own page templates in the Editor. (To find out how to create custom Web site templates, see the next section, "Custom Web Site Templates.")

Perhaps you want to create several similar pages that don't look much like any of the existing FrontPage templates. You can create your own template to use when creating these pages and minimize the number of changes you need to make to each. Of course, you can always open a FrontPage page template, alter it to suit your needs, and then use that as a new template.

Using a custom page template is a great way to streamline the gathering of employee information at a company. You can create a specific form with places for each kind of information you need from your employees, and then save that form as a template. You can then distribute that template within your organization for all to use.

Creating and saving a custom page template requires only a few steps:

1. Start with the Normal Page template in the Editor, and insert the content that you want to have appear in your new template; for example, custom logos, navigation buttons, and so forth.

2. Choose the Save As command from the File menu in the Editor. If you're running the Explorer, you see the Save As dialog box. If you're running the Editor only, you see the Save As File dialog box, with the Save As dialog box below it. The Save As File dialog box lets you save the file as a page independent of any other pages. To see the Save As dialog box, click Cancel in the Save As File dialog box.
3. In the Save As dialog box, click the As Template button. You do not need to supply a template name or a URL before you click this button.
4. In the Save As Template dialog box (see Figure 4-6), give your template a title and a name, and then enter a short description of the template in the Description text box. If you want to save the current template in place of another template, click the Browse button and find the template that you want to replace.

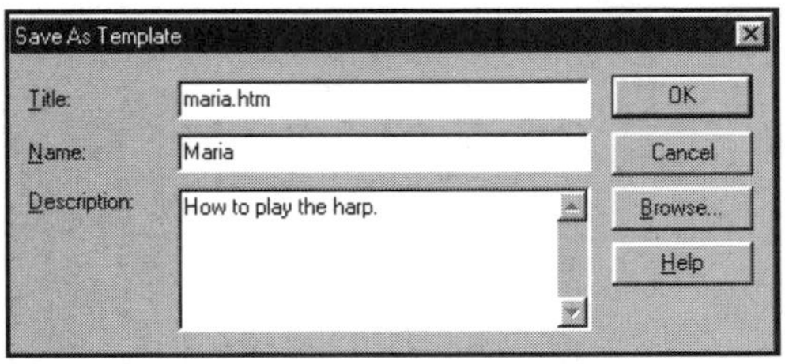

Figure 4-6

5. Click OK in the Save As Template dialog box. FrontPage saves the page as a template and returns you to the page.

After you save the template, any time you create a new page in the Editor, that template appears in the New Page dialog box along with all the page templates and wizards included with FrontPage. If you want to save your template to a different location, include a pathname in the Title field of the Save As Template dialog box.

Custom Web Site Templates

You can use the *FrontPage Developer's Kit* to create custom Web site templates, as well as custom Web and page wizards, which I discuss later. For information on obtaining this free kit, see the FrontPage area of Microsoft's Web site at www.microsoft.com/frontpage/.

Wizards

How long do you suppose it would take to create a Web site for your business from scratch that includes all of the following?

- A home page with places for an introduction, mission statement, company profile, and/or contact information
- A What's New page that contains links for press releases, articles, reviews, and information about your site
- Numerous products and services pages, each with room for a description of the product or service, images, pricing information, and more
- A Table of Contents page that indexes your site and is updated automatically as your site structure changes
- A feedback form that asks users for specific information, such as their name, title, address, phone number, fax number, and e-mail address

As you know by now, creating a Web site that includes all of this from scratch by writing it in HTML would take quite a long time. For many, it would be akin to putting an automobile together piece by piece—it's easy to see where the big pieces go, but incorporating the smaller pieces and getting it all to work smoothly is quite difficult. Would you believe that with FrontPage, creating a site like the one just described can take less than five minutes? You can do it all by using the Corporate Presence Wizard, which is one of several wizards included with FrontPage, and a couple dozen clicks of the mouse. And when you're done, you have a set of linked pages complete with elements that are ready for you to customize.

FrontPage offers two Web wizards that create the framework for entire Web sites, plus an additional Web wizard that allows you to import non-FrontPage Web sites. FrontPage also includes one page wizard that creates a form page that you can use to collect information from users, and save it back to a page on your site, or to a text file on the server.

Web Wizards

The two Web wizards that create brand new FrontPage sites for you are the Corporate Presence Wizard and the Discussion Web Wizard. The Corporate Presence Wizard creates the framework for a site that includes the items described in the previous section, and the Discussion Web Wizard produces a site in which users can participate in discussions on various topics. First, I walk you through the Corporate Presence Wizard; after that, I provide a description of the Discussion Web Wizard.

Keep in mind that you can easily change the resulting site later on if you want to, using the Editor. You can add to the pages, delete items or pages, and modify the pages in any other way you like.

Corporate Presence Wizard. Using the Corporate Presence Wizard, you can create a site to highlight your business without having to do much up-front work. Let's step through the process of using this wizard, as someone might when designing a site for the fictitious Snake River Winery:

1. From the File menu in the Explorer, choose New, and then choose FrontPage Web from the submenu. In the New FrontPage Web dialog box that appears, select Corporate Presence Wizard. You can also reach the New FrontPage Web dialog box by selecting Create a New FrontPage Web from the Getting Started dialog box.
2. Give your new site a title (for the purposes of this example, use *Snake River Winery*), and click OK. FrontPage begins to build the sites folder structure on the server location specified in the New FrontPage Web dialog box. For more information on changing the server location, see Chapter 3.
3. Next, you see the opening screen of the Corporate Presence Wizard (see Figure 4-7). It contains a brief description of the wizard and informs you that you need to answer a few questions about how you want your site to appear. Several buttons appear at the bottom of the screen:

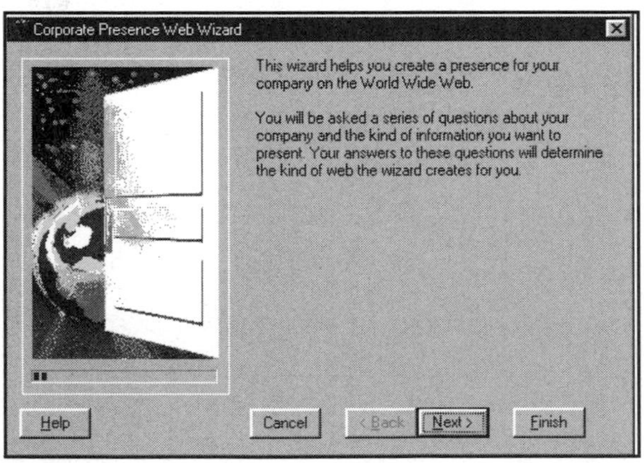

Figure 4-7

- **Help.** At any time, you can click the Help button to open a Corporate Presence Web Wizard topic in online help.
- **Cancel.** The Cancel button stops the wizard and takes you back to the Explorer. Because some of the material for the site has already been created, you are asked whether to delete the site.
- **Back.** When the Back button is enabled, you can click it to return to the previous screen or screens and change any information you have already entered.
- **Next.** Clicking the Next button takes you to the next screen in the wizard.
- **Finish.** The Finish button ends the wizard process at whatever point you click it. You can stop using the wizard anytime before the final wizard screen. When you click the Finish button, FrontPage immediately begins to populate the site with all the information you've supplied up to that point.

Click Next to proceed.

4. The next screen gives you several options for pages to include in your site. Notice that the Back button is now enabled.

   The Snake River Winery is building a sophisticated site and intends to include all of the available types of pages (see Figure 4-8). The site starts with a required home page, the contents of which you can customize in the next step of the wizard.

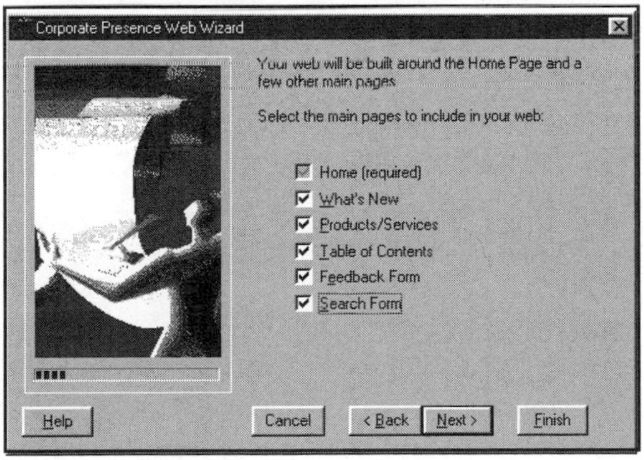

Figure 4-8

- **What's New page.** For any users who return to the site multiple times, this page can provide information on recent updates to the site. Perhaps a new Merlot is being offered in the fall, or maybe there's a special group rate for tours of the winery in July. The What's New page can link to these items in your site.
- **Products/Services page.** Simply because the winery sells products, and especially because the products have mass appeal, the Products/Services page is a wise addition to the site. Here the winery can highlight all its wines and other products, and this also might be a good place to tell people how to order.
- **Table of Contents page.** Those who want to see an overview of what the winery's site has to offer can go to this page, which links to all other pages in the site. It's wise to include some sort of overview page in your site. These pages can help prevent users from getting "lost" in your site.
- **Feedback Form.** The winery management wants to know what users think of the products offered in the site, and what they think of the site. Visitors to the site can use the Feedback Form to submit comments to the winery.
- **Search Form.** The winery considers a search form an attractive feature for its site. It allows users to search the site for any word that might appear on its pages. Enabling the search form is as easy as selecting the Search Form check box in the wizard. FrontPage automatically compiles a word list that the search form uses when someone searches the site.

For each page that you decide to include in your Web site, the wizard presents you with a subsequent screen that you can use to customize the page further. The wizard does not show screens for pages you do not select in this screen.

Click Next when you're ready to move on.

5. Next, a screen appears presenting several options for the format of your home page (see Figure 4-9). Your choices include creating spaces for an introduction, mission statement, company profile, and contact information for your company. You're not asked to supply the exact information, such as the text of your mission statement, at this time; you enter that later in the Editor. The wizard simply creates a space for you to fill with the actual content at your leisure.

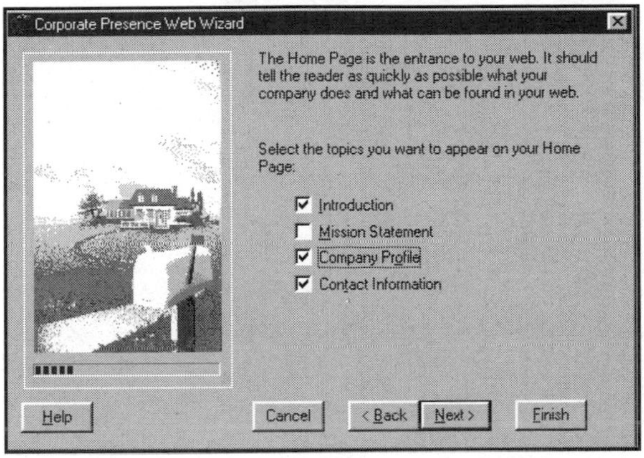

Figure 4-9

The folks at the Snake River Winery want their site to look professional, so at the very least they'll include the introduction, company profile, and contact information. Including the contact information is vital; potential wholesalers or individual customers who view the site might want to find out more about purchasing products.

After you select the check boxes for the topics you want to include, click Next.

6. Options for the What's New page are presented in the next screen. Select any of the three check boxes if you want to include that type of information on the page. FrontPage creates subsections for any items that you want to include on the What's New page.

   If a contact phone number changes at the Snake River Winery, the winery can alert its Web site viewers to the new number on the What's New page in the Web Changes section. You easily can add any other breaking news about the company to this page later on as well.

   The What's New page (see Figure 4-10) also is a great place to put information about the industry, such as a list of upcoming trade shows, positive information about stock trends, or other business news. It's great to have a place in your site where visitors can expect new, timely content. Such information can lure your customers back to your pages, where they'll be exposed to your products again and again. You can use the Press Releases section and the Articles And Reviews section for this purpose.

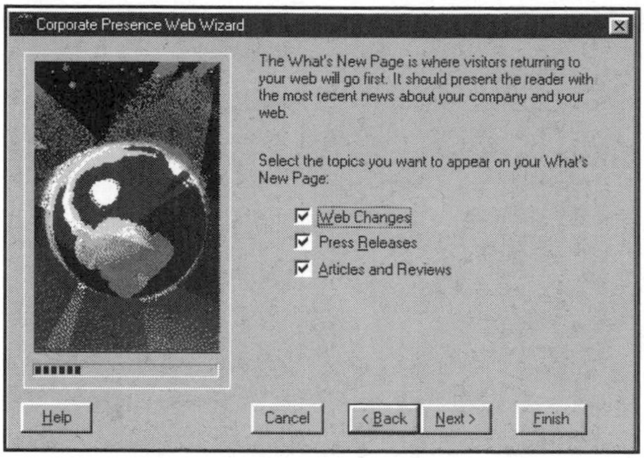

Figure 4-10

After you select the kind of information you want to include on your page to start with, click Next.

7. The next screen provides options for the Products/Services page (see Figure 4-11). Enter the values for the number of products and/or services you want to highlight on this page; FrontPage allows you to enter between 0 and 5 for each. The wizard creates sections on the page for the number of products and services you enter in this screen.

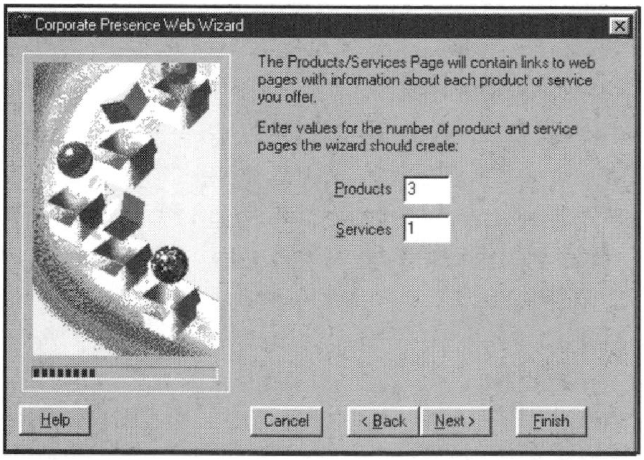

Figure 4-11

The Snake River Winery plans to highlight its three best wines in the Web site, so enter *3* in the Products text box. The winery also prides itself on providing top-flight customer service, so enter *1* in the Services text box to provide a section to highlight that aspect of the company.

Click Next to move to the next screen.

8. Next, you specify how you want to customize any product or service pages you have in your site. The wizard shown in Figure 4-12 gives you choices to provide placeholders for product images, pricing information, and information request forms on the Products pages, and to provide capabilities lists, reference accounts, and information request forms on Services pages.

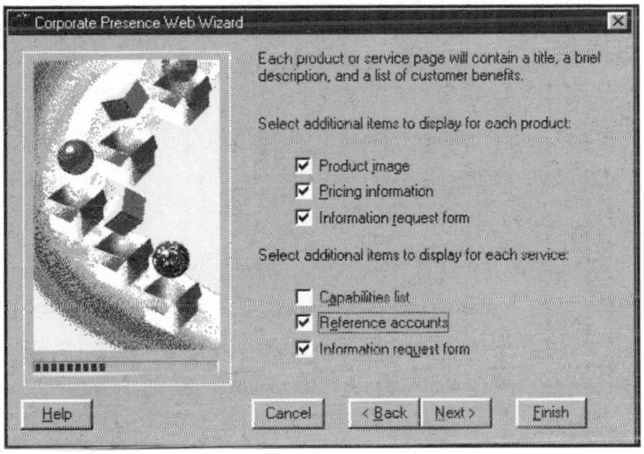

Figure 4-12

Select the options you want to include on those pages, and then click Next.

> **TIP** You can tab through the content options in the wizard screens instead of using your mouse. To select or deselect a check box, use the spacebar.

9. The next screen provides options for the Feedback Form, shown in Figure 4-13, where you specify the information you want to receive from your audience. Think carefully about this, keeping in mind what kind of audience you expect to view your pages. If the audience doesn't have plenty of time to fill out every item, seeing all of them at once might overwhelm them. Even though it takes only seconds to fill out a feedback form, Web surfers are keen on clicking out of a page if it looks like too much work.

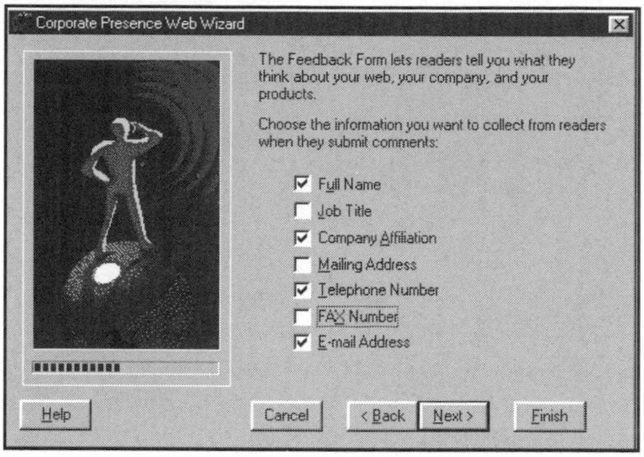

Figure 4-13

After you select the options you want for the Feedback Form, click Next.

10. The next screen, seen in Figure 4-14, features a neat option: It allows you to specify how to store the feedback you receive from your viewers. If you plan to manipulate the information using a database or spreadsheet application (such as Microsoft Access or Microsoft Excel), select the first option; FrontPage stores the information in tab-delimited format. If you don't plan to use such an application, select the second option and FrontPage stores the information in Web page format.

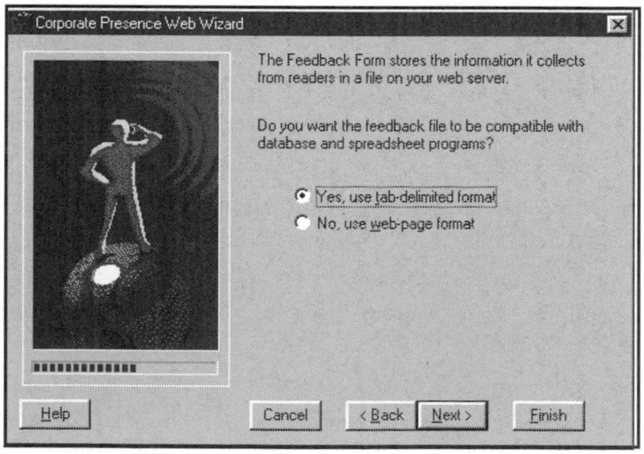

Figure 4-14

The Snake River Winery is not a large company, but management does expect its Web site to receive heavy traffic. It's easier to manipulate feedback information in Access and Excel—it reduces the workload significantly—so management wants to save the feedback information in tab-delimited format. That means that you should select the Yes, Use Tab Delimited Format option (see Figure 4-14).

After you make your choice, click Next to continue.

11. Next, you see a screen with options for customizing the Table of Contents (TOC) page shown here in Figure 4-15. Here you can select options to update the TOC automatically each time a page is edited, to show pages not linked to the pages that appear in the TOC, and to use bullets for top-level pages.

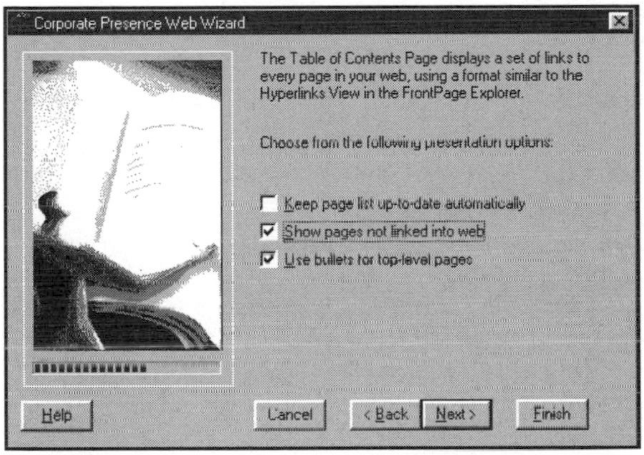

Figure 4-15

If you anticipate that your site will be small or that it won't be updated often, it's a good idea to select the Keep Page List Up-To-Date Automatically check box. If you anticipate that your site will be large or that it will grow significantly, however, you should not select this check box, because updating the page list can be time-consuming in these cases. You can update the TOC manually later on, so don't be overly concerned about this option.

After you select the options to customize your TOC page, click Next.

12. The next screen (see Figure 4-16) deals with the items that you want to appear at the top and bottom of every page in your site. You can include your company's logo, a page title, and links to your main Web pages at the top. You also can include links to your main Web pages at the bottom, along with your Webmaster's e-mail address, a copyright notice, and the date on which the page was last modified (which FrontPage automatically supplies).

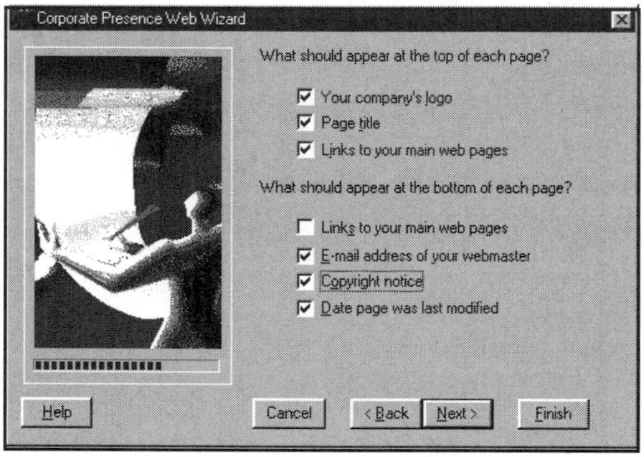

Figure 4-16

Again, these options control whether FrontPage leaves room for the item, not for the actual content for each item. Select the options you want, even if you plan to use different items on different pages.

The Winery Web site will sport a different logo for the pages in each section, so select the Your Company's Logo check box to include a space for the logo. Later, in the Editor, you can manually insert a different logo at the beginning of each page.

FrontPage doesn't check the contents of each space, so you can be flexible in how you use these options. If the winery wants to include the e-mail address of someone other than the Webmaster on the pages, for example, you should select the E-mail Address Of Your Webmaster check box to leave the space open. You can change the e-mail address in the Editor later on.

Select the options you want, and then click Next.

13. The next screen gives you the option of showing an Under Construction icon on all unfinished pages of your site, shown below in Figure 4-17.

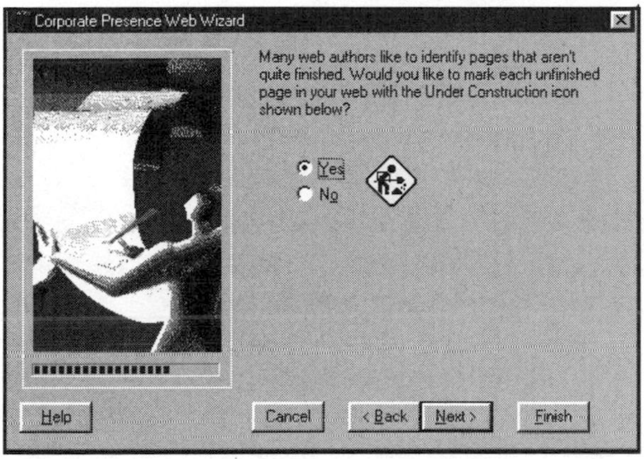

Figure 4-17

14. Select Yes, and then click Next. The next two screens, seen in Figures 4-18 and 4-19, offer *huge* potential time-savers. They ask for your company information, such as the company's full name, one-word name, address, phone number, and fax number; the e-mail address of the Webmaster; and a general-information e-mail address. These screens are time-savers because you enter the information once, and FrontPage inserts the information into the placeholders already in your site. In an earlier screen of the wizard (refer back to Figure 4-15), for example, if you requested that FrontPage display your Webmaster's e-mail address at the bottom of every page, all you need to do is type the address here, and FrontPage takes care of the rest.

If you need to make changes to this information later on, you only need to change it in one place. (You can change these settings later on by using the Web Settings command on the Explorer's Tools menu.)

The Snake River Winery wants to start with all this information on its pages, even though it might decide later not to include some of it.

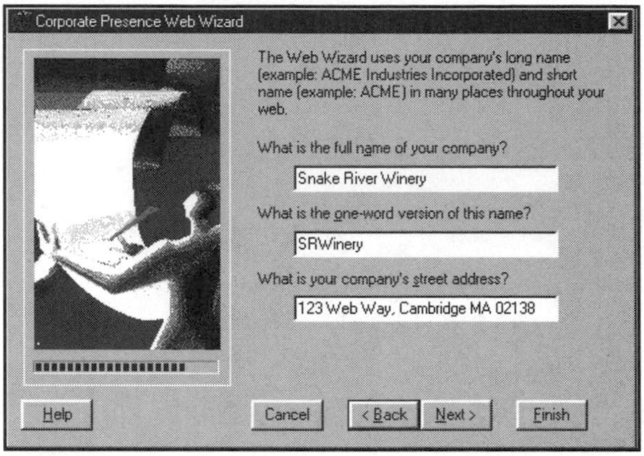

Figure 4-18

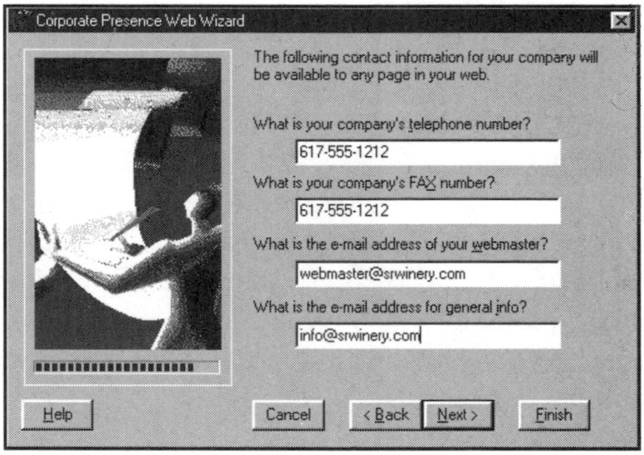

Figure 4-19

When you finish entering this information in both screens, click Next to move on.

15. In the next screen, you can control the "look and feel" of your site, via the FrontPage Web Themes, as seen in Figure 4-20.

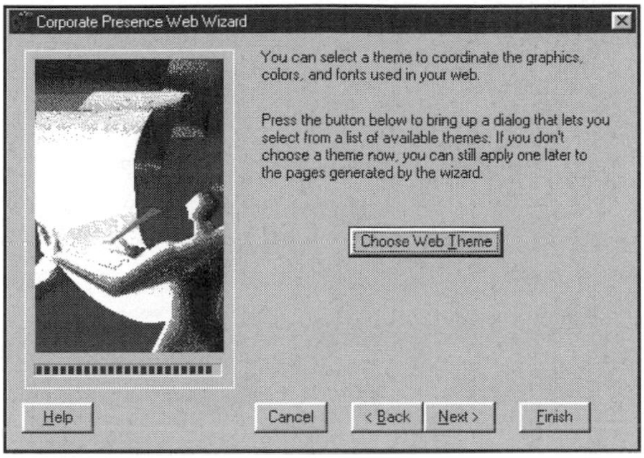

Figure 4-20

If you want to use one of the FrontPage Web Themes, click the Choose Web Theme button. The Choose Theme dialog box opens, shown here in Figure 4-21.

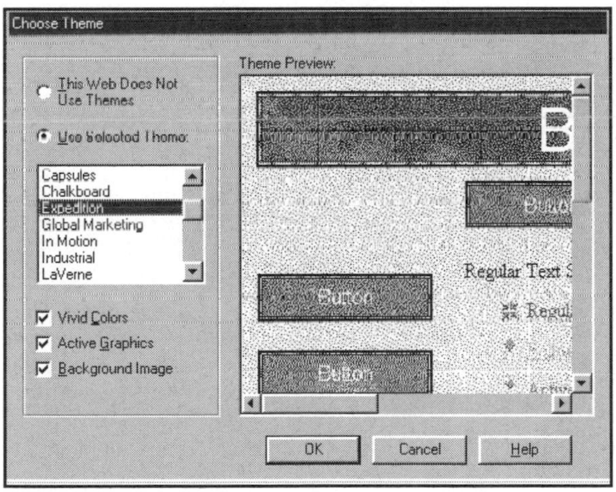

Figure 4-21

This dialog box works exactly the same way as the Themes view in the Explorer. For more information on the Themes view, see Chapter 3. Scroll through the list of themes and choose the one that best fits your site. Snake River Winery wants the site to have a rugged look, so let's use the Expedition theme, with Vivid Colors, Active Graphics, and Background Image selected.

After you choose a theme, click OK.

16. Now you're back in the Corporate Presence Web Wizard, right where you left off. Click Next to move on in the process.

The final screen, shown in Figure 4-22, tells you that FrontPage has gathered all the information that it needs to create your Corporate Presence site. It includes a Show Tasks View After Web Is Uploaded check box. The *Tasks view* is a list of tasks that need to be completed in your site. FrontPage adds several tasks to the list after it creates this site; among them are customizing various pages with specific text and other files, and replacing images. The Tasks view is explained in greater detail in Chapter 3.

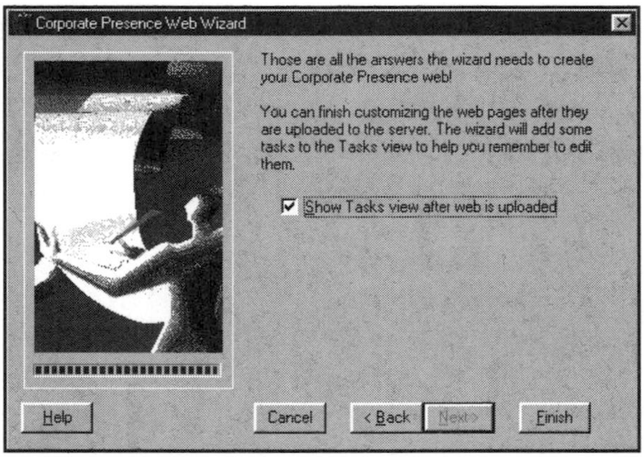

Figure 4-22

Click the Finish button, and FrontPage fills in the Corporate Presence site with the information you supplied and saves the site. Based on what you specified, it saves the site to the server or to a folder on your LAN or hard drive. After saving the site, FrontPage displays it in the Explorer (and in Tasks view, if you've directed it to). From this point on, you can fill in the fine details of your site and personalize it to give it your own "look and feel."

That's all there is to creating the structure for a Web site using the Corporate Presence Wizard—a bunch of tiny steps, all of which add up to a huge time-savings.

Discussion Web Wizard

The Discussion Web Wizard creates a threaded discussion group about a topic of your choice. Often this discussion group is added as part of a site. Each user can contribute thoughts and associate them with a particular ongoing conversation (thread). Each separate entry from a user is referred to as an article. The user also has the ability to search for existing articles. The wizard asks you to decide the following:

- What kinds of pages you want to include
- The title of the discussion
- Some input fields to separate topics of discussion
- Whether the discussion will take place in a protected site (meaning that only registered users can participate)
- How the table of contents should sort the posted articles
- Whether the Table of Contents page should be the site's home page
- The information you want reported about each article found in a search of past discussions
- The colors for the background and text
- Whether you want to create the site using frames

As always, you can change the look and feel and add or delete features to these pages later, using the Editor.

Administering a Discussion Group. You can administer a discussion group in FrontPage quite easily by using the Explorer and the Editor. All you need is author or administrative access to the discussion site. If you're in charge of administering a discussion group, here are a few things you can do:

- **Edit articles.** Each page that a user completes and sends to the discussion group is called an *article*; FrontPage saves it as an HTML file in a hidden folder, typically named _disc1. To see a list of articles, you need to tell FrontPage to show files in hidden directories. You can do this in the Explorer by choosing Web Settings from the Tools menu, clicking the Advanced tab, and selecting the Show Documents In Hidden Directories check box. When you click OK, a dialog box appears asking you if you want to refresh the Web site now. If you click the Yes button, the hidden pages will display in the Explorer.

You edit an article by first finding it in the discussion folder and then double-clicking it in the Explorer. The article appears in the Editor, where you can delete text—such as objectionable language. You can then save the modified article and users will be able to view the edited article.

- **Delete old articles.** If you can see the files in hidden folders, you can sort the files and delete old, no longer needed messages. In Folder view, sort the list of files in the discussion site by date, and then delete any files that you don't need by selecting them and pressing the Delete key.
- **Limit administrative access.** Any author can view and edit any message in the discussion group if he or she has access to the site. This amounts to little administrative control if a large number of authors are members of the discussion group. You can limit access to a discussion group so that users can browse the articles but not edit them. To do so, choose the Permissions command from the Explorer's Tools menu, apply the use of unique permissions settings for the Web site on the Settings tab, and then set Browse access for specific users on the Users tab (or specify that everyone only has Browse access). For more information on the Web Settings command, see Chapter 5.

  An easier way to limit access to your site is by specifying that only registered users can access the site. To do this, use the Discussion Web Wizard to create your site. In the wizard, a screen gives you the option to have all discussions take place in a protected Web site, which means that only registered users of the discussion site can access the articles. If you opt to use the protected Web site, FrontPage gives you some simple directions for steps to complete on a registration page in the Editor after you complete the wizard and create the site.

Import Web Wizard

If you have other Web sites that you'd like to turn into FrontPage Web sites, you can use the Import Web Wizard to do so. This wizard imports a folder of files from your hard disk or LAN and creates a new FrontPage Web site from them. The folder doesn't necessarily have to be a complete Web site; any folder of files that you want to use to create a FrontPage Web site will do.

The Import Web Wizard also is handy for importing any older FrontPage site that might be stored in folders that your current Web server does not search when you're opening a site in the Explorer. For example, the Microsoft Personal Web Server does not search folders in which early versions of FrontPage stored its sites. In these cases, you have to use the Import Web Wizard to import those older FrontPage sites.

Here are the sweet-and-simple directions for importing sites with the Import Web Wizard:

1. In the Explorer, choose New from the File menu, and then choose FrontPage Web from the submenu.
2. In the New FrontPage Web dialog box, select the Import an Existing Web radio button, and then click OK. The Import Web Wizard dialog box appears (see Figure 4-23).

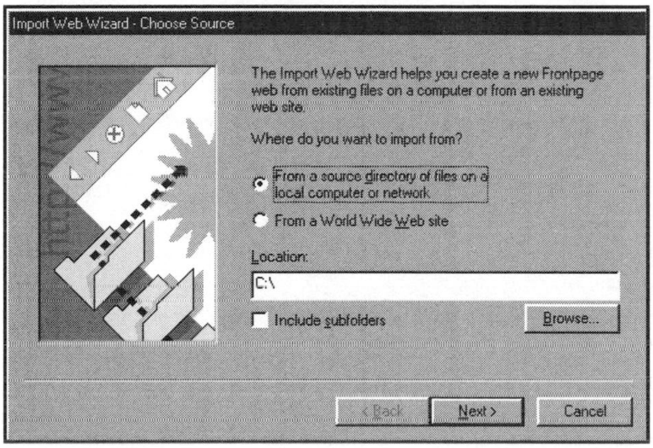

Figure 4-23

NOTE You can also access the Import Web Wizard by selecting Import from the File menu, and choosing From Web in the resulting Import File to FrontPage Web dialog box. You must have a site open in the Explorer before you use this method.

3. In the Import Web Wizard - Choose Source screen (shown above), choose whether you want to import from a local computer or network, or from a World Wide Web site.

   In you select to go with the first option, you must locate the folder of files you want to import. Click Browse, select the folder in the Browse For Folder dialog box, and click OK. If the folder includes subfolders of files you want to import as well, select the Include Subdirectories check box in the Import Web Wizard - Choose Source screen.

   If you choose From a World Wide Web site, the second option, you have to enter a Web location, and if the server requires SSL, select that check box. These options are shown in Figure 4-24.

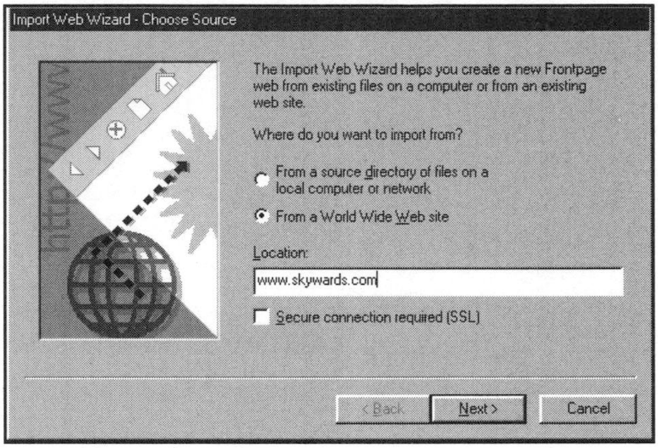

Figure 4-24

Click Next to continue.

4. It you choose to import from a local computer or network, you see the Import Web Wizard - Edit File List dialog box, seen in Figure 4-25, which contains a list of all the files, including files in subfolders, within the folder you selected. You can specify which files to import at this stage. If you plan to create a new site and are importing an older site as part of it, for example, you might not want to include certain files if you do not plan to use them.

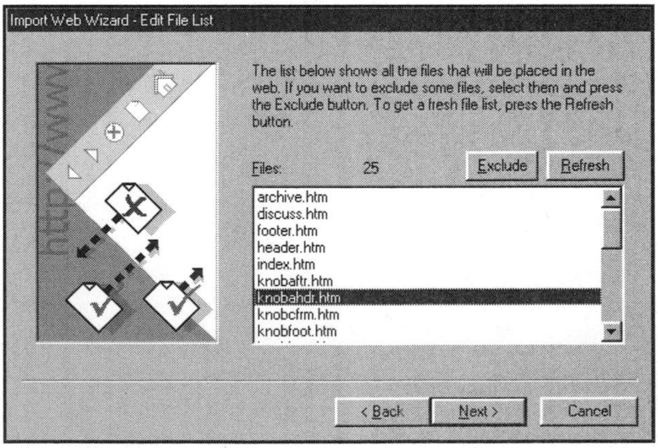

Figure 4-25

To omit a file from the list of files to be imported into your new site, select the file and click Exclude. If you remove some items from the list and want to start over with the original list, click Refresh, and the original list will appear again.

When you're satisfied that you want to include all the items in the list in your new FrontPage site, click Next.

5. If you choose to import from the World Wide Web, click Next, and then you get the Import Web Wizard - Choose Download Amount dialog box, shown in Figure 4-26. Here you set limits of levels and file size, and you have the option to limit to text and image files, as well.

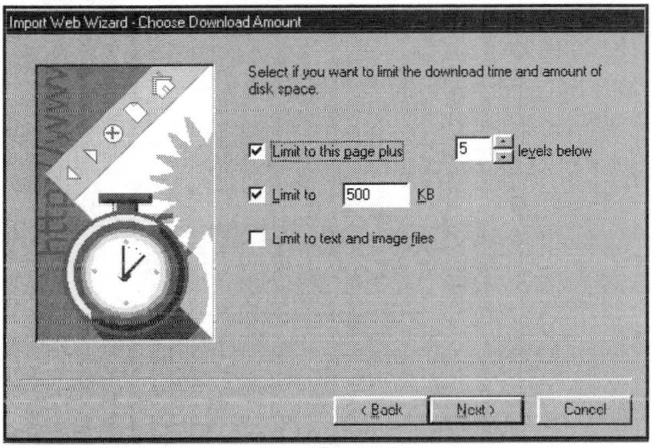

Figure 4-26

Select the options you require, and then click Next.

6. Next, you see the Import Web Wizard - Edit File List screen, which contains a list of all the files, including files in subfolders, within the folder you selected. You can specify which files to import at this stage. For example, if you plan to create a new site and are importing an older site as part of it, you might not want to include certain files if you do not plan to use them.

7. Now you've reached the Import Web Wizard - Finish screen, the last screen of the wizard. Click Finish to have FrontPage create the new Web site. If you want to change some information you've entered in the wizard, click Back until you reach the screen that contains the information that you want to modify, change the information, and then click Next until you once again reach this final wizard screen.

That's all it takes for FrontPage to import a folder of files and create a new Web site from them. FrontPage preserves the old folder structure that you've imported and adds its own folders to the site, such as the _private and images folders for storing private and image files, respectively.

Form Page Wizard

The Form Page Wizard creates a form that you can use to gather input from users and save the results to a Web page or text file on the Web server. This form can be very useful in situations where you need to gather contact information, account information, product information, and so on, from your viewers. You use this page wizard in the Editor. You can place the resulting page in your site and link it to other pages.

Using the Form Page Wizard

To add a page to your site using the Form Page Wizard, do the following:

1. In the Explorer, open the site that the new page will belong to. (You can skip this step if you want to; after you save the page, you can import it to any Web site.)
2. In the Editor, choose New from the File menu. The New Page dialog box appears, seen in Figure 4-27.

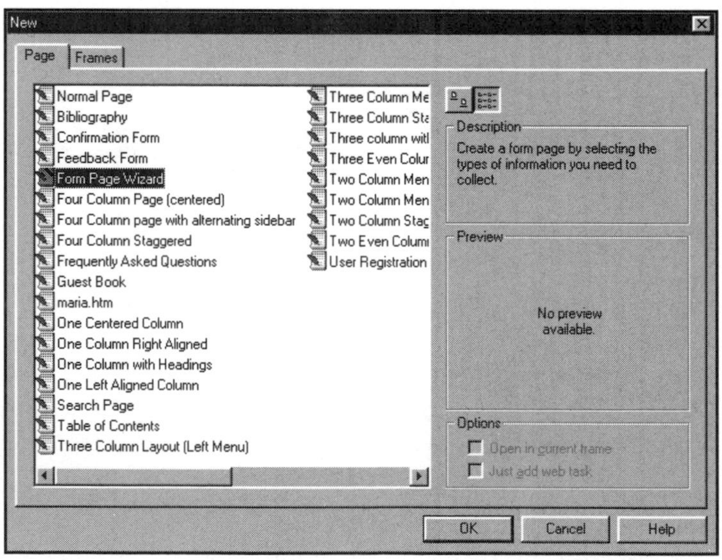

Figure 4-27

3. From the list of page templates and wizards, select the Form Page Wizard. Note that when you select a template or a wizard, a description of the item appears in the upper right portion of the New dialog box. After you select the wizard, click the OK button.
4. Move through the screens of the wizard and answer the questions that FrontPage asks you. The process of using these wizards is the same as that for using the Corporate Presence Wizard, described earlier in this chapter, but the questions are, of course, different. For example, you are asked to name the page instead of a site.
5. When you reach the final screen, click Finish and FrontPage creates the page and displays it in the Editor. You can then edit the page, adding text and/or images, linking it to other pages, and so on. When you save the page, you can save it as a file, or if you have a site open in the Explorer, you can add it to the site.

Custom Wizards

Anyone can create custom Web wizards and page wizards for FrontPage using Microsoft Visual Basic or Microsoft Visual C++. You can learn how by consulting the *FrontPage Developer's Kit.* Look in the FrontPage area of Microsoft's Web site at www.microsoft.com/frontpage/ for information on obtaining this free kit.

FrontPage templates and wizards can free up some extra time for you to get more things done in your life. Maybe they'll free up enough time that you can put up one of your favorite signs on your office door: "Gone to the Monster Truck Races!!!"

Coming Up

Speaking of freeing up time, FrontPage also helps you to administer a site after you have it up and running. FrontPage makes it easier for you to implement security, manage tasks, update content, do testing, and go live with your site. Chapter 5 looks at these topics.

CHAPTER 5

Managing Your Web Site

The Explorer Makes It Easy

You've worked hard to plan and design your Web site, and you've started putting it together. You've begun to turn all those ideas into actual pages, and now—whoa there, varmint! "How am I ever going to get all this done? Who's going to make sure it's kept up-to-date? How can I be sure it works perfectly before it goes online? And how can I be sure that my officemate, Georgio Trustnomore, who makes more than I do with half the talent, doesn't get into my site and mess it up?"

Dozens of questions like these can go through your mind at all stages of developing your site, especially if your company or organization has a large Web site development team. But even one-person development teams have to consider numerous Web site administration issues. Before those worries running through your head turn into a monster headache, read on and find out how FrontPage simplifies site administration.

Whenever you think of Web site administration, think "Explorer." The FrontPage Explorer is the starting point for most of your administrative tasks—it's where you can see what work needs to be done in your site, assign those tasks as necessary, deal with proxy servers (also known as *firewalls*), set permissions, and much more. This chapter explains how FrontPage helps you deal with all these issues, beginning with security.

Security

In the Old West, security came in the form of a weathered tough guy and his trusty six-shooter. Today, with information traveling over the air waves, and through phone lines at the speed of light, security is a little bit trickier. Especially when some 12-year-old hacker from Nebraska keeps finding ways to break through even the most complicated security measures. So, when it comes to protecting your Web site and restricting who sees it, you'll be glad to know that FrontPage makes available the toughest security components.

Making Use of SSL

Secure Sockets Layer (SSL) is a protocol that allows for secure communication between a server and a client. SSL doesn't protect access to the communicated data, but it does encrypt the data. In order for SSL to work properly, both the server and the client must support SSL. Both FrontPage and Microsoft Internet Explorer support SSL, as does Netscape Navigator. FrontPage also allows the creation of links that start with https:// instead of http://. Links that start with https:// indicate a secure link using SSL.

Before you go any further, you'll want to know whether the server you're communicating with supports SSL. There are a couple ways to find out:

- Check with the person administering the server. It's possible for the administrator to disable SSL support, so it's always a good idea to check first.
- If you're running Microsoft Internet Information Server or Netscape's Commerce, FastTrack, or Enterprise server, you're probably fine. But it can't hurt to check with the server's administrator in this case, too. (Note: The Microsoft Personal Web Server does not support SSL.)
- If you want to check for yourself, create a new Web site in the FrontPage Explorer, as described in Chapter 3. Specify the server and the name of the site, and select the Connect Using SSL check box. If the Explorer opens the site and you don't encounter an error message, support for SSL is available on your server.

With an SSL-enabled Web server and with SSL enabled in FrontPage, all communications between the FrontPage client and the server, including any commands issued from the Explorer, or the Editor, are secure. This means that the information is encrypted as it travels between FrontPage and the Web server, wherever they're located. This security comes in handy in several situations.

- If you're on the road and you need to make changes to a site that is on a server back home, you can open the site, make your changes, and save the changes back to the server.
- If your business or organization has more than one office but has only one Web server, someone at a remote office can make changes to the site.
- If your corporate Web site or personal Web site lies on an Internet service provider's "staging" server (a server that houses in-production Web sites), and you access that server to make changes to your site with FrontPage, the information is encrypted as it's being sent. This prevents a hacker from looking at the information before you go live with the site.

Permissions

Permissions give you, the Web site developer, the final say over who has access to your site. You can set permissions to control who can browse, author, or administer a site, no matter what kind of site you're developing—a site for an intranet or for the World Wide Web. If you've set permission to registered users only, someone on the Web who is not a registered user will not have access to your site, plain and simple. (You might want to limit access to a list of registered users while you are developing the site.) When your site is ready to go live, you can simply change the end-user permissions to allow access to everyone.

If you're using a World Wide Web server to author your sites in FrontPage, you can use the Explorer to administer the setting of permissions on each Web site, as well as to allow access to it for specified users. If you create your site and save it to a file location, such as a network drive, you can't use the Explorer to set permissions. You must use the tools available on your file system to manage access to these sites.

An adminisitrator can manipulate permissions in the Explorer by using the Permissions command on the Tools menu. By default, all Web sites on the server use the permissions that are set for the root Web site. You can, however, set permissions unique to a specific site. I discuss both options here.

Setting and Changing Permissions for the Root Web Site

Here's how to set and change permissions for the root Web site:

Open an existing FrontPage site in the Explorer, by choosing Open FrontPage Web from the File menu. In the Open FrontPage Web dialog box, enter or select a Web server. Click the List Webs button, select <Root Web> from the list of sites, and then click OK. With the site open in the

Explorer, choose the Permissions command from the Tools menu to open the Permissions dialog box, seen in Figure 5-1.

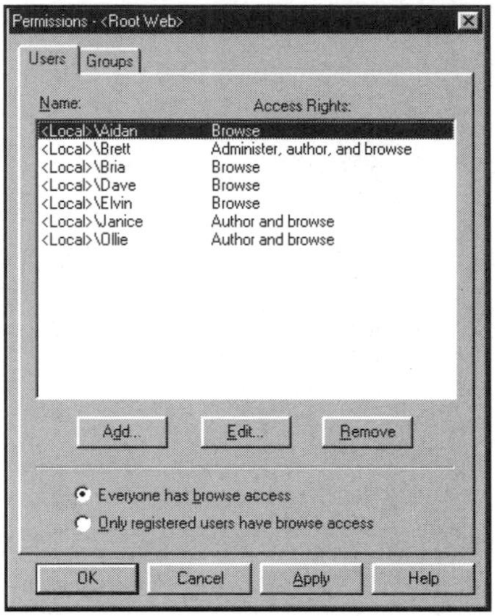

Figure 5-1

The first tab of the dialog box, Users, lists all users currently set for the root Web site, along with their current level of access. It gives you the option to add, edit, or remove users, and provides two option buttons, Everyone Has Browse Access or Only Registered Users Have Browse Access.

- To add users, click the Add button and specify their access rights.
- To edit a user, select the user from the name list and click the Edit button to change the access rights for that user. You'll see the Edit Users dialog box, where you can change the level of permission for the user. Figure 5-2 on the next page shows the Edit Users dialog box.
- To remove a user, select the user from the name list and click the Remove button to remove that user from the list.

The second tab, Groups, lists all groups currently set for the root Web site, along with each group's current level of access. It also gives you the option to add, edit, or remove groups. These options work in exactly the same manner as those on the Users tab.

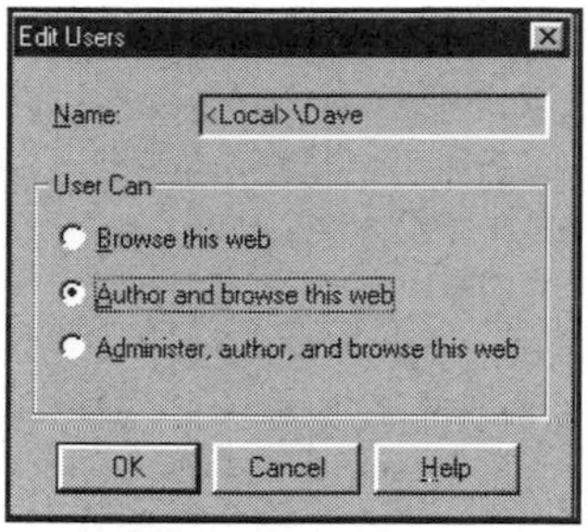

Figure 5-2

WARNING When removing administrators or authors from your permissions list, make sure that the users highlighted in the upper box are the ones that you want to remove—FrontPage does not prompt you to confirm your action.

Setting and Changing Permissions for a Specific Site

Here's how to set and change permissions for a specific site:

Open an existing FrontPage site in the Explorer, by choosing Open FrontPage Web from the File menu. Enter or select a Web server in the Open FrontPage Web dialog box. Click the List Webs button, select a site, and click OK. With the site open in the Explorer, choose the Permissions command from the Tools menu. You are greeted by the Permissions dialog box, which has three tabs, each of which deals with a specific level of access. Figure 5-3 on the next page shows the Permissions dialog box for a site named Project One.

- The first tab, Settings, includes two option buttons, one of which allows you to use the same permissions in the current site that are used by the root Web site, and the other of which allows you to set unique permissions for the current site. Selecting either option yields a description of the option at the bottom of the dialog box. If you want to assign administrative, author, and/or end-user permissions to certain people for this site but not for the root site, select the second option. Otherwise, the first option should be selected, and you must make any changes to permissions to the root site, as described earlier in this chapter.

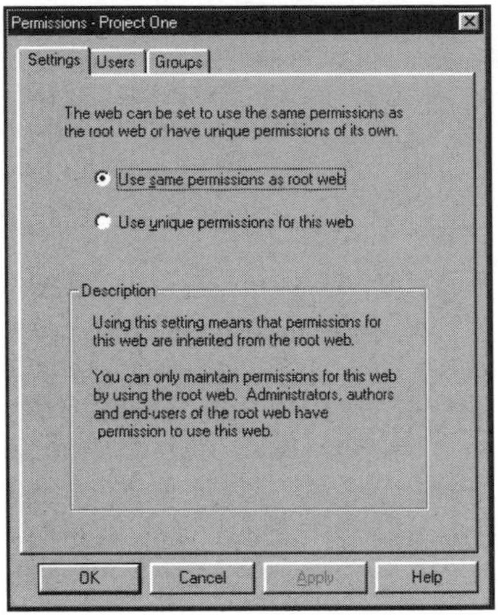

Figure 5-3

- The next two tabs deal with Users and Groups. Setting permissions for Users and Groups works the same way as described above for the settings for the root Web site. Be aware that when removing users and groups, FrontPage does not prompt you to confirm your action.

  When you finish updating the permissions, click OK to return to the Explorer.

NOTE If you make changes to settings on a tab, you must click Apply to keep those settings if you move to other tabs.

Server Permissions

Web servers often have built-in permissions mechanisms that allow you to restrict access by using a password/user name scheme, an IP address mask, or a combination. (Note: Microsoft Internet Information Server, the Microsoft Personal Web Server, and the Windows NT Workstation Peer Web Services restrict access using standard Windows NT security, and do not support access restriction via IP address masks.)

An IP address contains four numbers separated by periods; each number is less than 256. An example is 150.200.45.65. An IP address mask uses a combination of actual values and asterisks (also known as a *wild cards*) to create a model of an acceptable IP address. Masks are used to determine whether a computer has access to a location on the Internet; for example, a FrontPage site. An example of an IP address mask that would permit connections with the IP address above is 150.200.*.*. Computers with IP addresses beginning with 150.200 would be given access to a FrontPage site, and computers whose IP addresses did not begin with those numbers would be denied access. If an IP mask is in place, an administrator, author, or user must be working on a computer that has access to the location, and also must have the correct permissions to access the FrontPage site. By default, all computers are given permissions to access FrontPage sites.

For more information on server permissions, consult your server's documentation.

Passwords

FrontPage requires passwords to author and administer your sites, but depending on the Web server you use, you might rarely see a dialog box asking for them. The Change Password command on the Explorer's Tools menu might even be grayed out.

If FrontPage asks you to enter a user name and a password, it will be for one of the following reasons:

- Some Web servers always require user name and password confirmation, regardless of the user or situation.
- You're trying to access, author, or administer a site on a server and you don't have permission to do so.

When you install FrontPage, it asks you to supply a user name and a password for a single administrator to the sites you'll be creating. To add administrative access and to grant end-user and author access to others for your sites, you use the Explorer's Permissions command.

Changing Passwords

With several of Microsoft's Web servers, you're not allowed to change passwords in FrontPage. Microsoft Internet Information Server, the Microsoft Personal Web Server, and the Windows NT Workstation Peer Web Services use Windows NT user accounts, and FrontPage does not allow you to create, delete, or modify those accounts. Changing your password is the same as modifying your Windows NT account, and Windows NT considers that a breach of security.

So, if you're using one of these servers and you change access rights using the Permissions command in the Explorer, you'll notice that you are not allowed to change passwords for those users. Now you know why! That's also why the Change Passwords command on the Tools menu might be grayed out. When using these servers, FrontPage seeks the Windows NT user account information to verify user names and passwords. Therefore, in Windows NT, you must administer passwords at the system level. See the server-specific or network-specific documentation for information on changing passwords when using these Microsoft servers.

If you are using the Microsoft Personal Web Server with Windows 95, you administer users and passwords by using the Personal Web Server administration tool, which you can access by double-clicking the Personal Web Server icon in the Windows Control Panel. For more information, see Chapter 11.

With other Web servers, because the user list is completely independent of the system's user account list, you can freely add, delete, or modify passwords without fear of opening security holes. You do this through the Change Password dialog box, which you can reach by choosing the Change Password command from the Explorer's Tools menu. For more information, see Chapter 3.

Proxy Servers

A *proxy server,* or *firewall,* protects a network from uninvited outside access. FrontPage makes communicating with proxy servers very easy, in either direction. For example, communication can be inbound—communicating from the outside through the proxy server and to your internal server, or it can be outbound—communicating from your server, through a proxy, and to another server on the outside. Communications related to the Web site are permitted only through the proxy, so uninvited guests are barred from your system.

If your local network uses a proxy server, you must specify that server in the Explorer in order for FrontPage to communicate with it. To specify a proxy server for your machine or to specify any server that can be used without going through the firewall, follow this procedure:

1. Choose the Options command from the Tools menu in the Explorer, and then click the Proxies tab (see Figure 5-4) in the Options dialog box.
2. In the HTTP Proxy text box, enter the name of the proxy server and the port; for example, *itgproxy:1000.*

3. If your organization has servers that are inside the firewall, list them in the List Of Hosts Without Proxy text box. You can connect to these servers without using the proxy server. Port numbers are optional, and items in the list must be separated by commas; for example, jeffserver:345,deborahserver:222. To remove the proxy server or any servers in the list, select the information and press the Delete key.

   If you want to use all available servers inside the firewall, select the Do Not Use Proxy Server For Local (Intranet) Addresses check box.

4. After you update the information in the Proxies dialog box, click OK.

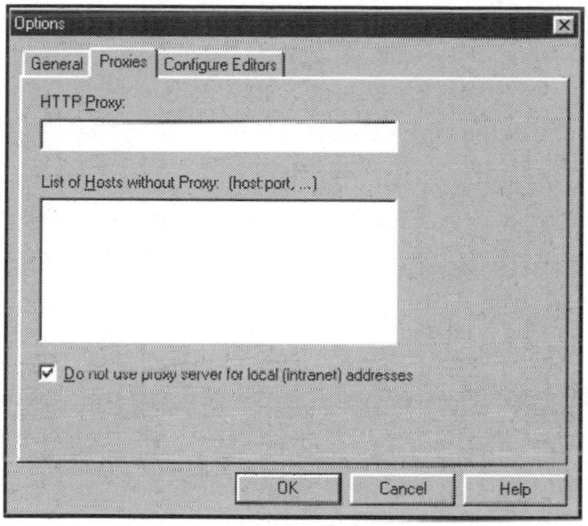

Figure 5-4

FrontPage saves the proxy server information and uses it for all future connections, so you don't have to enter the information again and again. Whenever you request a connection to a server (for example, when you are following a link), FrontPage checks whether Do Not Use Proxy Server For Local (Intranet) Addresses is selected and might check the List Of Hosts Without Proxy list. If the server is available internally, FrontPage makes the connection directly. If not, FrontPage first connects to the proxy server and has the proxy server connect to the server you want to use. This means that after you supply that information for the proxy server, FrontPage automatically handles all proxy communication, and you don't even have to be aware that a proxy server is in use.

Testing Your Site

Once your site is all nice and spiffy and you think it'll run just fine, it's always a good idea to test it. Testing can prevent the following from happening: It's the morning that you are scheduled to present your finished, working site to the CEO for final approval. It's a small site, but you're mighty proud of it. Your officemate, Joan Clueless, who is jealous over your recent raise and subsequent purchase of a red sportscar, drops by the office around 11:30 the night before. She gets into your site and makes a teensy-weensy change to one of your links. So instead of linking to a profile of the CEO from the See Profile button as you've set it up, the button links to the "Little Johnny Visits the Morgue" Web site.

But you're craftier than Ms. Clueless, and you show up a little early the next morning to make sure that your site runs fine. Here are three techniques you should use to check those links:

- You can check them individually in the Editor. It's a slow way to check links, but if you're ever in the Editor and want to make sure that a link works, you can put your cursor on the link, press Ctrl, and click the link. The Editor will take you to the page to which the link jumps.
- You can wander through your site using a browser, such as Microsoft Internet Explorer, Netscape Navigator, or any other popular browser, and test each of the links. This way, you can see first-hand that all the links work, including links to other sites on the Internet.
- You can have FrontPage verify all of your links in one step by using the Verify Links command on the Tools menu in the Explorer. This command is explained in Chapter 3. This command, however, only verifies that the targets of your links exist—it does not verify that what you linked to is what you *intended* to link to! If you want to save some time, you can view the status of your links in the Hyperlinks Status view in the Explorer. For more information on this view, see Chapter 3.

Finally, you can check that your image files are positioned on your pages where you want them. You should do this in the Editor and in the various browsers. When testing your images, you want to look for things such as download time and visual quality. For more information on optimizing graphics for the Web, see Chapter 8.

The easiest way to test your site in a browser is to use the Preview In Browser command on the File menu in the Editor. This command allows you to select any installed browser to view your site, and at different window sizes. For more information on the Preview In Browser command, see Chapter 7.

You often get different results when you test a site locally than when you test the same site through a network or over the Internet, because of variables that can affect speed and information transfer. If you can, test your site in as many ways as possible, such as

- Locally, on your own computer
- Over a network
- Remotely, over the Internet
- Through modems and other communication devices at different speeds
- On different operating systems
- With different browsers at different screen settings (such as different resolutions)

Going Live with Your Site

Maybe you have several thousand Benjamin Franklins to spare for the kind of party where you break bottles of champagne against your Web server, but most organizations don't. Nonetheless, going live with an intranet site or World Wide Web site is still a milestone event, and when it comes time, you have to know how to do it.

There are a few ways in which you can make your site accessible to your audience. One common way is to develop your site on the server on which it will be viewed, and let people visit your site as it matures. The Under Construction icons are very useful for this purpose; they let viewers know that a page isn't in its final form just yet. FrontPage can insert these icons if you use a wizard to create your site.

When you're not comfortable with people seeing your site under construction, and when there's simply not enough content to make a visit worthwhile, you can do one of two things: develop your site locally or limit end-user permissions.

Developing Your Site Locally

The Microsoft Personal Web Server, the FrontPage Personal Web Server, and the Microsoft Internet Information Server suit local development to a "T." They allow you to develop and test your intranet or World Wide Web site on your own computer or over a LAN. When your site is complete and you're ready to go live with it, you can copy it to its destination Web server with the push of a button by using the Publish command on the toolbar menu in the Explorer. With this command, you can copy the site to any of the most popular Web servers. For more information on the Publish command, see Chapter 3.

Updating Your Site

The World Wide Web is a perfect reflection of information technology in general today—it changes constantly. One day you can e-mail a friend about a great site you visited, and the next day your friend can't see what you saw because it's already changed. Even corporate intranets reflect this changing nature. One reason that some sites change so often is that it's so easy to make small changes to them. Once they're up and running, it takes little effort to replace a graphic, change a link, or even add a new page.

Another reason that sites change so often is that audiences demand it. You must keep your site updated with the latest information, or else your viewers will not return. Visiting a site is like turning up a playing card that's face-down; if your audience doesn't see a different card now and then, they'll move on to a different game.

With all that said, you need to be careful when making major changes too often. If you have a strong repeat user base, you don't want to confuse them by changing the location of your navigation buttons every month, or changing the names of the departments, or areas on your site so that they can't find what they're looking for. Just remember, regularly changing content, such as stories and images, is fine, but changing the structure can be a real pain for your regular users.

Updating large sites can be time-consuming, however, and the process can require more time as the site's size and the frequency of updating increase. You should have a plan for updating your site before you even begin to create your site. If you're planning a site now, or if you need to implement an update plan, read ahead for a few ideas on how to go about it.

Updating Content

You can use a similar process for updating content that you used for gathering the content originally, but watch for ways to streamline the process. When getting approval for your content, for example, you can try routing it to people in a different order if the process was slow the first time around. Or you can eliminate a step in the process if you determine that the step wasn't necessary; for example, the material might need only one editing stage, not two. Also, check employee schedules to make certain a folder with Web site content doesn't sit on someone's desk while he or she is lying on a beach in Tahiti.

If your company requires you to route material through a legal department, perhaps *all* of it doesn't have to be routed there, or maybe some of the material that you want to put on your site has already been approved for use elsewhere in the company. If you can save some of the material from being rerouted, you can save time and energy that you can apply elsewhere.

Never forget to *plan ahead.* If you put forth a major effort to implement a site that's to be updated monthly, and if you plan to create a test site for your new material before you go live with it every month, leave yourself plenty of time for that test. If you first went live in May, and you have an update planned for June, for example, allow enough time to develop and test the update before June 1 rolls around. That might mean that all content for the June release must be finalized by mid-May so you have enough time to test the site and fix any errors you find.

Consider the time that you and/or your team will need to write, edit, and approve content. You'll need resources from different departments around your company, and even if you or an assistant is the ultimate go-getter who loves to make personal office visits for every bit of information you need, be sure to allow plenty of time for gathering that material.

Updating Content Remotely

Updating site content from a remote location is one of FrontPage's strongest attributes: few other Web site authoring tools offer this feature. It's easy to do; here's all you need:

- You need to be able to connect to the Web server that contains the site you want to update. (Preferably, the server has the FrontPage Server Extensions installed.)
- You must have FrontPage installed on the computer that you're using remotely.
- The remote computer and user must have author or administrative permission to change the site.

If you utter a resounding "YES!" to all three of these requirements, it's time to lobby your boss to allow you to work on the site, sipping an espresso from your favorite café along the Champs-Élysées. *Oui, oui!*

Simultaneous Authoring

FrontPage makes changing the content of your site a simple task that multiple authors can perform at the same time. If you update content while you're on the go, piece by piece, you can be changing one page in your site while someone else is working on another page. The danger, of course, arises when two or more authors attempt to make changes to the same page simultaneously.

To help avoid this problem, FrontPage issues a warning if someone is overwriting a page that someone else has edited since you started working on your copy.

If you receive a warning like this, you'll need to decide which set of edits is retained. If you continue with your changes, the others might be lost. In the future, coordinate with the other person so that only one of you works on a given page at one time.

Your organization can avoid such complications by adhering strictly to the Tasks view. In the Tasks view, only one author is assigned a given task. If that author is not the one who should be performing that task, you should reassign the task. Even if multiple authors are changing content in a site from separate locations, they still use the same Tasks view for that site, and working on the same page simultaneously can easily be avoided if they are directed to work only on tasks assigned to them.

Updating for Traffic

Are you or your company prepared to receive heavy traffic on your site? If your site becomes a popular one on the Web, you need to have a high-volume Web server to handle the hits. FrontPage makes it easy to move sites from one server to another, using the Publish FrontPage Web command on the File menu in the Explorer. So if a server in one location is taking a beating and you have a higher-volume server that can handle increased traffic, you can simply move your site to the new server. It's as easy as point-and-click. For more information on the Publish FrontPage Web command, see Chapter 3. For more information on Web servers and the FrontPage Server Extensions, see Chapter 11.

Coming Up

This wraps up Part 2, which has gone over the basics of using the FrontPage Explorer to view, manipulate, and manage your Web site. Part 3 familiarizes you with the Editor and shows you how to fine-tune your site so that no visitor will want to leave.

PART III

6 Creating Your Pages

7 Fine-Tuning Your Pages

8 Getting into Graphics

9 FrontPage Components and Forms

Building Your Pages

CHAPTER 6

Creating Your Pages

HTML Got You Down?

We all know that the Web is where it's at right now, and it's where you want to be too, or you wouldn't be reading this. What you may not know, though, is that you used to have to be a HTML whiz to get anything respectable on the Internet, and who has the time to become a whiz at anything these days, especially computer programming. I mean, there's always a good rerun of *I Dream of Jeannie* on, right? Well, as you've learned so far, FrontPage had just these things in mind when they created the Explorer, and the FrontPage Editor is no exception to that thinking.

The FrontPage Editor follows right along with the ease-of-use philosophy at work in the Explorer. FrontPage doesn't require you to know a speck of HTML to produce professional-looking pages for your intranet or for the Web. If you're editing a page and want to italicize a word or change the color of a heading, you just select the text, click a button, and *voilà*—FrontPage creates the HTML behind the scenes. This allows you to concentrate on more important things, like creating a good Web presence. You may even have enough time left in your day to catch up on some of those old reruns on TV.

For all of those people who do have the time to become an HTML whiz, or already are one, FrontPage didn't forget about you, either. If you want to, you can edit the HTML right in the FrontPage Editor, and you can even see how it looks, right there, without even opening a browser.

Now it's time to get your hands dirty and find out how to use the FrontPage Editor to craft all the elements on your site's pages to get just the look and feel you want. To illustrate the many components you can add to your pages, we'll work with the pages from an intranet site of a fictitious company called Cascade Coffee Roasters. You'll see several examples of the integration between FrontPage and Microsoft Office.

The Editor in Brief: WYSIWYG

One reason the Editor is so easy to use is that it presents pages in WYSIWYG ("what you see is what you get") format. This means that whatever you see in the Editor is what you or your audience will see when viewing the pages using a Web browser. In the days when every detail on a page had to be formatted with HTML code, you would painstakingly make changes to the code and then *hope* that the changes looked right when you actually viewed the results. Now all you need to do is make sure it looks right in the Editor *once*. What you see is what you get!

Using the Editor is much like using a word-processing application such as Microsoft Word. The Editor includes many of the standard buttons and commands found in Word, such as buttons for bold, italic, and underline; numbered and bulleted lists; undo and redo; and so on. You type text in the Editor's screen just as you do in Word, and you can spell check the files in your site as you would a file in Word. You can also draw tables and use frames very easily in the Editor—with just a few clicks of the mouse.

And like Word, the Editor allows you to have more than one file open at a time. The Editor deals with pages, so it's correct to say you can have more than one *page* open at a time. This is useful for toggling back and forth between pages to ensure consistency, accuracy of information, and so forth. The Editor also allows you to copy a page (including all of its HTML) from the World Wide Web and edit it as you wish. This is useful if you own other sites and need to garner information from them quickly. Be careful, of course, about copying information from others' Web sites—there are copyright laws to heed, and plagiarism should be left to those who don't mind shelling out the bucks for a defense attorney.

Launching the Editor

How do you get to the Editor? Let us count the ways:

- By double-clicking a page in Folder, All Files, Navigation, or Hyperlinks views in the Explorer. The Editor opens with that page in its main window.
- By right-clicking a page in Folder, All Files, Navigation, or Hyperlinks views in the Explorer, and then choosing Open from the menu that appears.

- By right-clicking a task associated with a page in the Tasks view of the Explorer, and selecting Do Task from the pop-up menu. The Editor opens with that page in its main window.
- By launching the Editor on its own (either from Microsoft Windows, by clicking the Show FrontPage Editor button in the Explorer, or by choosing the Show FrontPage Editor command from the Explorer's Tools menu). In this case, the Editor opens with a blank screen. You can then open a page using the Open command on the File menu, and begin editing.

When the Editor launches, it appears in its own window, with toolbars and numerous menu commands at the top. An example of the Editor, with all of its toolbars visible, is shown in Figure 6-1.

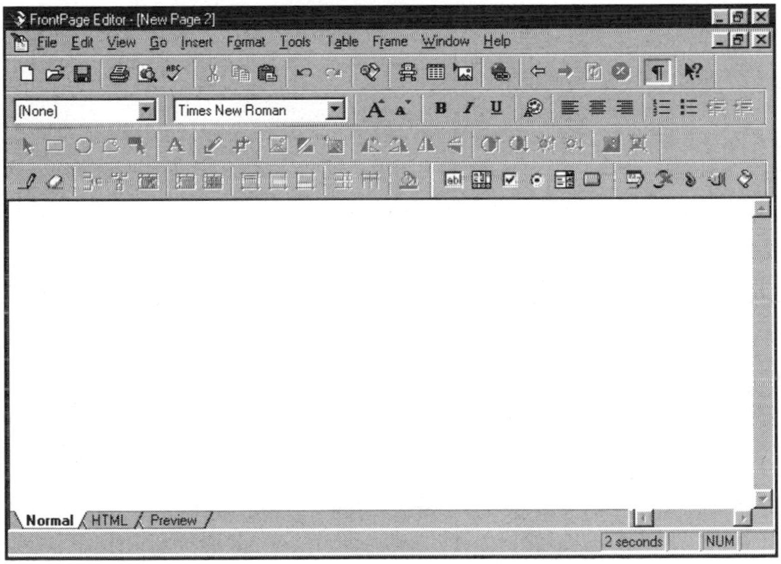

Figure 6-1

It might look a tad formidable at first, but don't worry—we'll describe what many of the toolbar buttons and commands do in this chapter. If you're an Excel user, you'll notice the sheet-like view tabs at the bottom of the Editor: Normal, HTML, and Preview. These tabs let you view your page in different ways. For now, we'll be using Normal view. Before you begin to use the Editor, though, you should learn how to customize it so that you can use it to your best advantage.

Adjusting Settings

Surely you have a preferred way to work on your computer. (Even if you don't, we'll stop calling you Shirley.) For example, maybe you don't like working with toolbars—so what's the purpose of keeping them on the screen? Or maybe you like working in a smaller or larger window. Adjusting these elements in the Editor is easy; here are a few ways to tailor your environment.

Changing the Window Size

It's often useful to maximize the Editor to a full screen so you can get the largest view of the page you're editing. To do this, click the Maximize button, which is the middle button of the three-button set in the upper right corner of the Editor's title bar when the window is not maximized. To restore the Editor to its previous location and size, click the Restore button that appears in the same position for maximized windows. That three-button set is the same one that you see in all applications for Microsoft Windows NT 4.0 and Windows 95.

You can also maximize and minimize individual pages in the Editor. To do so, click the Maximize button for the page. This button is the middle button of the set of buttons in the upper right corner of the *page's* title bar. You can *minimize* a page by clicking the leftmost button in the group of three. When you minimize a page, it's reduced to a button at the bottom of the Editor window, which makes it easy to see that you can have multiple pages open in the Editor at once.

Working with Toolbars

The Editor includes the Standard, Format, Image, Forms, Advanced, and Table toolbars, available from the View menu. When they are all displayed, as shown in Figure 6-1, they take up a fairly large chunk of space in the Editor window. If you don't need some of them, you can hide them. To hide a toolbar, choose that toolbar's name from the View menu (to remove the check mark beside it). To show a hidden toolbar, choose its name from the View menu (to add a check mark beside it), and the toolbar will appear in the same position it held before it was hidden. You can also access the Status Bar and Format Marks features via the View menu. For more information on these options, see the next section.

The Editor's toolbars can be placed anywhere on your screen. If you prefer to work with the toolbars off to one side or at the bottom of your screen, you're in luck. To move a toolbar, click a region of the toolbar outside the buttons and drag it to its new position. To have a toolbar "float," drag it from the toolbar region to a new position. To "dock" the toolbar again, drag it back to the toolbar region at the top of the Editor window.

Showing and Hiding the Status Bar and Formatting Marks

You can show or hide the status bar at the bottom of the Editor window by choosing the Status Bar command from the View menu. The Editor also uses formatting marks on the screen for some elements, such as paragraph marks, bookmark underlines, and form outlines. To show or hide these marks for the page you are currently working on, choose the Format Marks command from the View menu.

Now that you've learned how to adjust some basic settings, it's time to dive into Cascade Coffee Roasters' RoasterNet site.

SHORTCUT You can click the Show/Hide Paragraph toolbar button, which looks like a paragraph symbol, to show or hide format marks.

Let the Construction Begin

This section describes most of the elements you can add to a page in the Editor. You can add all of the obvious page components, such as text, links, and headings, plus some that you may not have thought of—such as *tables*, *frames*, *marquees*, *background sound*, and *video*. These are discussed in this chapter and in Chapter 7. You can also add images, which are another major component of a Web page; the procedures are detailed in Chapter 8. You can also add forms and WebBot components in the Editor; these procedures are fully explained in Chapter 9. Advanced features, like ActiveX components, and Java applets, are also easy to insert into a page. These features are discussed in Chapter 10.

When adding elements to your pages in the Editor, follow this simple guideline: Think as you would when using a word processing application such as Word. The Editor mimics many of the procedures and techniques you use in Word to add and manipulate page elements. Many of the menus and toolbars also closely resemble those in Word. If you've used a word processing application, you'll have no trouble using the Editor, and you'll learn it very quickly.

Moving Around in the Editor

Once you have material on your page, you can use your keyboard to navigate in the standard ways. For example, you can use the PgUp and PgDn keys to move one screen up or down. Ctrl+Home takes you to the top of a page, and Ctrl+End takes you to the end of a page. You can also use the cursor keys to navigate on your pages, and you can use a scroll bar, if one is present, to move horizontally or vertically.

TIP The Editor implements the top 25 keyboard shortcuts of Microsoft Word, so Office users can feel right at home.

Text

Adding text to a page is as simple as typing it in. Let's go through the motions of adding some text to a new Human Resources page in the RoasterNet site:

1. Create a new page in the Editor by choosing New from the File menu. In the New dialog box, select Normal Page, and then click OK. A blank page appears on your screen (see Figure 6-2), with the cursor blinking in the upper left corner.

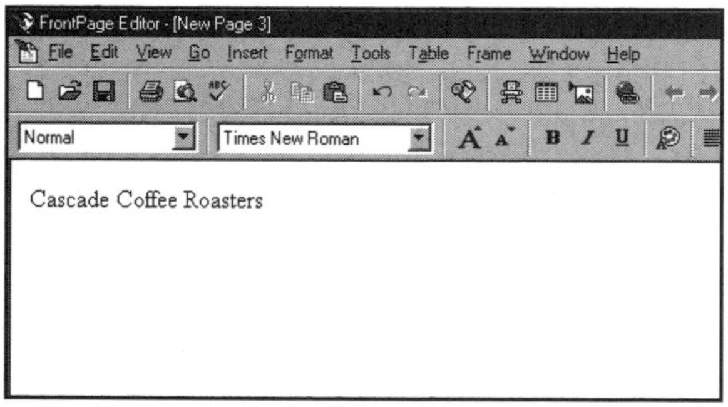

Figure 6-2

2. Type the words Cascade Coffee Roasters.

Notice that the text begins on the far left side of the current line. It doesn't have to stay there; you can indent the text, center it, or right-align it. You can also change the font and point size of the text, turn the text into a heading, and change its properties in many other ways. We'll discuss all those formatting techniques in the next chapter.

Whatever you type on the screen is what you see in the browser. And just as in Word, to start a new paragraph you simply press the Enter key.

SHORTCUT The Editor uses common keyboard and toolbar shortcuts for cutting, copying, and pasting. Cut: Ctrl+X; Copy: Ctrl+C; Paste: Ctrl+V. You can also right-click to cut, copy, and paste.

Cutting, Copying, and Pasting Text

You can cut, copy, and paste text (and any other elements, for that matter) in the Editor just as you do in Office applications. The Editor uses the Clipboard in the same way that Office applications do; you can cut or copy material to other pages in the Editor, or to other documents in other applications. Simply cut or copy the material, move to the destination document (opening it first if necessary), and paste it in. Depending on the application you move the material to, you might lose some of the formatting when you move the material. For example, if you're moving text of varying point sizes to a file in Notepad, all the text will appear in Notepad in the standard Notepad point size.

Deleting Text

Deleting text or other elements is also very simple, and you can do it in many ways. You can select the material you want to delete, and then press the Del key or choose Clear from the Edit menu.

TIP If you want to reinsert material you've just deleted, choose Undo from the Edit menu or click the Undo toolbar button. For more details, see "Undo/Redo" in the next chapter.

You can also delete words and characters in front of and behind the cursor. To delete a word to the right of the cursor, press Ctrl+Del, and to delete a word to the left of the cursor, press Ctrl+Backspace. Try these shortcuts to get comfortable with them; they're some of the least-used keyboard combinations in the FrontPage Editor and in Word, but they can make your editing work go much faster.

Material from Microsoft Office files

A significant advance in FrontPage is its ability to seamlessly incorporate material from Microsoft Office files. This integration can be a big timesaver. For example, if you have material in a Word or Excel file that you want to use on a page in a FrontPage site, you don't have to re-create that material in FrontPage. This applies to entire documents as well; if you have documents in Word or Microsoft Excel that you want to use, you can do that in a matter of seconds in FrontPage.

Copying and Pasting from Office Files

Figure 6-3 illustrates how easy it is to move material from Word into the FrontPage Editor. Susan from the Human Resources department at Cascade Coffee Roasters has started to write the text for RoasterNet's home page in Word, but her officemate, Robert, advises that she should use FrontPage. Susan had entered only a few lines in Word, but rather than lose those few lines, she cuts and pastes the text from Word…

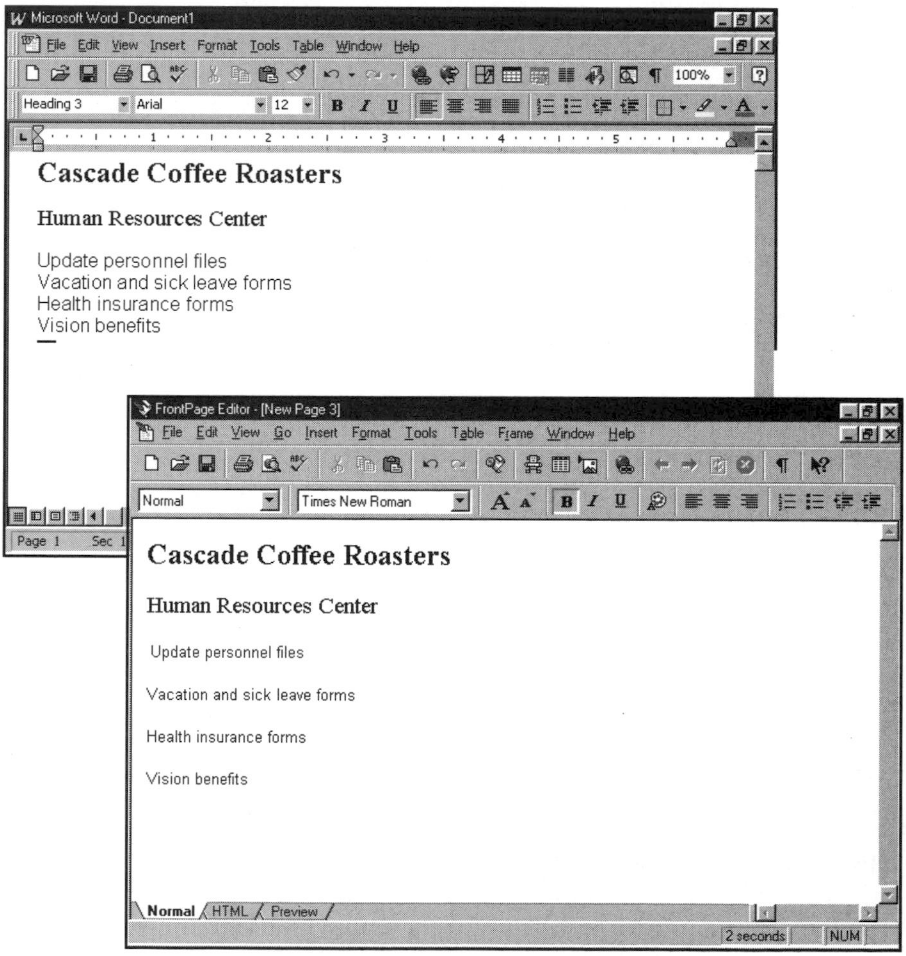

…into the FrontPage Editor.

Figure 6-3

Susan simply selects the text in Word, copies it, switches to the Editor, and pastes the text wherever she wants to on her open page. FrontPage automatically converts the material from Word into HTML for use on the page.

Dragging and Dropping Office Files into the Editor

Now let's get on to some bigger things. In the example above, suppose Susan has typed several *pages* of information into Word instead of just a few lines. Perhaps she was intending to type in the material and then use Word to turn it into an HTML file so she could use it in her company's intranet site. Nice thinking, Susan—but your fellow HR Generalist, Ashley, knows that this step is unnecessary because Cascade Coffee Roasters uses FrontPage.

Ashley shows Susan how to link to Office files or insert entire files into the FrontPage Editor and automatically convert them into HTML files:

- If an Office file has already been imported into the Explorer as a part of the site (in other words, with the intention of linking to it from within the site), you can drag that file from either view in the Explorer and drop it onto a page in the Editor. To do so, click the icon representing the file in the Explorer (such as a Word or Excel icon), and while holding down the left mouse button, drag the file onto an open part of the page in the Editor. FrontPage creates a link to the file, using the name of the file.
- You can drag and drop an Office file from anywhere in Windows onto an open page in the Editor. For example, you can drop files from the Windows Explorer or even from the Windows desktop. FrontPage converts the entire file into HTML and presents it on the open page. If the file has links, they are converted to FrontPage links and still link to the same places.

TIP You can also insert files onto a page in the Editor by using the File command on the Insert menu.

Remember when you're dragging and dropping that you don't need to have the Editor active on your screen when you begin. With the Editor open, you can drag the file over the Editor button on the Windows taskbar and wait for a moment (while still holding the mouse button down). The Editor will then become active on your screen, and you can then drop the file onto the open page.

TIP The Editor allows you to drag and drop or insert files with any document format that Office recognizes. For example, you can drop WordPerfect documents or Lotus 1-2-3 spreadsheets into the Editor.

Headings

One mark of an effective Web page design is the wise use of headings. Too many large headings can make a page difficult to read, and too few headings can make a page look dull and perhaps make it difficult to understand. Headlines help to prioritize the levels of information on a page, just like in a newspaper or magazine.

To show you a simple use of headings, let's follow along as another Cascade employee, Jeb, begins creating his Accounting home page. Jeb wants the names of his department's personnel to appear on the page, which will later serve as links to their own pages. Here's the process he follows:

1. Create a new page in the Editor by choosing New from the File menu. In the New Page dialog box, select Normal Page, and then click OK. A blank page appears in the Editor, with the cursor blinking in the upper left corner.
2. From the Style drop-down list on the Formatting toolbar, select Heading 1. You'll notice there are six levels of headings in the list. The page heading should be a fairly prominent one, such as Heading 1. FrontPage adds space for the heading as a separate paragraph, placing it on its own line, ready for you to type the heading text.
3. Type in the main heading for the page, *Accounting,* as seen in Figure 6-4.

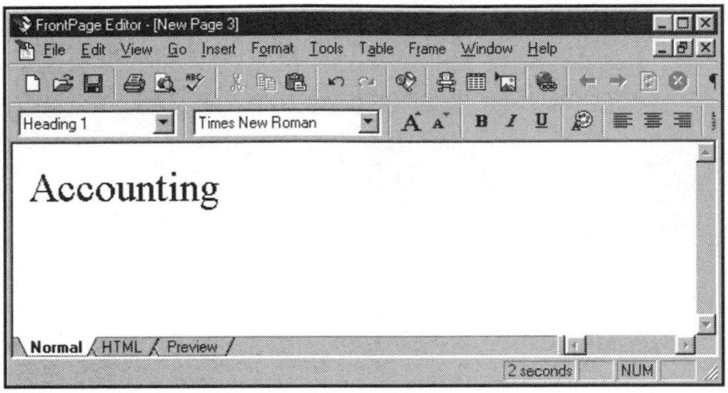

Figure 6-4

This heading is formatted as Heading 1. Notice the Heading 1 option in the Style drop-down list.

4. Now you want to add the names of your salespeople to the page. Press Enter to move the cursor to the next line, and then select Heading 3 from the drop-down list. A line formatted as Heading 3 appears below the title you just typed. Type *Kathy*.
5. Repeat step 4 to enter the names of your other salespeople: Eli, Tom, Janine, and Kevin. Your page should look like Figure 6-5 below.

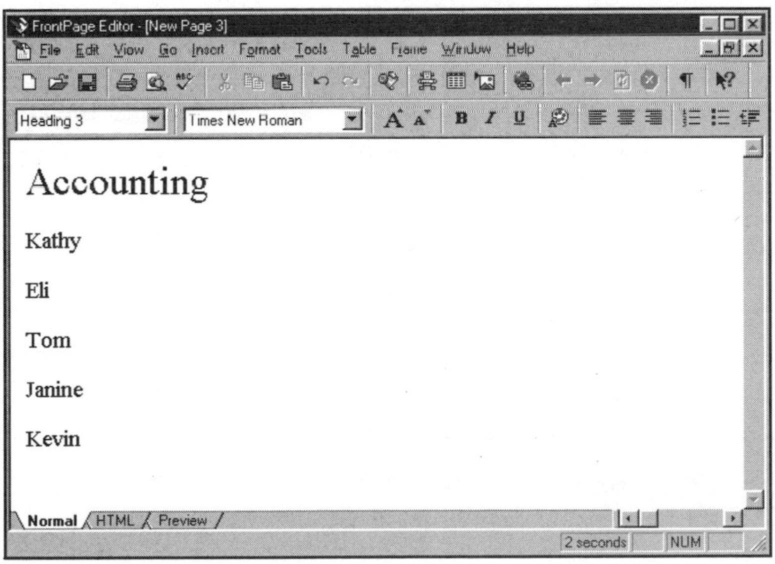

Figure 6-5

Figure 6-6 shows the relative sizes of the six heading formats.

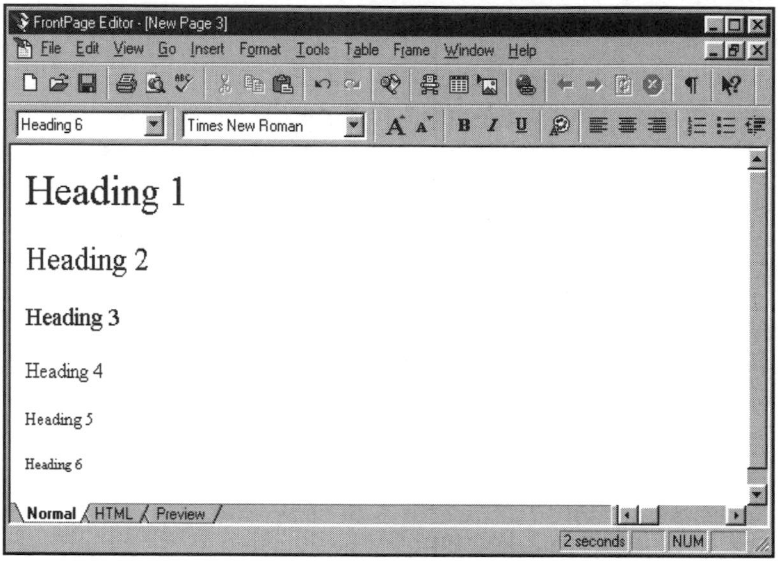

Figure 6-6

The Web browser you use will determine the exact formatting of the headings and might override FrontPage-specific formatting. No matter what, the formats are designed so that the higher level headings (starting with Heading 1) stand out more than the lower level ones (ending with Heading 6). Generally, the more important the heading, the larger the text, the more space above and below the heading, and so on.

Lists

When you're designing your pages, consider using a list instead of cramming material into paragraph form; lists are much easier to read, so they tend to make your pages more user-friendly. If you use too many lists, though, your pages can become dry and tedious to read, and your audience will dash off to read *Particle Physics Illustrated* just to clear their minds.

TIP It is possible to modify the numbered list attributes. For example, the list can be ordered using uppercase and lowercase Roman numerals and uppercase and lowercase letters. You can also modify the starting value. For more information, see the section titled "List Properties" in Chapter 7.

The exact formatting of each kind of list is determined by the Web browser used to view the page. Here's a rundown of the kind of lists that are available from the Style drop-down list:

- **Bulleted List.** Presents items with bullets. Bulleted lists are often used for related but nonsequential items.
- **Directory List.** Another bulleted list format. Some browsers recognize the coding for a directory list and format the list items differently than for a simple bulleted list. Generally, this format is used for very short items.
- **Menu List.** Another bulleted list format supported by most browsers.
- **Numbered List.** Presents items in an ordered sequence, typically using numerals and beginning with the number 1. Numbered lists are ideal for stating procedures.

Creating a List

Back to RoasterNet. Natalie, an HR Specialist, wants to create a numbered list to spell out the steps employees should take to declare their sick-leave days. (Of course, Cascade Coffee Roasters employees, honest folks that they are, wouldn't even think of *not* declaring those days.) Here are the steps that she followed:

1. On the page in the Editor, position your cursor where you want the list to begin. You can position the cursor at the beginning, middle, or end of a paragraph. If you position the cursor on a line that contains text, FrontPage will turn that text into the first item of the list. If you want to start a new list, position the cursor on a blank line.

SHORTCUT You can convert existing text to a numbered or bulleted list by selecting it and then clicking the respective toolbar button. For more on formatting, see the next chapter.

2. Select Numbered List from the Style drop-down list. FrontPage formats the first line of the new list with a number 1; type the text for the first item in the list.
3. After you type the text for the first item, press Enter. The Editor inserts the next number, and you can type that text in. Continue this process until you finish the list.
4. When you finish the list, press Ctrl+Enter. The Editor inserts a new line following the list and places the cursor at the start of that line.

Definitions

A *definition* is a type of formatting that is particularly useful for organizing a list of terms, called *defined terms*, and their definitions (although you can use definitions in any way you like). In many ways, a series of definitions is a special type of list. Rather than numbers or bullets, a word or a phrase is used to start each item. The remaining text for the item is formatted as the definition for that entry.

In many browsers, the word or phrase is positioned at the left margin and the definition text is indented next to it (similar to the way a bulleted list has the bullet at the left with the remaining text indented). In other browsers, the word or phrase appears on one line with the remaining text positioned below it.

Working with Page Files

Standard file management commands in the Editor are similar to their counterparts in the Explorer, except they work at the page level, not at the Web site level. For example, the Close command in the Editor closes a page, while the Close command in the Explorer closes a site. Also, you can perform a few additional tasks with files in the Editor, such as printing. In this section, you'll learn how to use the Editor's file management commands.

Creating New Pages

Creating new pages in the Editor is easy, and FrontPage allows you to create numerous kinds of pages with its templates and wizards. Most often, you'll create new pages to add them to a Web site that is currently open, but you're not limited to that scenario. You can also create a new page, save it separately, and add it to any other Web site later on. (See "Saving Pages" later in this chapter for more information.)

SHORTCUT You can quickly create a new Normal page template by clicking the New button on the toolbar.

1. To create a new page, choose New from the File menu or press Ctrl+N on the keyboard. You'll see the New dialog box, as seen in Figure 6-7.

   In the New dialog box, you can select any number of page templates, or click the Frames tab, and select from the frames page templates.

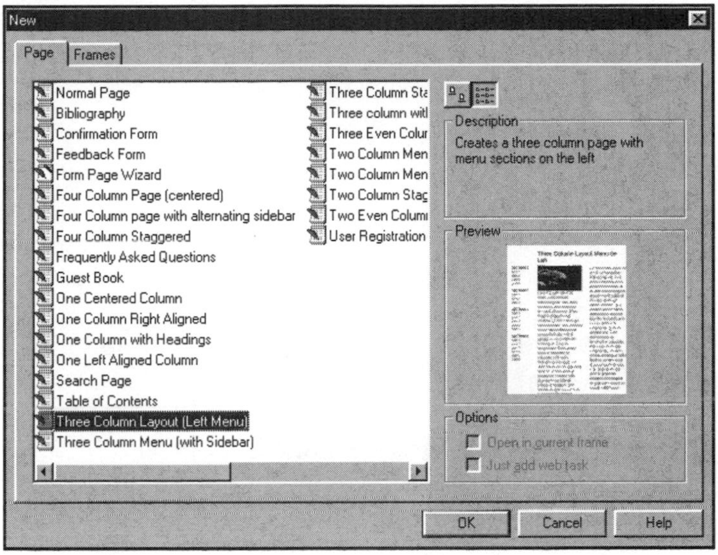

Figure 6-7

2. After selecting a template from the list, click OK. You can find full descriptions of the templates and wizards in Chapter 4.

Opening Pages

The Open command allows you to open pages in the Editor from the Web site currently open in the Explorer, existing pages that are stored as files in your system, and even pages from the World Wide Web. Not only can you open pages created with FrontPage, but you can open additional file types as well. This gives you many options for adding new material to your site. The file types you can open in the Editor include the following:

- HTML files (HTM, HTML)
- Preprocessed HTML (HTX, ASP)
- Rich Text Format files (RTF)
- Text files (TXT)
- Hypertext templates (HTT)
- Word documents
- WordPerfect files (DOC, WPD)
- Excel Worksheets (XLS, XLW)
- Works files (WPS)

If you have Microsoft Office installed, and if during the Office setup you selected a configuration that installs additional document converters, those converters will also be accessible to FrontPage.

Opening a Page from the Current Site

If you need to edit a page that's part of the current Web site in the Explorer, there are two easy ways to do it: You can go to the Explorer, find the page, and open it from there (perhaps by double-clicking it). Or (an even easier way), you can open it in the Editor by choosing the Open command from the File menu.

When you choose the Open command, you'll see the Open dialog box, shown here in Figure 6-8.

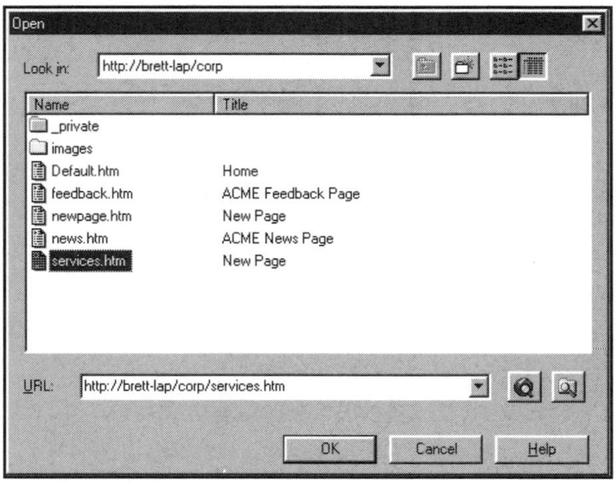

Figure 6-8

Select a file from the list, and click OK. The page opens in a new window in the Editor for you to edit to your heart's content.

Opening a Page from Your File System

Say you're editing your Web site, and you need to add a page that is saved as a file but not saved as part of any site. For example, suppose someone in your organization is creating custom pages for several different Web sites and is saving them separately for others to add to their respective sites as needed. If you want to add a page like this to your site, here's how to do it:

1. Choose the Open command from the File menu. If you're working with the Explorer open, you'll see the Open dialog box. Click the Select a File on Your Computer button, the second button to the right of the URL text box.

This brings up the Select Files dialog box. If you're working on a file without the use of the Explorer, choosing the Open command will bring up the Select File dialog box, seen here in Figure 6-9.

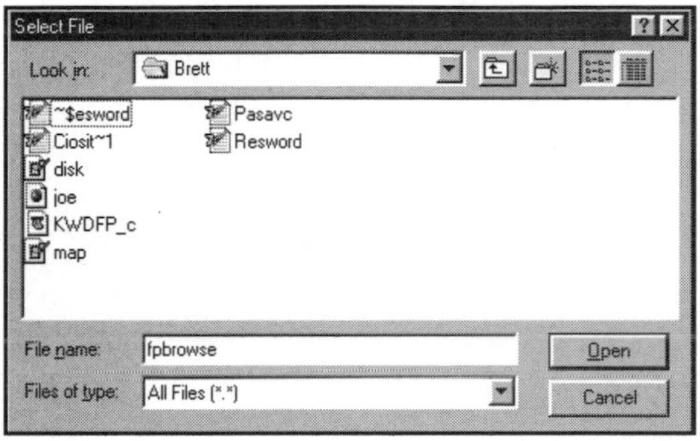

Figure 6-9

2. Select the file of your choice, and click Open. The file will be opened in the Editor.

SHORTCUT You can quickly access the Open File dialog box from the Editor by pressing Ctrl+O or by clicking the Open button on the toolbar.

The Editor will try to open actual HTML files as they are, without conversions, and display all of their elements. However, if the file contains HTML that FrontPage does not recognize, the Editor will preserve it.

Opening a Page from Any Web Site

You can open any page from any Web site you have access to—including those on intranets and the Web. All you have to know is the page's address. Here are the details:

1. To begin, choose Open from the File menu. This brings up the Open dialog box. If the Select File dialog box comes up, click Cancel to get to the Open dialog box.
2. Select the first button/icon to the right of the URL text field (that's the Use Your Web Browser To Select a Page button). This will launch your default browser, as seen in Figure 6-10.

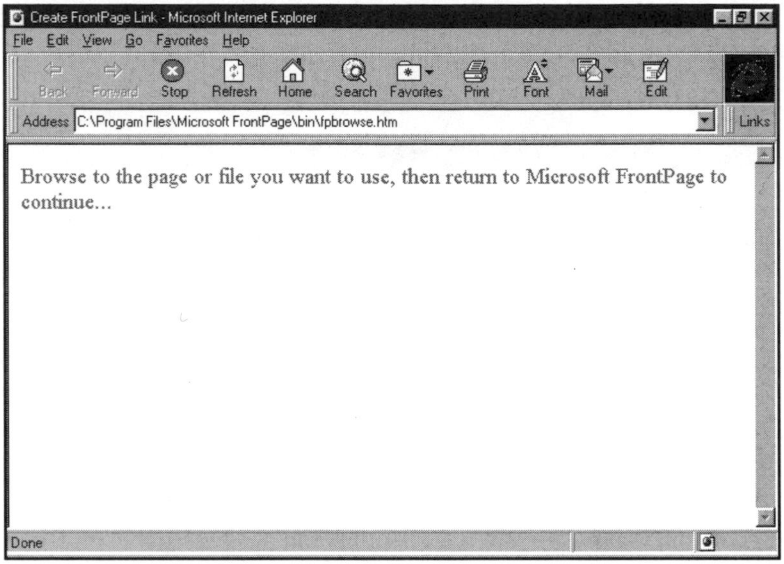

Figure 6-10

Browse to the Web page you want to open; FrontPage will automatically place the address in the URL text field for you.

4. Click OK in the Open dialog box, and the page will be opened in the browser.

If you're attempting to open a page from the Web and you get an error message, you might not be connected to the Web. Make sure your connection is live by viewing the page with your browser, and then try again.

You can also open a Web page in the Editor by typing its address in the URL text field of the Open dialog box. The address must be in the form of an absolute URL. An *absolute URL* is the full address of a page, including the protocol, host name, folder name, and filename. With absolute URLs, you can open pages from any system that can create a connection to that site. For example, say Cascade Coffee Roasters is testing a Web site called *RoasterTest1* on a local server named *BeanThere,* which includes a press release page (with the page URL *PR3.htm*) that you'd like to edit. If you have access to the Web site, you could open that page in the Editor by typing in *http://BeanThere/RoasterTest1/PR3.htm*—the absolute URL. It's that easy, even for bringing up World Wide Web pages in the Editor. Notice that an address on a local server begins with a directory name; for example, a Web address would begin htttp://www..., with the location coming after the www.

FrontPage might display a warning that the address you supplied is not a valid *IP address*. If you see this warning, check the address and try it again. Make sure you typed the correct characters; you'll need at least the server name at the beginning of the address. Be sure to use forward slashes instead of backslashes in the address.

Closing Pages

To close a page in the Editor, choose Close from the File menu. If FrontPage notices that you haven't saved the page, you'll be prompted to do so first, and then FrontPage will save the page and close it.

Saving Pages

Save your work in the same way that people in Seattle drink their coffee: early and often. Murphy's Law *will* strike you when it hurts the most; there will be times when the power goes down, or when your officemate, Tracy Tripsalot, rips the power cords from the wall sockets with her size-10 blue suede shoes. The Editor gives you three kinds of saving options:

- **Save.** Saves the active page in HTML format, to a Web site or to a file.
- **Save As.** Copies and saves the active page to a new page in the current Web site or to a file.
- **Save All.** Saves all pages that are open in the Editor.

Saving for the First Time

No matter which command you use, if you haven't saved the page before, you'll see the Save As dialog box, which gives you several options for how to save your file. You can also use the Save As command to save a page to a different location or with a different name. Figure 6-11 shows the Save As dialog box.

Here's how to use the Save As dialog box:

- Enter a page title in the URL text box. Give your page a unique and intelligent name so you can recognize it easily among other page names. After you enter that information, click OK.
- If you want to save the page as a file, such as to a floppy disk or hard disk, you don't need to fill in the title or URL. Click the Select a File on Your Computer button, the second button to the right of the URL text box. This takes you to the Save As File dialog box, where you can type the filename and specify a file type, along with the location where you want the file saved. You can specify an extension as part

of the filename, but if FrontPage does not recognize the extension, it will append an HTM extension to the filename when it saves the file.

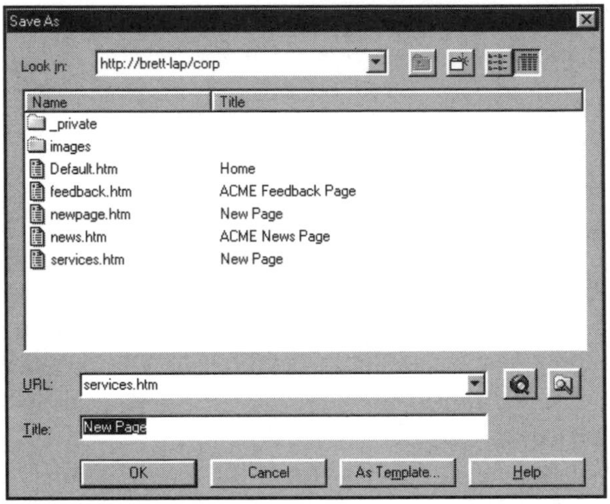

Figure 6-11

- You can also save the page as a template from the Save As dialog box. For details on this, see Chapter 4.

TIP You can quickly save a page by pressing Ctrl+S or by clicking the Save button on the toolbar.

Printing Pages

Sometimes in the virtual world of Web development, it's good to see a hard copy of a page you're working on, even if it's just to get a different "feel" for the page.

TIP Sometimes end users will print your pages to save them for later reading. Thus, you might want to print your pages from various browsers, too, to see what they'll look like to your end users.

The Editor prints your pages as they appear on-screen, provided that your paper size is large enough to accommodate the page. The following sections describe how you can use the Page Setup, Print Preview, and Print commands to produce a paper version of the page you are working with.

TIP If your page is wider than the paper you're printing on, portions of the page might not be printed. In these cases, you can try printing the page in Landscape orientation.

Page Setup

Choose Page Setup from the File menu to set up the header, footer, and margins of your printed page. These settings can be used to make your printed page easier to read and keep track of. You'll enter settings in the Print Page Setup dialog box, shown below in Figure 6-12.

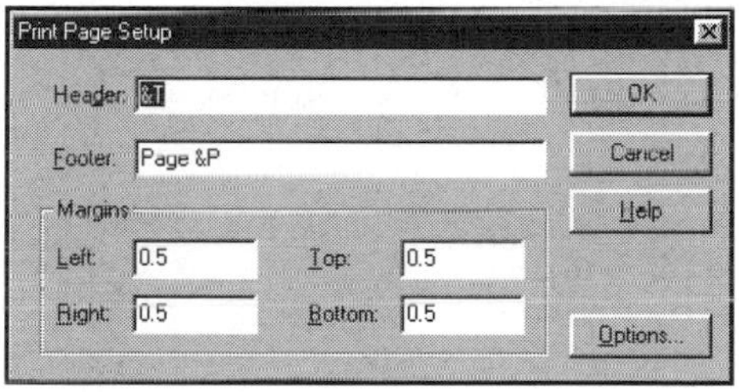

Figure 6-12

If you accept the default settings of the header and footer (shown as *&T* and *Page &P*), the Editor will print the page title as a centered header at the top of each printed page, and the current page number (with the word *Page*) as the footer. This emphasizes the difference between a Web page and the printed page. A single Web page might extend across several printed pages. Of course, your pages do not need to be numbered, but FrontPage numbers its printed pages in case you need to keep track of them.

NOTE If you do not want a header or a footer to appear on your printed pages, leave their text boxes blank in the Print Page Setup dialog box.

Clicking the Options button in the Print Page Setup dialog box takes you to the Print Setup dialog box for your printer. The Print Setup dialog box is different from the Print Page Setup dialog box—it is controlled by Windows and allows you to change settings for your printer, such as page orientation, paper size, and so on. When you're satisfied with your printer settings, click OK to return to the Print Page Setup dialog box. When you are finished in the Print Page Setup dialog box, click OK.

Print Preview

You can choose the Print Preview command from the File menu at any time to see what your page will look like when printed. This is not necessarily what the page will look like in a Web browser, however, so be careful not to rely on Print Preview for that purpose. After previewing the page, you might want to return to the Print Page Setup dialog box to adjust the margins or the header and footer.

When the Editor shows your page in Print Preview, it presents a series of view-adjustment buttons at the top of the screen. You can zoom in or zoom out, and you can view the next page, the previous page, or a two-page, side-by-side view. You can also print directly from Print Preview by clicking the Print button. To exit Print Preview without printing, press the Esc key or click the Close button.

SHORTCUT You can click the Preview In Browser button on the toolbar to preview your page in a Web browser. For details, see "Preview in Browser," in Chapter 7.

Print

Choose Print from the File menu to print your page. The standard Print dialog box will appear on your screen; if you need to change printer settings, click the Properties button. You can change printer settings in the Properties dialog box that appears.

SHORTCUT Press Ctrl+P or click the Print toolbar button to reach the Print dialog box quickly.

When you're satisfied with your printer settings, click OK in the Print dialog box to print your page. If your Web page runs longer than the length of paper you're using, the Editor will print it on multiple pages.

Making Tables

So many Web sites these days use tables to present information in a neat, orderly fashion. Tables allow you to design flexibility and control over layout of your pages. As a result, you can avoid having to format text and images manually so they appear in a structured way. Tables also allow for more consistency across Web sites, and especially across pages within a site. In addition, using tables increases the chance that information will appear the way you want it to regardless of the browser a viewer is using. Most browsers treat tables in similar enough fashion to ensure some consistency from browser to browser.

TIP If you open a Word document containing a table in the Editor, the table will be converted to an HTML table and can be modified in the Editor.

Tables in FrontPage have the same structure and are used in similar ways as tables in a Word document. Tables consist of columns and rows of cells that can contain text, images, background images, forms, FrontPage components, or even another table. If you create a table and find later that you need to change the size of cells or add or delete rows or columns, don't fret—it's easy to customize an existing table in the Editor. When you create a table, you don't have to consider cell width and height if you don't want to; as you add material to the cells, the width and height automatically expand to accommodate the material.

You can never have too many options, right? Well, at least not when it comes to adding a table in FrontPage. You have two ways in which to create a table in the FrontPage Editor. Just to help keep the day interesting, you can draw one right on the page, using the Table toolbar, or you can insert a table from the Table menu. If you're someone who has trouble making decisions, don't worry; FrontPage will let you use both table options on any table, in a variety of combinations. For example, you could insert a table from the Table menu, and then add rows to the table using the Tables toolbar. So you can mix and match between them as you wish. For clarity of instruction, though, we'll describe each method individually, starting with the Table toolbar, and then we'll follow up with what they have in common.

FrontPage Table Toolbar

FrontPage will let you draw tables in the Editor in almost exactly the same way Word lets you draw tables on a page, via the Tables toolbar as seen in Figure 6-13. To access the Tables toolbar, select Table Toolbar from the View menu, or select Draw Table from the Table menu.

Figure 6-13

The Tables toolbar lets you draw your table right on the page and then alter many aspects of it to suit your needs. The first button on the Tables toolbar, the Draw Table button, is also what you use in the first step you take in drawing your table.

1. If you selected Draw Table from the Table toolbar, the Draw Table pointer is automatically active; otherwise, select the Draw Table button from the Tables toolbar. Your cursor becomes a pen pointer.
2. Position the pointer where you want the table to begin, click, and then drag down and to the right to create the table. The table is automatically drawn at the left side of the page. You can change this later if you like. For more information on table properties, see "Changing Table Properties," later in this chapter.

   So that you can see how large your table is going to be, the table's outer border is represented as a dotted outline as you drag the cursor.

You've just a drawn a single-celled table, with one column and one row. When you draw a table, it's automatically drawn with a border. To remove the border, you need to access the table's properties dialog box. For more information on the Table Properties dialog box, see the section, "What These Methods Have in Common," later in this chapter. Your table should look something like the table shown in Figure 6-14.

In case you didn't get it right the first time, you can easily change the size of your table, without having to redraw it. Move your cursor to the border of the table. Notice how it changes into a two-sided arrow. You can click and drag to change the table width by dragging the right side of the table, or change its height by dragging from the bottom.

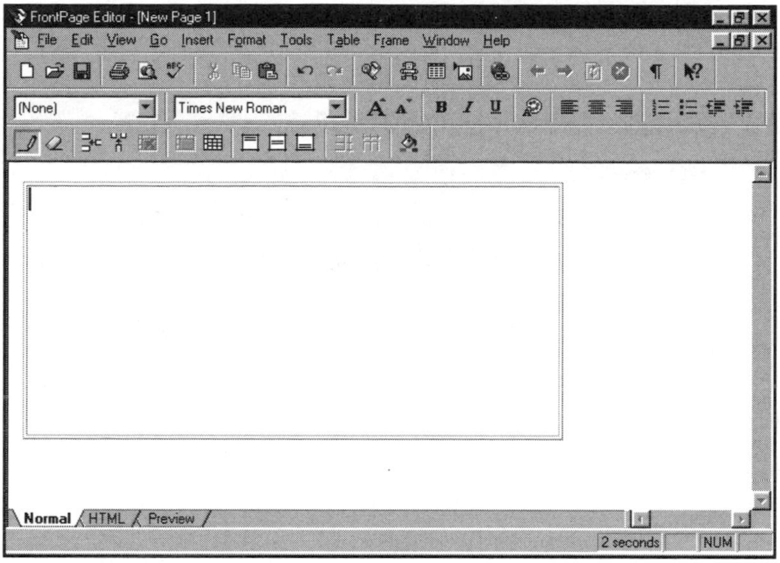

Figure 6-14

TIP If you hold down the Shift key while you drag a border all of the cells in that direction would retain their widths.

Adding Rows and Columns

Now that you have your table the size you want, you might want to add some rows and columns.

You can easily draw a row or column, dividing your table almost anyway you like, using the Draw Table pen pointer.

1. Select the Draw Table pen pointer, if it isn't already selected.
2. Position the pointer inside the cell you want to divide. Make sure that the pointer is *not* touching the table border. Doing this will draw a new table within the cell.
3. Click and drag, horizontally to create a row or vertically to create a column. As you drag, a dotted line will represent the new border. You don't have to worry about drawing straight; FrontPage will constrain the line either vertically or horizontally for you. All you need to do is start in the right direction.

Figure 6-15 shows the table divided into two columns, with the right column divided into two rows.

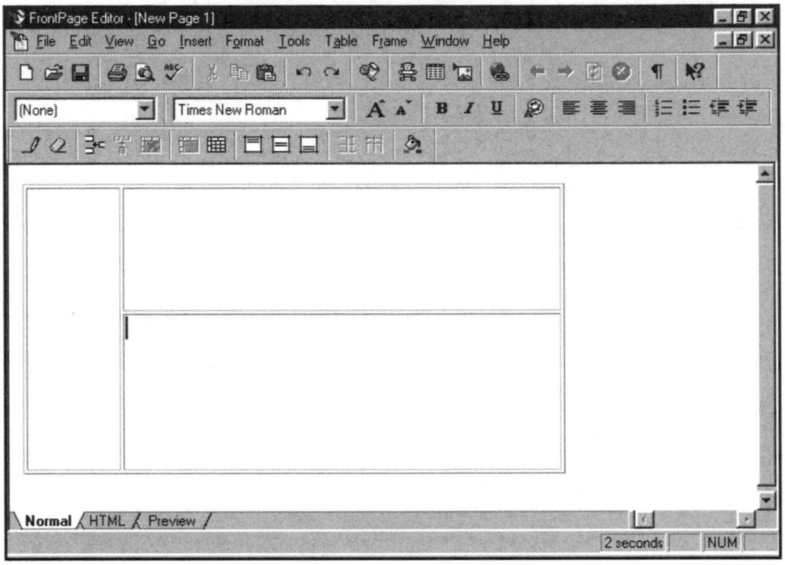

Figure 6-15

If you want to divide the table evenly with rows or columns, you can do that with the Insert Rows and Insert Columns buttons on the Table toolbar.

1. Place the cursor in the cell of the table you want to divide.
2. Select either the Insert Rows button or the Insert Columns button. FrontPage will automatically create a column equal to half of the cell, or create a row equal to the size of the cell. Your cursor will be left blinking in the new cell.

The example shown in Figure 6-16 shows the table divided using the Insert Column button on the Table toolbar. Notice that we now have one table divided into two equal columns. By repeating the steps above, you can divide each cell as often as you like. Once you've created a table with columns and rows, you can move the borders around to suit your needs, no matter which method you used to create them.

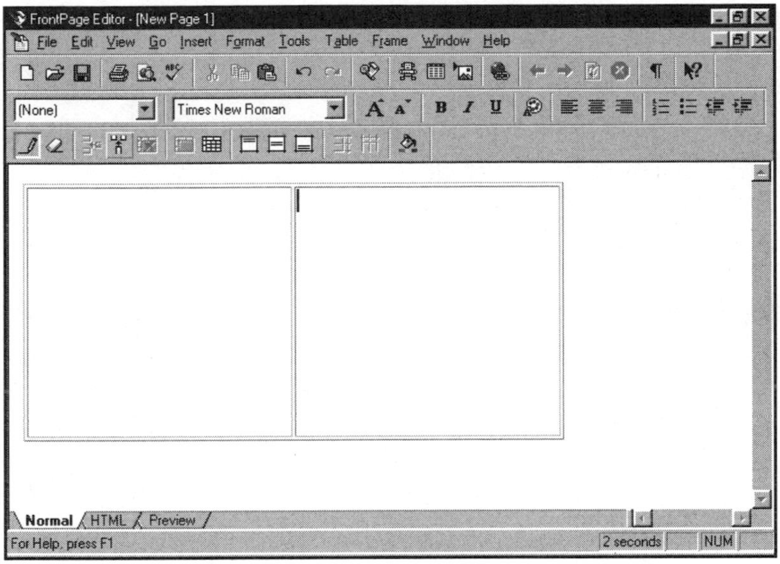

Figure 6-16

Erasing a Row or Column

If you've created a table and then notice that you have too many rows, or columns, you can easily erase a border, using the Erase button on the Tables toolbar.

1. Select the Erase button from the Tables toolbar. Your cursor becomes an eraser.
2. Place the Eraser cursor outside of the border you wish to delete.
3. Click and drag across the border line you wish to delete. As you drag, the border will be highlighted.
4. When you release the mouse, the selected borders are deleted.

You cannot erase a border that would result in an incomplete cell. In other words, all border lines must touch two complete borders. In the example shown in Figure 6-17, the interior borders are selected to be erased. The circled area could not be erased by itself, because this would result in an incomplete cell at the bottom.

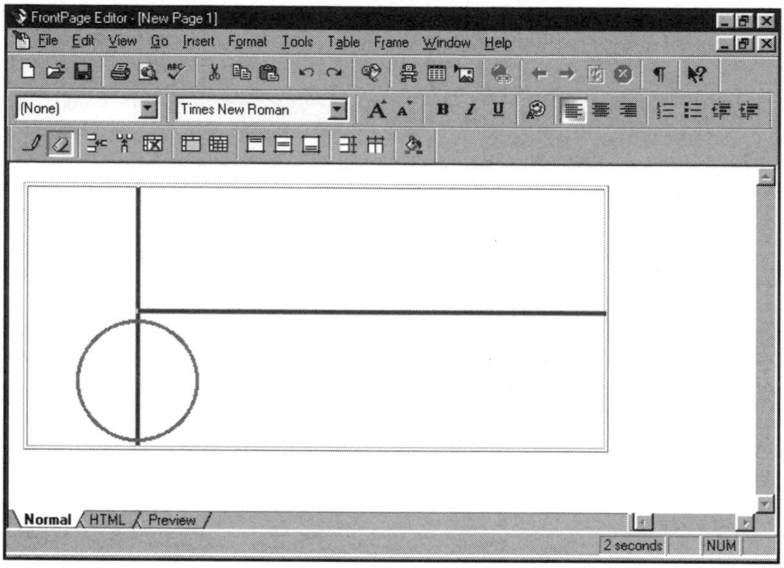

Figure 6-17

The Remaining Tables Toolbar Buttons

The other buttons on the Tables toolbar let you further adjust, and design your tables:

Delete Cells. You can delete cells by selecting the row or column containing the cells and choosing the Delete Cells button on the Tables toolbar. For more information on selecting rows and columns, see the section "Selecting Rows and Columns," later in this chapter.

Merge Cells. You can merge cells together by selecting the cells and choosing the Merge Cells button on the Tables toolbar.

Split Cells. You can split cells into columns or rows by selecting the cells and then choosing the Split Cells button on the Tables toolbar. This brings up the Split Cells dialog box. For more information on this dialog box, see "Splitting Cells," later in this chapter.

Align Top, Center Vertically, Align Bottom. By placing your cursor in the cell and selecting one of these buttons, any text in the cell will align accordingly.

Distribute Rows and Columns Evenly. If you want a selection of rows or columns to be distributed evenly in the table, select them and choose the appropriate button.

Background Color. If you want to add color to the background of a cell, or to the entire table itself, select the area, and then choose the Background Color button. This brings up the Color dialog box. Select a color and click OK.

Inserting a Table

Here is the process to follow if you want to insert your table using the FrontPage menu commands.

1. Position your cursor where you want the table to begin, and then choose Insert Table from the Table menu. You'll see the Insert Table dialog box, as seen here in Figure 6-18.

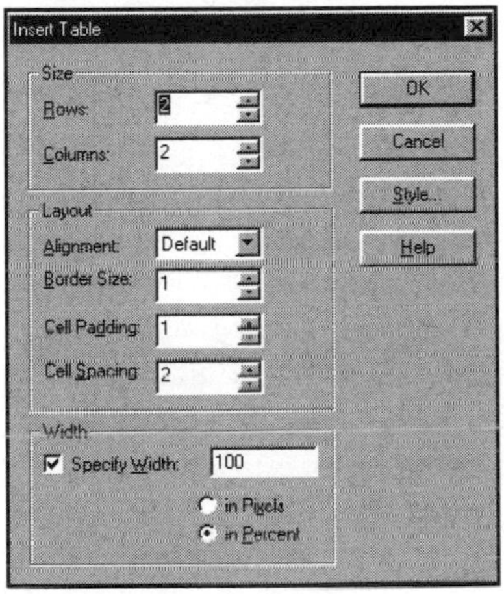

Figure 6-18

2. Enter the number of rows and columns you think you'll need in your table. You can add or delete rows and columns later.
3. Select an alignment option for the table: at the left side of the page, centered, or at the right side of the page.
4. If you want a border around the table, enter the width in pixels for the border size. This setting is for the border that surrounds the entire table; each cell in the table also has a border representing the cell spacing (see step 6). If you do not want a border, enter 0. If you choose to surround your table with a border, you can specify border colors later on. The exact format of all table borders is determined by the browser being used rather than by settings within FrontPage.

TIP

If you create a borderless table and want to see what the table looks like without formatting marks, you can choose the Format Marks command from the View menu or click the Show/Hide Paragraph toolbar button. You'll see cell outlines in the Editor that will not appear in a browser.

5. Enter a number, in pixels, for the cell padding. *Cell padding* is the space between a cell's contents and each of its borders. This number pertains to all cells in the table; cell padding cannot be set for individual cells. The default is 1.
6. Enter a number, in pixels, for *cell spacing*. This controls the spacing between the cells in a table and is represented as a border around each cell (including those at the outer edge of the table). The default is 2.
7. Specify the width of the table. You can set the number in pixels or as a percentage of the page width. For example, if you set the table width to 50 percent, the table will span half the width of the page.

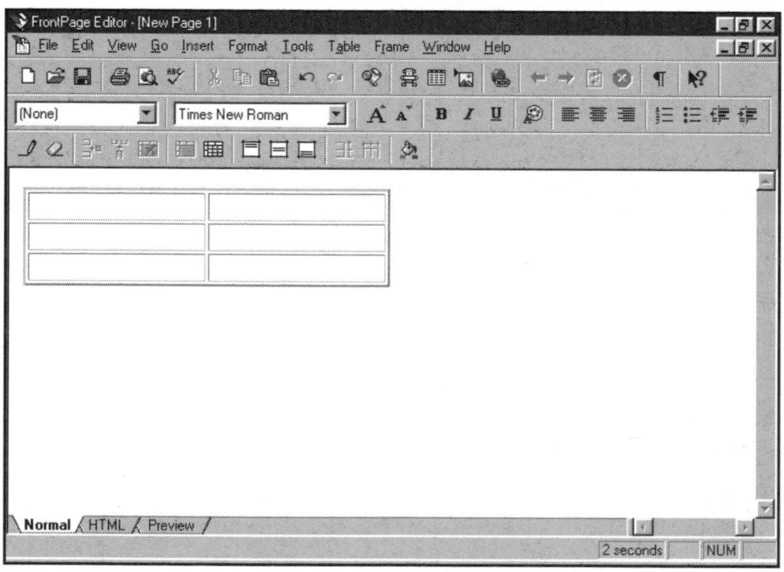

Figure 6-19

The table above is three rows by two columns. It is left-justified on the page; has a 2-pixel border, 1-pixel cell padding, and 2-pixel cell spacing; and has a width setting of 50 percent.

8. Click OK. The Editor creates the table and displays it on the page, as seen in Figure 6-19 on the facing page. FrontPage uses the number of columns and the width of the table to calculate the size of each of the individual columns.

What These Methods Have in Common

Once you've made a decision on which way you're going to get a table into FrontPage, you'll probably want to fine-tune it.

Adding Text

You can type in a table cell just as you would anywhere else on a page in the Editor. If you add more text than the cell is formatted to hold, the cell expands to accommodate it.

Changing Table Properties

At any time, you can change settings for table alignment, border size, cell padding, cell spacing, and overall table width by using the Table Properties command. Simply right-click on the table and choose Table Properties from the pop-up menu. You can also access table properties by placing your cursor in the table and choosing Table Properties from the Table menu. The Table Properties dialog box opens, as seen in Figure 6-20 on the next page.

TIP

You can quickly add a table to your page by clicking the Insert Table button on the toolbar and clicking the appropriate box on the grid that is displayed. The table properties are based on the last table property setting.

To get a "test view" of what your table might look like with different settings, you can change some settings in the Table Properties dialog box and then click the Apply button. You can change the settings and click Apply as many times as necessary.

NOTE

When you see the Style button on various dialog boxes, it means that you can create or modify a stylesheet associated with the page from within that dialog box. For more information on stylesheets, see Chapter 7.

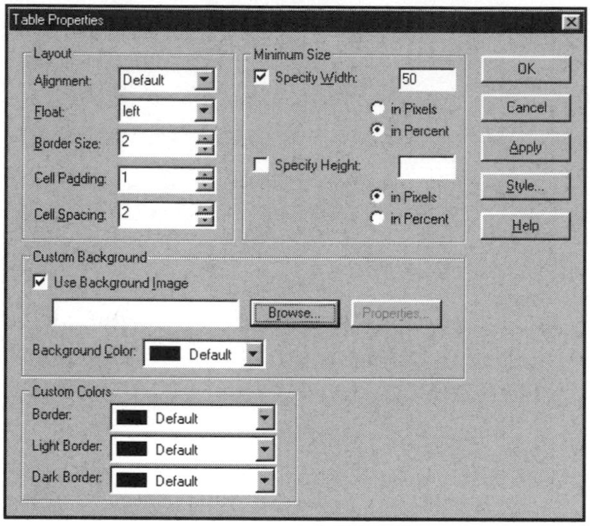

Figure 6-20

In addition, you cT2 insert a background image or add a background color by selecting the Use Background Image check box. When you make this selection, you'll see the Browse button become available. If you click the Browse button, you'll have a few different ways to choose an image. Do one of the following:

- If you want to use a background image that is currently in your Web site, find the file in the appropriate folder, and click OK.
- If you want to use a background image from another location, such as a floppy disk, hard drive, or LAN, locate the background image in the Select Background Image dialog box, and click OK. You can also select a background image from the World Wide Web or make a hyperlink to a file on your computer.
- You can also use FrontPage-provided clip art for your background image. To do so, click the Clip Art tab, click a background image, and then click OK.

If your table has borders, you can specify their colors in the Custom Colors section of the Table Properties dialog box. To use a uniform color for all borders, select that color in the Border drop-down list. Selecting colors from the Light Border and Dark Border drop-down lists allows you to give the table a three-dimensional look. The light border color specifies the highlight color and the dark border color specifies the shadow color. Experiment with these colors to give your tables a customized look.

NOTE An easy way to expand the number of rows in a table is to position your cursor in the lower right cell and press the Tab key.

Changing Cell Properties

You can also change some properties for cells, such as the alignment of text within them, their minimum width, the number of rows or columns they span, and their background images or colors. Here's how to view and change these properties:

1. Position your cursor in a cell whose properties you want to change. To change the properties for multiple cells at once, you need to select those cells first. To do so, position your cursor in one of the cells and then choose Select Cell from the Table menu. Then, hold down the Ctrl or Shift key to select additional cells with the cursor. Holding down the Ctrl key also lets you deselect selected cells. For information on methods for easily selecting entire rows or columns, see "Selecting Rows and Columns" later in this chapter.
2. Choose Cell Properties from the Table menu or right-click over the selected cell(s) and choose Cell Properties from the pop-up menu. The Cell Properties dialog box appears, as seen in Figure 6-21.
3. To change the alignment of text within the cell(s), alter the settings in the Layout section. For example, to align the text in the exact center of a cell, select Center for the Horizontal Alignment and Middle for the Vertical Alignment.
4. Enter new numbers in the Specify Width and Height text boxes to change the width and height of the cell(s), respectively.
5. In the Cell Span section, enter the number of rows or columns you want a cell to span. Changing this setting expands the cell to cross that number of rows or columns. This causes cells in the column to the right and/or the rows below to move accordingly to make room for the enlarged cell. One reason you might want to expand a cell in this fashion is to fill the area with an image.

   For example, suppose you have a two-row, two-column table, and you want an image to fill the area below the top two cells. You can expand the bottom left cell so it spans the two columns. To insert a background image or add background color to the cell(s), select the appropriate options in the Custom Background section.

6. To add colored borders to the cell(s), select those colors in the Custom Colors section.
7. Click Apply to view your changed settings before closing the dialog box. When you have the settings the way you want, click OK to exit the Cell Properties dialog box.

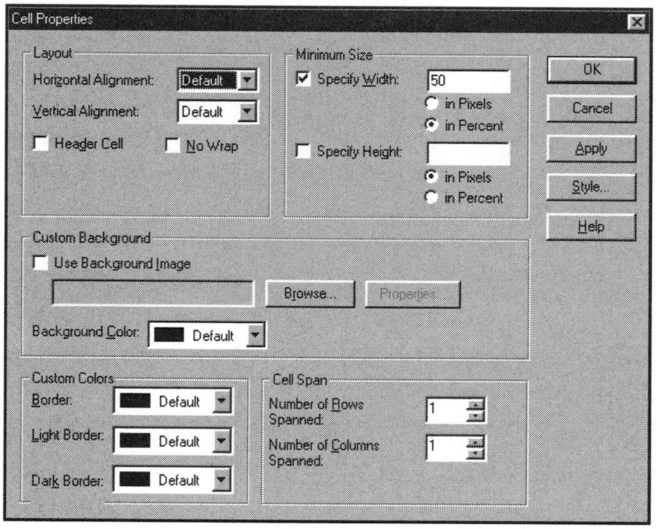

Figure 6-21

Creating Header Cells

Header cells are marked for special formatting; in FrontPage tables, the text is made bold. Often a header cell is used at the top of a column or at the left end of a row, and will contain a title for that row or column, but a header cell can be any cell that you want to make prominent in your table. You can turn any regular cell into a header cell by doing the following:

1. Select the cell you want to turn into a header cell. To select multiple cells, select the first cell and then hold down the Ctrl or Shift key while clicking on additional cells.
2. Choose the Cell Properties command from the Edit menu or right-click over the selected cell(s) and choose Cell Properties from the

pop-up menu. In the Cell Properties dialog box, select the Header Cell check box, and then click OK.

That cell becomes a header cell, and any existing text in the cell is shown in bold, and any additional text you type in the cell will also be bold. Be aware that different browsers might treat header cell formatting in different ways.

Selecting Rows and Columns

To select a row or a column, position the mouse pointer near the top of a column or near the left border of a row until it turns into a solid arrow, and then click. You can also place your cursor in a cell, and then choose Select Cell, Select Row, Select Column, or Select Table from the Table menu.

Moving Around within a Table

You use the arrow keys to move from character to character (or element to element) within a cell, and the Tab key to move from cell to cell.

Adding Cells

If you need to add a piece of information in your table but have nowhere to add it, you can always insert a blank cell. Inserting a cell into a table adds one more cell to the row it's inserted in, and can extend the row outside the original table boundary. In the following illustration, a cell was added to the right of the cell with *6* in it.

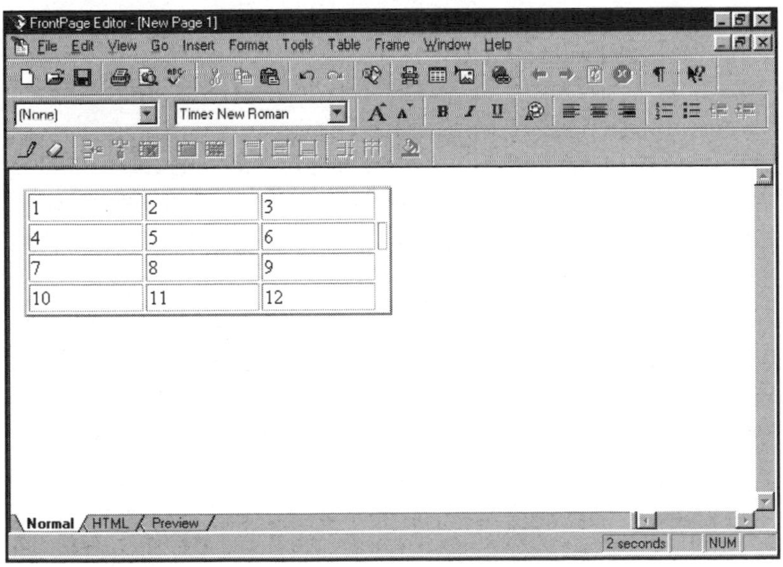

Figure 6-22

As you can see, inserting cells can make your tables asymmetrical, but that just might be your goal. To insert a cell, position your cursor in the cell directly to the left of where you want the new cell to appear, and choose Insert Cell from the Table menu.

Adding Rows

To add a row or rows to your table, do the following:

1. Position your cursor in the row above or below where you want the new row(s) to appear.
2. Choose Insert Rows Or Columns from the Table menu. You'll see the Insert Rows Or Columns dialog box, shown here in Figure 6-23.

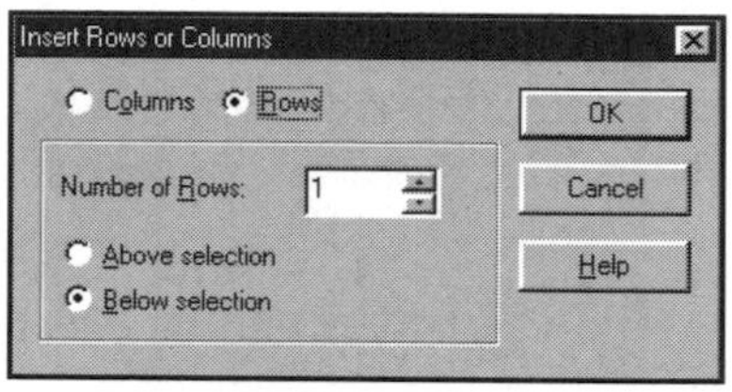

Figure 6-23

3. Select the Rows option, and enter the number of rows you want to insert. Then specify whether you want the row(s) to be inserted above or below the row you selected, and click OK.

Adding Columns

To add a column or columns to a table, position your cursor in the column next to where you want the new column(s) to appear, and then choose Insert Rows Or Columns from the Table menu. Follow the same procedure outlined above in "Adding Rows," but select the Columns option and enter the number of columns you want to insert.

TIP To add a blank paragraph after a table, position the cursor at the end of the lower right cell, and then press Ctrl+Enter.

Deleting Rows or Columns

To delete a row or a column, select the row or column you want to delete, and then press the Delete key.

Inserting a Caption

A *table caption* is a headline that appears at the top of your table. To insert one, select Insert Caption from the Table menu, and then type your caption.

Moving Rows or Columns

Here's how to move a row or a column to another place in a table. In FrontPage, as well as in Excel, when you paste a portion of a table, the pasted information replaces whatever was in the new location. Therefore, to move a row or a column without losing any other information, you must first insert a blank row or column into which you'll paste the row or column you want to move. For this example, we'll move a row, but the same procedure works for columns:

1. If there are no blank rows in the table, insert a row to serve as the destination row for the material you want to move.
2. Select the row you want to move, and then choose Cut from the Edit menu or press Ctrl+X.
3. Select the blank row you want to move the material to, and then choose Paste from the Edit menu (or press Ctrl+V). The material is pasted in the new row.

This procedure also works for material you want to copy from one row or column to another. You can also cut and copy multiple rows and columns at once in the same way.

Splitting Cells

To provide more detailed information in your table, or to clean up the formatting on a page, you might want to split a cell. When you split a cell, you divide a single cell into as many rows or columns as you need. Here's how:

1. Position your cursor in the cell you want to split.
2. Choose Split Cells from the Table menu. The Split Cells dialog box appears, as shown in Figure 6-24.

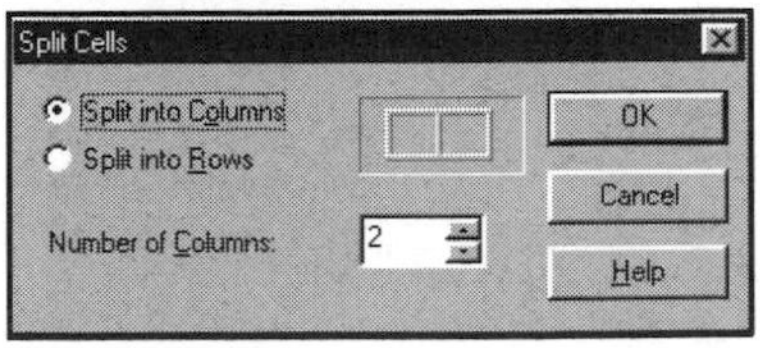

Figure 6-24

3. Specify whether you want to split the cell into columns or rows, and then enter the number of new columns or rows you want in that cell. Click OK.

Figure 6-25 shows an example of a three-column table whose center column is split into three rows:

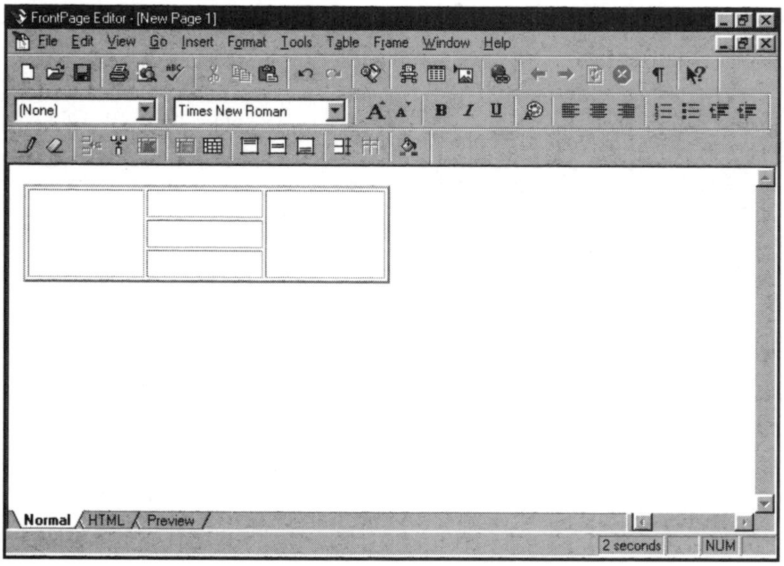

Figure 6-25

Merging Cells

There might be times when you want to combine material from several neighboring cells into one cell. This is called *merging cells*. Here's how to do it:

1. Select the cells you want to merge. To select multiple cells, select the first cell, and then click in the next cell while holding down the Ctrl or Shift key. When merging cells, you can select as many cells as you want, but ultimately you must have a rectangular area selected.
2. Choose Merge Cells from the Table menu. The Editor merges the cells. Any cell borders shared by the merged cells are removed, resulting in a larger cell. The content of each cell is retained and is formatted as a separate paragraph.

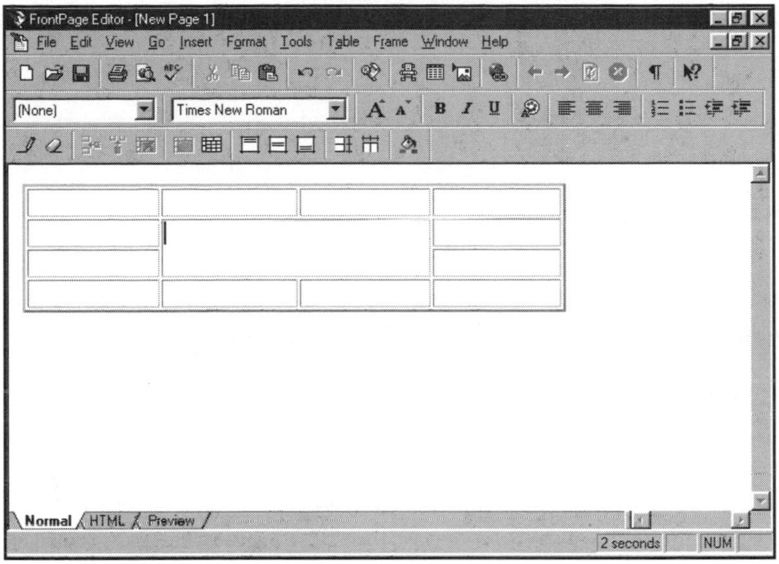

Figure 6-26

In the table above, the centermost four cells have been merged.

Adding Images to Cells

To add an image to a table cell, position your cursor in the cell, choose Image from the Insert menu, and then select an image from the resulting Image dialog box. You can also drag an image from the Windows Explorer or the FrontPage Explorer. For detailed information on inserting images, see Chapter 8.

Inserting Tables within Tables

The Editor allows you to insert a table within a table. You might want to use a table within a table to order your data in a special way. Or, you might want the look and feel of several bordered tables on a page. If you use tables for presenting thumbnail images for users to click on to obtain a larger version of the image, using a table within a table might help you to present the thumbnails in a more logical or graphically pleasing way than in an ordinary table.

Before you use the table-within-a-table strategy, consider if you can obtain the same results by splitting cells. Keeping your table design as simple as possible will probably save you time when you troubleshoot any problems on your pages.

To insert a table within a table, position the cursor in the cell where you want the new table to appear, and create the new table by using the Insert Table command on the Table menu or by clicking the Insert Table button on the toolbar. This process was described earlier in this chapter.

WYSIWYG Frames

Frames are rectangular regions on a Web page in which you can display other pages or images. In FrontPage, you can create frames pages using the frames templates; this process was described in Chapter 4.

Uses for Frames

Frames can be used in a wide variety of ways, and their use is limited only by your imagination. You should use a frame whenever you want particular content on a page to remain static while other content on the page changes. A common use involves inserting a company logo in a frame at the top of a page, and dividing the rest of the page among frames for other content.

Another use of frames might involve presenting a list of your company's products in a frame on the left side of a page, and having a description of each product appear on a page in a frame on the right side. The page in the left frame is static; you want the list of products to appear all the time. The page that appears in the right frame changes according to what product the user clicks on in the left frame. You can associate each of the links on the page in the left frame with a target frame, which in this case is the right frame. Thus, when a user clicks a link on a page in the left frame, the appropriate page appears in the target frame on the right side of the page.

In Cascade Coffee Roasters' RoasterNet site, one page might present a listing of each month of the year in the left frame, with each month linked to a sales report page for that particular month, which appears in the right frame. Or, a list of forms that employees need to submit periodically can be placed in a frame near the top of the page; the forms can appear in a larger window near the bottom of the page. The following figure shows an example of a Web page in progress, containing three frames, and viewed in the Editor.

As you can see in Figure 6-27, the page is divided into three sections, each separated by a gray border. Notice that it displays in the Editor in the same way as it would display in a user's browser.

Figure 6-27

Framesets

A *frameset* is actually a separate page that contains the combined information of the pages in the set. That information communicates with the server to display the pages in a browser. In the previous example, there are three pages visible; add to that the frameset page, and the total number of pages required to display the frames is four. Which means that the server is *hit* four times before it displays the pages. That's why it's a good idea to limit the number of frames in your frameset.

FrontPage displays all of the pages in a frameset together, in the Editor. You can create, manipulate, and view frames pages in the Editor. This WYSIWYG viewing is extremely helpful when designing with frames. In the old days, you had to open each page individually in order to work on them, and you could view the finished results only in a browser.

Working with Frames

When you create frames using the frames templates (described in Chapter 4), FrontPage automatically creates the individual pages, and the frameset, and displays all of the frames in the Editor. Now isn't that nice of them?

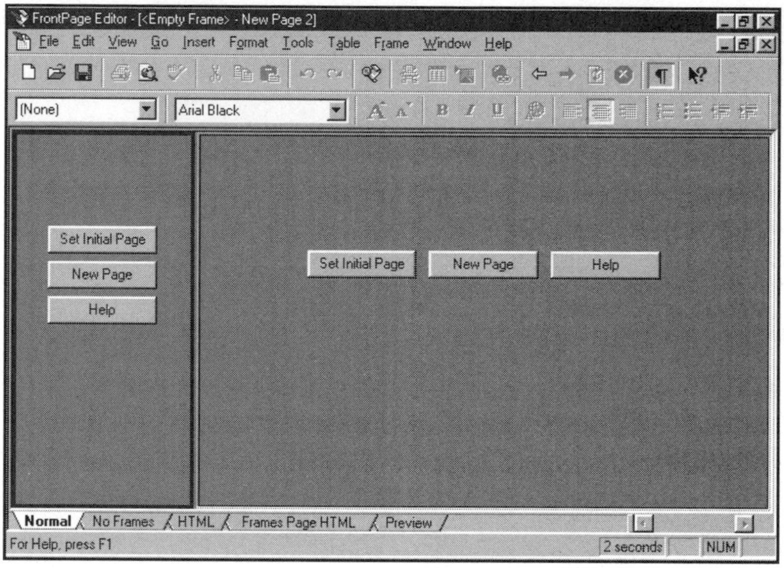

Figure 6-28

This is what it looks like when you create a new frames page. These pages were created using the Contents frame template.

Define Your New Frames Page

When you first create a frames page in the Editor, as seen in Figure 6-28 above, the pages are not set for you. You need to make a quick choice before you can begin to populate them with content:

- **Set Initial Page.** The *initial page* is the page initially displayed in a frame when a user firsts opens the frame. When you select this button, it brings up the Create Hyperlink dialog box. Here, you can create a new page and a link to it, or if you have the Explorer open, you can set the initial page to any page currently in the Explorer. For more information on the Create Hyperlink dialog box, see the section "Links," in Chapter 7.
- **New Page.** When you click this button, a new normal page is displayed in the frame. This is an unsaved page that is created using the Normal template. For more information on Page Templates, see Chapter 4.

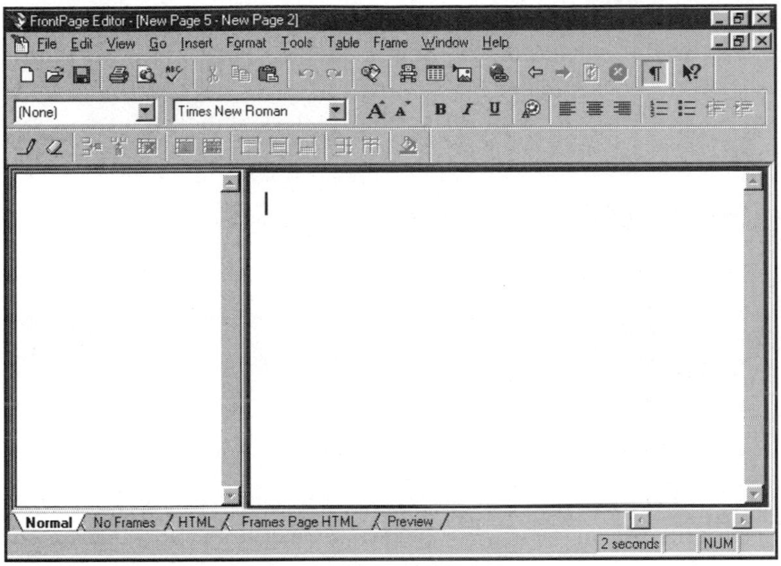

Figure 6-29
Once you set your pages in the frameset, you're ready to begin adding your content, and laying out the page.

Selecting a Page or a Frameset

When you click anywhere on a frame, that page becomes the active page. A active page is represented by a colored border around the individual page. Click anywhere on an outer border of the frameset, and the entire frameset is highlighted with a colored border.

Frames Page Properties

You can make changes to the frameset by selecting the frameset and choosing Frame Page Properties from the Frame menu. This brings up the Page Properties dialog box, with the Frames tab selected. You have two options here:

- **Frame Spacing.** You can add spacing between the frames by typing a number in the Frame Spacing box.
- **Show Borders.** You can show or hide frame borders by checking or unchecking the Show Borders check box.

For more information on the on the Page Properties dialog box, see Chapter 7.

Frame Properties

Select a single frame page and choose Frame Properties from the Frame menu, or right-click on the page and choose Frame Properties from the pop-up menu. This brings up the Frame Properties dialog box, shown here in Figure 6-30.

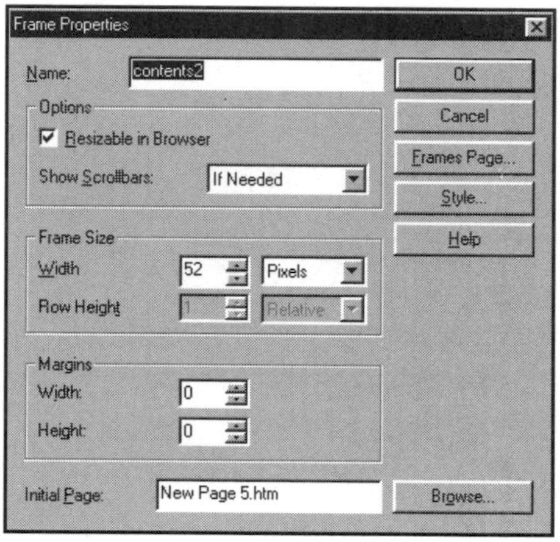

Figure 6-30

From here, you make changes to an individual frames page. Just in case you weren't happy with it the way it was, you can give the page a new name by typing the name in the Name text field. You can also set a new initial page by typing directly into the Initial Page text field, or by selecting the Browse button. Selecting the Browse button brings up the Edit Hyperlink dialog box, which is described in detail in Chapter 7.

There are three other areas on this dialog box that let you further customize your frames page: Options, Frame Size, and Margins.

- **Options.** Here you can specify whether the frame is resizable in the browser automatically, based on the browser the user is using. The box is checked by default, and for most pages, that's a good idea. You can also decide to show scroll bars: *If Needed*, *Never* or *Always*. If Needed is selected by default, and it's a good idea not to change this unless you have a very good idea that the content will not need to scroll. If you select Always, the page will have scroll bars no matter how much content is on the page and no matter what resolution the user is viewing the site in. In other words, don't do this unless you have a good reason. Unnecessary scroll bars not only look unprofessional, but they can put the user in a bad mood and make them want to leave you site—and we want them want to stay, right?

- **Frame Size.** Here you can adjust the Width or Height of the frame.

    Width: If the frame page is in a column alongside another frame, these options are enabled. Relative means that the frame size will be based on the other frames in the column; for example, a relative value of 1 means that the frames in the column will be of equal size. Percent means that the frame will be a certain percentage of the total window when displayed in a browser. And if you want to define an exact size for the frame, insert a value and select Pixels.

    Row Height: If the frame is in a row that has another row of frames to its left or right, these options are enabled. The values are defined in the same way as for Width.

  All frames in a row or column are changed uniformly when you change any one of the pages in that row or column.

- **Margins.** If you want to adjust the margins within the page, enter the value in the Width and Height text boxes. Anything displayed on the page will be offset by the number entered here.

You can access the Frames Page dialog box by selecting the Frames Page button. This dialog box is explained above in the section "Frames Page Properties" earlier in this chapter. If you want to create or edit a stylesheet associated with the page, select the Style button. The Style dialog box appears. For more information on this dialog box, see Chapter 7.

When you finish making changes to the frame, click OK.

Page Properties

You can change the properties of the page by right-clicking a page and selecting Page Properties from the pop-up menu. The Page Properties dialog box is displayed. For more information on the Page Properties dialog box, see Chapter 7. You can also change the default target frame. For instructions on doing this, see the section "Default Target Frames" later in this chapter.

Saving Frames and Framesets for the First Time

Saving the frames pages, and the frameset page itself, for the first time works exactly the same as saving a regular page for the first time, with one very cool difference. When you save a frame for the first time, the Save As dialog box displays a thumbnail version of your frameset, with the current page highlighted, ready to be saved, as seen in Figure 6-31. This way, you know exactly which frame is being saved, and what its name is. For more information on saving pages, see "Saving Pages," later in this chapter.

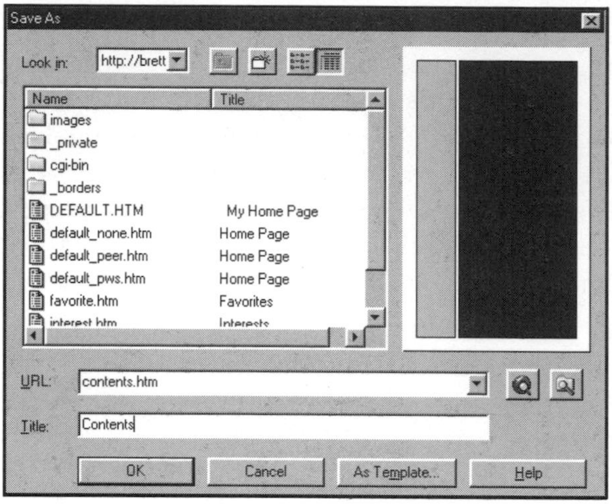

Figure 6-31

When you name the page and click OK, the next page will be highlighted in the thumbnail, ready to be saved. Once you've saved the frames, you'll be asked to save the frameset page.

NOTE It's a good idea, especially when saving frames pages and the frameset page that controls them, to use names that are easy to remember. Later on, you'll want links from one frame to open pages in another frame, and this can get confusing if the page names aren't clearly defined.

Saving in the Editor Only

If you're working without the use of the Explorer, you'll be greeted with the Save As File dialog box when you save for the first time. For more information on the Save As File dialog box, see the section "Saving Files" later in this chapter.

Saving When the Page Has Been Saved Before

Once you've saved the page for the first time, every subsequent save will save in the background.

Deleting a Frame

If you want to delete a frame from the frameset, select the frame and choose Delete Frame from the Frames menu. The frame is deleted and the remaining frames are expanded to fill the window.

Opening a Page in a New Window

If you want to view a frame in its own window, outside of the frameset, right-click the page and select Open Page in New Window from the pop-up menu.

Splitting a Page in a Frameset

After you've created a frameset with the Frames template, you may decide that you need another frame. You can do this in two different ways, from the Frames menu or by using a keyboard shortcut.

Using the Frames menu:

1. Select the frames page you want to split by clicking inside the page. The page should now be outlined in color.
2. Select Split Frame from the Frame menu. You'll see the Split Frame dialog box. This dialog box, shown in Figure 6-32, works exactly the same way as the Insert Rows Or Columns dialog box, explained earlier in this chapter.

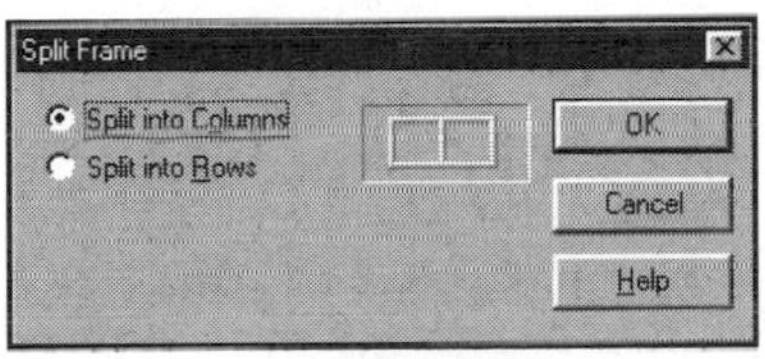

Figure 6-32

3. Choose either Split into Columns or Split into Rows, and then click OK.

Using the keyboard shortcut:

1. Move the cursor to the border of the frame you want to split. The cursor changes into a double-sided arrow.
2. Hold the Ctrl key and click and drag the cursor. You'll see your new frame as you drag the mouse.
3. When you've created the page to the desired width, let go, and a new unset frame is created.

Displaying a Page in a Frame

To designate a page to appear in a frame, you can create a link to the page and associate the link with the frame. This all happens in the Create Hyperlink or Edit Hyperlink dialog box. For example, suppose RoasterNet has a Table of Contents page with a word, *Sales,* in the frame on the left, that's already linked to a page containing sales information. You want to click the Sales link and have the Sales page appear in the frame on the right. Here's how to set this up:

1. Open your frameset in the Editor.
2. On the Table of Contents page in the Editor, right-click the *Sales* link and choose Hyperlink Properties from the pop-up menu to open the Edit Hyperlink dialog box, shown here in Figure 6-33.

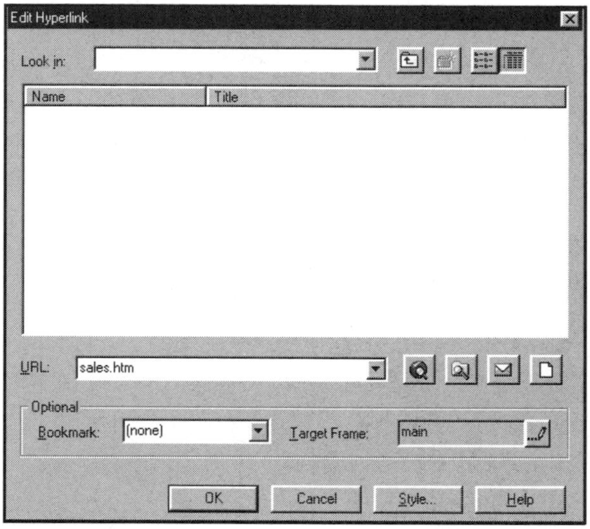

Figure 6-33

3. Specify the URL in the URL text box, or use the drop-down list to view the files most recently used by the Editor. For more information on the other options in the Edit Hyperlink dialog box, see Chapter 7.
4. Select the button to the right of the Target Frame text box, you'll see the Target Frame dialog box, enter the name of the frame you want the Sales page to appear in. You can also click on the frameset thumbnail, to select the target frame.

   You can skip step 4 if you've already set a default target frame for the page and you're happy with it. For more information on setting the default target frame, see "Default Target Frames," later in this chapter.
5. Click OK in each dialog box, to return to the Editor. That's it.

Back in the Editor, you can follow the *Sales* link in the left frame, which opens the Sales page in the right frame. To follow a link in the Editor's Normal view, right-click the link and select Follow Hyperlink from the pop-up menu, or Ctrl+click on the link.

Displaying Form Submission Results in a Frame

In the same way that you can direct a standard page to appear in a frame, you can direct the results of a form submission to appear in a frame. This is typically used with the Custom ISAPI, NSAPI, or CGI script, or with Database Region Wizard form handlers. Here's how to set this up:

1. In the Editor, right-click any form field and choose Form Properties from the pop-up menu to open the Form Properties dialog box, shown here in Figure 6-34.

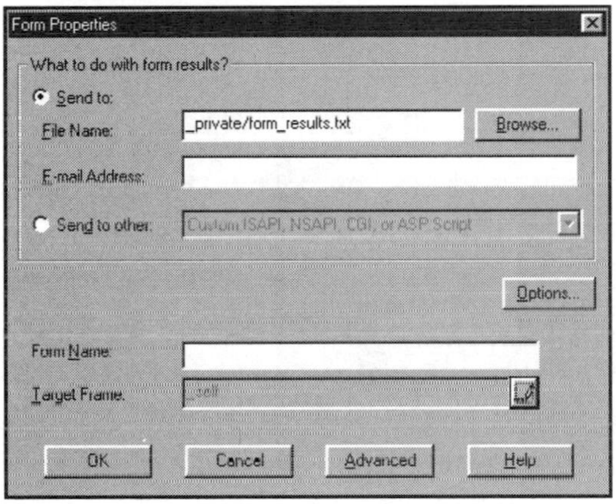

Figure 6-34

2. Select the button to the right of the Target Frame text box, and you'll see the Target Frame dialog box. Enter the name of the frame in which you want the form results to appear.
3. Click OK to close the Target Frame dialog box, and then click OK to close the Form Properties dialog box.

For more information on creating and using forms, see the section of the same title in Chapter 9.

Default Target Frames

If you have a page with many links and you don't want to assign a target frame to every one of them, you can associate them all with a default target frame. Default target frames specify a frame for any links on a page, including clickable images, that are not associated with a specific target frame. To assign a default target frame, do the following:

1. With the page open in the Editor, right-click anywhere on the page and choose Page Properties from the pop-up menu.
2. In the Page Properties dialog box, click the General tab, select the button to the right of the Default Target Frame text box, and you'll see the Target Frame dialog box. Enter the name of the frame in which you want the form results to appear, and then click OK.

You can still edit an individual hyperlink to a to a target frame other than the default target. This process is described above in "Displaying a Page in a Frame."

Frames View Tabs

When you first open a frameset in the Editor, you may notice a new series of view tabs at the bottom of the Editors window. Each of these tabs gives you a different look, behind the scenes of your frameset and frames pages:

- **Normal.** The Normal tab is selected by default. This is your "working" view in FrontPage, and the view we've been working in thus far.
- **No Frames.** If a user tries to open your frames site and they have a browser that doesn't support frames, they'll see the text on this page automatically. You can change this as you like.
- **HTML.** This tab shows the HTML for all the frames in the current frameset. This is a fully functioning HTML editor, so be careful what you change.
- **Frames Page HTML.** Here, you'll be able to edit and view the HTML for the frameset. Be careful here too: Don't change anything unless you're experienced using HTML and frames.
- **Preview.** You can preview your page right in the Editor by selecting this tab.

Coming Up

With that, the grand discussion of creating your pages in the Editor comes to an end. In the next chapter, you'll learn how to format your pages in the Editor, and you'll also learn some of the Editor's utilities and useful commands.

CHAPTER 7

Fine-Tuning Your Pages

I Wonder What *This* Would Look Like...

Once you've got the material you want on your pages, more than likely you'll want to fine-tune it. Your paragraphs don't have to stay left-aligned, your text doesn't all have to remain the same size and color, and the links and background of your pages don't have to stay the same, either. You can change all of this, and more, very easily in the FrontPage Editor.

You've probably noticed many Web pages that use plain, black text in a single size, which makes for plain, boring paragraphs. Even though the trend is moving in the other direction, there's still a long way to go before the majority of Web pages are pleasing to the eye. With FrontPage, you can format your pages so they really stand out. It's like a Ferrari next to a beat-up, rusted 1973 Pinto—your pages will catch more eyes and generate a positive reception if they're lively and clean.

With the integration of FrontPage with Microsoft Office, you have much more flexibility to format your pages than you had in earlier versions of FrontPage. Much of the formatting functionality is housed in the Format toolbar, which can be turned on and off by choosing Format Toolbar from the View menu.

Fonts

The Editor gives you many options for formatting characters in different sizes, colors, and styles. You can change most of this formatting with the buttons on the Format toolbar, but all of the options are included in various menu commands. The following sections provide a primer on your character formatting options.

Text Size

FrontPage follows the HTML standard and uses size levels rather than actual point size values for setting the size of regular text. The levels correspond to point size, and the smaller the number, the smaller the point size. For example, level 1 corresponds to 8-point text, level 2 corresponds to 10-point text, and so on. Even though this might seem confusing at first, you will quickly become accustomed to it. You can however, define custom point sizes, and other font and paragraph attributes, using stylesheets. For more information on stylesheets, see the section "Cascading Stylesheets," in Chapter 10.

Changing Text Size

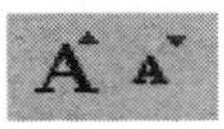

Here's the easiest way to change the size of your text. Select the text you want to change—it can be a single word, a line, a paragraph, or an entire page. (To select an entire page, press Ctrl+A.) Then, click the Increase Text Size or Decrease Text Size toolbar button. You can also use the Font command on the Format menu to change text size.

Text Color

An occasional change of color in your text can attract attention, but we stress "occasional." Too many different colors of text can make a page look busy and cluttered. One good way to use a second text color is to make the first words of important paragraphs a different color. This can help to "index" the page; readers pay attention to anomalies, and a different text color is just that if it's used sparingly.

Changing Text Color

You can make your text any of 48 standard colors supplied by FrontPage, or any other custom color. To change the color of your text, select the text you want to change, and then click the Text Color toolbar button.

In the Color dialog box that appears, click the color you want, and then click OK. If you want to use a custom color, click the Define Custom Colors button, define your color, and then click Add To Custom Colors to save it if you plan to use it again. When defining your custom color, remember that you can use the "elevator" arrow on the right side to adjust the color. This is a little-used tool in the Color dialog box. If you're designing your site using a 256-color "safety" palette, be sure when you create a custom color to make it part of that palette. For more information on color palettes, see Chapter 8.

Font Type

With a wide range of fonts and several styling options to choose from, you can easily craft the look and feel that you want for your pages. As with most other design considerations for your Web pages, however, try to strive for consistency. Don't use too many different fonts or font styles on a page; if you get carried away, your viewers will run screaming from your pages quicker than a runaway semi down Teton Pass.

TIP

Remember that in order for the font to be displayed in the user's browser, they must have that font on their computer. If you choose a font that's not part of the user's system, the browser will default to another font, usually Times. If you really want to use a particular font, and you don't want to take the chance that users wont have it, make the text a graphic. Image Composer is the perfect program to use to create graphics such as these.

Changing Fonts

You have oodles and oodles of fonts to choose from in FrontPage. If you've used the Font drop-down list in Microsoft Word, you'll have no problem getting used to that functionality in FrontPage. Here's the Change Font drop-down list:

To change fonts, select the text you want to change, and then select the font you want from the drop-down list.

Font Style

A change in font style can add just the right emphasis to words, phrases, or even entire paragraphs on your pages. Be objective in your use of this technique and consider how all of your audience members will see your pages. For example, consider the visitors to your site with less-than-perfect vision. Those people will have trouble reading an entire paragraph of italic text; that's why the overuse of italics on computer screens is a big no-no.

Changing Font Style

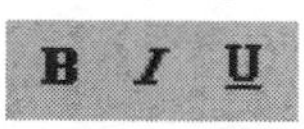

You can easily change font style—to bold, italic, or underline—with a click of a toolbar button. FrontPage includes these buttons on the Format toolbar.

To change font style, select the text you want to change, and then click one of these buttons.

Special Styles

The Editor includes some additional styles called *special styles*. FrontPage supports these because the pages you open might contain special styles. Try to use regular styles, not special styles, when you create new text. The special styles might not display in a browser as they do in the Editor, because some browsers do not support many of them. If you want to apply a special style to selected text, choose Font from the Format menu. You'll see the Font dialog box. Click the Special Styles tab, as shown in Figure 7-1.

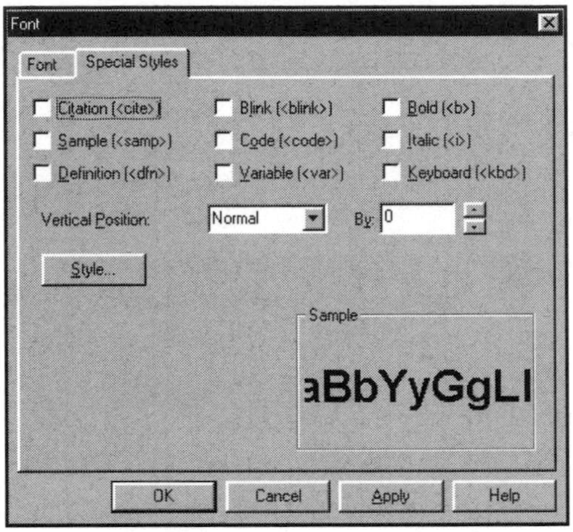

Figure 7-1

The following special styles are available. Selecting a check box displays an example of the style in the Sample section. To apply a special style, select the style and then click OK.

- **Citation.** An italic style that can be used for the name of a manual, section, or book.
- **Sample.** A typewriter-font style.
- **Definition.** A style that can be used for defining terms.
- **Blink.** A style that makes text blink in a browser. Many Web browsers do not support blinking text, however.
- **Code.** A typewriter-font style that can be used to represent code.
- **Variable.** An italic style that can be used to mark variable names.
- **Bold.** A simple bold style.
- **Italic.** A simple italic style.
- **Keyboard.** A typewriter-font style that can be used for text intended to be typed by the user.

You can also select multiple styles. For example, selecting both Italic and Keyboard will result in an italicized Keyboard style. By selecting the

Style button on the Special Styles tab of the Font dialog box, you can create and modify stylesheets associated with this page. For more information on stylesheets, see "Cascading Stylesheets," later in this chapter.

Superscript and Subscript

FrontPage supports authoring of superscript and subscript styles. These styles are supported by some browsers, but not by all.

You set superscript or subscript styles on the Special Styles tab of the Font dialog box, shown on the previous page. To reach the Font dialog box, choose Font from the Format menu. Select Superscript or Subscript from the Vertical Position drop-down list, and then set its numeric level. The numbers correspond to varying heights that the superscript or subscript can appear at, and not to the size of the superscript or subscript. Selecting a superscript level of 1, for example, sets the superscript slightly above the sentence. A level 2 superscript sets up shop a little higher than a level 1, and so on.

Symbols

Symbols are also called *special characters;* they contain characters beyond those found in the standard seven-bit ASCII character set. Say what? All you need to know is that the *ASCII character set* is the most widely used character-coding system in the world, but it does not include all of the characters from European languages that use accent marks, many other foreign characters, and symbols such as the copyright mark and the trademark. But you can use many of these special characters in FrontPage, and here's how:

1. Position your cursor where you want the symbol to appear on your page.
2. Choose Symbol from the Insert menu. This displays the Symbol dialog box, shown here in Figure 7-2.

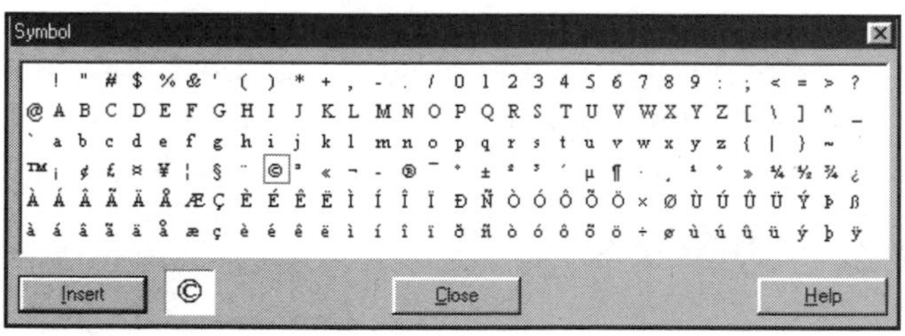

Figure 7-2

3. Select a symbol, and then click Insert. FrontPage inserts the symbol on the page, but does not close the dialog box. You can insert more symbols directly following the symbol you just inserted by repeating this step.
4. Click Close when you're finished.

Paragraph-Level Formatting

The other major type of formatting in FrontPage comes at the paragraph level. You can format lines and entire paragraphs, and you can implement such features as justification, different list styles, line breaks, and more. The following sections provide a hodgepodge of paragraph-level formatting options, many of which you'll probably want to get familiar with to give your pages a flash-and-dazzle touch.

Creating a New Paragraph

Let's start at the simplest level. To create a new paragraph, press the Enter key. A blank line will appear and the new paragraph will default to the Normal style.

To insert a new paragraph with a different style, do the following:

1. Position your cursor where you want the next paragraph to begin. If your cursor position is at the end of a line, press Enter once. If your cursor is in the middle of a paragraph, press Enter twice and the up-arrow key once.
2. Select a new style from the Change Style drop-down list. You can immediately begin typing in the new style.

If you insert a new paragraph in the middle of a paragraph, the Editor splits the original paragraph into two parts and adds the new paragraph between the two, keeping the original style for both parts. For example, inserting a Formatted paragraph in a Normal paragraph results in a paragraph containing the first portion of the Normal paragraph, followed by the new Formatted paragraph, and then the remaining portion of the original Normal paragraph.

Changing Paragraph Styles

Suppose you want to change the style of a paragraph from Normal to Heading 3. There are several ways you can do this. First select the paragraph whose style you want to change (or simply place your cursor anywhere within the paragraph), and then do one of the following:

- From the Change Style drop-down list, select a new paragraph style.
- Choose Paragraph from the Format menu. Select the new style for your paragraph in the Paragraph Properties dialog box, and then click OK.
- Right-click on any text in the paragraph and choose Paragraph Properties from the pop-up menu. Change the style in the Paragraph Properties dialog box, and then click OK.

Indenting a Paragraph

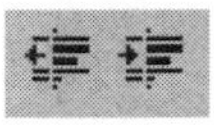

When you indent a paragraph in the Editor, the entire paragraph receives the indent. To indent a paragraph, position your cursor anywhere in the paragraph and click the Increase Indent toolbar button. To remove an indent, click the Decrease Indent toolbar button. You can indent as many times as your text will allow.

Aligning a Paragraph

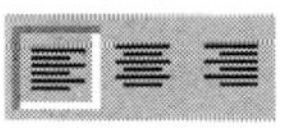

You can make a paragraph left-aligned, centered, or right-aligned with the click of a toolbar button. Just position your cursor anywhere in the paragraph, and then click the Align Left, Center, or Align Right toolbar button.

You can use these buttons to align paragraphs on a page or to align text in a table cell. Left-aligning a paragraph leaves a ragged right margin, right-aligning a paragraph leaves a ragged left margin, and centering a paragraph leaves both sides ragged and centers the paragraph within its margins.

> **TIP** If you're changing the style of a paragraph in the Paragraph Properties dialog box, you can also change the paragraph's alignment there at the same time.

List Properties

FrontPage gives you a vast array of list style options, including several variations of bulleted lists and numbered lists, and an option of using an image as a bullet. In Chapter 6, you learned how to create a list item-by-item; here you'll learn how to change the style of your lists once they're on the page.

Turning Regular Text into a List

Suppose you have a number of lines on your page that you would like to turn into a list. You don't have to follow the process in Chapter 6 to re-create that list. You can simply select all the elements of text you want to turn into the list, and then choose Bullets And Numbering from the Format menu. You'll see the Bullets And Numbering dialog box, as shown here in Figure 7-3.

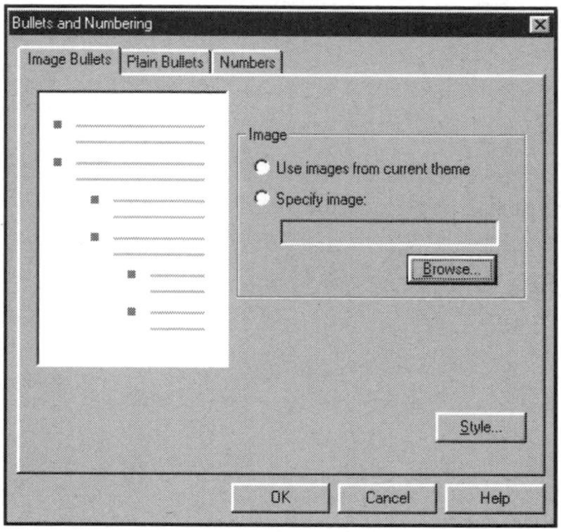

Figure 7-3

The Bullets And Numbering dialog box has three tabs. The first one lets you use an image for a bullet. If there is a theme applied to the page, FrontPage can use images from that theme to format your list. You can also specify an image by selecting the Browse button and choosing an image. Of course, the image you choose should be small enough to use in a list.

The other two tabs let you format either Plain Bullets or Numbers, by giving you a variety of choices, all displayed as thumbnails. If you want to turn your text into a bulleted list, select the Plain Bullets tab, and then select one of the styles by clicking it and clicking OK. The default style does not apply any formatting. If you want to turn your text into a numbered list, first click the Numbers tab. You can begin your list with a number other than 1 (or if you want a lettered list, a letter other than "a"). All you need to do is select one of the styles on the Numbers tab, and then select or enter a number in the Start At text box. Then click OK.

Changing the Style of an Entire List

To change a list from one style to another, right-click the list, and then choose List Properties from the pop-up menu. You'll see a List Properties dialog box, which is exactly the same as the Bullets and Numbering dialog box, except that it has an extra tab called Other. You can select from image bullets, bulleted or numbered styles on the Image Bullets, Bulleted, and Numbered tabs, or you can select a standard bulleted list, definition list, directory list, menu list, or numbered list on the Other tab, as shown in Figure 7-4. When you select a style and click OK, FrontPage changes your list to that style.

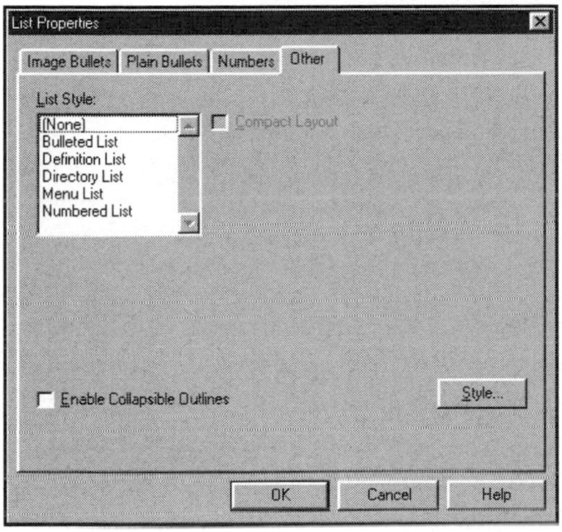

Figure 7-4

Changing the Style of Individual List Items

You also have the option of changing the style of individual items in a list—so all your list items don't have to be the same. It's a good idea to keep your list styles consistent, but if you ever want to change an individual entry to a different style, here's how: Right-click on a list item, and then choose List Item Properties from the pop-up menu. You'll see the List Item Properties dialog box with one tab pertaining to the type of list item that was selected. Select a different style, and then click OK to exit the List Item Properties dialog box.

Line Breaks

A line break forms a new line on a page without creating a new paragraph. In other words, when you insert a line break, the next line starts below the previous line with the formatting used for the other lines within the paragraph. When you start a new paragraph, it too begins on the next line, but unlike the line break, the new paragraph can have different paragraph formatting than the previous paragraph.

Inserting a Line Break

To insert a line break, position your cursor where you want the line break to appear, and choose Line Break from the Insert menu. This displays the Break Properties dialog box, seen here in Figure 7-5.

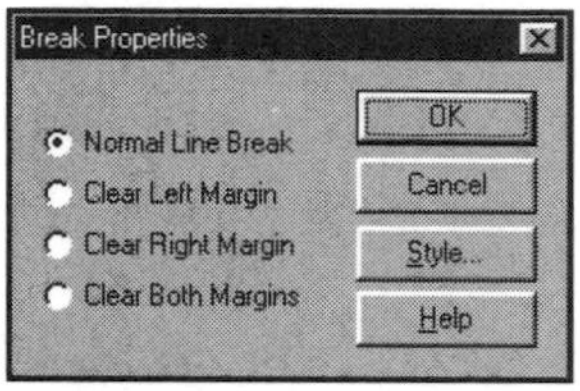

Figure 7-5

In the Break Properties dialog box, select among the following:

- **Normal Line Break.** Adds a line break and does not move based on any images in the left or right margins. In other words, even if there is an image in either the right or left margin, the new line starts immediately below the line break. (You can quickly insert a Normal line break by pressing Shift+Enter.)
- **Clear Left Margin.** Adds a line break, and if an image is in the left margin, moves the line following the line break down until the left margin is clear.
- **Clear Right Margin.** Adds a line break, and if an image is in the right margin, moves the line following the line break down until the right margin is clear.
- **Clear Both Margins.** Adds a line break, and if an image is in one or both margins, moves the line following the line break down until both margins are clear.

Formatting a Line Break

To change the way a line break works with images, select it, right-click on it, and choose Line Break Properties from the pop-up menu. This displays the Break Properties dialog box, where you can change the type of line break.

Deleting a Line Break

You can treat a line break as any other character. You can delete it with the Backspace or Delete key.

Horizontal Lines

Using horizontal lines on a page is a neat way to separate sections, topics, or other elements. You can insert shaded or solid horizontal lines and format them in a few ways.

Inserting a Horizontal Line

To insert a horizontal line, position your cursor where you want the line to appear, and then choose Horizontal Line from the Insert menu. A line appears, formatted the same way as the last horizontal line that was inserted in the Editor. The horizontal line will conform to any page margins or other formatting that may have been set for the page. Horizontal lines can also be placed inside table cells, and will follow any formatting applied to the table cell.

Formatting a Horizontal Line

To change the appearance of a horizontal line, right-click it and choose Horizontal Line Properties from the pop-up menu. The Horizontal Line Properties dialog box appears, as shown in Figure 7-6 here.

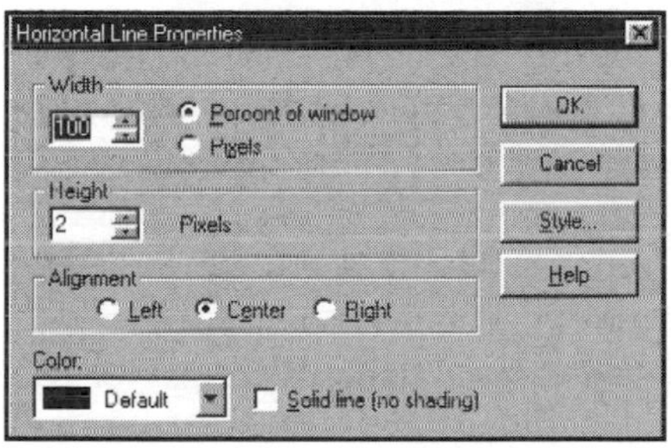

Figure 7-6

> **TIP** You can also use an image as a horizontal line. Select Image or Clipart from the Insert menu, and choose the image you wish to use. Since these lines are actually images rather than standard HTML horizontal lines, their properties are specified differently. You change their properties in the Image Properties dialog box instead of the Horizontal Line Properties dialog box. For more information, see Chapter 8.

In the Width section, specify the length of your line as a percentage of the browser window width, or as a length in pixels. Then enter the line's thickness in pixels in the Height section. In the Alignment section, specify

Left, Center, or Right alignment. From the Color drop-down list, select a color for the line. If the line color is set to the default color, you can also specify whether the line should be displayed with no shading by selecting the Solid Line check box. Solid lines set to the default color typically appear in gray, and shaded lines set to the default color appear shaded with the page's background color. Click OK to accept your settings and close the dialog box.

Deleting a Horizontal Line

To delete a horizontal line, select it and then press the Delete key or Backspace over it.

Further Enhancements

Now that we have covered some ways to format your pages, let's look into some other features that you can use to enhance your pages; for example, using bookmarks, links, sound, and themes.

Applying a Theme to a Page

As we discussed earlier, themes are a great way to get a consistent professional look, without having to be a graphic designer. In Chapter 3, you learned how to apply a theme to the entire Web site. In the Editor, you can apply a theme to single page or modify the theme that you applied in the Explorer. For example, let's say you choose a cool theme for your Web site in the Explorer and it includes a background image. You begin working in the Editor and come across the feedback page on your site, and decide that the background image distracts too much from the feedback form you want people to use. You can remove just the background image on that page, keeping the rest of the theme intact.

Choose Theme from the Format menu, to open the Choose Theme dialog box. This dialog box works exactly the same as it does in the Explorer, giving you the option to choose a theme (if one isn't already selected), use the theme from the current Web, or select a new theme. Remember: Any changes that you make here apply only to the page you're working on, not to the entire Web site.

Auto Thumbnail

Occasionally, you'll have no choice but to use a large image, or perhaps you'll find yourself faced with having to put a large number of images on a page. As you know by now, too many images, especially big ones, is no way to make happy surfers out of your visitors. Using the Auto Thumbnail command, you can have FrontPage create a small version of the graphic that automatically has a link to the larger one. This saves file size, which in turn reduces download time. So when visitors come to your site, all of your thumbnails will download quickly, and if users choose to, they can click an image for the large version to be displayed in its own window.

This is an excellent feature—when you can get away with showing a small version of the image. If you were creating a Web catalog, for example, you'd probably want to have a lot of pictures of products. Using the Auto Thumbnail feature, you could create small pictures, and display many of them on a single page. Users could then choose to view an enlarged version of only the products they're interested in.

To make an image a thumbnail, select the image first and then do one of the following: choose Auto Thumbnail from the Tools menu, or press Ctrl+K. FrontPage will create the thumbnail and display it in the Editor as a hyperlinked image. The way the thumbnail is displayed to the user is based on the choices you make in the Options dialog box. For more information on the Options dialog box, see the section "Options" on page 195.

When you make an image a thumbnail, FrontPage creates a new smaller version of the image, and when you save the page, you'll be asked to save the new image along with it. Although using this method does create two different graphics of the same image, it also boosts speed on your site, and gives users the control. They decide whether or not to see the larger image. Remember though, that this feature is best used when a small version of the picture is necessary or appropriate, and it shouldn't be used as a standard throughout your site.

Bookmarks

A *bookmark*, also known as an *anchor*, is a set of one or more characters on a page that is the target of a link. Using links to bookmarks allows a viewer of your Web site to jump to any point within a page (not just to the beginning of a page).

For example, suppose one of the pages in the RoasterNet site consists of a long, five-section document on the bright future of coffee bean sales in Seattle, and you link to that page from somewhere else within your site. When a user follows that link, the top of the page (that is, the top of the document) appears in the browser. But if the document includes bookmarks at the beginning of each section, you can create your links directly to those bookmarks. That way, a user can jump directly to any of those sections instead of jumping to the top of the document and having to scroll down.

Bookmarks appear in the Editor as text with dashed underlines. See "Links" on page 187 for information on linking to bookmarks.

Creating a Bookmark

To create a bookmark, do the following:

1. Select one or more characters of text that will become the bookmark (the text you want to jump to).
2. Choose Bookmark from the Edit menu. The Bookmark dialog box appears, as shown in Figure 7-7.

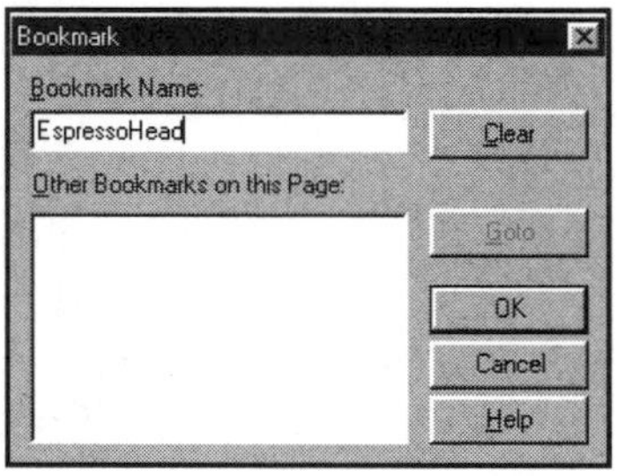

Figure 7-7

3. Enter a name for the bookmark in the Bookmark Name text box. Try to name your bookmarks intuitively, because later when you create a link to a bookmark, you'll need to enter the bookmark name or select it from a list. It'll help to be able to easily discern one bookmark from another. If your page already includes other bookmarks, they will appear in the dialog box.
4. Click OK after you enter the bookmark name. In the Editor, the selected text will now have a dashed underline, indicating that it is a bookmark.

SHORTCUT You can access the Bookmark properties dialog box by right-clicking any bookmark and selecting Bookmark Properties from the pop-up menu. You can also press Alt+Enter on any selected bookmark to bring up the Bookmark properties dialog box.

Finding a Bookmark

Suppose you have a list of bookmarks on the current page in the Bookmark dialog box, and you want to find one of them. To find any bookmark in the list, select the bookmark, and then click Goto. The page scrolls to the bookmark location, and the bookmark is selected. This is a quick and handy alternative to scrolling up and down a page to locate your bookmarks.

Clearing a Bookmark

To remove a bookmark, select the bookmark and choose Bookmark from the Edit menu, or right-click on the bookmark and choose Bookmark Properties. In the Bookmark dialog box, click Clear. The dialog box closes, and the bookmark is removed. This procedure does not remove the text; it only removes the bookmark reference.

Links

Links, also known as *hyperlinks*, are connections from one point to another. Viewers of a site can click on a link and jump to wherever it points to; this location is represented in HTML as a *URL*. You can link to and from text, images, other files (such as Microsoft Office files), or bookmarks. For information on creating links from images, see Chapter 8, and for information on changing the color of a link, see the section "Page Properties," later in this chapter.

If you have an intranet site populated with Office documents, those documents can be interconnected with links. For example, a Word file can have a link that jumps to an Excel file. When you click that link, the Excel file appears in Excel. You can link between Office files and FrontPage HTML files very easily, creating a dynamic and powerful Office—style intranet site. This book describes creating links from FrontPage to Office files. For information on creating links within Office files only, see the documentation or online help for the individual Office applications.

Creating a Link to Pages or Bookmarks

To create a link, select the text or image you want to link from, and press Ctrl+K, or choose Hyperlink from the Edit menu. The Create Hyperlink dialog box appears, as seen in Figure 7-8.

SHORTCUT You can quickly create or edit a link by selecting the text or link and then clicking the Create Or Edit Hyperlink toolbar button.

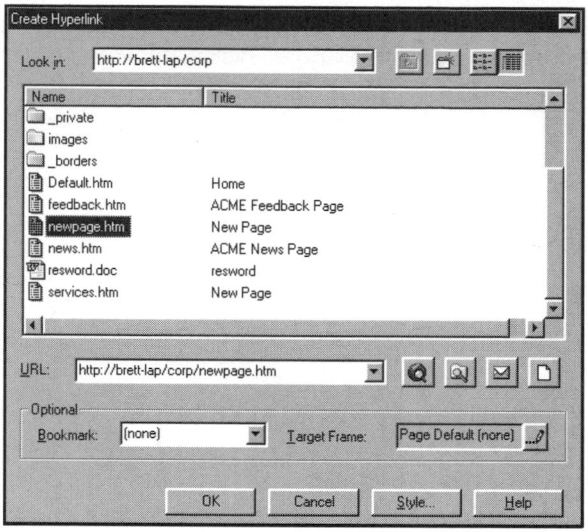

Figure 7-8

You can create hyperlinks in a few different ways: to a page in the Explorer, to any URL via your Web browser, to any file on your computer, and to any e-mail address; and you can also create a new page and link to that. You can also link to a bookmark and set the target frame for the link to appear in. Here's how you create hyperlinks in the various ways:

- **To a page from a site in the Explorer.** If you're working with the Explorer open, you'll see all of the pages in the current site listed in the dialog box, each one available to be linked to. Note: Once you select a file, its URL is placed in the URL text box.
- **To any World Wide Web URL.** Just as selecting a file places the URL into the URL text box, you can type the URL in the box. Or, you could select the Use Your Web Browser To Select A Page button. Your browser will launch, giving you a message to go to the page you want to link to. When you find the page on the Web, the URL is automatically placed in the URL text box for you.
- **To any file on your computer.** If the file you want to link to is located on your computer, you can select it by choosing the Make A Hyperlink To A File On Your Computer button. You'll see the Select File dialog box, where you can choose the file you need.

- **To an email address.** If you want your link to allow users to send e-mail to a certain address, select the Make A Hyperlink That Sends E-mail button. You'll see the Create E-mail Hyperlink dialog box, as seen in Figure 7-9.

  Just enter the address in the text box, and whammo, it's done.

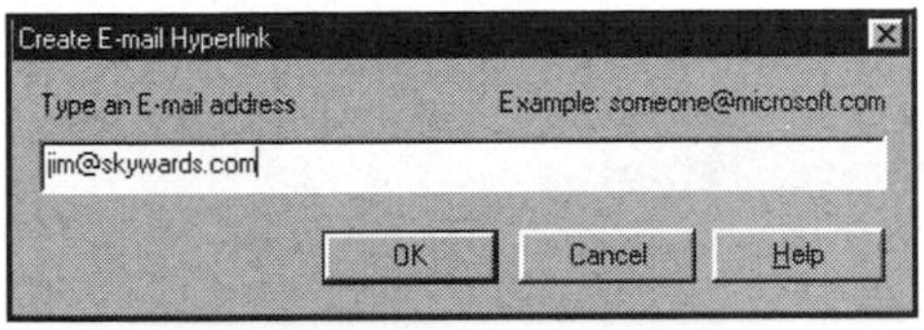

Figure 7-9

- **To a new page.** This allows you to link to a page in the current Web site that has not yet been created. Selecting the Create A Page And Link To The New Page button brings up the New dialog box. Select the type of page you want to create from the list of templates. FrontPage will create the new page, and either open it for you or assign it as a Task, depending on the choices you made. For more information on the New dialog box and using templates, see Chapter 4.

You can also choose from these two options in the Create Hyperlink dialog box:

- **Bookmark.** If your target link is a bookmark, you can enter its name in the Bookmark text box for the selected page.
- **Target Frame.** To specify a target frame for the page to appear in, enter the frame name in the Target Frame text box.

After you've made your link selections, click OK to return to the Editor. Your link is now highlighted with the link color of the page. You can test your new link by holding the Ctrl key and clicking the link.

Selecting a Link

Once you have created a link and you want to modify it, you must first select it. All you need to do to select a link is to click anywhere within the link. You can also highlight text associated with a link to select it, but you do not need to. If the cursor is in a link, the toolbar buttons and menu items pertaining to links are enabled.

Removing a Link

To remove a link, select it and then choose Unlink from the Edit menu. The link is removed, but the former link's text or image remains.

Automatically Created Links

Whenever you type in a supported protocol in the Editor followed by a destination, FrontPage detects that you want to make a link from the text and automatically creates one for you. All you need to do is simply type the text, like *www.microsoft.com,* in the Editor. Because *www* prefaces only World Wide Web addresses, FrontPage assumes that the HTTP protocol would be used, so you don't have to type it in. You can also create other supported links, like mailto: by just typing the link starting with the correct protocol.

Editing a Link

To change a link's properties, select it, and then choose Hyperlink, or Hyperlink Properties, from the Edit menu. You can also right-click the link and then choose Hyperlink Properties from the pop-up menu. You can change any of the link's properties in the Edit Hyperlink dialog box that appears. For more information, see "Creating a Link to Pages or Bookmarks" earlier in this chapter.

Dragging a Link from the Explorer

Here's another neat feature of FrontPage. If you have the Explorer and the Editor open simultaneously, you can create a text link to a page by dragging the page from the Explorer to a location on a page displayed in the Editor. Here's how to do it:

1. Make sure the Editor and Explorer are open so that the target for the link appears in the Explorer window and that the page on which you want the link to appear is open in the Editor. The Explorer can be in either Folder or Hyperlink view, and the target for the link can be any file you can create a link to, such as a page or an Office document.
2. Click the icon or file in the Explorer that will be the link's target, and drag it onto the page in the Editor. If you don't have enough room on your screen to drag the link directly into the Editor, drag the link to the Editor button on the Windows taskbar, and wait (while still holding down the left mouse button) until the Editor becomes active on your screen. Then finish the operation by dragging the file onto the page in the Editor. The cursor changes to the Windows shortcut cursor. Position the cursor at the exact spot where you want the link to

appear on the page in the Editor, and release the mouse button. The name of the target is inserted and a link is created from that text to the target itself. This is just like any other link you might have added manually, and it can be edited in the same way.

Creating Links to the Web Using a Browser

In FrontPage, you don't have to recall and retype Web addresses if you want to link to a page on the Web. You can easily create such a link in two ways.

- With your cursor positioned on the page where you want the link created, click the Create Or Edit Hyperlink toolbar button, and click the World Wide Web tab (as explained earlier in this section).
- While you are browsing in Microsoft Internet Explorer or Netscape Navigator, simply click and hold on any link you see on a page, and drag that link onto a page in the Editor. Ta-da! FrontPage automatically creates a link to that page.

Navigation Bars

You may be wondering why you spent all that time building a structure in the Navigation view in the Explorer. Well, besides it just being a whole lot of fun, it's also the foundation used to create navigation bars in the Editor. *Navigation bars* are a graphic representation of the structure of a site. They're placed on the page in the Editor, and appear as navigation buttons or hyperlinked text in the browser. They can be created in two different ways by designing the structure in the Explorer yourself, or, if you use a Web wizard to create your site, they'll be created for you. If you used a Web wizard, the navigation bars are based on the choices you made during the setup process. If you designed the structure in the Explorer, the pages are automatically linked on the navigation bar, based on their position in that structure.

If you've created or modified a navigation structure in the Explorer's Navigation view, you can use that structure to create navigation bars, automatically, in the Editor. If you wanted to create a navigation structure with a home page that has a feedback page set up as its peer, for example, the process would go like this:

1. Create the structure in the Navigation view of the Explorer, shown in Figure 7-10.

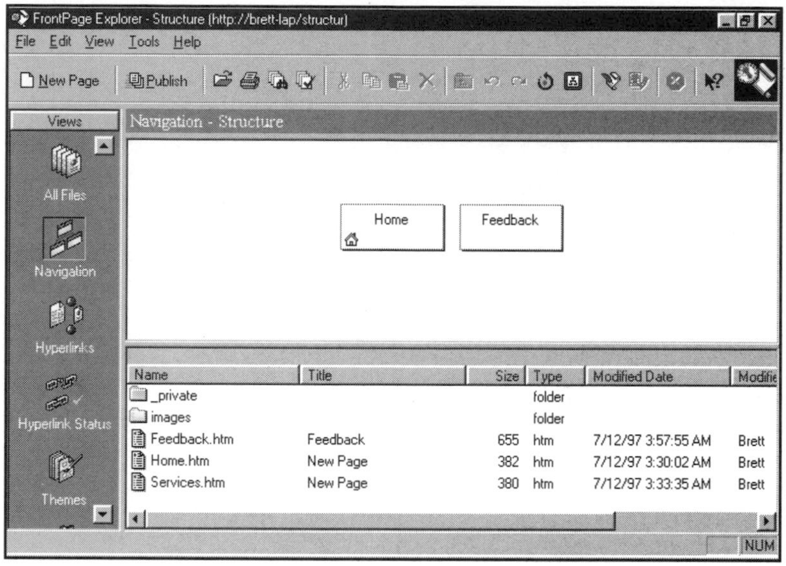

Figure 7-10

This figure shows the Navigation view in the Explorer. The Home page and Feedback pages are peers, and we want them to appear together as a navigation bar in the Editor.

2. Make decisions concerning how you want the navigation bar to look by using the Navigation Bar Properties dialog box, in the Editor, shown in Figure 7-11 below.

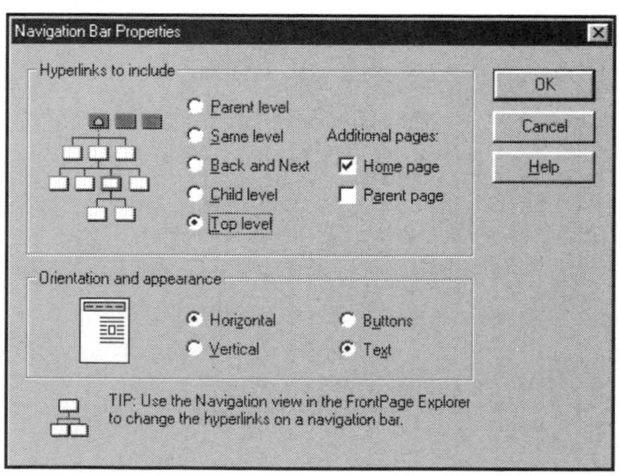

Figure 7-11

You can see we've selected our navigation bars to be Top level, with the Home page, and we want them to display horizontally on the page, and shown as text.

3. View your finished navigation bar. It should resemble that shown in Figure 7-12.

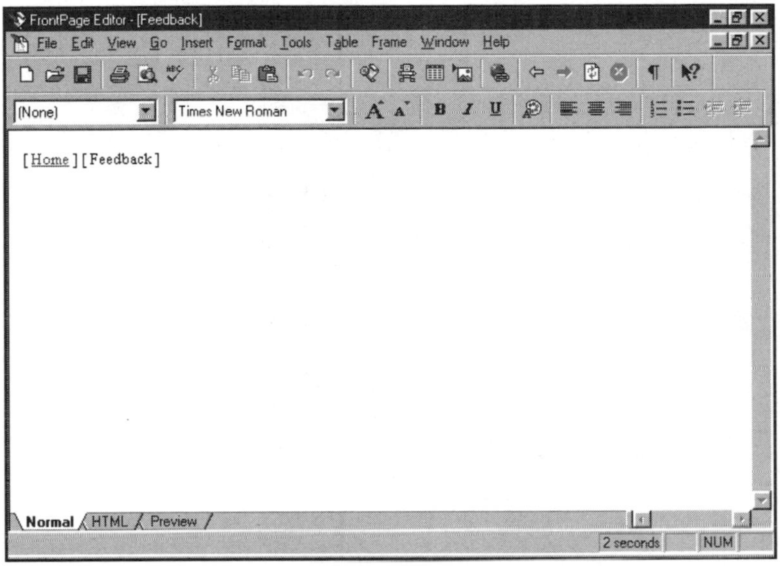

Figure 7-12

This figure shows the Feedback page, in Normal view. The links at the top of the page are the navigation bar, created automatically from the structure designed in the Explorer and defined in the Navigation Bar Properties dialog box.

Of course, you can get a lot fancier than the option shown here. If your Web has a theme applied to it, for example, and you choose to display the structure as buttons, FrontPage will choose the appropriate button style and create your navigation bars using those cool theme buttons.

Once the navigation bar is on your page, you can modify it in the Editor, via the Navigation Bar Properties dialog box. You can modify only how the structure is displayed, however, not the structure itself. You must make any structural changes in the Explorer. For more information on the Navigation view, see Chapter 3.

You can insert or modify a navigation bar on your page in a few different ways.

- Select Navigation Bar from the Insert menu in the Editor.
- If you currently have a navigation bar on the page, right-click the bar, and select FrontPage Component Properties from the pop-up menu.

- Double-click the navigation bar.
- Select the bar and press Alt+Enter.

The Navigation Bar Properties dialog box (shown in Figure 7-13) offers you a variety of options for displaying the navigation bar on the page.

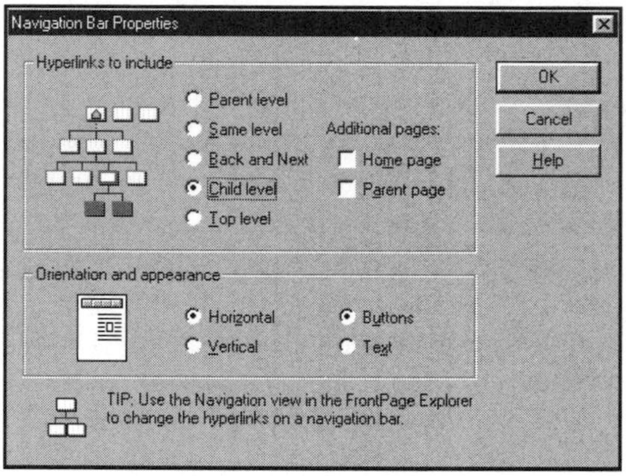

Figure 7-13

The dialog box is divided into two sections:

Hyperlinks to Include. Here you select which pages to have included in the navigation bar. As you select the various options, they are highlighted in the structure thumbnail on the left side of the dialog box. Many times, you'll be using navigation bars as your only source of navigation on a page, and you'll want to display the home page on the navigation bar. In these cases, select the Home Page check box. You can also choose to include the parent page of a selected level, by selecting the Parent Page check box.

Orientation and Appearance. You can position the navigation bar in either a Horizontal or Vertical position on the page. If you're not using a theme on the page, or if you just prefer text, select the Text check box, and the navigation bar will be displayed as hyperlinked text only.

Modifying a Navigation Bar

Since navigation bars are created automatically, based on decisions you've made, you'll probably be happy with them just the way they are. If not, you can modify them in a few different ways.

- The text labels on a navigation bar are based on the page titles in the Explorer. If you decide that you don't like a given name, go to the Explorer and rename the page title, and then apply changes.
- If the navigation bar was created automatically by a wizard and you want to change where it points to, open the page in the Editor, and then open the Navigation Bar Properties dialog box. Here you can adjust the settings.
- If you're not happy with the colors, button types, or fonts used in the navigation bar, you must select a different theme. If you change the theme in the Editor, it will apply to the current page only. If you want the theme to apply to the entire site, change the theme in Themes view in the Explorer.

Deleting a Navigation Bar

If you need to delete a navigation bar from a page in the Editor, select the navigation bar, and then press the Delete key or select Cut from the Edit menu. You can also right-click the navigation bar and select Cut from the pop-up menu.

Options

To set the parameters for the Auto Thumbnail feature, or to set the default font for the Editor, access the Options dialog box via the Tools menu. For more information on using an Auto Thumbnail, see the section "Auto Thumbnail" earlier in this chapter. Figure 7-14 shows the Auto Thumbnail tab.

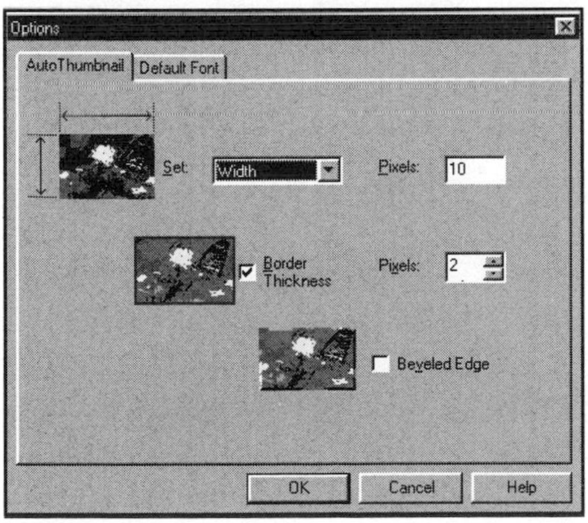

Figure 7-14

Here, you can set the default size for the thumbnail image in pixels. You can choose between Width, Height, Shortest Side, and Longest Side. FrontPage will create the thumbnail based on that setting and size the image in proportion to the original. For example, if you set the width to 50 pixels, the thumbnails will all be 50 pixels wide and their heights will vary depending on the original image.

You can also choose to have a border around the image, and adjust the border thickness that appears on the thumbnail hyperlink. Select the Beveled Edge check box if you want the thumbnails created with a beveled edge.

The Default Font tab lets you choose a default font language when no other font is defined for text. These settings do not effect the HTML Encoding; they effect only the font display in the Editor.

Shared Borders

Let's say that you want your company's logo to appear at the bottom of every page on your site. You might think that you'd have to add it to each page individually, or that you'd have to use frames—but wait! You have another, much easier, option. You can use a shared border at the bottom of the page, and any page that has a bottom-shared border will display the same information as any other page that has a bottom-shared border. That means that you only need to add your logo one time, on one shared border page. If you need to modify the information in a shared border, you only need to do that once too; and you can do it on any of the pages in your site that has the same shared border location.

To apply shared borders to the entire Web site, select Shared Borders from the Tools menu *in the Explorer*, or to apply shared borders to an individual page, select Shared Borders from the Tools menu *in the Editor*.

If you elect to apply shared borders to the entire site, you'll see the Shared Borders dialog box, seen in Figure 7-15 here.

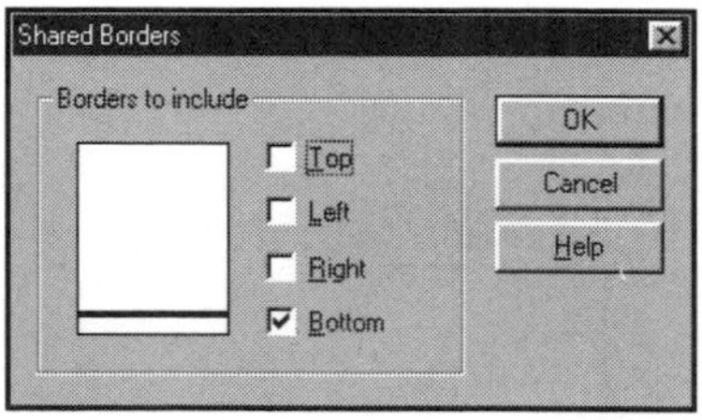

Figure 7-15

If you want to apply a shared border to a page in the Editor, you'll see the Page Borders dialog box, as seen in Figure 7-16 below.

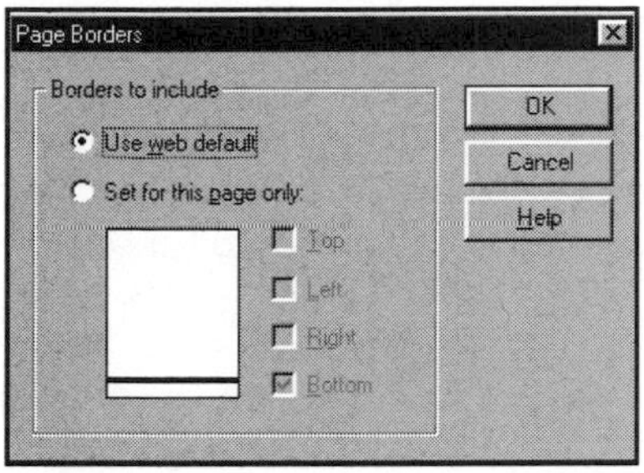

Figure 7-16

Both dialog boxes work in basically the same way, except that in the Editor you have the option to use any borders defined in the Explorer for the current site, or to set borders for that page individually.

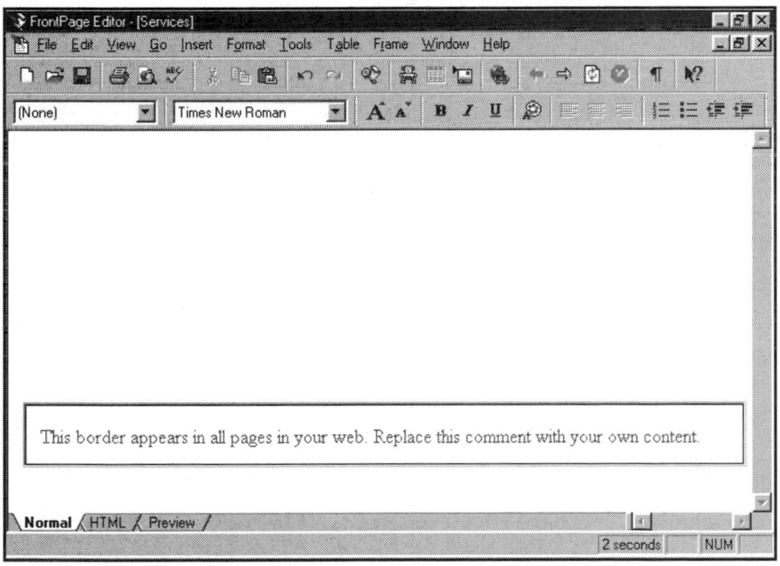

Figure 7-17
You can insert any text or image into the shared border, and it will appear on all pages in the site that use a bottom-shared border. The border around the shared border area will not appear in the user's browser; it's there only for layout purposes.

WARNING Since using a shared border creates a new page, using shared borders on a frames page is not recommended.

To use shared borders, select any one or more borders to include, and then click OK. You can share borders on the top, bottom, left, or right of a page. Figure 7-17, on the previous page, shows a page in the Editor with a shared bottom border. If the border is empty, FrontPage will add a comment that tells you about the border.

Sounds

A background sound can add another dimension to your site and give it more of a "multimedia" feel. A background sound plays whenever someone visits the page it's on, and it can play a specified number of times or loop continuously. Just as hearing a certain song can put us in a certain mood, background sound can set the tone for your viewers—and it can also annoy them if it's overused. Use background sound sparingly and wisely.

FrontPage supports several types of sound files, ranging from wave sounds (with WAV extensions) to midi sequences (MID), AIFF sounds (AIF, AIFC, AIFF), and AU sounds (AU, SND).

Inserting a background sound and setting its properties all happens in the Page Properties dialog box. For more information on the other options in the Page Properties dialog box, see the section "Page Properties," later in this chapter.

Here's how to insert the sound:

1. Right-click on the page, and choose Page Properties from the pop-up menu (or choose Page Properties from the File menu). The Page Properties dialog box appears, as seen in Figure 7-18.
2. On the General tab, type the path to the sound you want to use. You can also select a background sound by selecting the Browse button. The Background Sound dialog box appears, shown in Figure 7-19.

   You can select a sound from the current Web, use your browser to select a sound from the World Wide Web, or choose a sound from a local drive on your computer. When you've finished, click OK to return to the Page Properties dialog box.

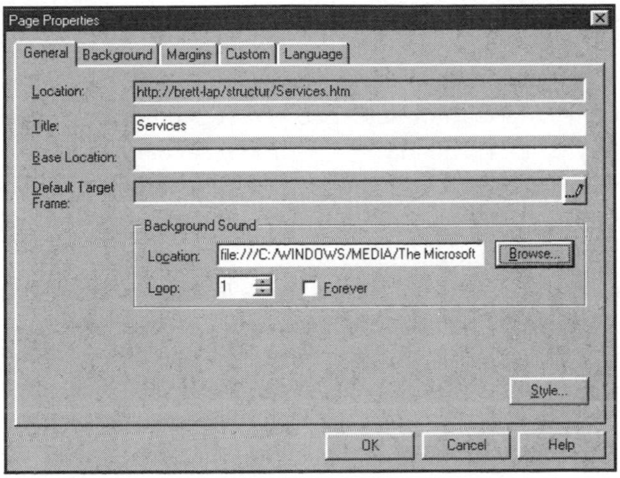

Figure 7-18

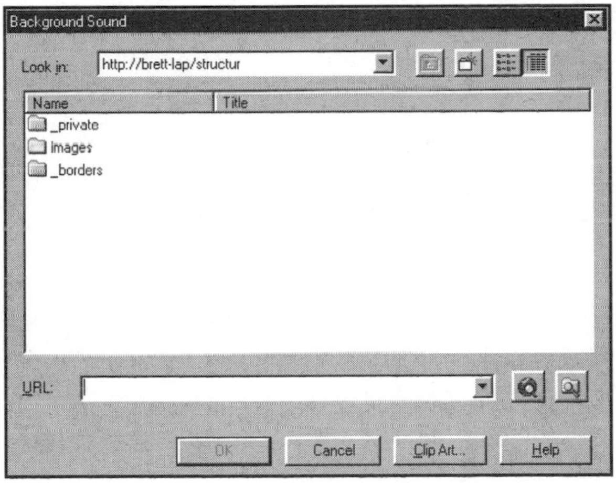

Figure 7-19

3. In the Page Properties dialog box, specify in the Loop text box the number of times you want the sound to play. If you want the sound to loop endlessly, select the Forever check box.
4. Click OK to exit the Page Properties dialog box.

Active Elements

Maybe you're tired of seeing all of those static Web sites; you know, the ones that just sit there and do nothing. But you're thinking "In order to have some fun on my page, I'll need to hire some ten-year-old kid to write me some code." Not to worry—FrontPage has some built-in features that let you add a little extra zip to your page without having to spend a lot of dough on that little programming genius.

Each of these features can be found by selecting Active Elements from the Insert menu, and making the appropriate selection from the pop-up menu.

Hover Button

Have you ever wondered how they get those cool buttons on a Web page—you know the kind, ones that change color, or bevel, when you roll your mouse over them? Well, you need a degree in computer code writing and graphic design, that's how. But you know that with FrontPage, you're not going to have to get a fancy degree, and you won't even need the aesthetic of Picasso. The only thing you need is the Hover Button feature.

Using the Hover Button feature in FrontPage, all you need to do is make a few simple choices, and wham-bam, there she is, a fully functional animated button, complete with mouseover effects and hyperlinks. To begin, select Active Elements from the Insert menu, and then choose Hover Button from the pop-up menu. You can also right-click an existing Hover button and select Java Applet Properties from the pop-up menu, or you can double-click a Hover button, or press Alt+Enter on a selected Hover button. Each of these methods will result in showing the Hover Button dialog box, shown in Figure 7-20.

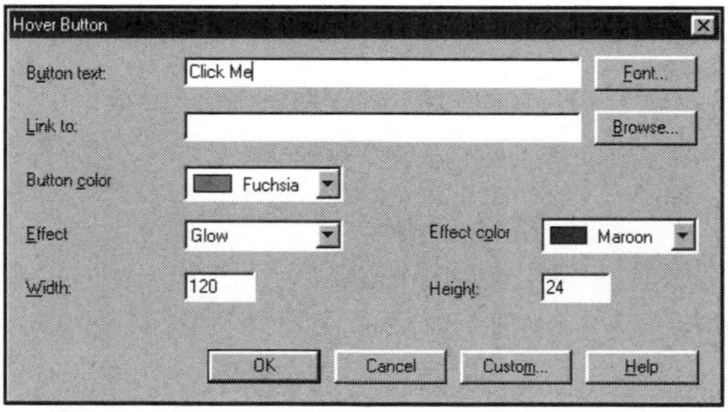

Figure 7-20

There are a number of standard options to choose from, as well as some interesting custom options that let you do things such as play a sound or display an image as a button. The standard options include:

Button Text. Most buttons on a Web page have text on them, telling the user what they can expect by clicking it. Type the text you would like to appear on the button in the Button Text text field.

Link To. If you want your button to be a hyperlink, type the URL in this text box, or click the Browse button to locate the URL. Remember that most people will naturally expect a button to be a hyperlink, so it's a good idea not to disappoint them.

Button Color. Use the drop-down Color list to pick a button color. If you choose an image for the button in the Custom dialog box, you don't need to enter a color here.

Effect & Effect Color. Select from the various visual effects in the Effect drop-down list. When you have an effect selected, you can select the color of the button when the effect is activated. Select a color in the Effect Color drop-down list. You have quite a few interesting options here, so experiment, and choose the one that best suits the mood you're trying to create on that page.

Width & Height. Type in the button's Width and Height values (in pixels), respectively. If you choose to use an image as a button, make sure that you enter the size of the image here.

To access the custom options available for a Hover Button, select the Custom button at the bottom of the Hover Button dialog box. This brings up the Custom dialog box, shown in Figure 7-21.

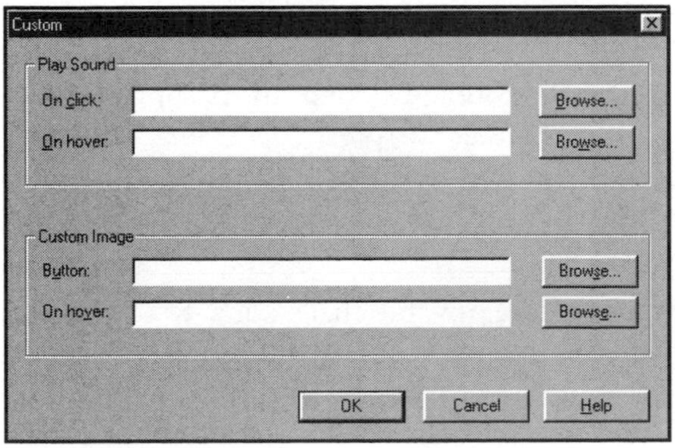

Figure 7-21

The Custom dialog box is divided into two sections, which, strangely enough, are your only two options in it.

Play Sound. In this section, you can choose to play a sound when the user clicks the button in the browser or when they mouse over the button. Technically, you could play a sound on both click and mouseover all on one button, but we know that that wouldn't be a very good idea, don't we? Use the standard browse buttons to locate your sounds.

Custom Image. If you would rather your button be in the form of an image, select the Browse button and choose an image for the button. If you would like an image to be displayed when the user hovers over the button, select browse and locate an On Hover image. Remember to put in the correct width and height in the Hover Button dialog box for any image you choose here.

Banner Ad Manager

One of the most popular ways people make money on the Web today is by selling ads on their pages. You've seen these banners all over the place, right? Have you ever noticed that if you stay on the page long enough, you sometimes see different ads rotating in and out in the same place? Well, with the Banner Ad Manager you can rotate between multiple banners, on any page, just like the big boys.

Of course, you aren't limited to rotating ads. You can rotate any image you like, and even apply transition effects between them. You could, for example, create your own little slide show, and tell a story as each new image shows itself.

FrontPage creates the rotating banners in the form of a Java applet, and you configure its properties in the Banner Ad Manager dialog box, seen in Figure 7-22. You can access the Banner Ad Manager dialog box via the Active Elements menu list or by double-clicking an existing banner. You can also right-click an existing banner (or press Alt+Enter), and then select Java Applet Properties from the pop-up menu.

Here, you can configure how your banners are displayed in the browser. You have a variety of choices.

Width & Height. Be sure to enter a value that's equal to the largest image being rotated. All other images will be centered in the space and display on a neutral colored background. If you really want to make the most of this feature, try to make all of your images the same approximate size.

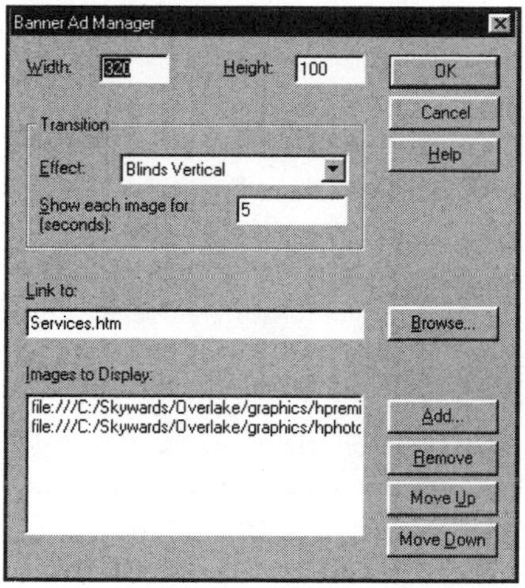

Figure 7-22

Transition. You can choose between Blinds Horizontal, Blinds Vertical, Dissolve, Box In, or Box Out. Selecting None displays the images without a transition effect. You can also set a time, in seconds, for the banner to display before the next one comes in. If your banner contains text, be sure to leave enough time for the user to read it. It's a good idea to keep the time under ten seconds. If you don't think that's enough time for anyone to read your banner, you probably have way too much text on it. Think of these banners as if they were billboards you see when you're driving. You have only a second or two to read a billboard, and they're designed with that in mind, just as you should design yours here.

Link To. If you want the banner to be a hyperlink, add the URL for the link here. Try to anticipate what users will do when they come to a page. If you make your banner look like an ad, your users will think it's an ad, and they'll want to click it—and you don't want them to click if nothing's going to happen. You can use the standard Browse button to locate your link.

Images to Display. Here you can add and remove images to be rotated. Click Add to add images to the list, and click Remove to remove a selected image. The images will play in a top-down order. The image listed first displays first, and so on. You can adjust the order of the images by selecting the image in the list and choosing between the Move Up and Move Down buttons.

The Banner Ad Manager will rotate through the list of images indefinitely as long as the user is on the page.

Marquees

Marquees can turn people's heads and get them to pay more notice to your site. As Sheriff Buford T. Justice, of the movie *Smokey and the Bandit,* would say, they're "attention gettas." But as with any other catchy design element in your site, be careful not to overuse them—users might find them annoying or might ignore their messages.

Marquees are HTML elements that allow text to move on a page. They turn an otherwise static page into one that's dynamic and lively. Let's use another example from RoasterNet to show what marquees can do for a page.

Richard, who's in charge of the National Sales department at Cascade Coffee Roasters, realizes the importance of evangelizing the sales message within the company, so he has instructed his department to create a Sales section for RoasterNet. He plans to have sections detailing general sales patterns, news from the competition and reactions to it, and up-to-the-minute news of the big "scores" his department earns. In the early stages, his pages are under construction, and he doesn't have much time to build them as he'd like. But one of his salespeople, Natalie, has just made the company's largest-ever sale, and Richard wants the news to go up on a page on RoasterNet. If he just types the news on the page, it will look static and people might read past it, especially since his page is under construction and they might think that nothing has changed unless they look carefully. So Richard will use a marquee to get their attention. Here's the process he'll use to insert it:

1. Position your cursor where you want the marquee to be inserted. Choose Active Elements from the Insert menu, and then select Marquee from the pop-up menu. You'll see the Marquee Properties dialog box, as seen in Figure 7-23.
2. In the Text field, type in the text you want displayed with the marquee.
3. In the Direction section, specify whether you want the marquee to move toward the left or the right. (If you select Alternate in the Behavior section in step 5, you won't need to specify a direction here.)

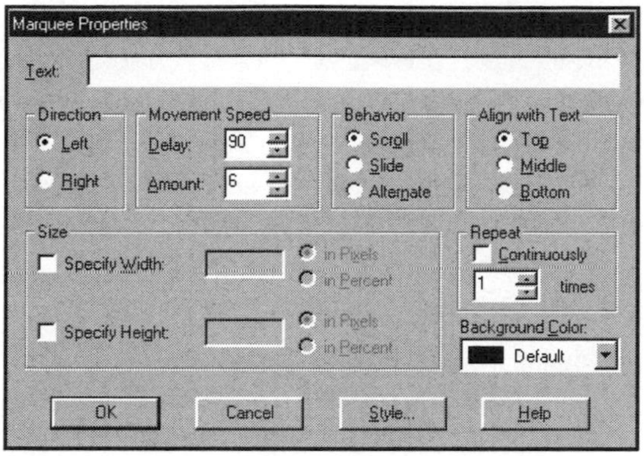

Figure 7-23

4. In the Movement Speed section, specify numbers for Delay and Amount. Delay sets the length of time in milliseconds between each movement of the marquee. The higher the number, the longer the delay, and the slower the marquee moves. Amount refers to the distance in pixels between each movement of the marquee. You can make your marquee move faster, therefore, by increasing this number. You can adjust the Delay and Amount values to make your marquees move at any speed, from very fast to very slow.
5. In the Behavior section, select one of the following options:

    Scroll. This moves the text in the direction across the screen that you specified in the Direction section. Text appears and disappears from the sides of the marquee area.

    Slide. This moves the text across the screen in the direction you specified in the Direction section. But instead of scrolling off the screen, the text stops when it reaches the end of the screen, and remains on screen.

    Alternate. This moves the text back and forth across the screen. The text never leaves the screen when you select Alternate.

6. In the Align With Text section, you specify how you want the text to be aligned in the marquee area. (You set the marquee area in the Size section.) You can align the text at the top of the marquee area, in the middle, or at the bottom.

7. The Size section is where you set the marquee area. To specify the width of the marquee area, select the Specify Width check box. If you want to specify the width of the marquee area in pixels, enter a number and then select In Pixels. If you want to set the width as a percentage of the screen, enter the number and then select In Percent.

   Select the Specify Height check box if you want to set the marquee area height. This number determines the amount of room, from top to bottom, that the text in the marquee area moves in. Enter a number and select either In Pixels to specify the height in pixels or In Percent to specify the height as a percentage of the page.

TIP To give your marquee "space to breathe" from top to bottom so it can be easier to read, specify an ample height and select Middle in the Align With Text section. This centers the marquee from top to bottom in the area you've specified.

8. In the Repeat section, select the Continuously check box if you want the marquee to run all the time. If you want the marquee to move only a certain number of times when a reader comes to your page, deselect Continuously and enter that number in the text box below it.
9. Select a Background Color if you want the marquee to move against a colored background. Sometimes using a different background color than the rest of the page can have a pleasing effect, but beware of "overstunning" your audience with this option. The movement of the marquee might be enough to grab their attention.
10. When you're satisfied with all your settings, click OK to exit the Marquee Properties dialog box.

Changing Marquee Settings

To change the settings of a marquee on your page, right-click the marquee and choose Marquee Properties from the pop-up menu. This brings up the Marquee Properties dialog box. Change the settings, and then click OK. You can also double-click the Marquee to access the Marquee Properties dialog box.

Search

You can easily add search functionality to your page using the FrontPage Search form. This feature is discussed in depth in Chapter 9, "FrontPage Components and Forms."

Hit Counter

A *hit counter* is a popular way to visually *see* how many visitors have been to your page. Most of the time, you'll see hit counters on the home page, and usually at the bottom of the page. A hit counter is not the type of thing you'll want to put on every page in your site. You can add a hit counter to your page by selecting Active Elements from the Insert menu and choosing Hit Counter from the pop-up menu. You'll be greeted with the Hit Counter Properties dialog box, shown in Figure 7-24.

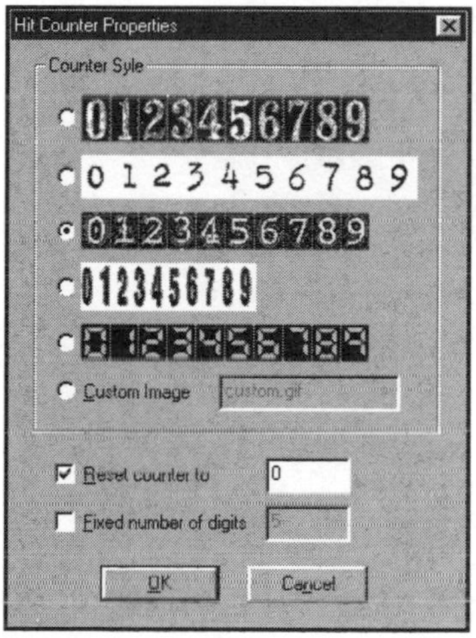

Figure 7-24

You can choose from one of the five Counter Styles, or you can create your own Custom Image. The one big drawback of having a hit counter is that it shows how many people *didn't* visit your site. If someone comes to your page and they see a bunch of zeros on the counter, they might think that there's nothing good to see there and move on. By inputting a number in the Reset Counter To text box, you can make it look like plenty of people have been to your site. Think of it as a little white lie. You can also fix the number of digits displayed by entering a number in that text box.

PowerPoint Animation

As many Microsoft Office users know, PowerPoint easily creates slideshow animations, and now with FrontPage, you can just as easily add these animations to your Web page. A PowerPoint animation file is inserted onto your Web page as an ActiveX control or as a plug-in.

To view a PowerPoint animation on a Web page, you must have the PowerPoint Animation Player installed. (You can download it from Microsoft's PowerPoint Web site at www.microsoft.com/powerpoint/.) When you install the PowerPoint Animation Player, it will detect the type of browser(s) you are using and install the ActiveX version, plug-in version, or both. The PowerPoint Animation Player can display standard PowerPoint animations, which have a PPT extension. The PowerPoint Animation Player for ActiveX can also display compressed PowerPoint animations, which have a PPZ extension. The advantage of using compressed PowerPoint animations is that they are smaller files and can be downloaded more quickly. Compressed PowerPoint animations can be created using an add-in to PowerPoint, called the PowerPoint Animation Publisher. For information on downloading, installing, and using the PowerPoint Animation Player and the PowerPoint Animation Publisher, visit Microsoft's PowerPoint Web site.

To add a PowerPoint animation to your page, choose Other Components from the Insert menu, and choose PowerPoint Animation from the submenu. This brings up the PowerPoint Animation dialog box, seen in Figure 7-25.

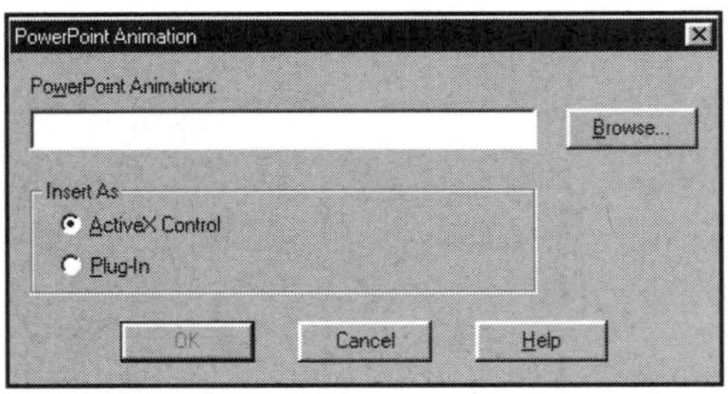

Figure 7-25

In the PowerPoint Animation File text box, enter the name of the PowerPoint animation file you want placed on your page, or use the Browse button to select a file.

In the Insert As section, select how you want the animation to be inserted. The ActiveX Control option inserts the animation as an ActiveX control; a graphic placeholder will display in FrontPage when the animation is inserted as an ActiveX control. The Plug-In option inserts the animation as a plug-in; a graphic placeholder will display in FrontPage when the animation is inserted as a plug-in.

Once you have the PowerPoint Animation Player installed, you can watch the animation play by previewing it in a browser.

Videos

Another great way to liven up your sites is to add video to them. As you might know, however, video files tend to be huge, and even though the bandwidth of the Internet is increasing gradually, it's not yet sufficient to transfer large video files in a speedy way. The situation can be different within a corporation if the intranet uses local connections where bandwidth is less of a concern.

TIP In the Editor, the download time for a page at 28.8 kbps is displayed (in seconds) in the lower right part of the screen. As you change your page—adding or deleting videos, sounds, images, and other elements—the download time updates appropriately.

FrontPage supports the viewing of Windows-based AVI files in its Web sites. First, you insert the video file on your page, and then you set its properties.

With your cursor on the page where you want to insert the video, choose Active Elements from the Insert menu, and then select Video from the pop-up menu. You'll see the Video dialog box. This standard dialog box lets you select a video located in the current Web site, use your browser to locate a video, or select a video from a local drive. Select your video file and click OK.

The opening frame of the video file will appear on the page as a "placeholder."

TIP If you double-click the placeholder, the Editor will try to launch a video-editing application. Since most of us don't have one, you'll get a message that says that there is no editor configured.

Once you've inserted the video file, you might need to adjust its properties. Here's how:

1. Right-click the video-file placeholder on the page, and choose Image Properties from the pop-up menu. The Image Properties dialog box appears, with the Video tab selected, as shown in Figure 7-26.

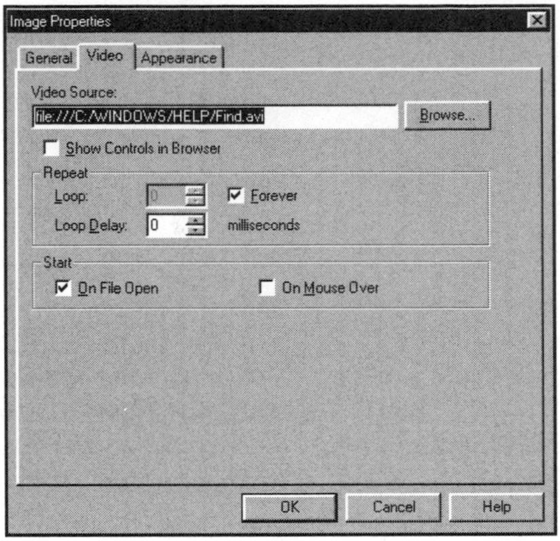

Figure 7-26

2. If you want to replace the video with another, click Browse, locate the replacement AVI file in the Video dialog box, and click OK.
3. Select the Show Controls In Browser check box if you want to show a set of controls—Play, Stop, and a slider—along with the video when it's displayed in the browser at runtime.
4. In the Repeat section, specify in the Loop box how many times you want the video file to play, and specify in the Loop Delay box the amount of time (in milliseconds) between playing of the video. If you want the video to play endlessly, select the Forever check box.
5. In the Start section, specify when you want the video to begin playing. Selecting On File Open starts the video whenever a person opens the page it's on, and selecting On Mouse Over starts the video whenever a user moves the mouse pointer over the video in the browser.
6. When you're satisfied with your settings, click OK to exit the Image Properties dialog box.

Page Properties

You can set the properties for a page in the Editor by choosing the Page Properties command from the File menu or from the pop-up menu that appears when you right-click on the page. In the Page Properties dialog box, you can change general file information such as the page's title; set a page's background image, color, or sound; set default colors for text and links; and specify margins and custom settings. You must have a page open in the Editor in order to set these properties. (To open a page or create a new page, see Chapter 6.) Here's a primer on the properties, starting with the General tab, shown in Figure 7-27.

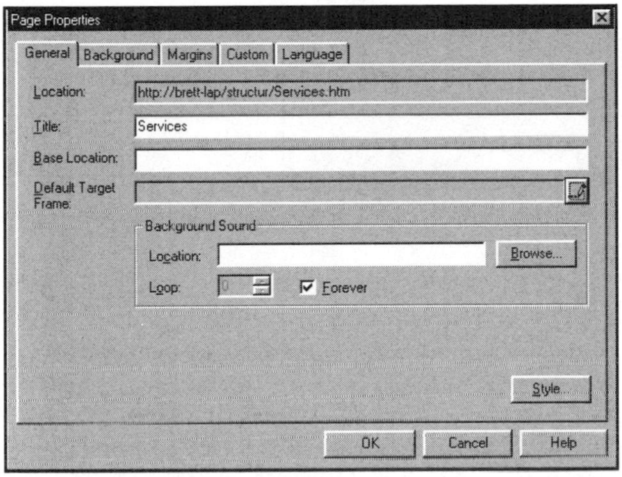

Figure 7-27

You can change the page's title by entering a new title in the Title text box, change the optional base URL by entering it in the Base Location text box. To assign a frame as the default target of all the links on the page, enter its name in the Default Target Frame text box, or select the Target Frame button. This brings up the Target Frame dialog box. For more information on working with frames, see Chapter 6. In the Background Sound section, you can change the properties for a background sound. For details on this, see "Sounds" earlier in this chapter.

The Background tab, shown in Figure 7-28, is where you can specify background colors and colors for various links.

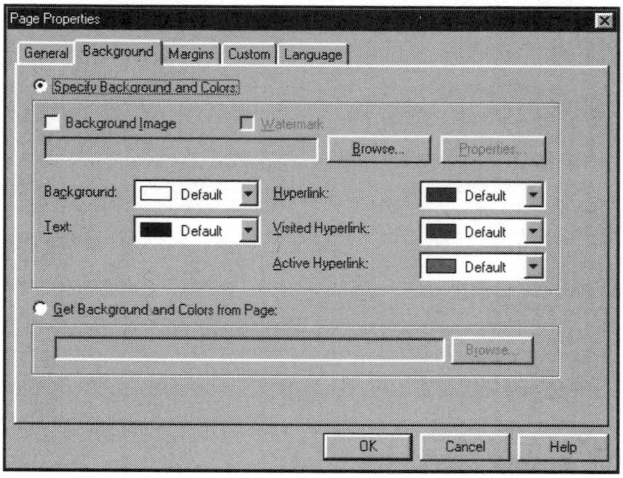

Figure 7-28

In the Specify Background And Colors section, you can set the following properties:

Background Image. By selecting the Background Image check box, you can specify an image to use as your page background; most browsers will tile this image automatically. You've probably seen this on the Web; a tiled background can be effective if it adds to the "viewability" of a page and does not impair viewing of text or other images on the page.

TIP To adjust the properties of an existing background image, open the Page Properties dialog box and click the Properties button in the Specify Background And Colors section. This brings up the Image Properties dialog box. See Chapter 8 for information on this dialog box.

Watermark. A watermark is a background image that does not scroll when you scroll the page. Select the Watermark check box if you want this feature. Click Browse to specify the image. (Note: This may not work as expected in certain browsers.)

Background Color. You can specify a background color for your page if you don't want to use a tiled image. You might consider using a color with more flair. Just make sure your text and images are easy to read against whatever color you select. Use the Background drop-down list to select your color.

Default Text Color. You can use the Text drop-down list to specify the default color of the text that appears on your page. Black is a safe standard, but don't hesitate to experiment with other colors that might look good against the background you selected. Any text that is formatted in a different color in the Editor will override the default color specified here.

Hyperlink Color. You can use the Hyperlink drop-down list to specify a color to use for all links on a page that have not been visited.

Visited Hyperlink Color. Links change to this color after they have been used. If a link appears on more than one page, following one instance of the link triggers the visited link color for all instances of that link in your site. You can specify the visited link color using the Visited Hyperlink drop-down list.

The default Hyperlink color is Blue, and the default Visited Hyperlink color is purple. It's a good idea to change both of these, just so that people know that you're paying attention to the details.

Active Hyperlink Color. The active link color is the color of a link as it is being clicked. To specify such a color, use the Active Hyperlink drop-down list.

In the Get Background And Colors From Page section of the Background tab, you can specify use of the same background color, background image, text color, and link colors that are used on another page. Select the option button, and then click Browse to specify the page from the current site that you want to use for this purpose. If you've already set up those properties elsewhere, this saves you time by not having to set them up again for the current page.

TIP The Get Background And Colors From Page option is a feature unique to FrontPage and is a great way to set up a "style page." For example, if you make changes to the background and colors on the style page, the changes will be reflected on all of the pages that this style page was applied to when you reopen them.

To specify top and left margins for your page, click the Margins tab, select one or both check boxes, and enter the numbers, in pixels, in the appropriate boxes. If you are trying to move text or an image to the very edge of the browser window, set the margins to zero.

The Custom tab displays a list of meta tags that are used on your page. *Meta tags* live in the page's HTML and contain information about the page; for example, the content type, the character set, and the application that generated the HTML. They are never displayed, but they can supply information to a browser that recognizes them. You can add, modify, or remove meta tags for system variables and user variables on this tab.

The HTML Encoding section is used to specify settings to control the HTML character encoding for the page, which is used for Web pages of different languages. You can make changes to the HTML Encoding on the Language tab.

The Editor View Tabs

Since most people like to see things from different angles, and because a lot of people like to get a behind-the-scenes view of their site, FrontPage gives you a couple of different ways to look a page.

Normal View

For most people, HTML can be a scary thing. That's one of the reasons you're using FrontPage in the first place, right? So, for you people who don't want anything to do with that HTML stuff, you'll want to be working in the Editor's Normal view (shown in Figure 7-29).

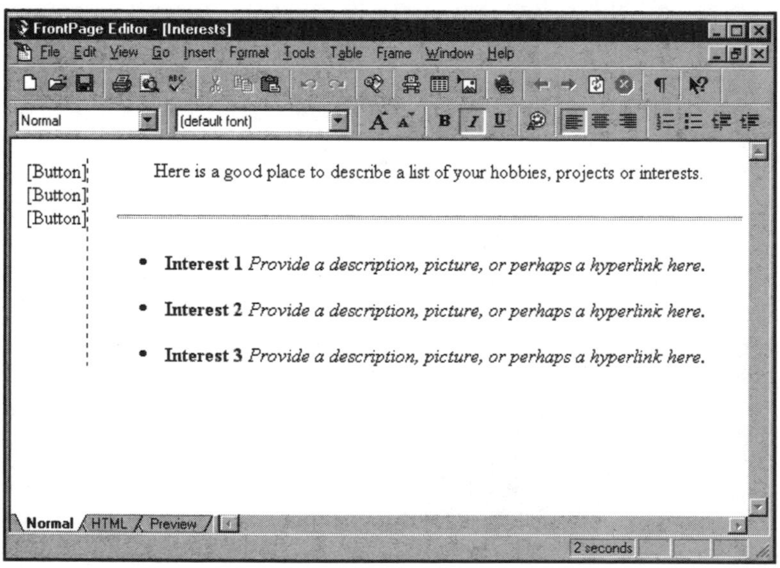

Figure 7-29

This is the view we've be using throughout most of this book, the layout view, and if you never want to see any code, it's the place you'll want to stay.

HTML View

When you're working in FrontPage, you may feel like you're in the "HTML free zone," and you can stay there, never looking at any HTML, forever, if that's what gets you going. If you're an HTML enthusiast, though, or in case you're just curious, we don't want you to feel neglected, so you can view and edit the HTML right in the Editor. To view the HTML for any given page open in the Editor, select the HTML view tab, at the bottom of the Editor window. Figure 7-30 shows a page in HTML view.

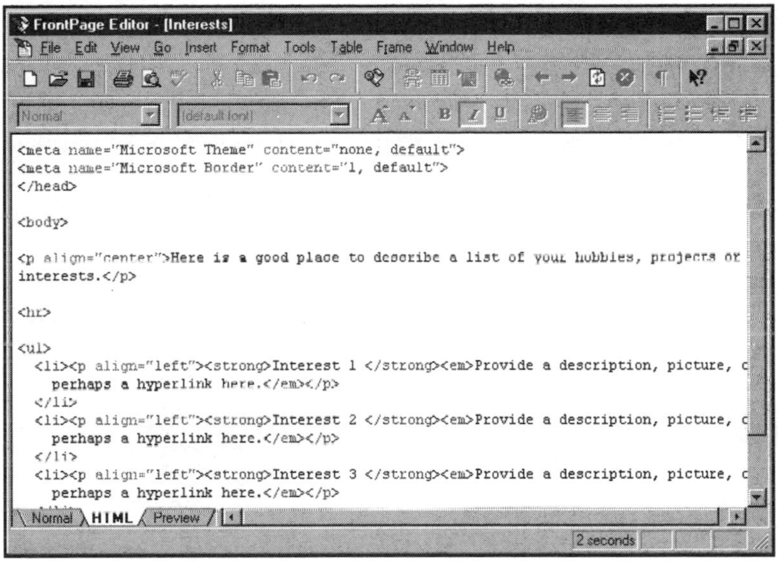

Figure 7-30

You can edit the code you see in HTML view, using the same keyboard shortcuts you use on a page in the Editor, such as those for copying, cutting, and pasting. The HTML view is colored coded; that is, it separates things like HTML tags, attributes, and page text into different colors. This makes sorting though the code a little easier to manage.

This is fully functioning HTML editor, so be careful. If you make a mistake, or get in over your head, remember those Undo/Redo commands. FrontPage will, however, help you when it can. If, for instance, you begin typing in text without HTML tags, FrontPage assumes that you wanted to start a new paragraph and automatically places your text between the <p> and </p> tags. It will also help you when typing in a table by adding <tr><td> and </td></tr> tags if necessary. FrontPage will also help out with many other common HTML tags you may forget to put in, but it's no substitute for learning your way around HTML for yourself.

> **TIP** If you're a bit overwhelmed looking at all of that code, and you're trying to find a certain place in the code to edit, you can try this little trick. In Normal view, place your cursor in the area you want to edit, and then switch to HTML view. The area that your cursor was placed in is right where HTML view opens to, with the cursor blinking, ready to go.

Preview View

Let's say you're working on a site off-line. Maybe you're using a laptop in the middle of the beach, on some remote tropical island, with no phones. Although, if you were in that situation, I don't know why in the world you'd be working on your Web site—but let's just pretend, okay? Once you begin building your pages, you may want to see how they're going to look, but with no phones and no way to post the pages to your server, what will you do, what will you do? Enter the Preview view. To see a preview of your site in the Editor, select the Preview tab (see Figure 7-31).

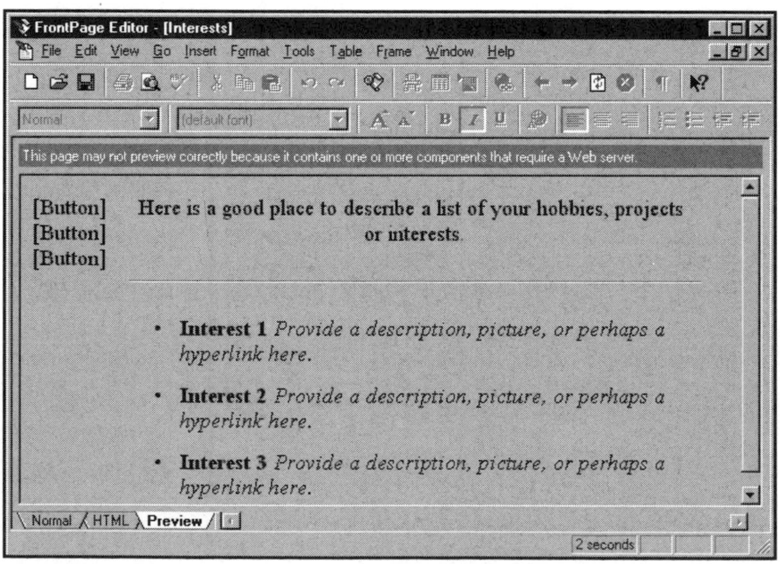

Figure 7-31

I know what you're thinking: "If I haven't saved the file to the server, then what am I looking at?" Well, when FrontPage edits a file, it's really editing a copy of the file, locally on your machine. The file is stored locally until you actually save it to your Internet server. When you use the Preview tab in the Editor, what you're seeing is that local file, presented as if it were on a server. Since you're not actually "on" a server, though, some of the active elements you may have on your page won't work. The Preview view is a great place for off-line viewing of your site, but to get the real deal, especially when testing, you'll want to view the site in a browser connected to the Internet.

If you're building a site that uses frames, you'll see additional view tabs at the bottom of the Editor. For explanations of these frames view tabs, see Chapter 6.

Utilities and Useful Commands

You'll find numerous utilities and other commands in the Editor to make your work a little easier, and maybe even save your rear end if you make a mistake somewhere along the line.

Preview in Browser

Believe it or not, many people use browsers other than Internet Explorer and Netscape Navigator. If your site is going to be accessible to the world, you should test it with as many browsers as possible. Therefore, you might want to install a variety of browsers on your computer and view your site using each one. You should also consider testing your site with different browser versions.

At any time, you can see the progress of your work and how it'll appear to the throngs that will rush to see your pages online. You can choose the Preview In Browser command from the File menu, to have FrontPage launch the current page in the Web browser of your choice. When you choose the command from the File menu, you'll see the Preview In Browser dialog box, shown in Figure 7-32.

Select an available browser in the Browser section. You can add new browsers to the list by clicking the Add button. You'll then see the Add Browser dialog box, where you'll need to enter a name for the browser and the path and name of the executable file (EXE). You can click the Browse button in the Add Browser dialog box to find the executable file for browsers you want to add.

In the Preview In Browser dialog box, you can also edit or delete browsers you have added to your list.

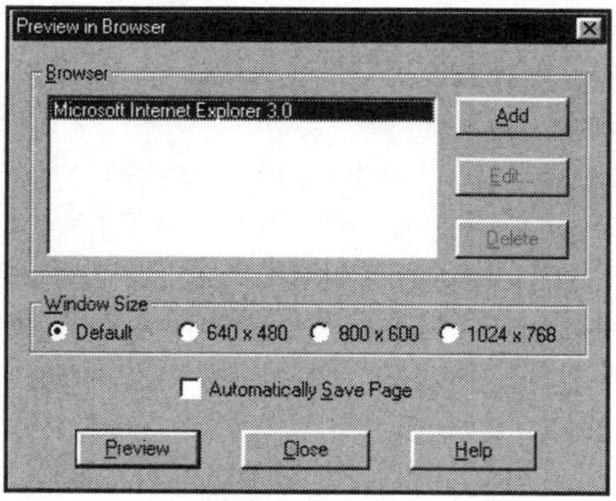

Figure 7-32

To edit a browser, select it from the list and click Edit. To delete a browser, select it from the list and click Delete. If FrontPage has automatically added a browser to the Preview In Browser dialog box, the Edit and Delete buttons are typically not available for it.

You can also set the browser window size by selecting one of the option buttons in the Window Size section. This is a great reason to use the Preview In Browser command—so you can test your site in different browser window sizes. Maybe you designed your Web pages using 1024 x 768 resolution but you want to see what the browser window size will look like to users with normal VGA (640 x 480) resolution. In order for the different window sizes to work properly, your display must have the same or higher screen resolution than the one you select. Clicking the Preview button causes the current page to be displayed in the selected browser and window size.

Undo/Redo

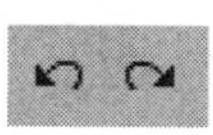

The 3-2 hanging curve balls, interceptions in the end zone, and missed lay-ups are on the record books to stay, but not the mistakes you make in the Editor. The Undo command can save you on the job. Use Undo to reverse the last action you made on a page, up to the last 30 actions. To undo an action, choose Undo from the Edit menu or click the Undo toolbar button.

To reverse the effect of an Undo command, you can choose Redo from the Edit menu or click the Redo toolbar button. You can redo up to the last 30 Undo commands.

TIP For a quicker way to Undo, press Ctrl+Z, and for a quicker Redo, press Ctrl+Y.

Following a Link

You can use the Editor as a mini-browser by using the Follow Hyperlink command. To see the actual page, file, or bookmark that a link goes to, select the link and choose the Follow Hyperlink command from the Go menu.

If the link leads to another page, the Editor opens that page if it is not already open. If the link is to a file, such as a Microsoft Excel document, the Editor opens the application configured for the file type and presents the file in its native environment.

SHORTCUT To quickly follow any link on a page, you can press Ctrl and click the link, or right-click the link and choose Follow Hyperlink from the pop-up menu.

Using Show Explorer and Show Image Editor

If the Explorer is open, you can bring it to the front of the desktop by choosing the Show FrontPage Explorer command from the Tools menu or by clicking the Show FrontPage Explorer toolbar button. If the Explorer is not already open, these operations will launch it.

If you have an image editor configured in the Explorer, you can launch it by choosing the Show Image Editor command from the Tools menu. You can install Microsoft Image Composer from the FrontPage CD, and it will become the default image editor.

Creating a Task

If you want to add a task to the Tasks view in the Explorer, you can choose the Add Task command from the Edit menu. This option is not available if you're viewing the page with the Preview tab selected. Of course, the Explorer needs have a Web open before you can perform this function.

In the New Task dialog box that appears (see Figure 7-33), you can add details to the task that appears in the Tasks view, such as the task name, who the task is assigned to, the priority of the task, and a description. The task will be linked to the active page in the Editor. Chapter 3 discusses using the Tasks view in the Explorer.

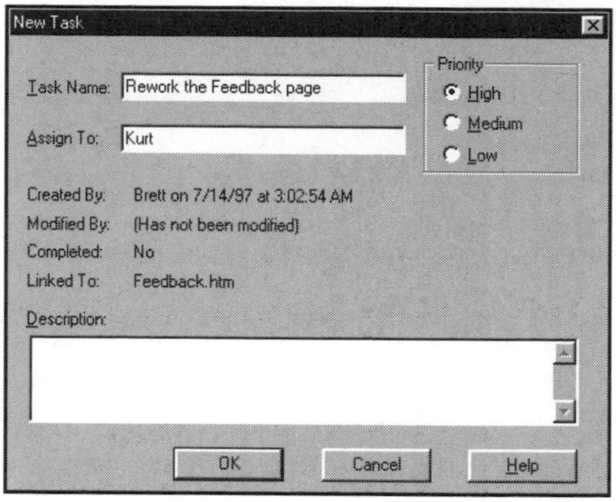

Figure 7-33

Using Spell-Checker

FrontPage is equipped with the Microsoft Office spell-checker, which provides outstanding consistency between Office documents and FrontPage Web sites. You can check the spelling of selected text, selected pages, or all the HTML pages in your Web site.

SHORTCUT You can quickly access the spell-checker in the Editor by clicking the Check Spelling toolbar button.

Spell-checking a Page Currently Open in the Editor

Here's the steps for doing this:

1. To spell-check a selection of text, select it. To spell-check the entire page, you don't have to select anything.
2. Choose Spelling from the Tools menu, or press F7. The spell-checker begins checking at the top of the page if no text is selected. If it finds no unrecognized words, it presents a dialog box informing you that the spell-check is complete.
3. If the spell-checker finds words that it doesn't recognize, you'll see the Spelling dialog box, shown in Figure 7-34.

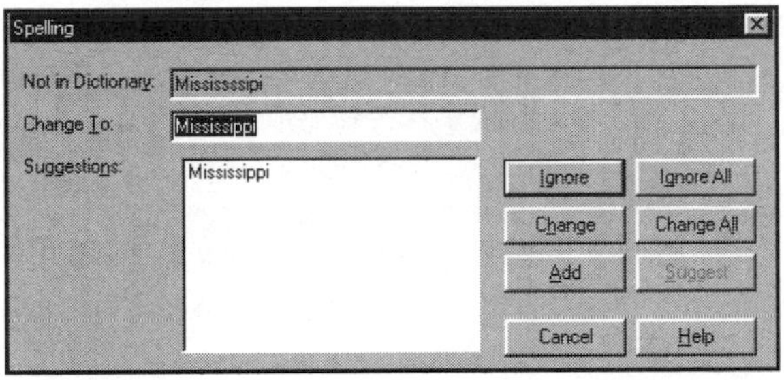

Figure 7-34

Use the dialog box as follows:

- **Not In Dictionary.** This text box displays words that are not in the Office dictionary or the custom dictionary.
- **Ignore.** Click this button to ignore the current word and search for the next unrecognized word.
- **Ignore All.** Click this button to ignore all instances of the current word and continue.
- **Change.** Click this button to replace the selection in the Not In Dictionary text box (the unrecognized word) with the selection in the Change To text box.
- **Change All.** Click this button to change all instances of the current word on the page with the contents of the Change To text box.
- **Add.** Click this button to add the selection in the Not In Dictionary text box to the custom dictionary and make no changes to the word. (Note: FrontPage shares the custom dictionary with Office, so any custom words you add while using Office applications are available in FrontPage, and vice-versa.)
- **Suggest.** When this button is enabled, you can click it to list alternative words in the Suggestions list, based on the word in the Change To text box.
- **Cancel.** Click this button to close the dialog box and quit the spell-check. Changes that have been made to the page and to the custom dictionary remain.

The spell-checker does not check the spelling in a file included on the page by a FrontPage Include Component. You must open these files separately to check their spelling. For more information on FrontPage Components, see Chapter 9.

Spell-checking Multiple Pages in a Site

To spell-check all the HTML files in a site, you need to have that site open in the Explorer. Choose Cross File Spelling from the Tools menu in the Explorer, or press F7. In the Spelling dialog box (see Figure 7-35), specify whether you want FrontPage to spell-check all HTML pages in the site or just the ones you've selected in the Explorer. (To select multiple pages, press Ctrl while clicking individual page icons in Folder view.) Then click Start.

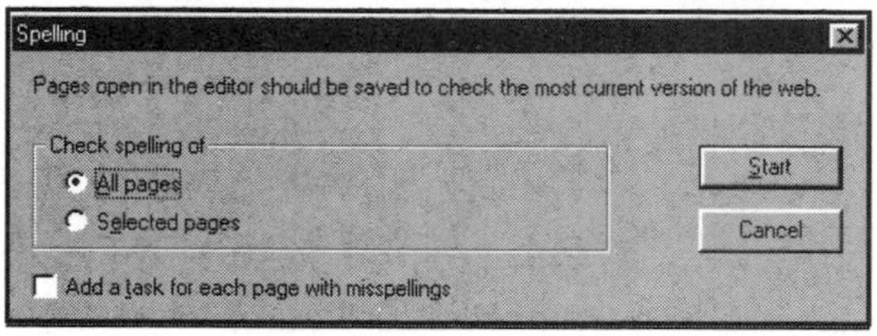

Figure 7-35

SHORTCUT You can quickly access the spell-checker in the Explorer by clicking the Cross File Spelling toolbar button.

FrontPage presents the results of the spell-check in the Check Spelling dialog box. In this dialog box, you can see details such as the pages containing misspelled words, as well as the number of misspelled words per page. If you find yourself saying "Whoopsie," and you want to correct the error right away, click the Edit Page button. The page will be opened in the Editor, with the first misspelled word displayed in the Spelling dialog box, ready for you to change. If you don't feel like making the changes now, or would rather have Kraig down the hall do it because the game starts in half an hour and you've got to pick up the pizza on the way home, click Add Task to add the tasks to the Tasks view. (From the Tasks view, you can assign Kraig's name to the tasks.) When you're finished with the Check Spelling dialog box, click Close.

Find and Replace

You can use Find and Replace in either the Editor (to search for and/or replace words on the current page) or in the Explorer (to search for and/or replace words across multiple HTML pages in your site). Take a second to imagine how useful this functionality can be. If your site contains dozens of instances of the word *board* that happen to be spelled *bored,* you have a big problem on your hands. But luckily you have a tool for searching the pages across your site and fixing any errors you know of in a straightforward fashion. We'll get to that Explorer tool in a moment; first, let's see how to use Find and Replace in the Editor.

Finding and Replacing Words on a Current Page

Unlike in Word, when you use the Find command in the Editor you do not have the option to open the Replace dialog box when you find matching text. If you know you need to replace a selection of text with another, you must use the Replace command.

Use the Find command to find instances of text on an active page. To use the command, choose Find from the Edit menu, or press Ctrl+F. The Find dialog box appears, as shown in Figure 7-36.

Figure 7-36

Type in the text you want to find. If you only want to find whole words, select the Match Whole Word Only check box. For example, if every word on your page is *the*, and you search for *t*, you won't find any instance of *t* if the Match Whole Word Only check box is selected. If the box is not selected, every instance of the letter *t* will be found.

Select the Match Case check box if you only want to find text that exactly matches the case of the selection you're searching for. You can specify the direction of the search, Up or Down, from the insertion point. When an instance of the selection is found, click the Find Next button to continue searching. Click Cancel to close the dialog box and stop the search.

To replace text with other specified text, use the Replace command on the Edit menu, or press Ctrl+H. The Replace dialog box appears, as shown in Figure 7-37.

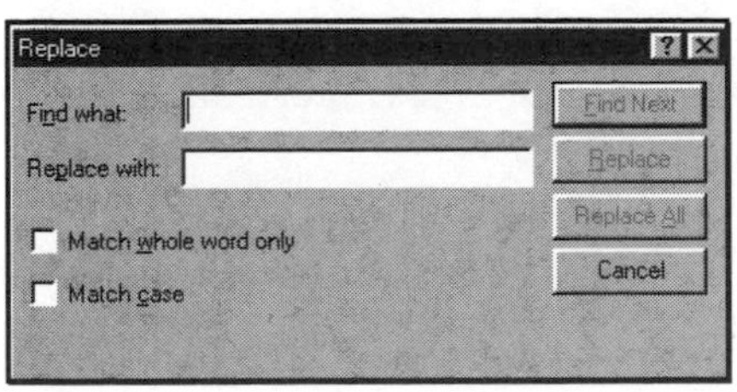

Figure 7-37

Type what you want to replace in the Find What text box, and enter your replacement text in the Replace With text box. To find text only if it matches a whole word or only if it matches the case of the text you're searching for, select the appropriate check box. To replace all instances of the text on the page, click the Replace All button. To locate the first matching instance, click the Find Next button to begin the search. When the Editor finds an instance of the text you're looking for, the text is selected on the page. To replace the text, click the Replace button. To move on without replacing the text, click the Find Next button.

Finding and Replacing Words across an Entire Site

The Explorer can find and replace words across an entire site. To use this feature, you must have the site open in the Explorer. Let's suppose that most of the good typists at your company are on vacation, and the people filling in for them can't spell their way out of a bowl of alphabet soup. Someone has typed in *iz* for *is* all across the site, and you've got to fix it.

You can use the Find command to search for instances of *iz* in the HTML pages in your site. Choose Find from the Tools menu, or press Ctrl+F. You'll see the Find In FrontPage Web dialog box, as shown in Figure 7-38.

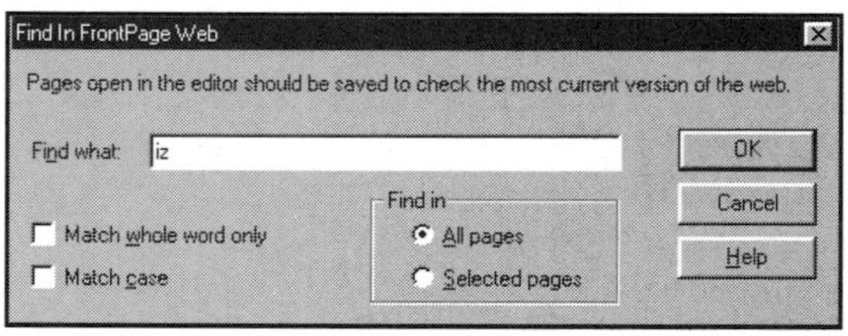

Figure 7-38

Type the word or words you want to find in the Find What text box. In the Find In section, you can specify all pages or selected pages. (To select multiple pages, press Ctrl while clicking on individual page icons in Folder view.) Make the appropriate selections in the Match Whole Word Only and Match Case check boxes. Click OK to begin the Find. When FrontPage finishes searching, you'll be presented with a Find Occurrences Of dialog box, seen in Figure 7-39, that contains summary information about the search.

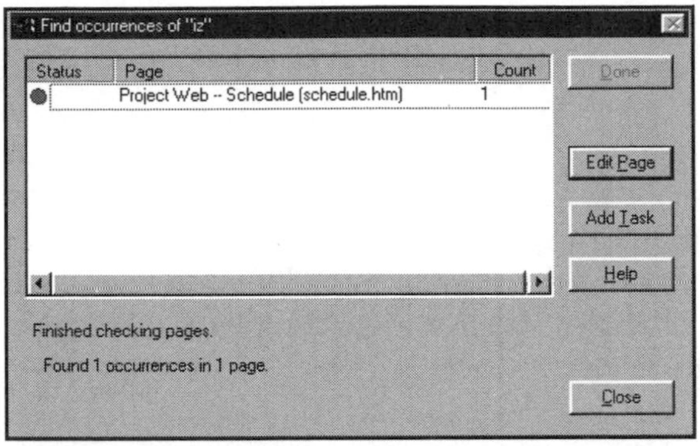

Figure 7-39

SHORTCUT You can quickly access Find in the Explorer by clicking the Cross File Find toolbar button.

If FrontPage finds instances of the text you searched for, it will indicate the number of occurrences, and in how many pages, at the bottom of the dialog box. You can immediately open the pages in the Editor to fix the mistakes one by one by selecting the page from the list and clicking Edit Page. If you'd rather work on the task later, or if you have the power to assign the task to someone else and your tee time is rapidly approaching, click the Add Task button to add the tasks to the Tasks view. When you're finished with this dialog box, click Close.

If you want to replace instances of text with different text in your site, choose Replace from the Tools menu, or press Ctrl+H. You'll see the Replace In FrontPage Web dialog box, as seen in Figure 7-40.

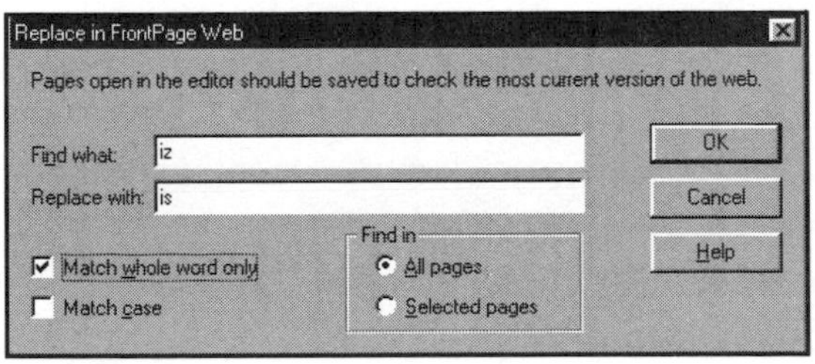

Figure 7-40

You use this dialog box the same way as described in "Finding and Replacing Words on a Current Page." When you use this command, you'll see a summary dialog box.

It looks like the same dialog box as the one that appears when you use the Find command, doesn't it? It is, and you can use it in much the same way. But you'll see the difference when you click the Edit Page button: With Find, FrontPage opens the page in the Editor and selects the text you searched for, but to change the text, you must replace it manually. With Replace, FrontPage allows you to replace each instance or all instances of the text you searched for, with the text you entered as replacement text in the Replace In FrontPage Web dialog box. You can also specify other replacement text if you so choose.

Thesaurus

You now also have the power of the Microsoft Office thesaurus in the Editor. The thesaurus comes in handy on those rainy days when you're sitting at your desk trying to find the right word that's on the tip of your tongue, and it doesn't help that your mind continually drifts back to the vacation you just spent in Cabo.

To use the thesaurus for help on a specific word, select the word and choose Thesaurus from the Tools menu, or press Shift+F7. You'll see the Thesaurus dialog box, seen in Figure 7-41, which you use in the same way that you use one in an Office application.

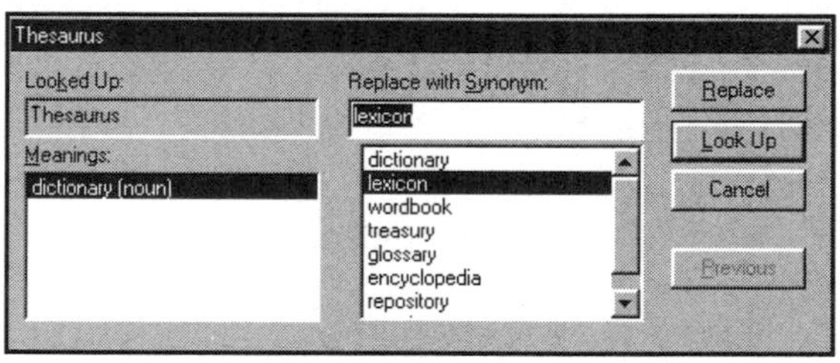

Figure 7-41

- The Looked Up text box displays the word you're currently checking.
- The Meanings list displays meanings for the word you're looking up. If you select a meaning here, you'll see a list of synonyms in the Replace With Synonym list.

- Click a word in the Replace With Synonym list if you want to use it in place of the selected word in the Editor, or if you want to use that word to search further. To use the word in the Editor right away, click Replace, and you'll be returned to the Editor with the new word in place. To keep on searching with the selected word as the new word you're looking up, click Look Up.
- If you don't want to use any new words from the thesaurus, click Cancel.
- If the Previous button is enabled, you can click it to return to the previous word you looked up.

Moving Among Currently Open Pages

Use the Back and Forward toolbar buttons to move among pages that are currently open in the Editor. The pages are listed at the bottom of the Window menu in the order that they were opened, and you can move to a new page via that menu as well. You can also use the Back and Forward commands on the Tools menu.

Refreshing a Page

To refresh an active page in the Editor with the last saved version of that page, click the Refresh toolbar button or choose the Refresh command from the View menu. If you have made changes since the last save, a dialog box will appear asking whether you want to save the changes. Click Yes or No, and the page will be refreshed. The Refresh command is handy when you've made changes to a page that you do not want to save, and you want to start over from the last version that was saved. It's also handy for viewing changes made to a page by another person.

Stopping an Action

To stop an action in the Editor, click the Stop toolbar button (if it is enabled). This command is handy for ending actions that are taking a long time to finish or that might be "hung up," such as communications between the Editor and a Web server.

Coming Up

With that, the grand discussion of formatting and using FrontPage's file commands and utilities comes to an end. In the next chapter, you'll learn how FrontPage works with images.

CHAPTER 8

Getting into Graphics

Images: A Balancing Act

Ask a writer and he'll tell you "Content is king." Ask a graphic artist and he'll tell you, "Content is one thing, but if you want anyone to read it, you'd better add some graphics." As a Web site developer, you'll be walking this fine line and addressing the content versus graphics issue for every page in your site.

The number one issue when dealing with graphics in a Web site is file size, which translates directly to how long an image will take to display in the average browser. You can discuss graphic formats, resolution, image editing software, color palettes, browsers, and so forth until you're blue in the face, but the bottom line is that the best graphics are the ones that have reasonable image quality and small file sizes.

Since many people are still using 14.4-baud modems, many site developers set size limitations on their pages. Typically, a page in your site, including any images on that page, should not exceed 35–40 KB. That loud noise you just heard was a collective scream from the graphic designers of the world, saying, "Yeah, right!" That size doesn't sound like much to work with, and it's not, but with some helpful tips to optimize your images, you'll be surprised at what you can do.

This chapter will discuss four aspects of using images in your sites:

- The types of graphic formats used in Web site development.
- How to optimize those formats, using color management, to achieve fast-loading images that still look good.
- Using FrontPage to handle your images, including placement, creating image maps, text on GIFs, and creating transparent GIFs directly in the FrontPage Editor.
- The new and improved image toolbar—adjust contrast and brightness, and flip, rotate, and crop images, all in the Editor.

Graphic Formats

As you might know, graphic formats are all referred to by an acronym or by the file extension associated with the format, and the names can get a little confusing. You've got BMP, GIF, EPS, TIF, JPEG, WMF, and many others. While working on your Web site in FrontPage, however, you'll be dealing primarily with two types of images: JPEG and GIF. Both are compressed graphic formats and are the most commonly used in Web site development. But what if you have some graphics that are not JPEGs or GIFs, and you want to use them on a Web page? Well, you're in luck, because FrontPage can import many graphic formats, which are listed here:

CompuServe GIF (GIF)
JPEG (JPG)
Bitmap (BMP)
TIFF (TIF)
Windows Metafile (WMF)
Sun Raster (RAS)
Encapsulated PostScript (EPS)
Paintbrush (PCX)
Targa (TGA)

When you save a page that contains images you've inserted that haven't been saved yet, FrontPage will ask you whether you want to save each image to the current site. By default, FrontPage saves each non-GIF, non-JPEG image as a GIF. If you want the image saved as a JPEG, be sure to specify this in the Image Properties dialog box before you save the page.

The JPEG (Joint Photographic Experts Group) format is a scalable compressed format that can deliver high compression with very little image degradation. It's not uncommon for an image to lose some of its crispness in electronic form, especially when it's converted from one format to another. Because JPEG images handle compression and image degradation well, they're ideal for a Web site environment in which they are often resized, converted, or otherwise altered. The JPEG format is most suitable for photographs or images with more than 256 colors. FrontPage looks at the number of bits used to represent each color in the image, also known as the file's *bit depth*. Images with eight bits of color information per pixel are capable of supporting 256 different colors. More bits mean more colors supported.

The GIF (Graphics Interchange Format) format is a compressed format for images that contain 256 or fewer colors. The GIF format is typically used with images that contain primarily solid colors, such as illustrations. The GIF format can also support transparency and interlacing.

Bit Depth	Number of Colors
8 bit	256 Colors
7 bit	128 Colors
6 bit	64 Colors
5 bit	32 Colors
4 bit	16 Colors
3 bit	8 Colors

Figure 8-1
Various bit depths and their corresponding number of colors.

In FrontPage, you can do a little something extra to a GIF image. With the click of the mouse, you can make one color in your GIF transparent. You can also type text anywhere on top of a GIF, in any color, font, or size. We'll get into all of that, later in this chapter.

Color Management

The idea of color management might be new to a lot of graphic artists, but if you plan on being successful with your Web site, it will become your new best friend. The basic idea behind color management is this: How can I decrease the number of colors in my images and still have them look good? Decreasing the number of colors decreases the file size of the image, and smaller files download faster in a browser.

TIP Start with a good color palette, which is a collection of colors (usually 256) that is designed to perform well across a variety of browsers and platforms. There are many so-called "safety palettes" available on the Web.

If you want users to see those impressive graphics you're about to create, you need to make sure they're built for speed. The last thing you want is for users to become frustrated as they watch their screens draw and redraw a bunch of large file-size graphics. Keep in mind the following tips for making your image file sizes smaller. (You can use Microsoft Image Composer, which comes with the FrontPage Bonus Pack, to manipulate your images.)

- Typically, the JPEG format works well for photographic images, and the GIF format works well for images containing solid colors, such as illustrations and line art.
- Size your images using your image editing software. Even though you can dimensionally size images in the Editor, this doesn't actually change the image file size. For example, if you insert a 2-inch square image that has a file size of 10 KB into the Editor and you size it to a 1-inch square, the image file size is still 10 KB.
- If you are creating an image that contains only black and white colors, save it as a black and white image. This will make the image file size smaller. In Microsoft Image Composer, you can do this by setting the color format to Black and White when saving.
- If you are creating an image that will be saved as a GIF and it contains a gradient or straight lines, try to make these horizontal. Since the GIF format performs its compression by looking at each horizontal line, it can make the file size smaller if an entire line has the same color value.
- Experiment with the different JPEG compression levels. Try to use as much compression as possible and still retain acceptable image quality.
- View your images at different resolutions and bit depths, and view them in different browsers. A JPEG image of more than 8 bits will dither when displayed on a monitor that only supports 256 colors.
- If you're using Photoshop and you want to save an image as a GIF, change the RGB Color mode to Indexed Color mode, specify the bit depth (the smaller the better), and select the adaptive palette with no dither.

- If you're using Photoshop and you're saving images as GIFs and you know your image uses fewer than 256 colors, try using the Exact palette. Exact palettes contain exactly the number of colors in your image and thus decrease the image file size.

The key is to experiment. You might notice some flattening of colors, but you'll also notice a decrease in image file size. It's a judgment call, but it's one you'll have to make if you want graphics to display faster in a browser.

As crazy as this might sound, some people don't like to wait for graphics *at all,* so remember to take advantage of the alternative text feature (explained later in this chapter, in the section "Alternative Representations"), and think about designing your pages so those "graphics haters" out there can still navigate through your Web site.

Colors in HTML

If you're new to HTML, and you've always wondered how colors are defined in the code to be displayed in a browser, you're in luck, because that's exactly what you're about to find out.

You may already know that your monitor uses RGB (Red, Green, and Blue) values to display all of the colors you see on your screen. Since HTML can't understand the RGB values your monitor uses, HTML uses a hexadecimal (hex) color value to display colors in a browser. You may be asking yourself, "So, what the heck are hex color values, and why should I care?" If you're creating original graphics, and you don't want them to dither, or if you just want a little insight into the HTML for color, you'll want to know this stuff. Since we already know that it's a good idea to use a 256-color "safety" palette, we'll concentrate on the hex, and on the RGB values that make up that palette.

If you look at the HTML for a page, you might notice the *color* tag. For instance, if you have black text on your page, the code would look like this: <font color="#000000"</font>. Hex colors are a series of three sets of two numbers or letters. Each set of two relates to an R, G, and B value, which is why you end up with a total of six. In the example above, 000000 represents black, which is the absence of all color. The other extreme is FFFFFF, which is all colors, making white. In an RGB value system, black would be 0,0,0, and white would be 255, 255, 255. In reality, you could type in just about any combination of six numbers or letters and come up with a hex color, but in order to stay within our 256-color palette, we'll use only hex values that match an RGB value of 255 or less. Of course, 255 plus 0 is where we come up with the 256 colors in the palette.

Okay, here's the simple method for determining whether your color is part of the 256 color palette. Hex colors must be a value of 00, 33, 66, 99, CC, or FF, and they can be in any combination of three sets. The RGB equivalent is a value of 0, 51, 102, 153, 204, or 255. So, for example, if you wanted to use a safe orange color, its RGB value would be 255, 102, 51, and its hex value would be FF, 66, 33, and in HTML it would look like this: <font color="#FF6633"</font>. Figure 8-2 shows hex/RGB values for the 256-color palette.

256 Color Value Chart						
HEX	00	33	66	99	CC	FF
RGB	0	51	102	153	204	255

Figure 8-2

Now when you're working with your favorite image editing software, like Image Composer, you can create RGB colors with confidence, knowing that they're part of the 256 color palette. And if you're the type of person who likes to fiddle with the HTML code, you'll know exactly what all of those color tags mean, and how to change them if you want.

Optimizing Your Backgrounds

If you want that cool background to appear quickly and still have acceptable quality, these tips can help you:

- Since a background image is just a tiled graphic, follow the guidelines described on the previous two pages to decrease the file size.
- Decrease the physical dimensions of the background image to decrease the file size.
- Don't put too much detail in a background. Remember that in most cases text will have to be read on top of it.
- Experiment with the backgrounds that are available with FrontPage. Many of these backgrounds are very small in size. See the next section for information on inserting them. You can also use your favorite Web search, and do a search on the word backgrounds, you'll get plenty of hits, with lots of pages offering free backgrounds.

- Consider using a background color instead of a background image. This will decrease download time, sometimes significantly.

NOTE Here's an easy way to convert an image so that it is suitable as a background: Open it in Image Composer and choose Warps And Filters from the Tools menu. From the Warps And Filters toolbar, select the Color Enhancement category, and then select the Wash effect. You can adjust the amount of wash effect by adjusting the Wash Opacity slider on the toolbar and then clicking the Apply button. This "washing out" effect makes the image an attractive and nondistracting background for a Web page.

Bringing in Those Images

Okay, now that you know a little bit about graphic formats and color management, it's time to find out how to get images on your pages. You do this in the Editor, by choosing the Image command from the Insert menu. Just follow these steps:

1. In the Editor, place the cursor where you want the image to appear.
2. Choose Image from the Insert menu. If you're working with the Explorer open, you'll see the Image dialog box, shown in Figure 8-3.

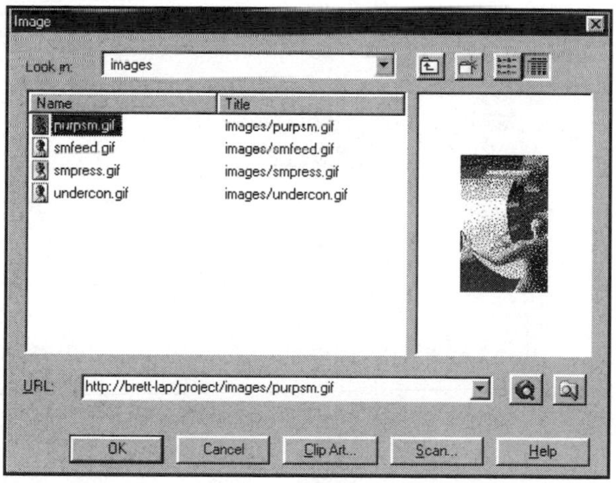

Figure 8-3

Here you can select from any file currently in the open Web, and browse throughout the folders in that site. Just click the file to see a preview displayed in the area on the right side of the dialog box. You can also just enter the URL in the text box, if you know it. You can also use your Web browser to select an image, or make a hyperlink to a file on your computer, by using the buttons to the right of the URL text box. If you choose the later, you'll see the Select File dialog box, described below.

If you're working in the Editor, by itself, you'll see the Select File dialog box, seen in Figure 8-4.

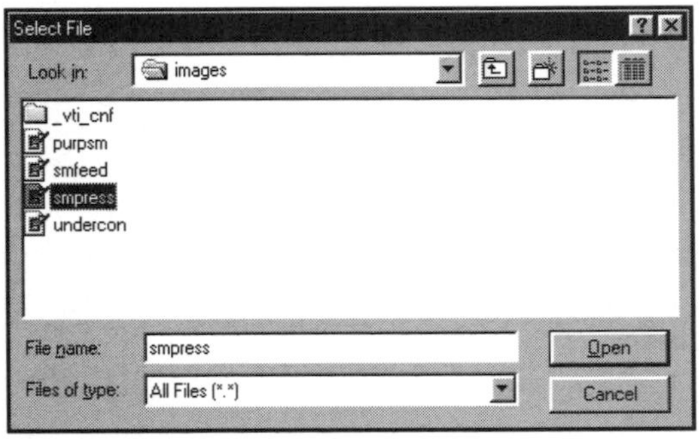

Figure 8-4

From this dialog box, you can select any file on your local machine. You can also hit the Cancel button, and you'll see the Image dialog box. Of course, without a site open in the Explorer, you'll only have the option to use your Web browser to select an image this time.

If you are connected to a scanner or digital camera, you have a very cool feature at you disposal. Anytime you're in the Image dialog box, you'll have the option to select the Scan button to launch any input device you're connected to. You can then scan an image directly into the Editor, with any name you choose and into any folder you like. If you don't feel like making that decision, FrontPage will name the file for you, and place it in the Temp folder, located in the directory you installed FrontPage in.

Saving Images

Images on a page are not saved within the same file that contains the HTML. Images are saved as separate files in their image formats (GIF or

JPEG). The HTML only references the location of the image. In FrontPage, images are saved differently, depending on how you're working; that is, either with the Explorer or without it.

Working without the Explorer

If you're working without the use of the Explorer, then FrontPage will not ask you to save the image at all. It will assume that the location you inserted it from is correct, and will reference that location. Remember though, that FrontPage will need access to that location in order to display the image later. So in other words, don't insert an image from a floppy disk or from the Web unless you save it locally first.

Working with the Explorer

If you're working with the Explorer open and you've inserted an image from any location other than from the site open in the Explorer, you'll be asked to save the image the next time you save the page. You save these new images using the Save Embedded Files dialog box, shown in Figure 8-5.

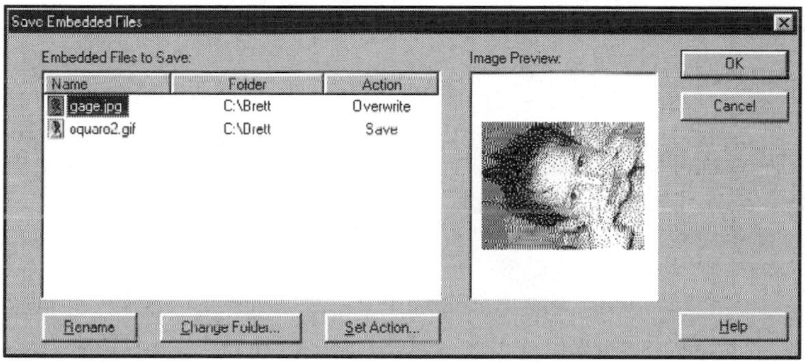

Figure 8-5

You'll see a list of the files that need to be saved listed on the left, with their name, location, and what action will take place when you click OK. If you click a file in the list, you'll see a thumbnail of the image in the Image Preview window. You can also rename the file, change its folder, or set a new save action, by clicking the appropriate button. When you're finished, click OK, and FrontPage will save the images.

Clip Art

FrontPage has a collection of hundreds of clip art images, as well as access to the Microsoft Office clip art library if you have Office installed. You can access clip art in two ways: via the Clip Art tab in the Image dialog box, or by selecting Clip Art from the Insert menu. In either case, you'll see the Microsoft Clip Gallery dialog box, shown here in Figure 8-6.

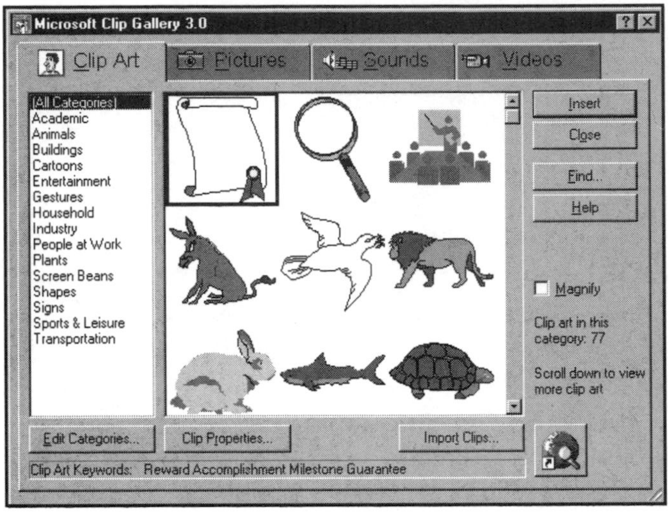

Figure 8-6

Select the category you want from one of the four tabs: Clip Art, Pictures, Sounds, or Videos. When you find an image you want, click the image in the preview window and then click Insert. If you're looking through the Sounds or Videos, you can play them on the spot, before you insert them, by pressing the Play button. If you don't find anything you like here, you can click the Internet button at the bottom right of the dialog box. You'll be transported to a clip art area at www.Microsoft.com, where you'll find dozens of free clips. Any images you select here will automatically be added to your Clip Gallery.

The Images Are In—Now What?

After you insert an image, FrontPage gives you many ways to manipulate it by using the Image Properties dialog box. Here, you'll find useful information about your image, such as its type, dimensions, and much more. You also have a whole suite of image editing tools available on the Image toolbar. (These are discussed in detail later in this chapter.)

Changing Image Properties

If you want to alter an image and the way it appears on a page, you can manipulate that information to your heart's content. To change any of the image properties, here's what to do:

1. Select an image in the Editor by clicking it.
2. Choose Image Properties from the Edit menu. You'll see the Image Properties dialog box, seen in Figure 8-7, which has three tabs: General, Video, and Appearance.

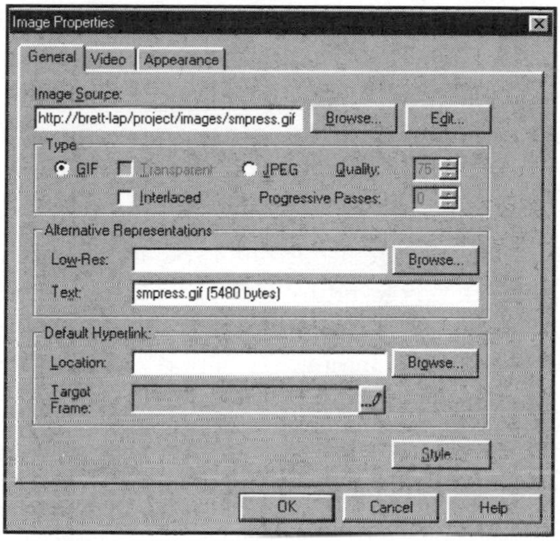

Figure 8-7

3. Adjust the settings as necessary. When you finish adjusting the settings, click OK. Remember that the settings are not permanent; you can always return to the Image Properties dialog box to change them.

The following is a detailed look at the settings in the dialog box, starting with the General tab.

SHORTCUT You can right-click an image and choose Image Properties from the pop-up menu to reach the Image Properties dialog box. With an image selected, you can reach the Image Properties dialog box quickly by pressing Alt+Enter.

Your options on the General tab are as follows:

Image Source. This text box displays the image's page URL if the image is in the current Web site, its absolute URL if the image is from the World Wide Web, or its path and filename if the image is in a file. If you want to change the image, click the Browse button, which brings up the Image dialog box. If you want to open the image to work on it in your image editor, click the Edit button.

Type. This section displays the graphic format of the selected image, either GIF or JPEG. The selected option is the image's current format. By selecting the other option, you can convert the image to that format.

When the GIF option is selected, you have two options for presenting the image: Transparent and Interlaced. You can use one or use both at the same time.

> **Transparent.** Available only for GIF images, this check box is selected if a color in the image is currently specified as transparent. Deselect the check box to return the transparent portions of the image back to their normal color and make the image nontransparent. Later in this chapter, you'll find out how to make a color transparent (which automatically selects this option).
>
> **Interlaced.** If the Interlaced check box is selected, the image will progressively render in the browser. A progressively rendered image slowly comes into focus as it downloads into a browser.

If the JPEG option is selected, the Quality text box becomes available.

> **Quality.** You can adjust the image quality by entering a number between 1 and 100. A higher number means less compression, resulting in a better quality image, but it also means a larger image and slower performance. (Larger files take longer for the browser to download and display.) A lower number means more compression, resulting in a lower image quality but smaller file size. By default, the Quality setting is 75.

Alternative Representations. Not all browsers support images, and most browsers can be set to disable images. Some browsers can display a low-resolution image in place of a high-resolution image while downloading the high-resolution image from the server. For all these cases, you can supply an alternative representation for the image.

Low-Res. Specifies a lower-resolution image to display in place of a higher-resolution image while the latter is downloading. Click the Browse button, select an alternate image, and then click OK. For you HTML buffs, this alternative image is the same as the LOWSRC attribute.

> **TIP** Neither FrontPage nor the browser checks that the low-res image is actually a low-res version of the real image, but an easy way to create a low-res image is to use Image Composer to create a grayscale version of the image, with very few colors.

Text. Specifies alternative text that will appear instead of the image if the user's browser cannot display images or is set to disable the displaying of images. This is useful if you anticipate that some users will view your site without its graphics. (Actually, it's a good idea to do this for all of your images.) In some browsers, this text will appear while the image is loading. By default, FrontPage will insert the name of the image in this field, along with its size in bytes. You can, however, change this to anything you like.

Default Hyperlink. You can turn part or all of your image into a hotspot that links to other locations. (See the section titled "Creating Image Maps" later in this chapter, to learn how.) If an image has multiple hotspots, you can set a default link for the parts of the image that are not covered by a hotspot.

To set a default link: Click the Browse button, and you'll see the Edit Hyperlink dialog box. For your link, you can select from a list of currently open pages; pages or files from World Wide Web, Gopher, Newsgroup, or FTP sites; or a new page. By selecting the mail button, you can also set a hyperlink that sends mail. Set your link, and then click OK to return to the Image Properties dialog box.

To change a default link: If the image already has a default link, when you click the Browse button, you'll see the Edit Hyperlink dialog box. You can change the link in exactly the same way that you set it. Edit the link, and then click OK to return to the Image Properties dialog box.

You can also specify a target frame for the default link in the Target Frame text box. For more information on setting a target frame, see Chapter 6.

Use the Style button to attach or edit a cascading stylesheet associated with the image. For more information on cascading stylesheets, see Chapter 10.

The second tab of the Image Properties dialog box, Video, seen in Figure 8-8, lets you insert an AVI (Audio Video) file onto your page. The image file you designated on the General tab is used as a placeholder that is displayed until the AVI is loaded and ready to run. Adding a video to your page using the Video command on the Insert menu is slightly different. For more information on using the Video command, see Chapter 7.

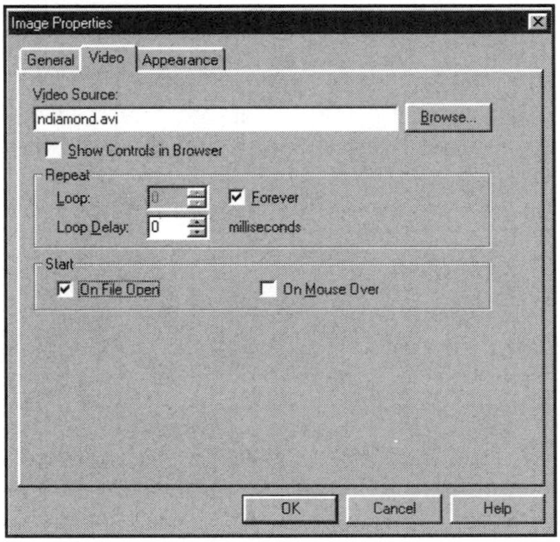

Figure 8-8

Video Source. You can type in the path and filename to your video in the Video Source text box, or use the Browse button to locate the video file.

Show Controls in Browser. Selecting this check box will show a set of controls: Play, Stop, and a slider, along with the video when it's displayed in the browser at run time.

Repeat. This section lets you set how often and when the video will play.

Loop. Enter a number for the amount of times you want the video to play.

Loop Delay. Entering a number will delay the playing of the video between each playing. The delay is specified in milliseconds.

Forever. Select this check box if you want the video to loop indefinitely while the page is displayed.

Start. This section lets you determine when the video will be played.

On File Open. Selecting this check box tells the video to play as soon as it's downloaded in the browser.

On Mouse Over. Select this check box if you want the video to play when the user positions the mouse pointer over the image.

The third tab of the Image Properties dialog box (shown in Figure 8-9), Appearance, lets you manipulate the appearance of your image in a number of ways:

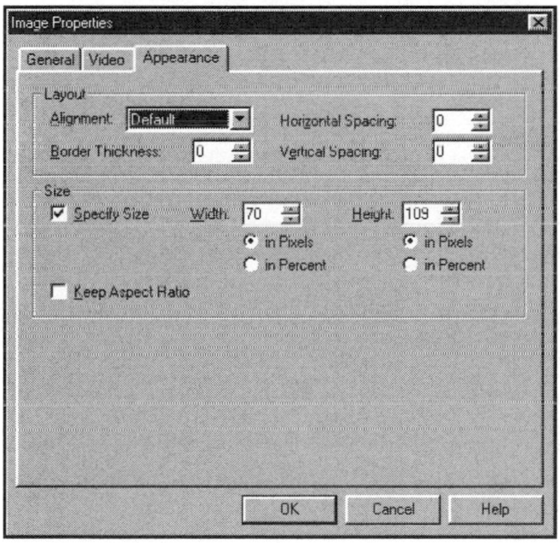

Figure 8-9

Layout. In the Layout section, you control the position of the image on the page.

Alignment. Specifies a type of alignment between the image and the text around it. You can align the image in several ways.

Bottom: Aligns the text with the bottom of the image, so that the text begins at the bottom of the image.

Middle: Aligns the text with the middle of the image.

Top: Aligns the text with the top of the image.

Absbottom: Aligns the image with the bottom of the current line.

Absmiddle: Aligns the image with the middle of the current line.

Texttop: Aligns the top of the image with the top of the tallest text in the line.

Baseline: Aligns the image with the baseline of the current line.

Left: Places the image in the left margin and wraps the text preceding the image down the right side of the image.

Right: Places the image in the right margin and wraps the text preceding the image down the left side of the image.

TIP You can also position the image on the left side, center, or right side of a page by using one of the alignment toolbar buttons in the Editor. The image alignment is WYSIWYG in the Editor, so you can see how the image will look from within a browser.

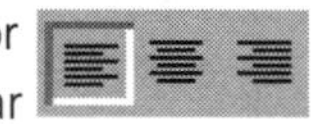

These settings apply only to images that appear on the same line as text. If an image is the only element on a line, the setting will default to Bottom.

Border Thickness. Specifies a black border around the image; the width of the border is expressed in pixels. To change the width, select the number in the text box and type in the new number.

Horizontal Spacing. Sets a specified horizontal spacing in pixels from the image to the nearest image or text on the current line, on both sides of the image.

Vertical Spacing. Sets a specified vertical spacing in pixels from the image to the nearest image or text on the line above and/or below it.

Size. This section displays the height and width of the image in pixels. Select the Specify Size check box to include width and height tags in the HTML, or change the Width and Height of your image by entering new numbers yourself. Sizes are measured either in pixels or as a percentage.

Keep Aspect Ratio. Check this box to keep the ratio of the image to its width or height if its been changed. In other words, if you change the width or height, but not both, checking this box will maintain the proportions of the image.

SHORTCUT You can resize an image by selecting it and then dragging the sides or corners of the image. If you drag from the corners, the image is resized proportionally. Remember, this has no effect on the file size, just the image dimensions.

NOTE When a browser begins to load a page, it looks for tags in the HTML. One of those tags references any images on the page. By specifying an image's width and height, the browser will leave room for it on the page, even before it downloads the image. Without the width and height tags, the browser has to wait for the image to download before it makes room for it on the page. When this happens, you'll see text and other elements on the page jump and move to make room for the image. You can ensure that these tags are included for every image by selecting the Specify Size check box, on the Appearance tab of the Image Properties dialog box.

Cool Stuff You Can Do to an Image

Once an image is on your page, you can do many cool things with it beyond setting or changing its properties, and you'll do all of these cool things via the Image toolbar, as seen in Figure 8-10. You can make the toolbar visible, if it's not already, by selecting Image Toolbar from the View menu. The toolbar floats, which means you can move it anywhere you want on your screen, even outside the Editor. To move the toolbar, click inside the toolbar in an area not occupied by a button, and then drag the toolbar to its destination. You can dock the toolbar by dragging it and dropping it anywhere in the toolbar region of the Editor.

Figure 8-10

With the Image toolbar, you have a miniature image editing studio right at your fingertips. You can create image maps, transparent GIF's, type text on a GIF, crop images, make adjustments to image quality, as well as a few other things. We'll walk through each of these features, starting with image maps.

Image Maps

FrontPage makes use of client-side image maps. Traditionally, for an image map link to work, the client (for example, a browser) would have to communicate with the server to figure out where the link goes to when the user clicks a hotspot. However, with client-side image maps, the link destination information is stored at the client end, so the image map is no longer server dependent. This results in less communication between the client and the server, taking pressure off the server and reducing the time it takes to determine the link destination when a user clicks on a hotspot.

You set the image map style in your Web site via the Web Settings command on the Tools menu in the Explorer; this command is explained in Chapter 3. By default, FrontPage generates both client-side and server-side image maps, so that any browser can use the image maps on the page. The server-side image maps take advantage of the FrontPage Server Extensions. If you don't have the FrontPage Server Extensions installed, you can select a different server-side standard for image maps (NCSA, CERN, or Netscape standard) on the Advanced tab of the FrontPage Web Settings dialog box.

Creating Image Maps

You can turn part or all of an image into a hotspot that links to other locations. For example, if you own a toy store and advertise your products on the Web, why not use an image of a teddy bear as a link to the section highlighting your stuffed animals? Or, in an intranet site, you can use an image of a dollar bill as a link to the Sales section.

You can create an image map in FrontPage in a matter of seconds, using the image map buttons, seen in Figure 8-11 below, on the Image toolbar.

Figure 8-11

To create an image map, use these buttons on the Image toolbar. They are, from left to right, the Select, Rectangle, Circle, Polygon, and Highlight Hotspots buttons.

1. Select the image that you'll be creating the hotspot on. Notice that the Image toolbar becomes active and that the Select button is depressed.
2. Decide which areas of the image you want "hot." For example, on an image of a house you might want the user to be able to click on the door and jump to an image of the foyer. If possible, make sure that the entire portion of the image you want to work with is visible on the screen.
3. Click the Rectangle, Circle, or Polygon toolbar button, depending on the area you want to define as a hotspot. The Rectangle and Circle buttons create rectangular and circular hotspots, respectively, and the Polygon button allows you to create a hotspot of any shape. When one of these buttons is depressed, the cursor changes to a pencil when it's over an image, indicating that you're ready to draw the hotspot.
4. Carefully draw the hotspot around the portion of the image that you want to be clickable. Here's a rundown of how:

   Rectangular and circular hotspots: Position the cursor near where you want the hotspot to appear. Click and drag the cursor to draw and size the hotspot.

   Polygonal hotspots: Position the cursor where you want to begin drawing the hotspot. Click once to insert the first point of the polygon. Move the mouse and click again to draw the first side of the polygon. Continue drawing sides until your hotspot is complete; it's complete when you connect to the original point where you first clicked.

   Once the hotspot is drawn, you can always move and resize it if it's not quite what you wanted. See the next section for more information.
5. After you draw the hotspot, the Create Hyperlink dialog box appears. This is where you set the target link for your hotspot. For more information on creating links, see Chapter 7.

Moving and Resizing Hotspots

Once you draw a hotspot on an image, you have complete control over its size and location. You can click and drag it to anywhere on the image, or use the arrow keys to move it and adjust its location. To resize a hotspot, select it and then click and drag a size handle (one of the small squares at the corners of the hotspot). To return a hotspot to its original position, press the Esc key; this is similar to an Undo command. You must use the Esc key *before* you release the mouse button.

TIP If you resize an image that already has hotspots defined on it, the hotspots are not also sized. You have to size the hotspots individually.

Editing a Hotspot Link

To change the target link of a hotspot, double-click the hotspot to bring up the Edit Hyperlink dialog box. You can also right-click on a selected hotspot and choose Image Hotspot Properties from the pop-up menu to display the Edit Hyperlink dialog box. Another way is to select the hotspot and click the Create Or Edit Hyperlink toolbar button. Change the target link, and then click OK.

TIP You can press the Tab key to jump between hotspots on an image; you can press Shift+Tab to select the previous hotspot.

Highlighting Hotspots

Sometimes it's difficult to see all the hotspots you've created, especially on a complex image. Click the Highlight Hotspot toolbar button to see all the hotspots on a selected image. The image is removed and replaced with a white background, and only the borders of the hotspots are shown. Click on a hotspot and its borders are filled in black. The toolbar button toggles between the two views.

Text on a GIF

A Let's say that you're in charge of putting the pages together for your company Web site, and this whole Web thing is confusing enough. You've already proved your intelligence, you've chosen to use FrontPage to create the site. Then all of a sudden your boss looks at the page and says, "Hey! We wanted that illustration of the hamburger at the top to say, 'Eat at Jeff's — You won't be Sorry!' the company's slogan, and we want it to link to our nutritional facts page." And you're already over budget on the graphics. Since you can't afford to have the illustrator do it, you remember that you can type the text in yourself in the Editor, right on top of the image, and even make the text a hyperlink. With the Text button on the Image toolbar, the problem's solved and everyone's happy—even your cranky boss, Jeff.

This is one of the coolest new features on the Image toolbar. The Text On GIF tool lets you type formatted text right on top of any GIF image, and you can even turn the text into a hotspot, using the Create Hyperlink dialog box. This is a great way to incorporate text into an image that didn't have any to begin with.

To use the text on GIF tool, first you must insert a GIF image on your page, in the Editor. Then select the GIF by clicking it, the Image toolbar becomes active. Select the Text button on the Image toolbar, and FrontPage automatically creates a text region, centered on the image, with a blinking cursor, ready to go.

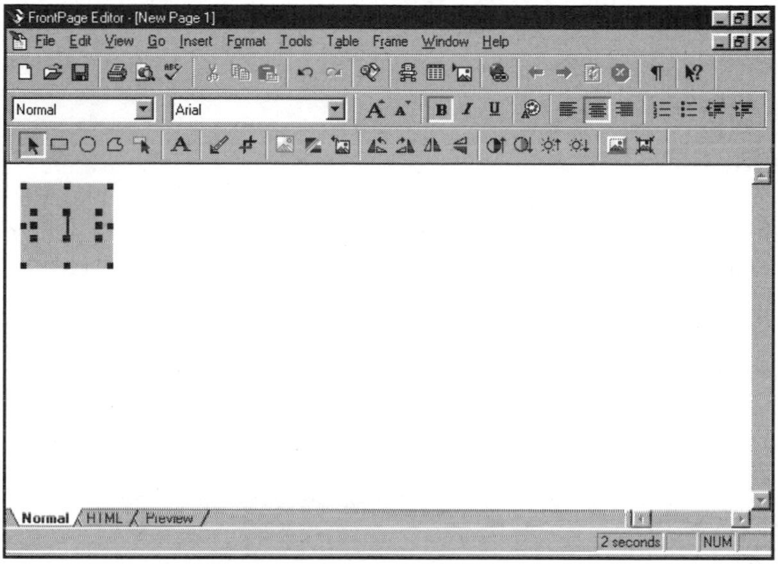

Figure 8-12

Formatting the Text

Figure 8-12 above shows a selected GIF image, just after pushing the Text button on the Image toolbar. The rectangular area in the middle of the square is the text field. As soon as you use the Text button, you can start typing in your text. The default text is 12 pt Arial black, centered, but you can easily change that. You can also change fonts, colors, size, and alignment, by selecting the text and using any of the buttons on the Format toolbar. For information on the Format toolbar, see Chapter 7.

The text is displayed in a single line, so if you want it to wrap, you'll need to adjust the width to suit your needs. You do this by resizing the text region, anywhere within the boundaries of the image it's on. Select a border anchor (the little boxes in the corners and in the middle of borders) and drag them out. Top and bottom border anchors adjust height, left and right border anchors adjust the width, and corner border anchors adjust height and width together. You can also move the text region to another location on the image by clicking a border and dragging it around into place, but you must stay within the image.

Making the Text a Hyperlink

If you want the text to be *hot*, right-click the text region, and then select Image Hotspot Properties from the pop-up menu. This will launch the Create Hyperlink dialog box. You can also create a hyperlink by selecting the text area, and pressing Alt+Enter, or by double-clicking the border. In the Create Hyperlink dialog box you can easily make the text area of the image a hotspot. For more information on using the Create Hyperlink dialog box, see Chapter 7.

Transparent GIFs

Okay, so you've been on the edge of your seat, waiting patiently to find out how transparency works. The truth is, it doesn't take Houdini to make a color disappear in an image—it's very easy. You use the Make Transparent button, which is the last button on the Image toolbar. This enables you to make one color in a selected GIF image transparent, allowing the background to show through. Unfortunately, because of a limitation in the JPEG format itself; namely, JPEG images cannot be made transparent. Figure 8-13 shows a before and after of using Make Transparent.

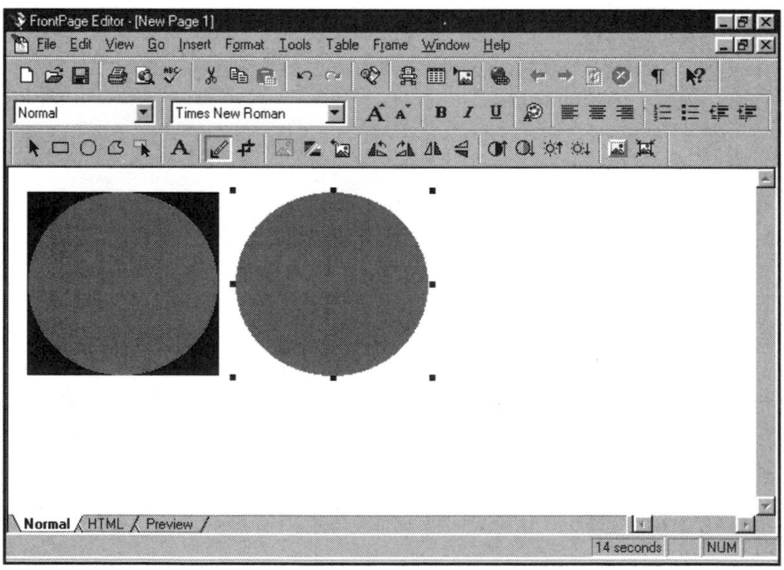

Figure 8-13

An image before and after using the Make Transparent option. The dark area around the circle has been made transparent, letting the background show through.

Here's how to make a color transparent:

1. Select an image to activate the Image toolbar.
2. Click the Make Transparent button. Once you click this button and move the mouse pointer over the image, the pointer changes to the Make Transparent pointer, which looks like a pencil.
3. On the image, click the color you want to make transparent.
4. *Voilà*—every part of the GIF that contained that color is now transparent, and the background of the page shows through the image.

WARNING If the image you're making transparent is in JPEG format, FrontPage displays a warning dialog box telling you that the image must be converted and asking if you really want to convert it. If you click Yes, the image is automatically converted to a GIF.

Only one color at a time can be transparent in a GIF image. If you select a new transparent color on an image that already has one transparent color set, the first transparent color reverts to its original color.

GIFs are used for transparency because they contain fewer colors and more solid areas to make transparent. Because JPEG images can contain a wide tonal range, using transparency on a JPEG image would be similar to poking holes sporadically through a photograph with a pin. The image would be transparent only where the holes appear.

TIP Many graphics packages try to use dithering in a GIF image to give it a more high-resolution appearance. The problem with dithering is that it actually uses many similar colors instead of a single color, which prevents transparency of a single color from working the way you would expect. When creating images that you want to make transparent, make sure that the background of the image is a single, solid color.

Image Manipulation—In the Editor

Most of the time when you insert an image, it'll look just the way you want it. It will be at the right size, with perfect color, clarity, and orientation, and you won't need to do anything to it. But, in those cases when the image does need a little tweaking, you'll be happy to learn that FrontPage has included a mini-editing suite on the Image toolbar. With the click of a button, you can fine-tune each image to get the look you're after. With a little experimentation, you may even create a whole new look, taking you in a direction you may not have thought of before.

Each of the remaining tools on the Image toolbar, with the exception of the Reset button, lets you change the appearance of an image from within the Editor. In all cases, you must select the image first, activating the Image toolbar, and then you can choose between the toolbar buttons. Only one effect can be applied at a time.

Cropping Images

Use the Crop tool on the Image toolbar to crop any image in the Editor. Cropping the image leaves a portion of the image visible, and removes the rest from view, altering the look and dimensions of the image.

With an image selected, click the Crop button. A selection border appears on the image, which you can resize to form the border of the area you want to keep. Any portion of the image remaining outside the border will be removed when cropped. Click any of the little cropping squares around the border, and then drag to resize to the area you want to keep. After you've resized the cropping border, you can move it around anywhere within the image by clicking inside the border and dragging it. You can resize, and drag the cropping border, as much as you like. When you have the portion of the image you want to keep positioned within the border, click the Crop tool again (or press Enter), and the area outside of the selection border will be cropped and removed.

Washout

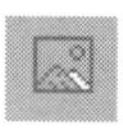

If you've inserted a background image on the page or in a table, you'll want to make sure it's light enough for text to appear on top of it. The Washout tool "ghosts" the image back, giving you a perfect background image. Although the Washout tool is great for creating background images, it can also be used to create an interesting effect for any image on your page.

Black & White

You can change any color image into a black and white grayscale image by using the Black & White button on the image toolbar. Since grayscale images contain no color, they have a smaller file size, which makes for a quicker download in the browser. When the image is saved, all of the color information is discarded, so if you think you might be changing your mind, keep that backup image that you made close at hand. Of course, we already know that we should always make a backup copy of our images *before* we edit them, right?

Reset

Having all of these cool tools at your fingertips could make you tempted to use too many of them at once on the same image. If you've become "button happy" and your image shows it, there is a cure: the Reset button. Clicking the Reset button removes all of the image editing you've done since the last save. Pay close attention to that last part: *since the last save*. We're always telling you to save, save, save, before lightning strikes and toasts your computer. Well, in this case, it's best to play around with the editing tools, get the image the way you want it, and then save. If you're worried about losing any information, it's always a good idea to have a backup copy of the image available, just in case.

Rotate, Reverse, and Flip

You can easily flip and flop you image, around and around if you like, by selecting the Rotate Left & Right, Reverse, and Flip buttons on the Image toolbar. This can be a real time-saver; for example, if you insert an image and it was accidentally saved upside down, you can easily make it right in the Editor. In the old days, you'd have to get the graphic artist to open the image themselves, resave the file the right way, and get it back to you. Whew! Look at the hassle you just saved yourself. Figure 8-14 shows the same image with these various effects applied to it.

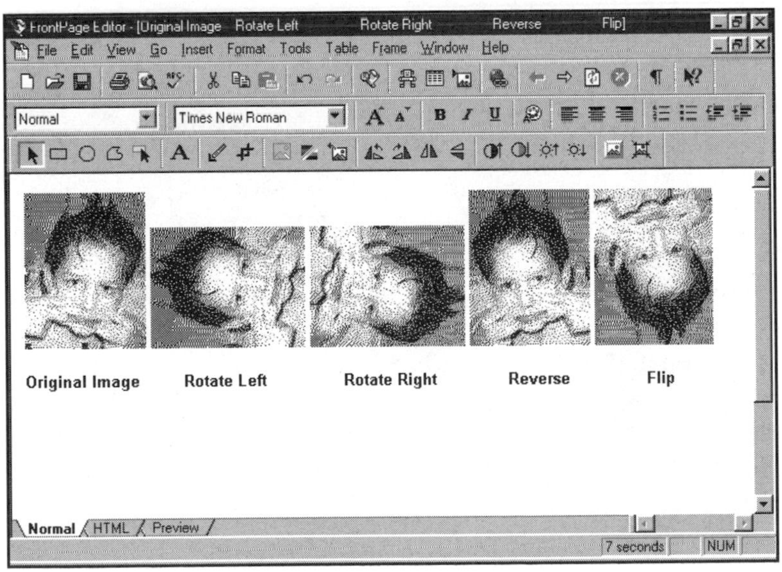

Figure 8-14

This screen shows the effects these buttons have when applied to the same image.

Contrast and Brightness

You can adjust the contrast and brightness of an image, incrementally, one click at a time, by using the More/Less Contrast and Brightness buttons on the Image toolbar. Remember that your images will be seen by a wide variety of people, with a wide range of vision. What looks too good to you on your machine may not look good to someone else on theirs. If you're trying to improve image quality, be careful when using these buttons; it's easy to make a mistake and actually create an image that's harder to view. These tools should be used for minor adjustments only. Use an image editing program, such as Image Composer, for any major work that may need to be done to an image.

Bevel

If you want your image to have a 3-D button look, select the image and click the Bevel button on the image toolbar. This is a great effect if you're making an image a hyperlink and you want to give it that pushbutton look. When you use the Bevel tool, FrontPage will darken the image itself alongside the top and right borders, and lighten it alongside the left and bottom borders, creating the 3D effect. This technique doesn't add any width or height to the image.

Resample

If you resize an image up or down in the Editor by dragging its borders, it may become blurred or out of focus as the image tries to compensate for the extra dimension. The Resample button can help clean up minor flaws in a resized image, but it's not a miracle worker. If you plan on doing major resizing, do it in your image editing software before you insert it into FrontPage. When you use the Resample technique, it will either resample down, decreasing the number of pixels in the image, or resample up, increasing the pixels in the image. When you resample down, pixels are deleted, and when you resample up, they're added, based on the surrounding pixel colors. Because you're either adding or deleting pixels, resampling will change the file size of the image. Once you've resampled an image and saved it, don't try to return the same image back to its original size; if you do, you'll have a mushed pixel mess on your hands. That's another good reason to always have a backup copy of the image around while you're playing with the editing tools.

Manipulating Background Images

If your page has a background image, you can apply any of the manipulation effects on the Image toolbar by clicking the effect of your choice when no other images are selected on the page.

Coming Up

The next chapter details the powerful FrontPage Components and forms, which let you add numerous types of functionality to your Web sites.

CHAPTER 9

FrontPage Components and Forms

We All Need a Break

Traditional hunters and gatherers knew how to make the most of their time—they conserved their energy by optimizing their food gathering, tool making, and other tasks. They also knew how important it was to rest; many hunting and gathering cultures worked fewer hours than we do today, and they allocated more time for leisure activities.

FrontPage lets you live a life like that again. You'll save so much time by using FrontPage's components and forms to create your Web sites that you'll be able to live in a cave and gather roots for dinner if you want to. It might be a little rough, though—there won't be an outlet to plug your television and food processor into, so you won't be able to watch *Melrose Place* and *Seinfeld* while you're chopping up those roots. Think you can handle it?

What Are Components?

FrontPage components are drop-in programs that add functionality to a Web site. For instance, you can add a Search Component to a page with a few clicks of the mouse, and instantly your page has a full-text search engine for your users. Using the traditional way, a Web site developer would have to do the following:

1. Create an HTML form that initiates the search.
2. Install a third-party full-text search engine on the Web server.
3. Write a CGI program on the Web server that connects the HTML form to the full-text search engine.

With components, you can forget all of this—there's no more need for complicated HTML and/or CGI programming to create sophisticated, interactive Web sites. Keep in mind that in order for components to work properly, the server hosting the site must have the FrontPage Server Extensions installed. These extensions are automatically installed with the Microsoft Personal Web Server and the FrontPage Personal Web Server, but must be manually installed with other Web servers. For more information on the Personal Web Servers and the FrontPage Server Extensions, consult Chapter 11.

You can insert FrontPage components in a couple of different ways, each one accessed via the Insert menu in the Editor. As each component is described throughout this chapter, the method by which you add it to the page is also described. When you select a component, you'll see one or more dialog boxes that let you configure it, and then the component is inserted on the page where your cursor was positioned. Some components are associated with forms, which are described later in this chapter.

The following sections provide a brief examination of the FrontPage components.

Implementing Search Functionality

To give your users the ability to look for matching words or phrases in the text of a site's pages or in the text of all the messages in a discussion group, you can insert a Search Component on your page. The Search Component can be configured to check every word used within the site for a match. (This feature is called *full-text searching*.)

Adding a Search Component

The Search Component, as seen in Figure 9-1, creates a form that allows users to enter one or more words to locate in the site.

FrontPage doesn't actually have to examine each page of the site; instead, it searches a list of words that's maintained by the FrontPage Server Extensions. FrontPage returns a list of pages that contain the word or words the user is searching for.

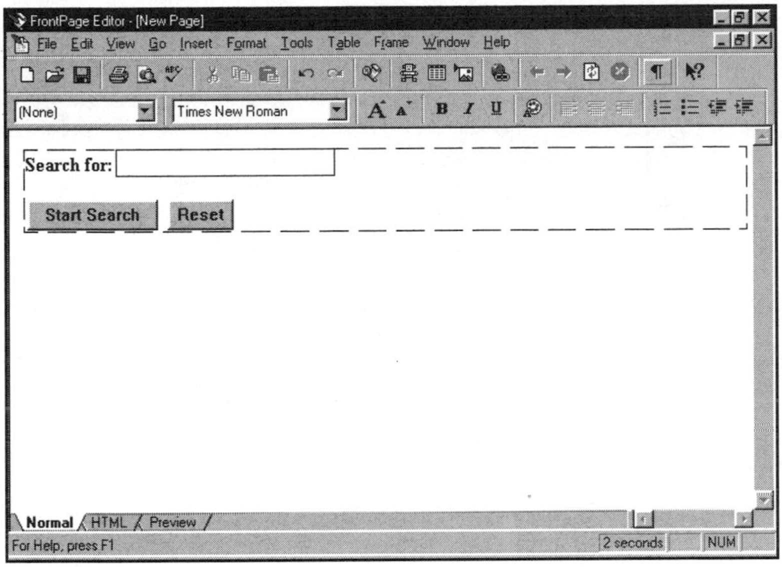

Figure 9-1

To add the ability to search for matching words or phrases in your site, do the following:

1. In the Editor, position your cursor at the place on your page where you want the upper-left corner of the search form (the label, text box, and buttons created by the Search Component) to appear.

TIP If you want to exclude certain pages from a search, you can save them directly in the _private folder under the folder for your site on the Web server. (FrontPage typically does not search a folder with a name that starts with an underscore.) If you save the page to a different location and then move it to the _private folder with the Explorer, it is recommended that you use Explorer's Recalculate Hyperlinks command to update the search index.

2. From the Insert menu, choose Active Elements, and then select Search Form from the pop-up menu. You'll see the Search Form Properties dialog box, as seen in Figure 9-2, which has two tabs, Search Form Properties and Search Results. Select the Search Form Properties tab.

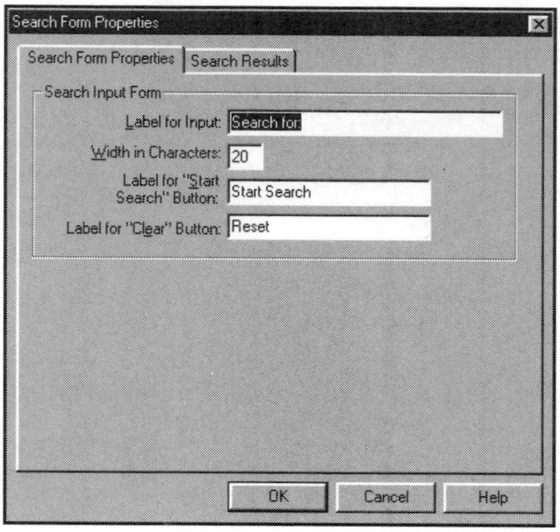

Figure 9-2

3. In the Label For Input text box, enter the text you want to use for the label of the text box. The default is *Search for:*.
4. In the Width In Characters text box, enter the width (in characters) of the input field.
5. In the Label For "Start Search" Button text box, type the text that will appear on the button that starts the search.
6. In the Label For "Clear" Button text box, type the text that will appear on the button that clears the search.

To configure the results of the Search component, select the Search Results tab on the Search Form Properties dialog box, seen in Figure 9-3.

1. In the Word List To Search text box, enter *All* if the search is intended for an entire Web site. If you created a discussion group using the Discussion Web Wizard, you can enter the name of a discussion group folder. This restricts the search to only entries in the discussion group.
2. You can also select check boxes to display the following information in the search results list:

   Score. This indicates the quality of the match, or how closely the results match what you searched for.

   File Date. This indicates the date and time the document containing the match was most recently modified.

File Size. This indicates the size of the document containing the match, in kilobytes. This can be especially useful for users on slow dial-up connections, who can see how large a document is before they download it.

3. When you finish entering the information in the Search Form Properties dialog box, click OK. FrontPage inserts the search form on your page in the Editor.

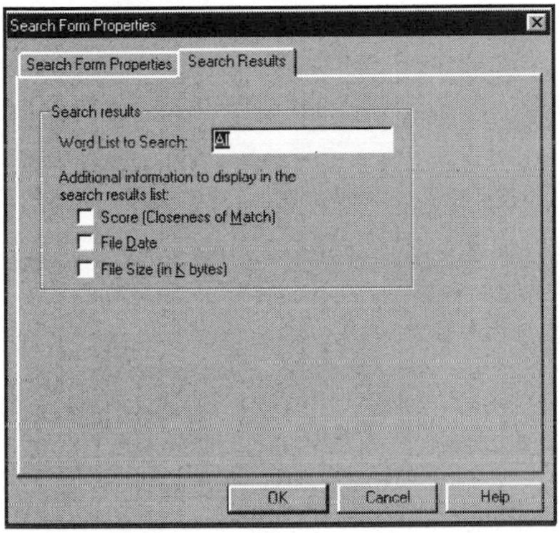

Figure 9-3

You can easily reconfigure the properties of your Search Component, by right-clicking on the component in the Editor, and selecting Form Page Component Properties from the pop-up menu, or by selecting the component and pressing Alt+Enter on your keyboard.

Limitations of the Search Component

One limitation of the Search Component concerns the updating of the search index. Suppose a page called test.htm has the word *Alice* on it when you save it to your Web site. The index maintained by the Search Component will record the fact that *test.htm* has *Alice* on it. However, suppose that you delete the word *Alice* from *test.htm*. The search index does not get updated automatically, so it will still show that *Alice* is on test.htm. Thus, if someone were to use the Search Component to search for *Alice,* they would get a false hit for *test.htm*. The way to fix this problem, and to update your search index so it has the correct information, is to use the Recalculate Hyperlinks command on the Tools menu in the Explorer. For more information on this command, see Chapter 3.

Creating a Timestamp

To insert a *timestamp*, which denotes the date and time the page was last edited or automatically updated, you use the Timestamp component.

Adding a Timestamp Component

To insert a timestamp on your page, do the following:

1. In the Editor, position your cursor at the place on your page where you want the timestamp to appear. Often, the component is placed following a phrase such as *This page was last modified.*
2. Select Timestamp from the Insert menu. Figure 9-4 shows the resulting Timestamp Properties dialog box.

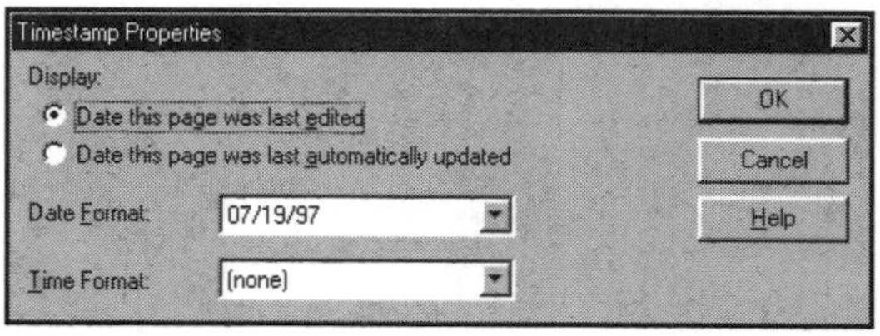

Figure 9-4

3. In the Display section, select the option for the date you want to display: either the date the page was last edited or the date the page was last automatically updated. There's a slight difference in meaning between "edited" and "updated." A page is considered to be *edited* when it is changed and saved to the Web server. A page is considered to be *updated* when it is changed and saved to the Web server or when an included page is changed. You can include pages on other pages using the Include Component, which is discussed later in this chapter.
4. From the drop-down lists, select a format for the date and time that you want displayed by the timestamp. The time format options containing the letters *TZ* indicate Time Zone. If you don't want to include either the date or the time, select None from the respective drop-down list.
5. When you finish entering your information in the Timestamp Properties dialog box, click OK. The timestamp is inserted on your page. You can then format the text used for the timestamp information using the standard tools within the Editor.

Figure 9-5 shows an example of the Timestamp component in the Editor.

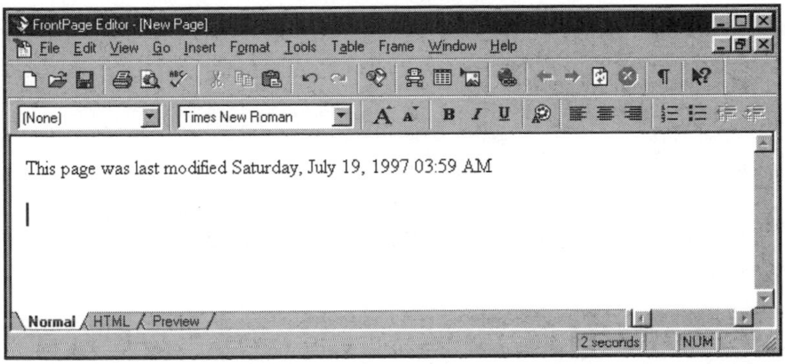

Figure 9-5

Including a Table of Contents

You can use the Table Of Contents component to create an outline for your Web site, with links to each page. You can direct the component to update the outline each time pages are added, deleted, or edited.

Adding a Table Of Contents Component

To insert a table of contents (TOC) on your page, do the following:

1. In the Editor, position your cursor at the place on your page where you want the TOC to appear.
2. From the Insert menu, choose Table of Contents. You'll see the Table Of Contents Properties dialog box, as shown in Figure 9-6 below.

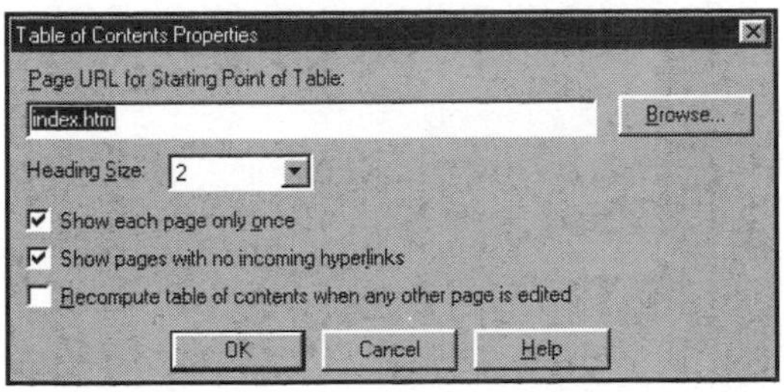

Figure 9-6

3. Enter the page URL of the page you want the TOC to begin with. The TOC will include all pages that have links that originate from the page you select. Specify the home page, often called *default.htm* or *index.htm,* of your Web site if you want a full TOC. If you have a site open in the FrontPage Explorer, you can click the Browse button to see a list of pages in the site. If you do so, select a page in the Current Web dialog box, and then click OK.
4. From the Heading Size drop-down list, select a heading size for the first entry in your TOC. You can select a number from 1 (the largest size) to 6 (the smallest size), or select None if you want to use the default size.
5. You can select check boxes to have FrontPage do the following:
   - **Show each page only once.** Select this check box to allow each page to appear in the TOC only once. If a page in your site has multiple links that can be traced back to your starting page, it can appear more than once unless you check this option.
   - **Show pages with no incoming hyperlinks.** Select this check box to include orphan pages in your TOC. (These are pages that do not have any incoming links from other pages in the site.)
   - **Recompute table of contents when any other page is edited.** Select this check box to automatically re-create the TOC whenever pages are added, deleted, or edited in your site. If your site is large and if pages are edited often, having this option selected can slow down your work; for example, when saving. An alternative is to manually re-create the TOC by opening and saving the page containing the Table Of Contents component.
6. When you finish entering your information in the dialog box, click OK. Your TOC appears on the page in the Editor. You cannot format the individual entries in the TOC, any formatting changes you apply will be applied to all of the entries. For example, you can't set both the heading in italics and the list as normal.

Figure 9-7 shows the Table Of Contents component as it appears in the Editor.

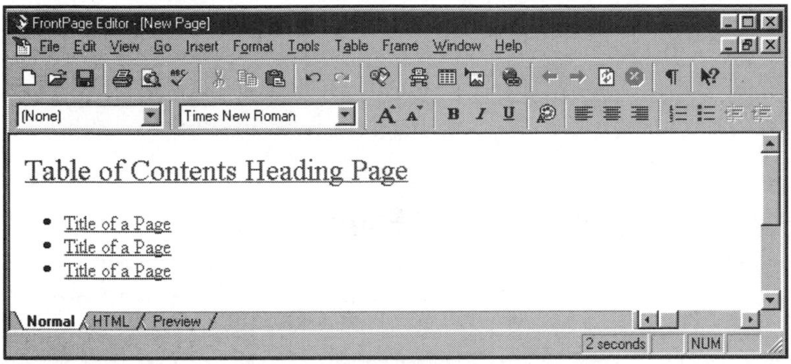

Figure 9-7

Inserting a Comment

Sometimes you'll be the person adding all of the pages in the site and creating the structure but someone else will be actually placing content on the page in the Editor. You can leave them a comment on the page, and that text will appear only in the Editor, not in the browser. This is also very useful if you want to leave yourself a reminder of an important piece of information about the page that you don't want to forget. Comments are kind of like sticky notes in HTML.

Adding a Comment

To insert a comment on the page, do the following:

1. In the Editor, position your cursor at the place on the current page where you want the comment to appear.
2. From the Insert menu, choose FrontPage Component. Then select Comment in the Insert FrontPage Component dialog box, and then click OK. You'll see the Comment dialog box, as seen in Figure 9-8.

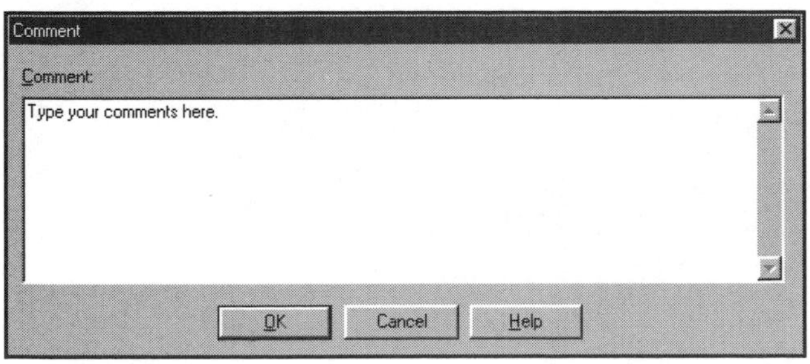

Figure 9-8

In the Comment dialog box, you can type the message you want to leave on the page. When you're finished entering the comment, click OK. In the Editor, you'll see the text in color, just as you've typed it, with the word "Comment:" preceding it. This text will be visible only in the Editor, and not in the browser.

Presenting One Page on Another Page

With the Include Page Component, you can present the entire contents of a page wherever you want on another page. The page you insert must be a page from the current Web site. The Include Page Component differs from the Scheduled Include Component (discussed later in this chapter) in that it presents a page on another page *at all times,* and not just at specified times.

Suppose you have a "Site in Summary" section in your company's Web site, which presents the most important pages in the site in one place, such as pages for urgent news and company information that your sales force needs to know. This kind of section might be good to include for those viewers who are "on the go" and who only need to see certain pages of your site. Plenty of business people don't even have the time to look at specific pages of your site one by one—if they're scanning the site for information in addition to their other daily tasks, you can understand how their time is limited. Your "Site in Summary" section can be a one-page section, in which you use several Include Page components, one for each page you want to pull in from the rest of your site. The included pages can be presented in full, one after another, and all of the content will be scrollable as a single page.

Adding an Include Page Component

To insert the contents of a page on another page, do the following:

1. In the Editor, position your cursor at the place on the current page where you want the inserted page to appear.
2. From the Insert menu, choose FrontPage Component. Then select Include Page in the Insert FrontPage Component dialog box, and click OK. You'll see the Include Page Component Properties dialog box, as shown in Figure 9-9.

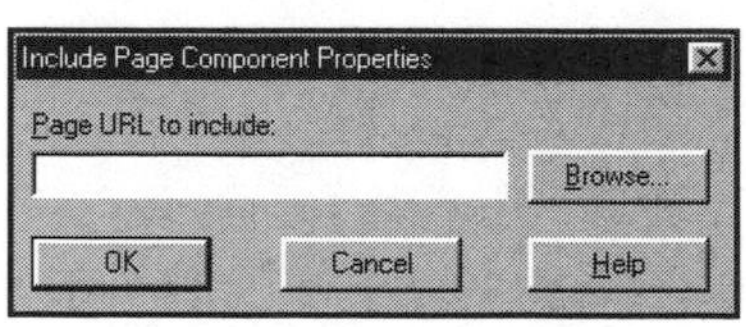

Figure 9-9

3. In the Page URL To Include text box, enter the page URL of the page you want to have appear. You can click the Browse button to see a list of pages in the current site; if you do so, select a page and click OK.
4. After you enter the page URL, click OK. The contents of that page are inserted on your page in the Editor.

TIP You cannot perform the previous steps without first having a "current" page open in the Editor.

Another fun use for the Include Page component is to include the copyright information for your company on every page, or if you want to include a special note or disclaimer, you can include that as well. And if you ever need to change the contents of the Include, just open the page it's calling and make any changes you need to, and those changes will appear on each page that uses that Include component.

Figure 9-10 shows an example of a note included at the bottom of a page, using the Include Page component.

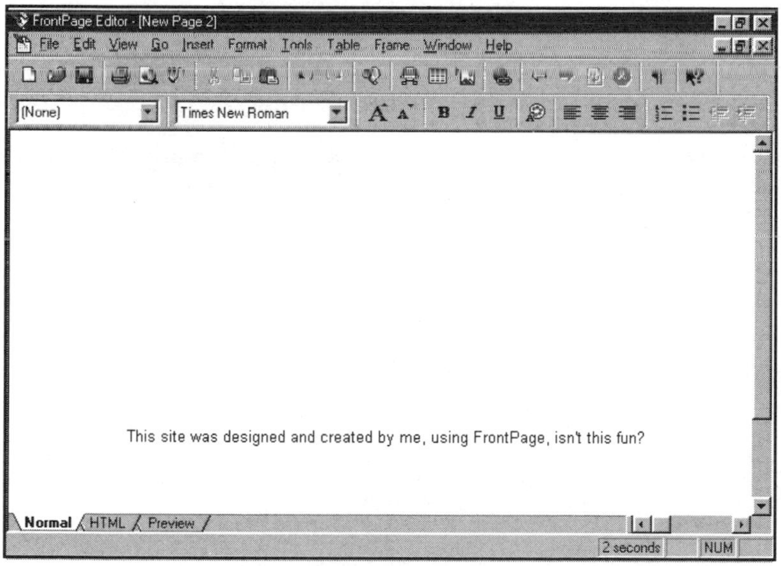

Figure 9-10

Making Images Appear at a Certain Time

You can use the Scheduled Image component to make an image available to users during a specified time period. The image is displayed on a page when the time period begins, and it's removed when the time has expired.

For example, suppose your human resources department is trying to increase employee enrollment in the company's 401K plan, and it's running a seven-day special sign-up event on its intranet pages. The pages will feature different "catchy" images each day. To avoid having to update the images manually every day, you can insert several Scheduled Image components to make those images appear automatically when you want them to.

TIP To be certain that a Scheduled Image component works on the day that the image is scheduled to appear or disappear, either make a change to your site or use the Recalculate Hyperlinks command in the Explorer on the same day to "refresh" the links and other information on the pages. These actions act as a reminder to FrontPage to update the information related to the components.

Adding a Scheduled Image Component

To make an image appear during a specified time period, take the following steps.

1. In the Editor, position your cursor at the place on your page where you want the image to appear.
2. From the Insert menu, choose FrontPage Component. Then select Scheduled Image in the Insert Component dialog box, and click OK. You'll see the Scheduled Image Properties dialog box, as seen in Figure 9-11.

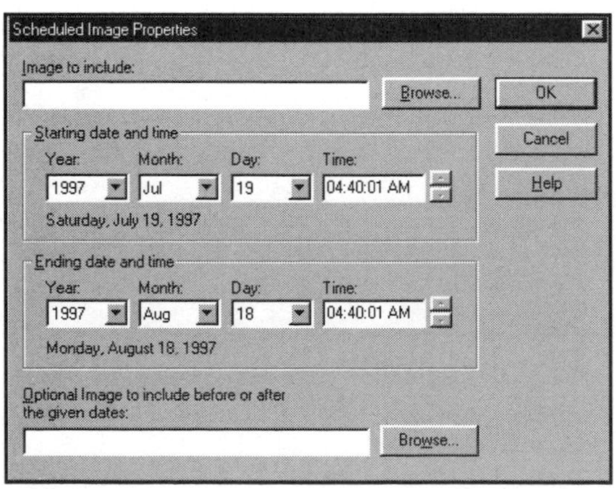

Figure 9-11

3. In the Image To Include text box, enter the name of the image you want to have appear. You can click the Browse button to see a list of images available in the currently open site in the Explorer; if you do so, select an image and then click OK.
4. Enter the starting date and time and the ending date and time for the period that you want the image to appear.
5. You can also specify a placeholder image that will appear in the same location before and after the scheduled image appears. If you want to do so, type the name of the image in the text box near the bottom of the dialog box, or click Browse to see a list of images available in the current site. This placeholder image will fill up the space when the scheduled image does not appear.
6. When you finish entering your information in the Scheduled Image Properties dialog box, click OK.

If you're within the time period you specified for the image to appear, the image will appear on the page. If you specified the image to appear at a future time (a more likely scenario) and did not specify a placeholder image, the words *Expired Scheduled Image* will appear in the component on the screen in the Editor (but not in a browser). If you see these words, don't worry—the image will appear at its scheduled time. If you specified a placeholder image to appear when the scheduled image does not appear, that image will appear in the Editor and in the browser when the scheduled image does not appear.

Making Content Appear at a Certain Time

You can use the Scheduled Include component to make specific content available to users in the same way that the Scheduled Image component works with images. In fact, using the same 401K scenario discussed in the previous section, you can make an entire page of 401K information appear at a certain time. The Scheduled Include component inserts an entire page at a specified time.

Like the Scheduled Image component, the Scheduled Include component works only if a change is made to the site or the Recalculate Hyperlinks command is executed on the day the content is scheduled to appear.

Adding a Scheduled Include Component

To make the contents of a page appear during a specified time period, do the following:

1. In the Editor, position your cursor at the place on your page where you want the content to appear.
2. From the Insert menu, choose FrontPage Component. Then select Scheduled Include in the Insert FrontPage Component dialog box, and click OK. You'll see the Scheduled Include Page Component Properties dialog box, as seen in Figure 9-12 below.

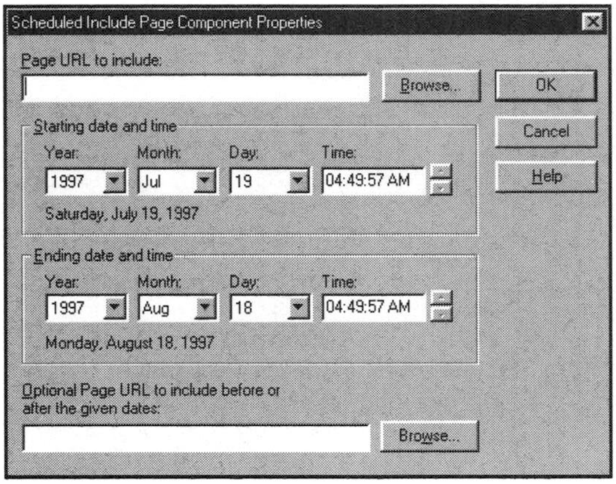

Figure 9-12

3. In the Page URL To Include text box, enter the page URL of the page you want to have appear. You can click the Browse button to see a list of pages in your site; if you do so, select one and click OK.
4. Enter the starting date and time and the ending date and time for the period that you want the page to appear.
5. To present the contents of another page in the same location before and after the scheduled page appears, type the name of the page in the text box at the bottom of the dialog box, or click Browse to see a list of pages currently available in your site. You can specify that a simple placeholder page appear at these times, which fills up the space when the scheduled page does not appear.
6. When you finish entering your information in the Scheduled Include Page Component Properties dialog box, click OK.

Confirming User-Entered Information

When you are using your site to collect information from users, you want to do everything you can to make sure that the information they provide is correct. In particular, you should give them an opportunity to review the text that they've submitted. Not only does this give them an opportunity to discover any typing errors, but it emphasizes that the information they provide is important. Maybe they'll read it a second time to make sure it really says what they want it to say.

TIP In FrontPage, you can specify validation rules for a form field; for example, you can specify that numbers be within a certain range, or that a text field contain only certain characters. FrontPage automatically generates the JavaScript or VBScript directly onto the page so that the browser will enforce those validation rules. For more information on validation rules, see the section "Validating Form Fields," later in this chapter.

If you've seen Web pages or other forums where information that you've entered is presented to you later for your confirmation, you've seen an example of this process. If you find that some of the information is incorrect, you can usually go back to the original page, change it, and resubmit it, and if all the information is correct, you can click a button to say so. The Confirmation Field Component manages this process of presenting the information back to the viewer. (For more information on confirmation pages, see the section titled "Creating a Confirmation Page" later in this chapter.)

The Confirmation Field Component presents the contents of one form field—a single item such as name, age, or occupation—on a form confirmation page. (We'll discuss forms and form fields later in this chapter.) Each form field requires a separate Confirmation Field Component, but several such components can be combined on a single page. So if a user has entered lots of information in different form fields, you can use a page of Confirmation Field components to replicate that information in one place for the user to confirm.

TIP Confirmation Field components are case-sensitive. That means that *FirstName* is not the same as *firstname*.

Adding a Confirmation Field Component

To present the contents of one form field on a confirmation page, do the following:

1. In the Editor, position your cursor at the place on the confirmation page where you want the Confirmation Field component to appear.
2. From the Insert menu, choose FrontPage Component. Then select Confirmation Field in the Insert FrontPage Component dialog box, and click OK. You'll see the Confirmation Field Properties dialog box, as shown in Figure 9-13.

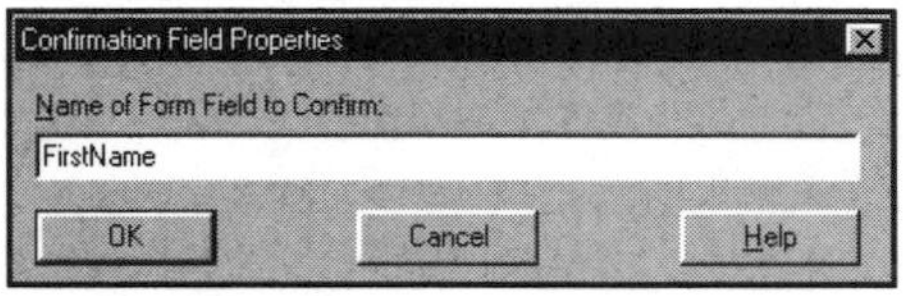

Figure 9-13

3. Enter the name of the form field whose contents you want to confirm.

When you click OK, the Confirmation Field component appears in the Editor as a set of brackets surrounding the name of the field you just typed in. In a browser, the field's contents are shown to the user in place of the Confirmation Field component. It's a good idea to provide appropriate text on the page to make sure users know what information is being shown back to them.

Inserting a Configuration Variable

You can insert the contents of a configuration variable (also called a *parameter*) on a page by using the Substitution Component. This is useful for many purposes, such as for noting who created or modified a page, or the page's URL. The Substitution component can also be used to present text strings that you might want to modify later, such as a company's fax number.

Adding a Substitution Component

Here's how to insert the value of a configuration variable on a page.

1. In the Editor, place your cursor on the page where you want to insert the Substitution component.
2. From the Insert menu, choose FrontPage Component. Then select Substitution in the Insert FrontPage Component dialog box, and click OK. You'll see the Substitution Component Properties dialog box, shown in Figure 9-14.

Figure 9-14

3. From the drop-down list, select a configuration variable. If you've added parameters to your site, they will appear in this drop-down list.

   When you click OK, the Substitution component appears on the page in the Editor, filled in with the value of the configuration variable.

For more information on adding configuration variables and setting their values, see Chapter 3.

Editing a Component's Properties

If you want to modify a component's properties, you don't have to replace the entire component—you can change its properties instead. To edit a component's properties, simply right-click the component (when you move your cursor over the component, the cursor will appear), and choose Component Properties from the pop-up menu. The Properties dialog box for the component appears; you can make your changes here. When you finish, click OK to exit the dialog box and return to your page in the Editor.

Creating and Using Forms

A *form* is a collection of text and *form fields* that allows users to enter information. FrontPage form fields include one-line text boxes, scrolling text boxes, check boxes, option buttons (called *radio buttons* in FrontPage), and drop-down menus. In addition, you can add command buttons (known as *pushbuttons* in FrontPage) to your form to perform actions. Each of these fields are located on the Forms toolbar, which you can make visible, if it's not already, by selecting Forms Toolbar from the View menu. Figure 9-15 shows an example of the form fields in the Editor.

You use a combination of these form fields to collect the information you want from the user. For instance, in an intranet setting, forms can be used to gather and store employee identification information. Or perhaps you want to find out what users think of your Web site or the products showcased in your site. Users provide answers to your questions in the form fields.

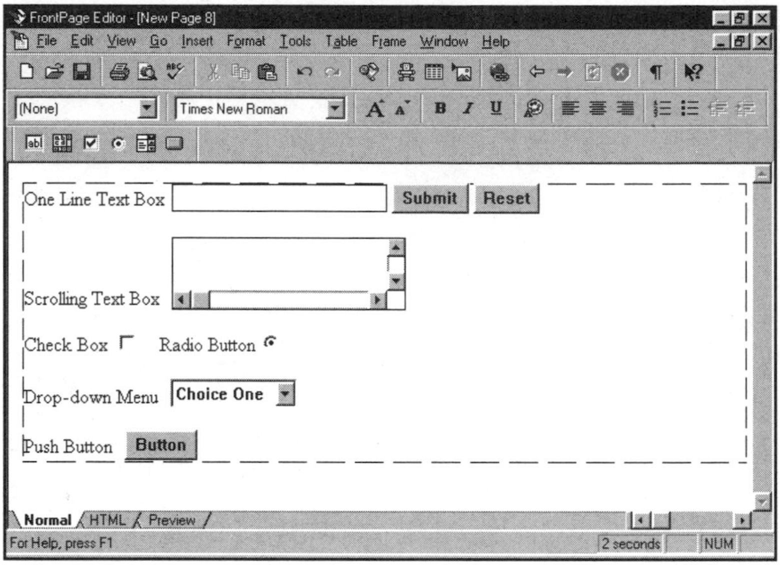

Figure 9-15

You create a form whenever you add a form field to a page. Some templates (such as the User Registration, Feedback Form, and Confirmation Form templates) and some wizards (such as the Discussion Web Wizard) create pages that already contain forms.

Forms use applications called *handlers* on Web servers that take the data from the form fields and process it. The handler can also respond to the user when it receives the input, by presenting a confirmation page so that the user can confirm the information he or she submitted. So, in a sense, the handler is a go-between for the form and the Web server. For example, a handler can be a Discussion component, Registration component, custom ISAPI DLL, NSAPI module, or CGI script. (These handlers are discussed in the section "Assigning a Form Handler," later in this chapter.)

Creating a Data-Collection Form

Once you know how to create a form, the process will seem fairly simple, but learning it can be a little tricky. We'll step through the process by modifying two pages created using FrontPage's Feedback Form and Confirmation Page templates. The templates already contain working examples of forms and confirmation pages; we'll create more examples on these pages so you can learn how to build them yourself.

Let's get going with some preliminaries.

Creating a Feedback Form Page

We'll begin by creating a Feedback Form page in the Editor.

1. Choose New from the File menu, select Feedback Form from the list of templates and wizards on the Page tab, in the New dialog box that appears, and click OK.
2. When the page appears in the Editor, save it with the title *Feedback Form* and give it the name within the current site, *feedback.htm*. We'll refer to this page from now on as the Feedback Form, an example of which is shown in Figure 9-16.

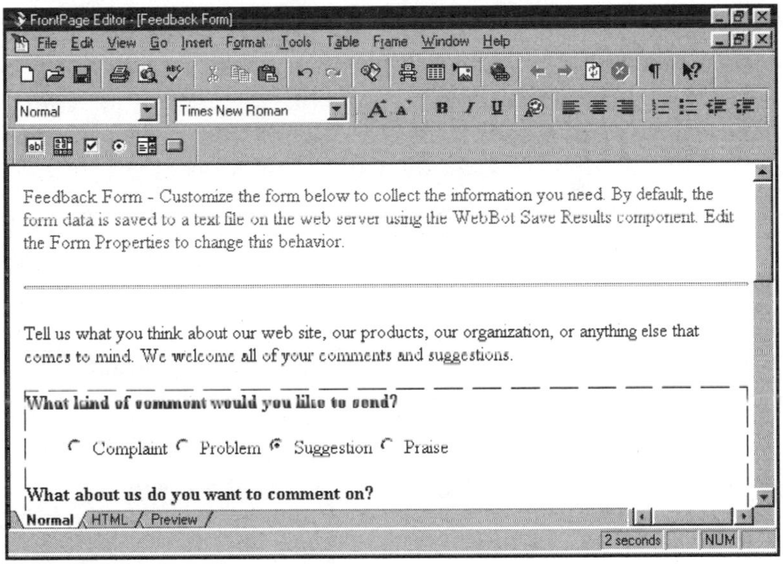

Figure 9-16

The Feedback Form includes several fields. In fact, it includes at least one of each of the five field types, plus two command buttons (push-buttons):

Option button. The buttons on the page under the line "What kind of comment would you like to send?" are option buttons (radio buttons). These buttons act as a group; you'll find out more about their group functions shortly. Each of the buttons was added to the form separately, and the text for each was typed next to that button. You use option buttons when you want the user to be able to select a single option from a group of options. (You can also use a drop-down menu for this purpose.)

Drop-down list. The field below the line "What about us do you want to comment on?" is a drop-down list. You can customize the list choices when you modify the field properties. A drop-down list allows the user to select one or more items (which is why these form fields are often called *drop-down menus*).

One-line text box. The text box next to the drop-down list is a one-line text box. Users can type text in this box. You set the width of this box as part of its properties.

Scrolling text box. The large box under the line "Enter your comments in the space provided below:" is a scrolling text box. This type of text box allows users to type lengthy comments.

Check box. The box near the bottom of the page next to the line "Please contact me as soon as possible regarding this matter" is a check box. When a user clicks a check box, a check mark appears in it. Use check boxes to offer the user a Yes/No choice.

Command button. The two buttons at the bottom of the Feedback Form labeled *Submit Comments* and *Clear Form* are command buttons (pushbuttons). A user clicks these buttons to perform either of these tasks.

Now we'll replicate some of these fields and the buttons directly below them on the Feedback Form, to show you how to create them.

Creating an Option Button Group

Let's create a group of two option buttons that resembles the group of four on the Feedback Form.

1. Position your cursor following the option button labeled *Praise* below the line "What kind of comment would you like to send?" (The cursor should be blinking beside the *e* in *Praise*.) Hold down the Shift key and press Enter.
2.  With the cursor on the blank line you just created, just below the Complaint option button, click the Radio Button button on the Forms toolbar. (Remember, FrontPage uses the term *radio button* rather than option button.) If the Forms toolbar is not visible, choose the Forms Toolbar command from the View menu. The button appears on the screen.
3. Right-click on the button you just inserted, and choose Form Field Properties from the pop-up menu. Figure 9-17 shows the resulting Radio Button Properties dialog box.

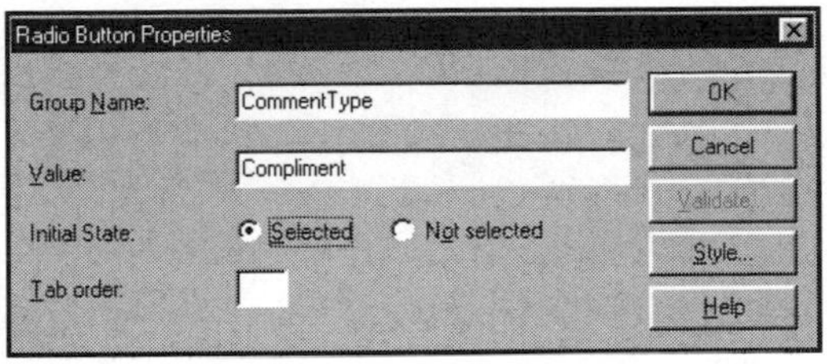

Figure 9-17

4. Fill in the following information:

   Group Name. Enter the word *CommentType*. This is the name of the group of option buttons you'll be creating. You'll use this name later on the confirmation page. If you give the same group name to a series of buttons, only one of them can be selected by a user. Assigning the same group name is what actually creates a group of option buttons.

   Value. Enter the word *Compliment*. The word will appear on the confirmation page if the user selects this option while using the Feedback Form. You'll see how this works shortly.

   Initial State. Select the Selected option. When the user sees the Feedback Form, this option will be selected as the default. Only one option button in a group can be initialized as Selected (because only one option in a group can ever be selected). FrontPage doesn't require you to initialize any option button as Selected; this is your choice.

5. Click OK to exit the Radio Button Properties dialog box, and then position your cursor next to the Option button you just inserted and type the word *Compliment*. You've just created an option button that, when selected, indicates that the user is sending a compliment back to you.
6. Using the same procedure, create another option button immediately to the right of the Compliment button. (You might want to press the spacebar to create a little space between the buttons.) In the Radio Button Properties dialog box, give the option button the same group name, *CommentType,* but give it the value of *Criticism*. Select the Not Selected option for its initial state. When you finish, click OK to exit the Radio Button Properties dialog box.
7. Type the word *Criticism* following the option button you just inserted. The option button is now complete. Figure 9-18 shows a sample of how the option button section of your page should look.

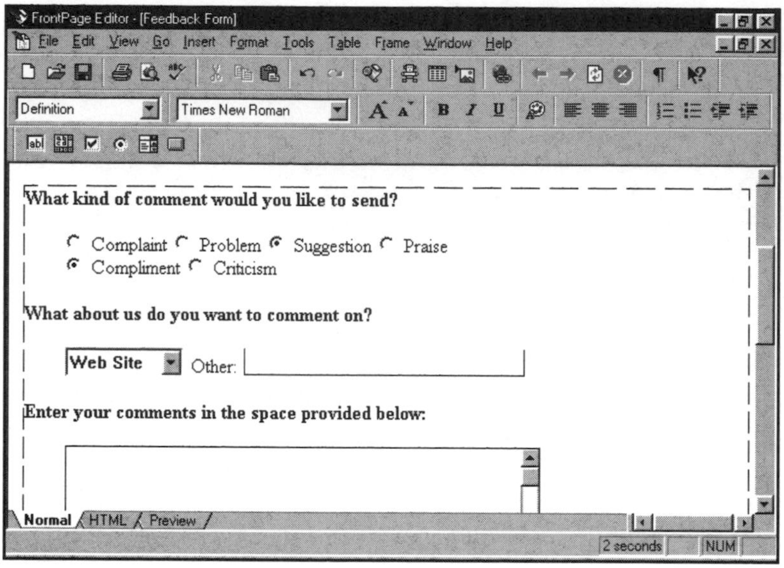

Figure 9-18

Make sure you save your changes as you go along.

You've just created a two-button group called *CommentType*. If you look at the properties for the buttons directly above (the Complaint, Problem, Suggestion, and Praise buttons), you'll see that their group name is *MessageType*. You've just created a similar group. You can create any option button group in the same way.

Creating a Drop-Down List

Next, we'll create a four-element drop-down list (known as a drop-down menu in FrontPage) directly below the existing one.

1. Position the cursor following the one-line text box below the sentence "What about us do you want to comment on?" and then hold down the Shift key and press Enter.
2.  With the cursor just below the existing drop-down list, click the Drop-Down Menu toolbar button. A drop-down list appears on the page.
3. Right-click the new drop-down list and choose Form Field Properties from the pop-up menu. You'll see the Drop-Down Menu Properties dialog box, as seen in Figure 9-19.

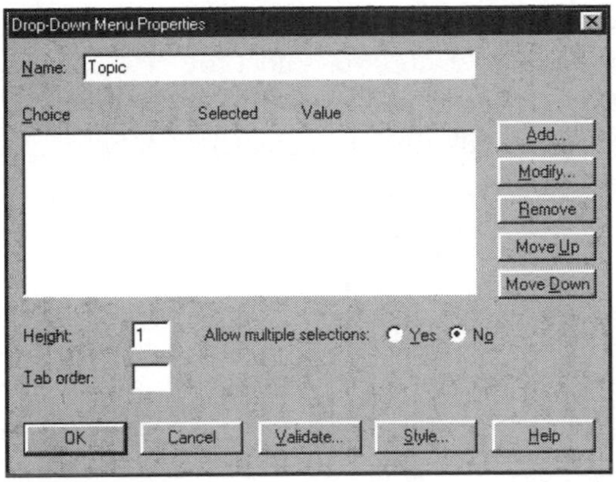

Figure 9-19

4. Enter the name *Topic* in the Name text box. You'll use this name later on when you configure the confirmation page.
5. Click the Add button to add an element to the box. You'll see the Add Choice dialog box, shown in Figure 9-20 below.

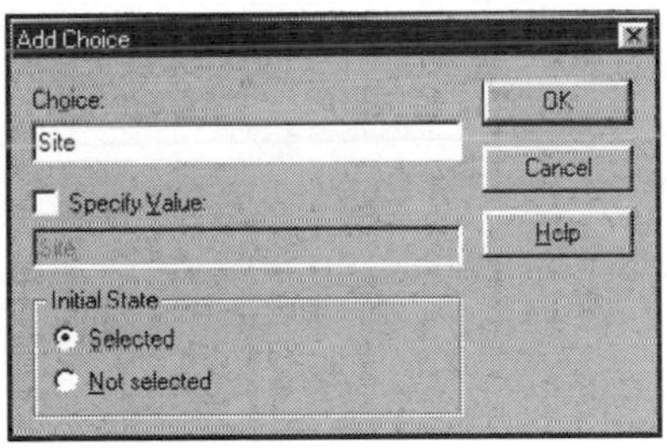

Figure 9-20

6. In the Choice text box, enter the word *Site*. By default, the value of this element is the same as its name; if you want the value to be different from the name, select the Specify Value check box, and then enter the value. In the Initial State section, select the Selected option. This sets the Site element as the item displayed in the drop-down list when the user first sees it in a browser.

   Click OK when you finish entering information in the Add Choice dialog box.

7. Add three more elements, named Technical Support, Prices, and Other, using the same procedure. For each one, select the Not Selected option in the Initial State section of the Add Choice dialog box. The width of the drop-down list will automatically expand to accommodate the widest element you add. Figure 9-21 shows the Drop-Down Menu Properties dialog box after all the elements have been added.

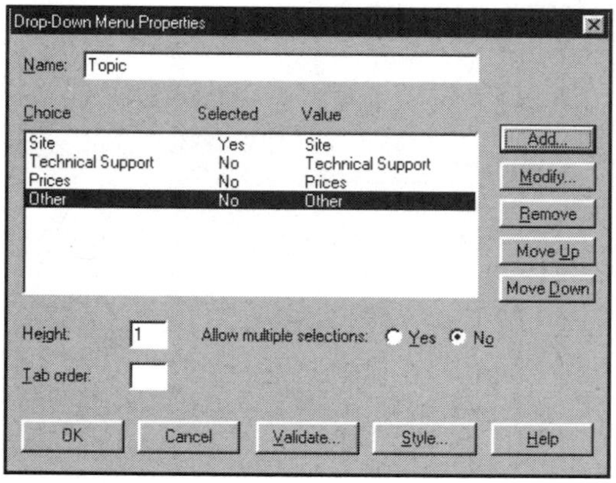

Figure 9-21

8. You can click the following buttons in the Drop-Down Menu Properties dialog box to perform some additional functions:

   Modify. To modify any element in the list, select the element and click Modify. You'll see the Modify Choice dialog box for that element.

   Remove. To remove any element from the list, select the element and click Remove.

   Move Up. To move an element up in the list, select the element and click Move Up. (The elements will appear in the drop-down list in the order that they appear in this list.)

   Move Down. To move an element down in the list, select the element and click Move Down.

   In addition, you can enter the height of the list in the Height text box. Keep the height at 1 for now. The height of the list determines how the list is displayed. In most browsers, if Height is set to 1, the drop-down list displays only one element and you can click the down arrow button to view the rest of the elements. If Height is set to a value greater than 1, the list typically behaves like a scrollable text box, where the number of elements displayed at one time equals the Height.

Finally, for the Allow Multiple Selections option buttons, select the No option to disallow multiple selections. Clicking Yes allows the user to select more than one element from the list. This is useful in many situations, such as when offering the user choices of receiving information about multiple products that you can display in a drop-down list.

9. When you finish entering the information, click OK. Figure 9-22 shows a sample of how the drop-down list section of your page should look.

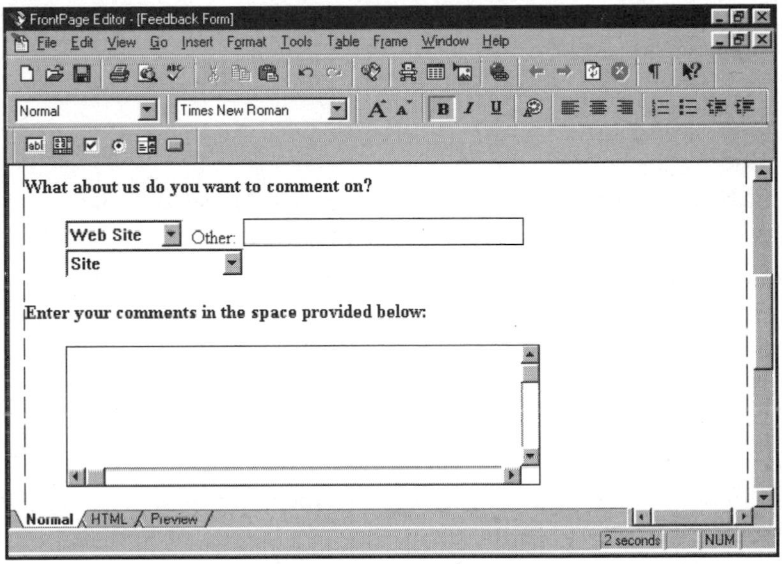

Figure 9-22

You've created a four-element drop-down list. You can create a drop-down list with as many items as you like, in the same fashion.

Creating a One-Line Text Box

Next, we'll create a one-line text box that appears next to the drop-down list, for users to enter an element if they selected (Other) from the drop-down list.

1. Position the cursor to the right of the drop-down list you just created. Press the spacebar to create a little space between the drop-down list and the text box. Type *OTHER:*, and then press the spacebar one more time.

2. 

Click the One-Line Text Box toolbar button. A one-line text box appears.

3. Right-click the new one-line text box and choose Form Field Properties from the pop-up menu. You'll see the Text Box Properties dialog box, as seen below in Figure 9-23.

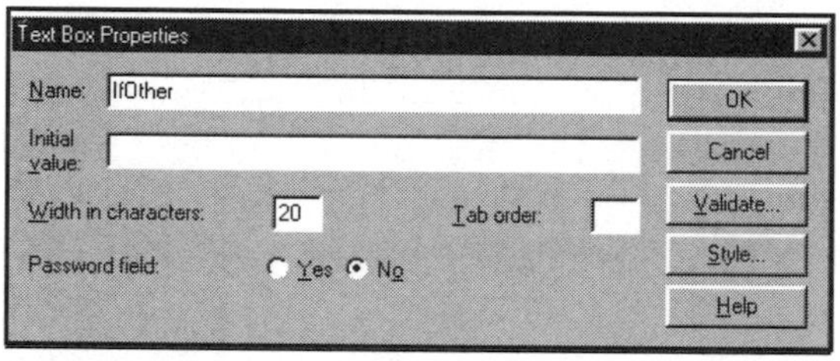

Figure 9-23

4. In the Name text box, enter *IfOther*. You'll use this name later on when configuring the confirmation page.

5. Do not enter anything in the Initial Value text box. In this instance, because the user will enter additional elements in the text box, there's no need to add an initial value. If you do enter an initial value, it appears in the text box when the user first views the form. The user can change the text if desired.

6. Type *20* in the Width In Characters text box if the current value is different. This sets the initial width of the text box to a rather wide 20 characters, giving it a user-friendly look. If you want to reset the size later, you can click and drag the text box's size handles in the Editor.

7. Select No in the Password Field section to specify that the text box will not be used as a password field in this instance.

8. You can click the Validate button if you want to set restrictions on the information that a user can enter in the one-line text box. For instance, you can set a maximum amount of characters that the user can enter in the text box, or restrict the entries to text or numbers only.

9. Click OK after you finish entering information in the Text Box Properties dialog box. Figure 9-24 shows a sample of how the drop-down lists and the one-line text boxes should look on your page.

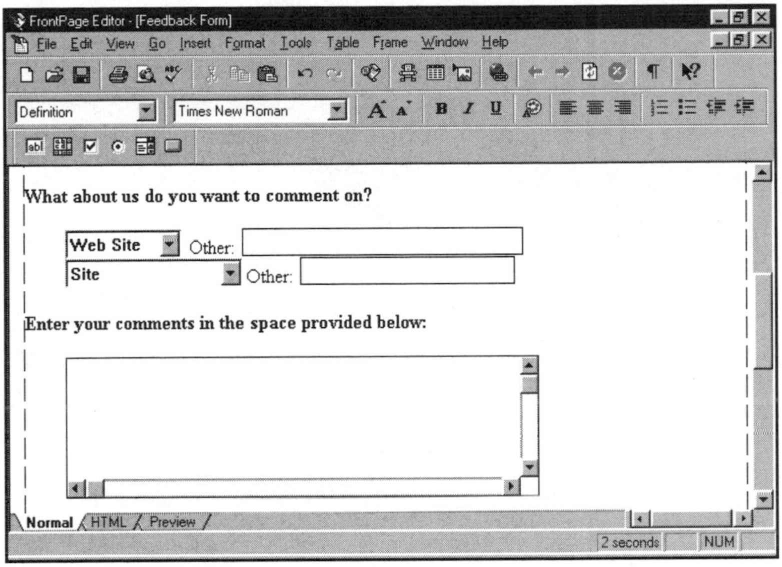

Figure 9-24

You've just created a one-line text box in which a user can enter additional comments.

Creating a Scrolling Text Box

Next, we'll create a scrolling text box directly below the existing one on the Feedback Form.

1. Position the cursor to the right of the existing scrolling text box, below the line "Enter your comments in the space provided below:" and then press Enter twice.
2.  Click the Scrolling Text Box toolbar button, and a scrolling text box appears on the page.
3. Right-click the new scrolling text box and choose Form Field Properties from the pop-up menu. You'll see the Scrolling Text Box Properties dialog box, as seen in Figure 9-25.
4. In the Name text box, enter *UserComments*. You'll use this name later on when configuring the confirmation page.
5. Do not enter anything in the Initial Value text box. In this instance, because the user will enter additional elements in the scrolling text box, there's no need to add an initial value.

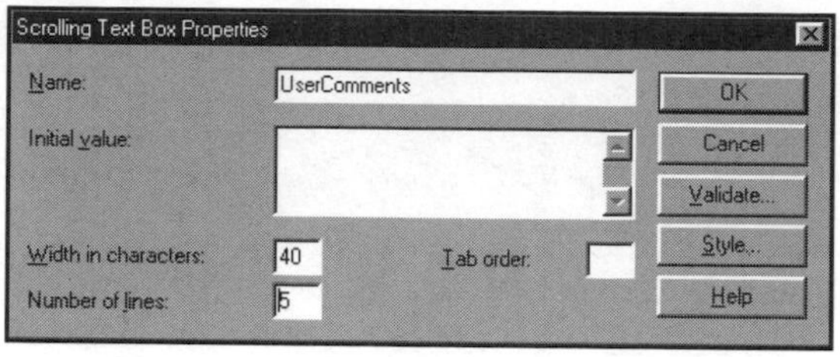

Figure 9-25

6. Type *40* in the Width In Characters text box. This sets the initial width of the text box to a wide 40 characters, giving it a user-friendly look. If you want to reset the size later, you can click and drag the text box's size handles in the Editor.
7. Type *5* in the Number Of Lines text box. This sets the height of the scrolling text box in number of lines, and 5 is a good number to start with. Because the text box is scrollable, a user can enter more than five lines of text, and it's often unnecessary to set the initial height to more than five lines.
8. You can click the Validate button if you want to set restrictions on the information that a user can enter in the scrolling text box. For instance, you can set a maximum amount of characters that the user can enter in the text box, or you can restrict the entries to text or numbers only.
9. Click OK after you finish entering information in the Scrolling Text Box Properties dialog box. Figure 9-26 shows a sample of how the scrolling text box should look on your page.

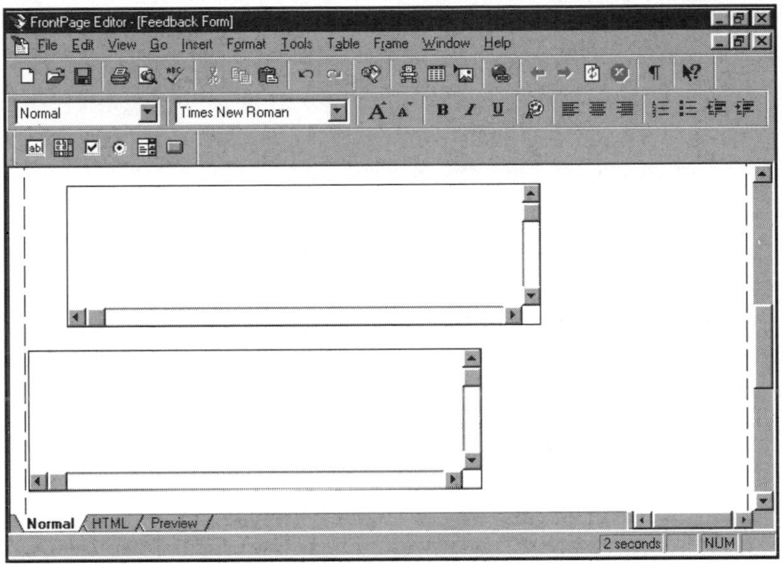

Figure 9-26

Creating a Check Box

Next, we'll create a check box below the existing check box at the bottom of the Feedback Form. The check box will allow the user to indicate that he or she wants more information sent via e-mail.

1. Position your cursor at the end of the line that reads "Please contact me as soon as possible regarding this matter." Hold down the Shift key and press Enter.
2.  With the cursor underneath the check box, click the Check Box toolbar button. A new check box appears on the page.
3. Right-click the new check box and choose Form Field Properties from the pop-up menu. You'll see the Check Box Properties dialog box, as seen in Figure 9-27.

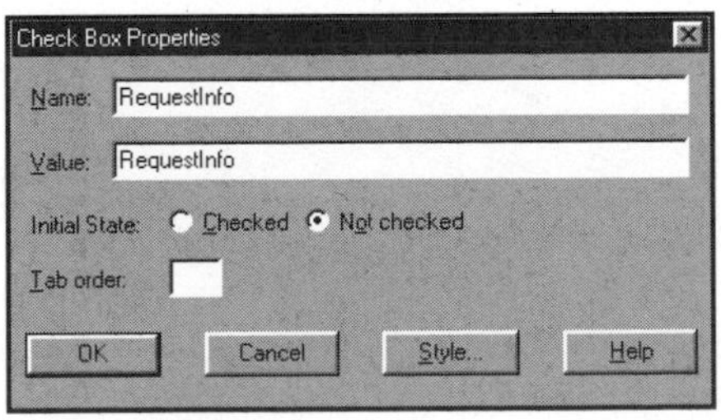

Figure 9-27

4. In the Name text box, enter *RequestInfo*. You'll use this name later on when configuring the confirmation page.
5. In the Value text box, enter the same value, *RequestInfo*. You'll see this value later when you're reviewing the information the user has sent to you with the Feedback Form. When you see this value, you'll know that the user wants more information sent.
6. In the Initial State section, select the Not Checked option, if it isn't already selected. The check box will be deselected (unchecked) when the user sees it in a browser. In instances like this, it's wise to leave check boxes deselected so that you'll know for certain whether a user actually wants information sent.
7. Click OK after you finish entering information in the Check Box Properties dialog box.
8. Position the cursor right of the check box you just inserted, and press the spacebar to create a little space between the check box and the text label you're about to add. Type the following sentence: *Please send me more information via e-mail.* Figure 9-28 shows a sample of how the check box should look.

You've just created a simple check box and labeled it for users to indicate they want more information from you. You can create all your check boxes in FrontPage in the same way.

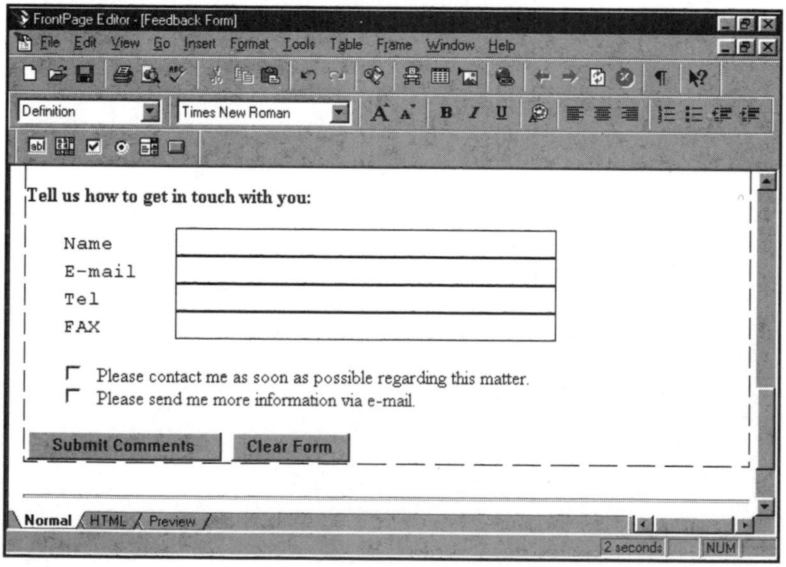

Figure 9-28

Creating a Command Button

Next, we'll create a command button (pushbutton) for users to click when they finish entering information on the form and are ready to send it to you.

1. Position your cursor after the command button labeled *Clear Form* at the bottom of the screen, and then press Enter.
2.  Click the Push Button toolbar button. A command button appears on the page.
3. Right-click the new command button and choose Form Field Properties from the pop-up menu. You'll see the Push Button Properties dialog box, as seen below in Figure 9-29.

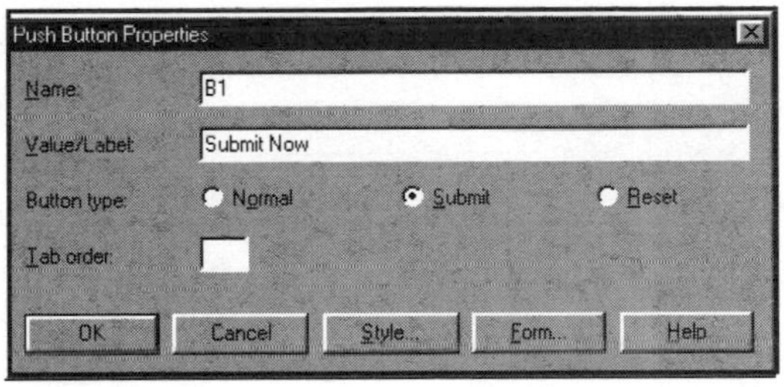

Figure 9-29

4. In the Name text box, leave the name as B1. If you supply your own handler by using a CGI script or other script, you can enter a name here and process the form based on the name. But for the purposes of this exercise, do not enter a name now.
5. In the Value/Label text box, enter the text that will appear on the command button: *Submit Now.*
6. In the Button Type section, select the Submit option. This allows the button to submit all information that a user has entered in the form to the handler on the Web server. Selecting the Reset option turns the button into one that resets the form to its initial state when a user clicks the button in a browser. You'll select Normal when you want to assign a script to the button.
7. Click OK after you finish entering information in the Push Button Properties dialog box. Figure 9-30 shows a sample of how the command button should look on your page.

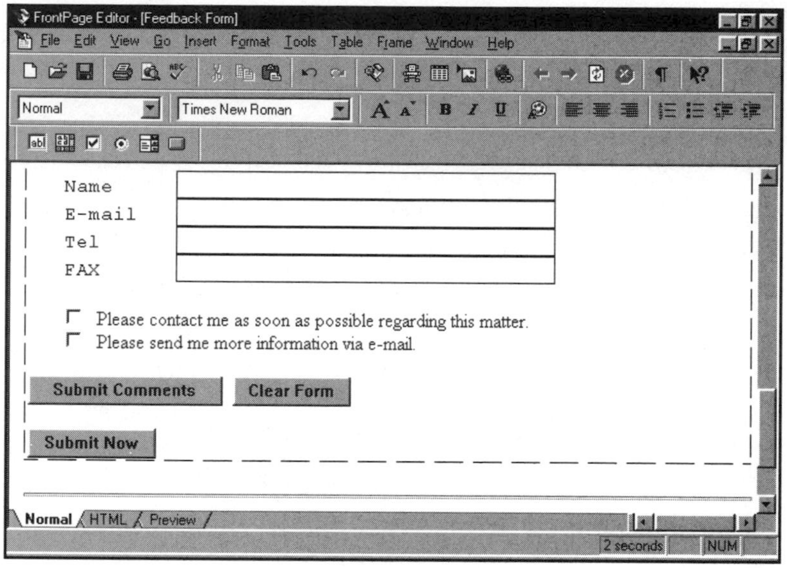

Figure 9-30

Using Alternative Command Buttons

FrontPage provides several additional styles of command buttons that you can use on your pages, so you're not limited to the style of the standard command button. These buttons don't give you the same options as standard command buttons; for example, you can't set them to reset or submit information. You can, however, assign your own scripts to these buttons. To reach the buttons, you must use a menu command. Here's how to add them to your page:

1. Position your cursor where you want the button to appear.
2. Choose Form Field from the Insert menu, and then choose Image from the submenu. The Image dialog box appears.
3. Select an image from the current Web open in the Explorer, from a file on your local machine, or from a file on the World Wide Web. For more information on the Image dialog box, see Chapter 8.
4. After selecting an image, click OK. The image appears as a button on the page.

You can right-click on the button and choose Form Field Properties from the pop-up menu to display the Image Form Field Properties dialog box, as seen in Figure 9-31.

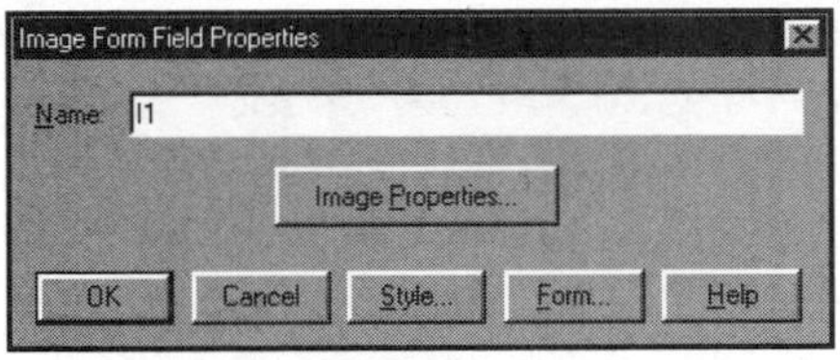

Figure 9-31

In the Image Form Field Properties dialog box, you can adjust the image properties by clicking the Image Properties button and making the appropriate settings in the Image Properties dialog box. In the Image Form Field Properties dialog box, you can also assign a handler by clicking the Form button and making the appropriate settings in the Form Properties dialog box.

Validating Form Fields

FrontPage allows you to confirm that certain information you receive from users in form fields is the type of information you want, or that it's in the correct format. For instance, you can specify that a text box contain a minimum or maximum number of characters, or that a selection is made from a drop-down list or group of option buttons. This process is called *form field validation*.

To specify validation rules for a form field, right-click on the field and choose Form Field Validation from the pop-up menu. You'll see a dialog box specific to the form field you're validating, such as the Text Box Validation dialog box shown in Figure 9-32.

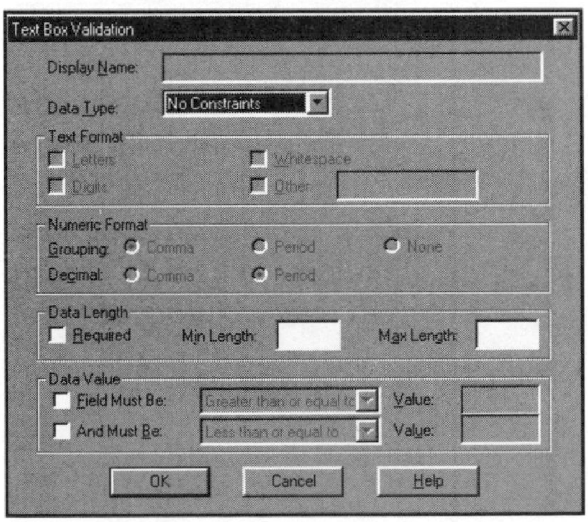

Figure 9-32

This is one of the most complicated Validation dialog boxes. It allows you to set validation rules for the type of data a user enters in the text box, as well as the format of text or numeric characters, minimum and maximum data length, and values for the data. When you finish specifying the rules you want for the form field, click OK to exit the Validation dialog box.

You can also reach the various Validation dialog boxes by clicking the Validate button in the Form Field Properties dialog box for the following form fields: text box, scrolling text box, option button, and drop-down list.

If you set up validation rules for a field, it's a good idea to explicitly tell users on the page (next to the form field, if possible) what you expect from them; for example, that a text field requires a value. If users submit information that does not fit within the rules you've specified for a particular form field, they will receive a validation error message in the browser notifying them that they must enter the correct type of information in the form.

How the validation error message is presented is based on a setting in the Explorer's FrontPage Web Settings dialog box. If you choose Web Settings from the Tools menu in the Explorer, the FrontPage Web Settings dialog box is displayed. On the Advanced tab, in the Validation Scripts section, you can select the language of the validation script. If you select VBScript or JavaScript, the validation error message will be displayed as a message box. If you select <None>, the validation error message will display as an HTML page. In either case, the user can click a button or link to return to the form to make corrections to the entered information.

NOTE When a user receives a validation error message, the information from the form *has not yet been submitted* to the Web site; only when a user submits all information according to any specified validation rules does the information get sent to the site.

A neat technique with drop-down list validation is to specify that the first item be something like "Pick One," to remind users that they really do need to make a selection. This also helps you determine, after the information has been submitted, whether the user made a valid choice. To do this, make sure that "Pick One" is selected by default. Another technique is to display an error message if the user does not make a valid selection from the drop-down list. To do this, make "Pick One" the first item in the drop-down list and select the Disallow First Item check box in the Drop-Down Menu Validation dialog box. The user will see a validation error message if he or she tries to submit the information with the first item in the drop-down list still selected.

Creating a Confirmation Page

A confirmation page displays information to a user confirming some action. For example, the user can receive confirmation that the information submitted in a form was received by the server. Users do make mistakes; the confirmation page can help them catch many mistakes and allow them to resubmit the form with the correct information. Also, a confirmation page can add a professional touch to your site.

Note that once a user submits a form to a Web site, that information is stored at the site (or wherever the site creator specifies) and cannot be changed. Confirmation pages simply allow the user to confirm that the information is what he or she wanted to submit. It's a good idea to advise users to review all information on a form before they submit it. You can take some steps to ensure that information is submitted correctly; see "Validating Form Fields" earlier in this chapter for more details.

A confirmation page is just a standard page that can be specified in the Form Properties dialog box for a form. (You'll learn more about this in the section "Specifying Form Settings" later in this chapter.) A confirmation page typically uses Confirmation Field components to present information back to the user for review.

Let's step through the process of creating a confirmation page. For this example, we'll use the form fields we created earlier in this chapter. First we'll start the easy way—by using a template to create a confirmation page.

1. In the Editor, choose New from the File menu, select the Page tab, select Confirmation Form the list of templates and wizards in the New dialog box, and click OK.
2. When the page appears in the Editor, save it with the title *Confirmation Form* and give it the name within the current site, *confirmation.htm*. We'll refer to this page from now on as the Confirmation Form, shown in Figure 9-33.

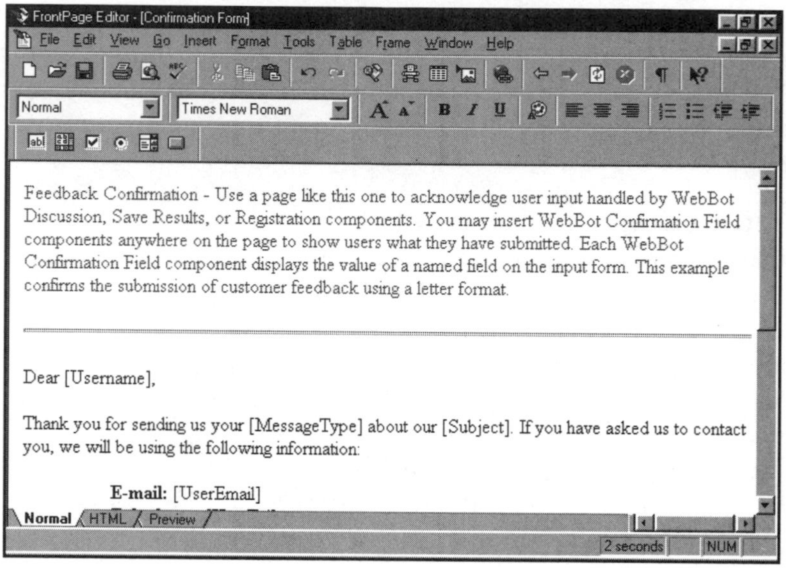

Figure 9-33

You'll see that the Confirmation Form is a template that's ready for you to customize. It's designed to be used with the Feedback Form template, and it includes many of the form field names used in that template. These names appear in brackets; they're actually individual Confirmation Field components.

If you move your cursor over one of these components, such as the component labeled *[UserName],* you'll see that the cursor turns into the cute little robot cursor. The value of the UserName field will replace the string *[UserName]* when the Confirmation Form appears to a user in a browser; whatever name the user entered will appear there. All Confirmation Field components on the Confirmation Form work in the same manner.

The Confirmation Form also includes some introductory and concluding sentences that you can use; you can change any of this information if you want to.

Inserting a Confirmation Field Component

When you know what information you want to present to the user for confirmation, you're ready to insert Confirmation Field Components on the page. Using the fields you created earlier, here's how you can do it:

1. First, you delete the component labeled *[MessageType]* and replace it with the one you created earlier called *[CommentType]*. Position your cursor immediately to the right of the [MessageType] Confirmation Field component and press the Backspace key. (This is an easy way to delete any component on a page.)
2. Next, you insert a Confirmation Field Component for the form field called *[CommentType]*. From the Insert menu, choose FrontPage Component. In the Insert FrontPage Component dialog box, select Confirmation Field, and then click OK.

   The Confirmation Field Properties dialog box appears, as seen in Figure 9-34 below.

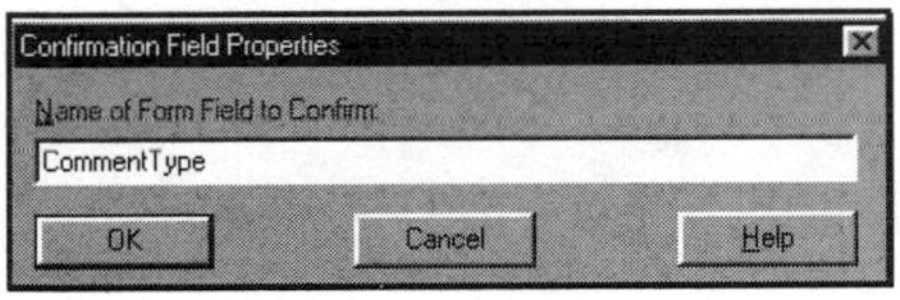

Figure 9-34

3. Enter the name of the form field whose information you want presented; in this case, enter *CommentType*. Then click OK.

> **TIP** For option buttons only, the name you enter is the group name.

   You'll see that the Confirmation Field Component with the label *[CommentType]* has been inserted in the middle of the sentence. This example only shows how you can replace a component, but of course you can create original sentences and insert components in the same fashion for presenting form field information on a Confirmation Form. Figure 9-35 on the next page shows a sample of how the Confirmation Form should look after the component has been added.

4. Using the same procedure, you can create original sentences or replace existing components for the other form fields you created earlier. Among these fields are the drop-down list named *Topic,* a one-line text box named *IfOther,* a scrolling text box named *UserComments,* and a check box named *RequestInfo*.

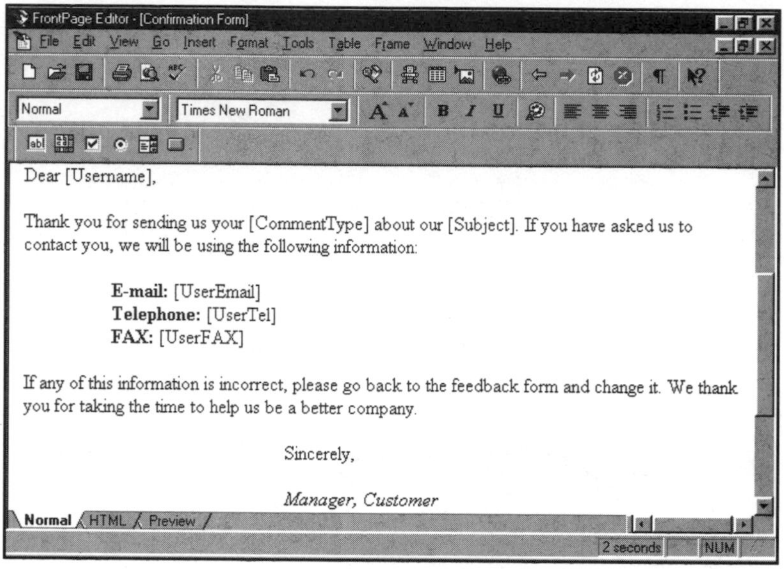

Figure 9-35

It's a good idea to include a link at the end of the Confirmation Form that returns the user back to the Feedback Form if he or she needs to resubmit information. It's also wise to include other navigational links on this page, such as links to the site's home page, a Table of Contents page, or the major sections of the site, so the page doesn't seem like a dead end to the user.

Our form field and confirmation field examples end here. Read on to learn how to process the information in a form.

Specifying Form Settings

Here's where it all comes together. You create forms by assembling a collection of form fields on one page, and you can present the information back to the user for confirmation on another page using a Confirmation Form. But in order for the two pages to work together, you must specify their relationship in the Forms Properties dialog box. You also specify the type of handler you want to use on the Web server for processing the information a user enters in a form.

FrontPage includes two forms in addition to the traditional data-collection forms: the discussion form and the registration form. Their handlers are specified in the Forms Properties dialog box. If you create a site using the Discussion Web Wizard, you're actually creating a form for users to "fill out" as the site is in use. When a user submits a message to the discussion group, the Discussion Component handler saves the information on the server so it can be accessed by others in the forum. You'll learn more about the discussion and registration form handlers later in this chapter.

Assigning a Form Handler

A *handler* is an application on a Web server that communicates between the server and the user in relation to a form. Handlers can send messages to the user (via Confirmation Pages, or e-mail, for example), and they can process the information in a form that a user submits to the Web server. You assign and configure a form's handler in the Form Properties dialog box.

You can open the Form Properties dialog box for the form you're assigning the handler to in one of two ways. You can right-click on any open space of the form, and then choose Form Properties from the pop-up menu; or, if you're already in the Push Button Properties dialog box, you can click the Form button to reach the Form Properties dialog box, seen in Figure 9-36 below.

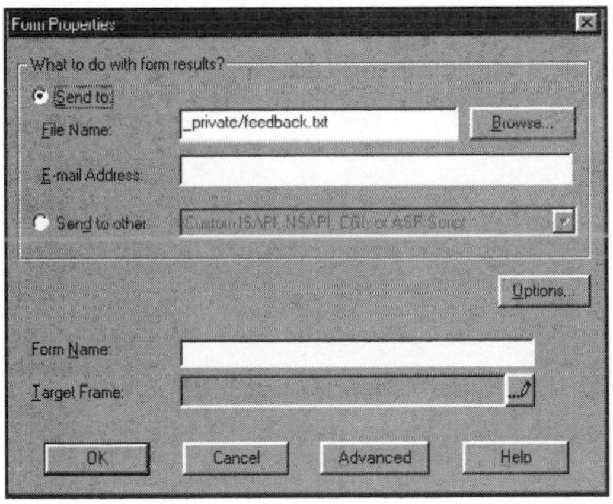

Figure 9-36

What to Do with Form Results?

There are two options in this section of the Form Properties dialog box.

- **Send to.** This is the default handler for a form.

  File Name. The results of the form can be saved to a text file on your server. The default location and name is *_private/feedback.txt*. Remember that the *_private* folder is invisible to a search of your site. You can select the Browse button and choose between any other page in the current Web, or you can type in a relative URL.

E-mail Address. This is a very cool feature that lets you send an additional results file to an e-mail address. You can choose from various e-mail options, in the Options for Saving Results of a Form dialog box, described below.

- **Send to other.** You have three "other" choices to use as a form handler, a Custom handler, or one of two FrontPage handlers. Select the Send to other: radio button and choose an option from the drop-down list.

  Custom ISAPI, NSAPI, or CGI Script. In terms of forms, these are software components on a Web server that process the information submitted using a form. These software components can be written to add functionality to your Web site beyond what FrontPage's components can offer. For example, a company might want a handler that allows a user special access to certain areas of the site.

  Discussion Form Handler. A component that allows users to participate in an online discussion. FrontPage allows basic discussion group administration abilities. The Discussion Component gathers information from a form, formats it into an HTML page, stores the page on the Web server, and adds the page to a Table of Contents and a text index. It can also gather other information from the form and store it on the Web server. Note that it's much easier to use the Discussion Web Wizard than to configure settings here. The Discussion Web Wizard does all of this for you.

  Registration Form Handler. A component that allows users to register for a service offered in your site. It adds the user to the service's authentication database, and then collects other information from the form and stores it on the Web server in the file and format you specify.

  - **Form Name.** If you're using a custom form handler, you may want to type a form name here and refer to it from the custom handler.
  - **Target Frame.** Here you can select a frame to display the results of a form. You can type the name of the frame, or use the Target Frame button to locate a frame.

- **Options.** You can configure various options for saving the results of a form, by selecting the Options button on the Form Properties dialog box. You'll see the Options For Saving Results Of A Form dialog box, which has four tabs: File Results (see Figure 9-37), E-mail Results, Confirmation Page, and Saved Fields.

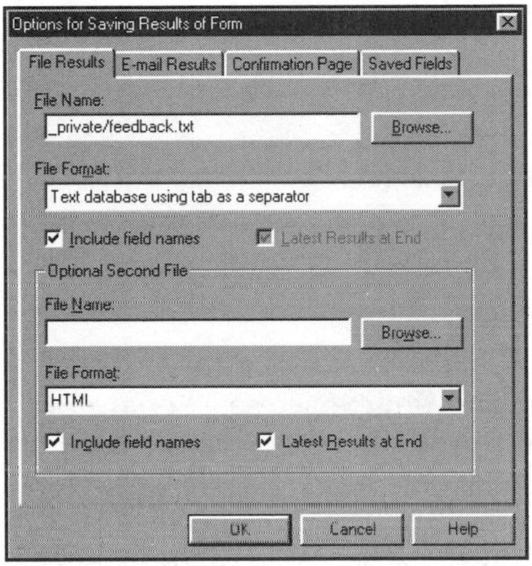

Figure 9-37

File Results Tab. If you've configured the results to be sent to a file, you can do a little fine-tuning here on the File Results tab.

File Name. Enter the name and location of the file you want the results saved to. The location can be either within or outside the current site. If it's in the current site, you might enter *_private/feedback.txt.* The results will be saved to the file called FEEDBACK.TXT in the *_private* folder in your Web site. If a results file does not exist when the first results are saved, FrontPage creates the file. If a results file exists, the information is appended to the end of the file.

File Format. Select the file format of the results file from the drop-down list in the File Format section. You have numerous choices:

- **HTML.** Formats the file in HTML using normal text with line endings.
- **HTML Definition List.** Formats the file using a definition list to format name-value pairs.

- **HTML Bulleted List.** Formats the file using a bulleted list for name-value pairs.
- **Formatted Text Within HTML.** Formats the file in HTML using formatted text with line endings.
- **Formatted Text.** Formats the file in an easy-to-read text format.
- **Text Database Using Comma as a Separator.** Formats the file in a text format with commas separating the elements. If the Include Field Names In Output check box is selected, names are listed on the first line, enclosed in quotes, and separated by commas. Values are listed on the second line, enclosed in quotes, and separated by commas. Use this format if you want to manipulate the information in a database or similar application.
- **Text Database Using Tab as a Separator.** Formats the file in the same way as above, but using tabs instead of commas to separate elements.
- **Text Database Using Space as a Separator.** Formats the file in the same way as above, but using spaces instead of commas to separate elements.

Include Field Names. Select the Include Field Names check box to save the field name along with the field value in the results file. If you don't check this box then only the values of the fields are saved.

Latest Results as End. This option is only available is you choose HTML as a file format. In which case the latest information will be saved to the bottom of the file. This is the default option for all other file formats, and will be grayed out if you choose one of those other formats.

Optional Second File. If you want to use the results of the form for different things, like spreadsheets, or databases, you can select a second file to save them to, and configure the format differently. So in essence, you get the same results saved in two different formats—cool huh?

E-mail Results Tab If you want results of a form to be sent via e-mail to someone—a very cool feature by the way—you can configure the specifics here. See Figure 9-38.

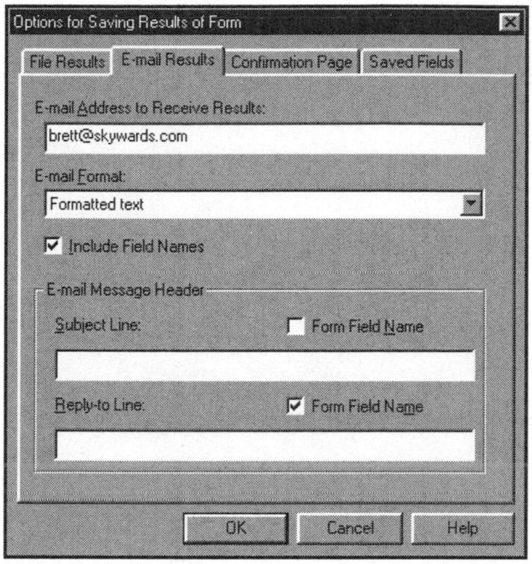

Figure 9-38

E-mail Address to Receive Results. In the text box., type in the full e-mail address that you want to receive the form results, for example, *donna@mycoolweb.com.*

E-mail Format. If you want the form results to read by most e-mail programs, like Microsoft Exchange, stick with the default format, Formatted Text. The other options available are described above in the section, "File Formats."

Include Field Names. If you would like the form field names included along with the form information, select this check box.

E-mail Message Header. If you would like to customize the Subject Line, and the Reply To line of the E-mail response, fill in that information here. The default subject line is Form Results. If you check the Form Field Name check box, enter the form field name that you want listed in the response mail. The Reply To line is a good place to enter the form field that lists the user's e-mail address; that way, you can quickly see who filled out the form.

Confirmation Page Tab. If you want the results of a form to be delivered to a confirmation page, make your selections here.

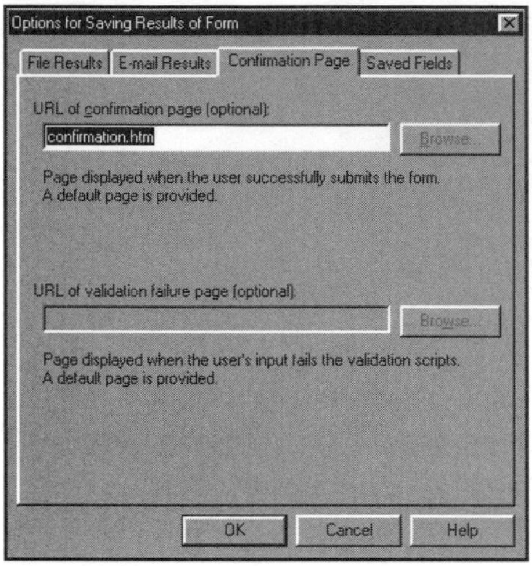

Figure 9-39

URL of confirmation page. If you've created a confirmation page for users to confirm the information they've entered, type its page URL in the URL Of Confirmation Page text box. This page will be displayed by the browser whenever the form is successfully submitted to the Web server.

If you do not specify a confirmation page here, the Save Results component will create and maintain one automatically.

TIP If the URL Of Validation Failure Page text box appears grayed out, you have not specified any validation for your form fields.

URL of validation failure page. You can also specify a validation failure page in the URL Of Validation Failure Page text box. A field validation failure page is displayed when the form is submitted and it contains data that violates any defined form field validation. This page is typically used only when the validation script language in the Explorer's FrontPage Web Settings dialog box is set to <None>. Otherwise, if a validation failure occurs, a failure message is generated with either a VBScript or JavaScript message box. If you do not specify a field validation failure page here, FrontPage will create and maintain one automatically.

Saved Fields Tab. Here, as seen in Figure 9-40, you can specify which fields the form will save, and in which order, as well as some other interesting information available from the server, like the user name or browser type.

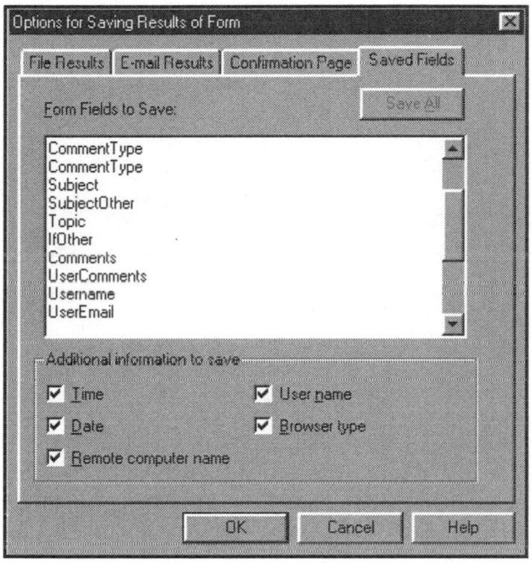

Figure 9-40

Form Fields to Save. Here you can write in the name of the form fields that you want saved along with the form results, one field per line. The fields will be saved in the order they appear in the list. If you leave the list empty, the form will save all fields, in the order they appear on the form, and list them in the results file.

Additional Information to Save. You can choose between these additional bits of information, each checked item will be listed after the form fields in the results file. Time lists the time the form was filled out. Date lists the date the form was completed and sent. Remote Computer Name will list the name of the computer that accessed the form User Name will list the name of the user that accessed the page. And Browser type will tell you the name of the browser that accessed the page.

When you've finished configuring the options for saving the results of your forms, click OK to go back to the Forms Properties dialog box. Notice that some of the fields may have changed, based on information you supplied in the Options for Saving Results of a Form dialog box.

Configuring a Discussion Component

You can create a discussion Web site using the Discussion Web Wizard, described in Chapter 4. You can configure the settings of a Discussion component in the Options for Discussion Form Handler dialog box, which you can reach in the following way:

1. Open the Form Properties dialog box for the discussion form.
2. Select the Options button. The Option for Discussion Form Handler dialog box appears, as seen in Figure 9-41, with three tabs.

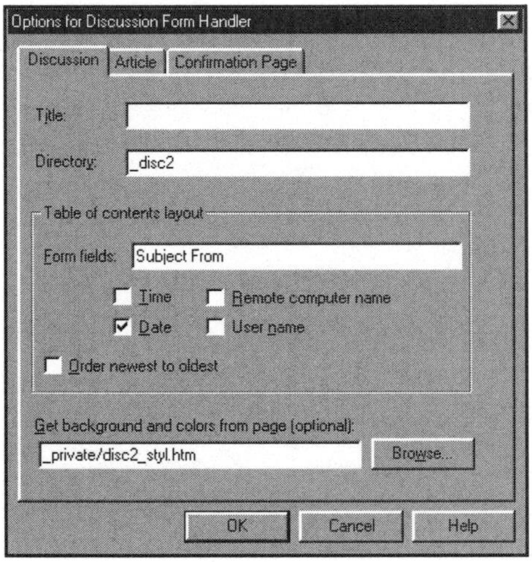

Figure 9-41

On the Discussion tab, you can enter the following information:

- Name the discussion group in the Title text box. The name will appear on pages containing articles.
- Enter the name of the discussion folder in the Directory text box. If you used the Discussion Web Wizard to create your discussion Web site, the folder you specified in the wizard will appear as the default. The folder name must be eight or fewer characters, one of which is a beginning underscore (_).
- In the Form Fields text box in the Table Of Contents Layout section, enter the names of the form field(s) you want displayed in the Table of Contents in the discussion group. If you enter multiple names, you must separate them with blank spaces.

- Select the appropriate check boxes if you want to display the time and/or date the article was submitted, the remote computer name the article came from, or the user name of the article's author.
- To place the most recently submitted articles first in the Table of Contents, select the Order Newest To Oldest check box.
- If you want to use the background and colors from another page in your site, you can do so by specifying the page in the Get Background And Colors From Page text box.

You specify the layout of each article in the discussion group on the Article tab, seen here in Figure 9-42.

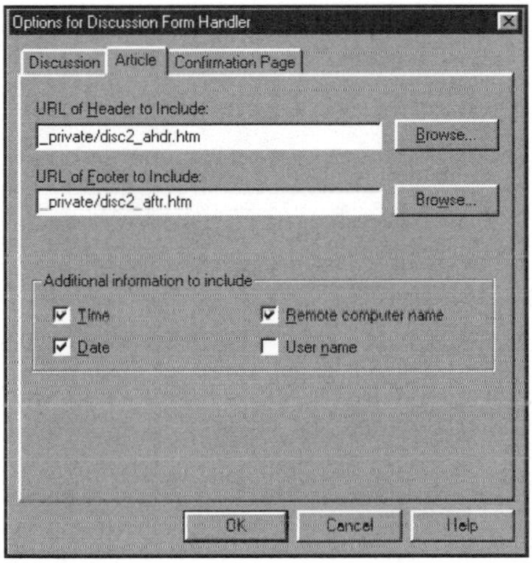

Figure 9-42

- To use a page as a header or footer of each article, you can specify the page in the URL Of Header To Include text box or the URL Of Footer To Include text box
- In the Additional Information To Include section, select the appropriate check boxes if you want to include the time and/or date the article was submitted, the remote computer name the article came from, or the user name of the article's author.

On the Confirmation Page tab, shown in Figure 9-43, you can specify an optional configuration page and an optional validation failure page.

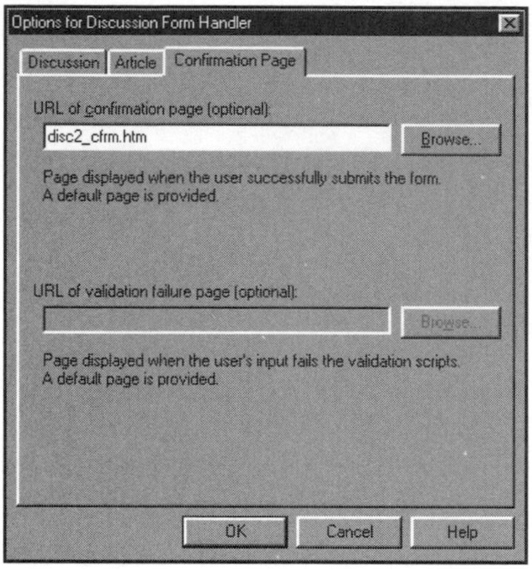

Figure 9-43

- If you've created a confirmation page for users to confirm the information they've entered, type its page URL in the URL Of Confirmation Page text box. This page will be displayed by the browser whenever the form is submitted to the Web server.

  If you do not specify a confirmation page here, the Discussion component will create and maintain one automatically.

- You can also specify a validation failure page in the URL Of Validation Failure Page text box. A field validation failure page displays information pertaining to fields with invalid data on a form. If you do not specify a field validation failure page here, FrontPage will create and maintain one automatically.

After you finish entering all the information you need to configure the Discussion Form handler, click OK to close the Options for Discussion Form Handler dialog box.

Configuring a Registration Component

You configure a Registration Component in the Options for Registration Form Handler dialog box, which you can reach in the following way:

1. Open the Form Properties dialog box for the registration form. You can create your own form to use as a registration form, or you can use the User Registration template for this purpose. The registration form must be located in the root Web site. Be aware that registration forms

do not work on the Microsoft Internet Information Server or the Microsoft Personal Web Server.

2. Select Registration Form Handler from the drop-down list in the Send To Other section, as seen in Figure 9-44 below, and then click the Options button.

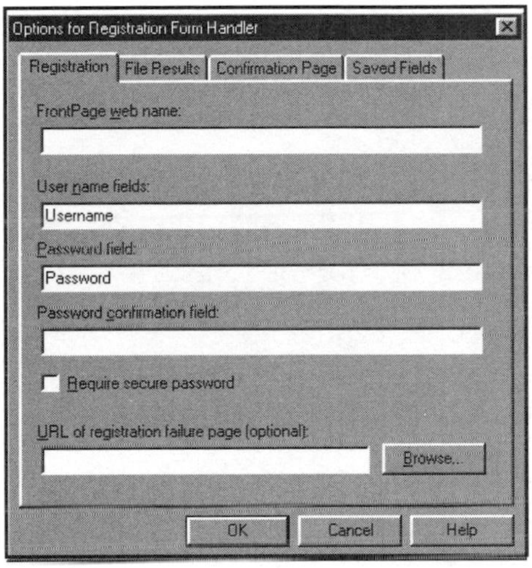

Figure 9-44

To configure the Registration component, do the following:

- In the FrontPage Web Name text box, enter the name of the Web site you're allowing the user to register for.
- In the User Name Fields text box, enter the name(s) of the field or fields on the form, separated by commas or spaces, that the user inputs his or her name into. The user name is constructed from the contents of these fields.
- In the Password Field text box, enter the name of the field for the user's password.
- In the Password Confirmation Field text box, enter the name of the field for the user's confirmation password.
- If you want to require that the user supply a secure password (which consists of six or more characters and does not partially match the user name), select the Require Secure Password check box.
- You can also supply a failure page, which notifies the user that a registration attempt failed. Supply the page URL for this page in the

text box at the bottom of the dialog box. This page is optional, but it's a good idea to include a page like this in your site.

The Settings For Registration Form Handler dialog box also includes File Results, Confirmation Page, and Saved Fields tabs. These are configured the same as described in "Configuring a Save Results Component," earlier in this chapter.

Configuring a Custom ISAPI, NSAPI, or CGI Handler

You can also configure settings for a custom ISAPI, NSAPI, or CGI handler if you decide to use one in your Web site.

You configure the custom handler in the Settings For Custom Form Handler dialog box, which you can reach in the following way:

1. Open the Form Properties dialog box for the form.
2. Select Custom ISAPI, NSAPI, Or CGI Script from the drop-down list in the Send to other section, and then click the Options button.

   The Options for Custom Form Handler dialog box appears, as seen here in Figure 9-45.

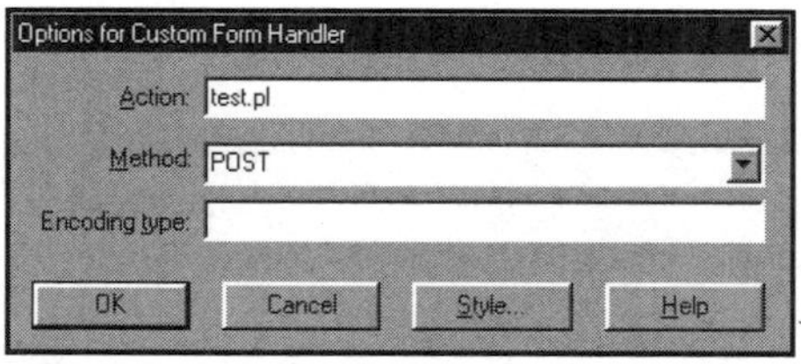

Figure 9-45

To configure the custom form handler, do the following:

- In the Action field, enter the *absolute URL* of the form handler.
- Use the Method drop-down list to select a method of submitting information to the handler—Post or Get. The Post method passes the name-value form field pair directly to the form handler as input, and the Get method encodes the form's name-value pairs and assigns the information to a server variable, QUERY_STRING.
- In the Encoding Type text box, enter the standard used to encode the form data that's passed to the handler. The default encoding method is *application/x-www-form-urlencoded;* leave this field blank to use the default.

Coming Up

You've now explored the big, amazing world of FrontPage components and forms. In the next chapter, you'll be introduced to some of FrontPage's more advanced features.

PART IV

10 Advanced Features
11 Web Servers

Finishing Touches

CHAPTER 10

Advanced Features

Getting Interactive

By now you pretty much know your way around FrontPage. You've learned about the Explorer and the Editor. You know how to build a Web site, manage it, and work with it page by page. Maybe you're saying to yourself, "Geez, there has to be more than this. What about all of those cool features I keep hearing about? I want my Dynamic HTML!" Well, this is your lucky day. FrontPage directly supports advanced features—such as ActiveX controls, Java applets, JavaScript, Visual Basic, VBScript, Netscape plug-ins, and yes, even Dynamic HTML. We'll even show you how to use *cascading stylesheets* and how to take advantage of one the hot Web buzz topics, *push technology*—via the Channel Definition wizard.

TIP When you add a control, script, or applet to your pages in the Editor, FrontPage typically inserts an icon representing that feature. You can double-click or right-click the icon and choose Properties from the pop-up menu to reach the Properties dialog box. With an icon selected, you can reach the Properties dialog box quickly by pressing Alt+Enter.

There are plenty of books specifically dedicated to many of these new features. You can hardly walk into the computer section of your favorite bookstore without bumping into a couple dozen books on Java alone. So, for the purpose of this chapter, we'll only discuss how FrontPage uses these features, and how you get them on your page and in your site.

The Advanced Toolbar

To get many of the advanced features onto your page, you use the Advanced toolbar as seen in Figure 10-1. To see the toolbar if it's not already visible, select Advanced Toolbar from the View menu in the Editor.

Figure 10-1

Inserting HTML

Since HTML is a rapidly evolving language, new tags will be introduced that FrontPage might not directly support. Therefore, FrontPage allows you to insert any HTML directly, including new HTML. Be aware, however, that FrontPage will not check to see if the text you insert is valid HTML. To insert HTML, you use the Insert HTML button, the leftmost button on the Advanced toolbar. Clicking this button brings up the HTML Markup dialog box, as seen in Figure 10-2 below.

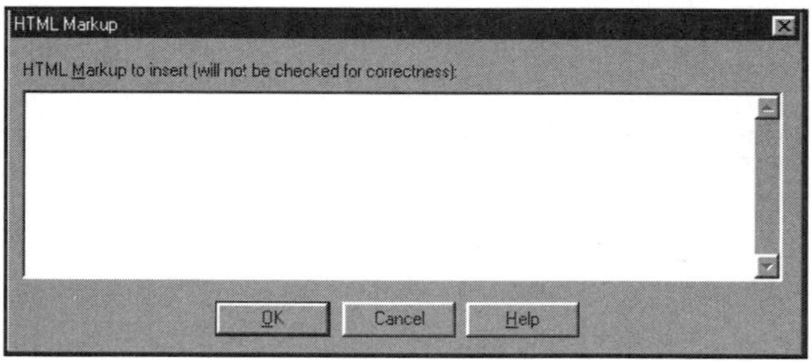

Figure 10-2

Enter your HTML, and then click OK to return to the Editor. The text you entered is shown in the Editor using the Unknown HTML placeholder icon. This icon reminds you that you created the HTML, not FrontPage. To rework HTML that you created using the HTML Markup dialog box, right-click the unknown HTML icon and select HTML Markup Properties from the pop-up menu. You can always edit the HTML that FrontPage creates by using the HTML View tab; to learn how, see Chapter 7.

Inserting an ActiveX Control

ActiveX controls are software components that add functionality to your page that can't be created using standard HTML. Examples of ActiveX controls include a label control that can display text at different sizes and angles, a timer control that can generate timed events, a stock ticker control that can display stock information, and an animation control that can display animations. ActiveX controls can be created with a variety of programming languages, including Visual C++ and Visual Basic 5.0. Be aware that some browsers do not recognize ActiveX controls on a Web page. For more information on ActiveX and ActiveX controls, as well as information on how to download free ActiveX controls, check out Microsoft's ActiveX site at www.microsoft.com/activex/ on the World Wide Web.

The second button from the left on the Advanced Toolbar is the Insert ActiveX Control button. Clicking the button brings up the ActiveX Control Properties dialog box, as shown in Figure 10-3.

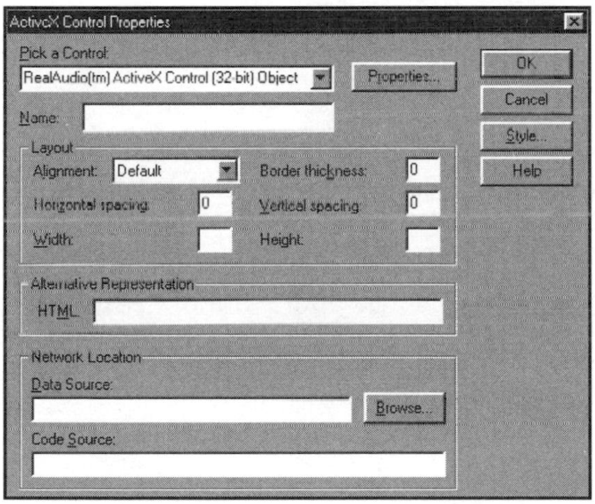

Figure 10-3

You use this dialog box to select and then configure an ActiveX control. Only the Pick A Control drop-down list is active at first, and the other areas are grayed out. When you select a control, the other areas of the dialog box become active.

Pick a Control

Select a control from this drop-down list, which displays all of the ActiveX controls currently installed on your computer.

To alter the properties for the control, click the Properties button. If the control you selected is installed on your computer, and if it takes advantage of local editing, you'll be presented with the Edit ActiveX Control dialog box as well as a Properties dialog box for that control.

Figure 10-4 shows these dialog boxes for the RealAudio ActiveX control.

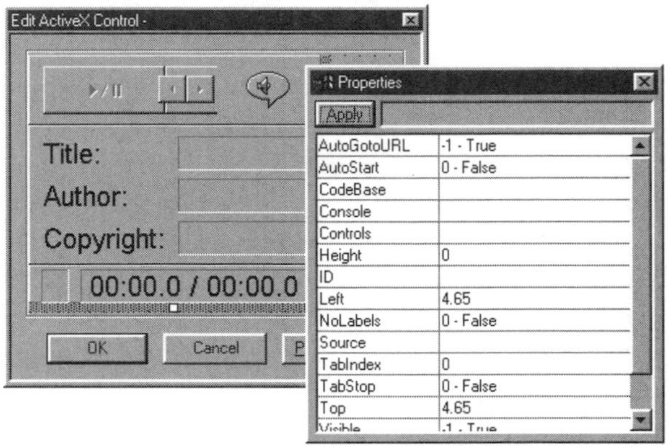

Figure 10-4

The Properties dialog box lists the current properties for the control. You can edit these options as needed.

If the control you selected is not loaded on your computer or does not support local editing, clicking the Properties button brings up the more generic Object Parameters dialog box, as seen below in Figure 10-5. To use this dialog box, you need to know all of the properties for the control and their values.

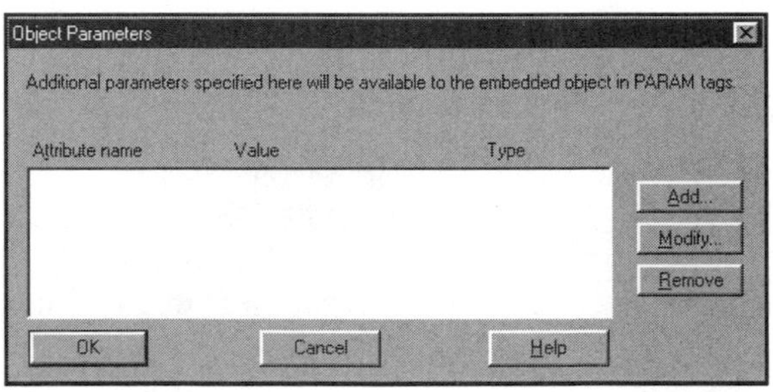

Figure 10-5

Name. The Name text box in the ActiveX Control Properties dialog box allows you to specify a name that represents the ActiveX control when it's used along with a script on the page.

Layout. In the layout section, you specify how the control will be placed on the page.

- **Alignment.** Specifies the type of alignment between the ActiveX control and the text around it.
- **Border Thickness.** Sets a black border around the control. The width of the border is measured in pixels.
- **Horizontal Spacing.** Sets a specified horizontal spacing (in pixels) from the control to the nearest object or text on the current line, on both sides of the control.
- **Vertical Spacing.** Sets a specified vertical spacing (in pixels) from the control to the nearest object or text on the line above and/or below the control.
- **Width.** Specifies the width of the control in pixels.
- **Height.** Specifies the height of the control in pixels.

TIP You can adjust the size of an ActiveX control on a page by selecting it and then dragging its border controls with the mouse.

Alternate Representation. For browsers that do not support ActiveX controls, use this text box to enter text or HTML that will be displayed in place of the control. For example, typing *Pebbles* will cause that word to appear in the browser in place of the control. You can also type HTML to add font, size, and other attributes to the text. You can also enter HTML in this text box to show an image in place of the control, such as *<img src="images/Pebbles.gif">*. In this case, Pebbles.gif is in the Images folder of the Web site the page belongs to.

Network Location. If the ActiveX control is not on the user's computer, you can specify a network location that the browser will search for the control or for data.

- **Data Source.** Use the Data Source text box to specify the network location or URL of the file containing the parameters, or use the Browse button to select a file. Certain ActiveX controls might take advantage of run-time parameters.

- **Code Source.** If the control is not on the user's computer, enter the network location or URL of the control in the Code Source text box to point the browser to that location when the page is opened. If necessary, this will allow the browser to download and install the control.

Figure 10-6 shows the ActiveX RealAudio control as it appears in the Editor.

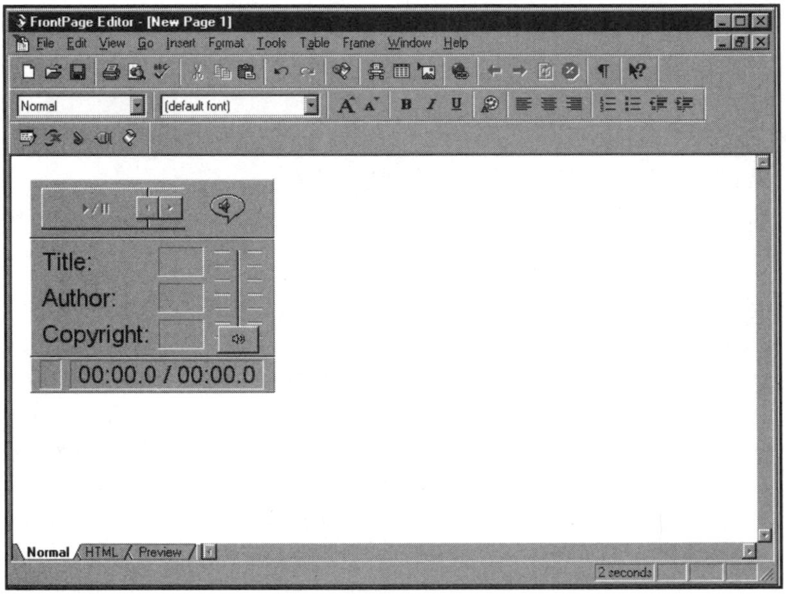

Figure 10-6

Inserting a Java Applet

The third button from the left on the Advanced toolbar is the Insert Java Applet button. Java applets are created in a programming language called *Java* and are very much like an ActiveX control in that they add dynamic functionality to your Web page. Clicking the Insert Java Applet button displays the Java Applet Properties dialog box, as seen here in Figure 10-7.

Applet Source. Source files for Java applets typically have the file extension CLASS. Enter the name of the Java applet source file in the Applet Source text box. Keep in mind that Java is case sensitive, so using the correct uppercase and lowercase letters is important.

Applet Base URL. In this text box, enter the URL of the folder that contains the Java applet source file.

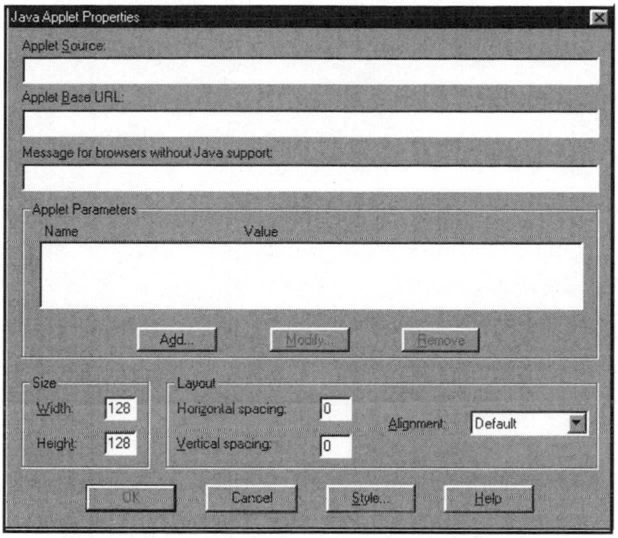

Figure 10-7

Message for browsers without Java support. For browsers that do not support Java applets, use this text box to enter text or HTML that will be displayed in place of the applet. For example, typing *BamBam* will cause that word to appear in the browser in place of the applet. You can also type HTML to add font, size, and other attributes to the text. You can also enter HTML in this text box to show an image in place of the applet, such as *<img src="images/BamBam.gif">*. In this case, BamBam.gif is in the Images folder of the Web site that the page belongs to.

Applet Parameters. In this section, you specify parameter names and values for the applet. You must use the documentation that came with the Java applet to determine the names and values for the applet.

The text box lists the names and values of any parameters that have been added. You can use the Add, Modify, and Remove buttons to configure this list.

Size. In this section, you can adjust the width and height (in pixels) of the Java applet.

TIP You can adjust the size of a Java applet on a page by selecting it and then dragging its border controls with the mouse.

Layout. In this section, you specify the spacing and alignment of the applet on the page.

- **Horizontal Spacing.** Sets a specified horizontal spacing (in pixels) from the applet to the nearest object or text on the current line, on both sides of the applet.
- **Vertical Spacing.** Sets a specified vertical spacing (in pixels) from the applet to the nearest object or text on the line above and/or below the applet.
- **Alignment.** Specifies a type of alignment between the Java applet and the text around it.

Figure 10-8 shows how the Java applet appears in the Editor.

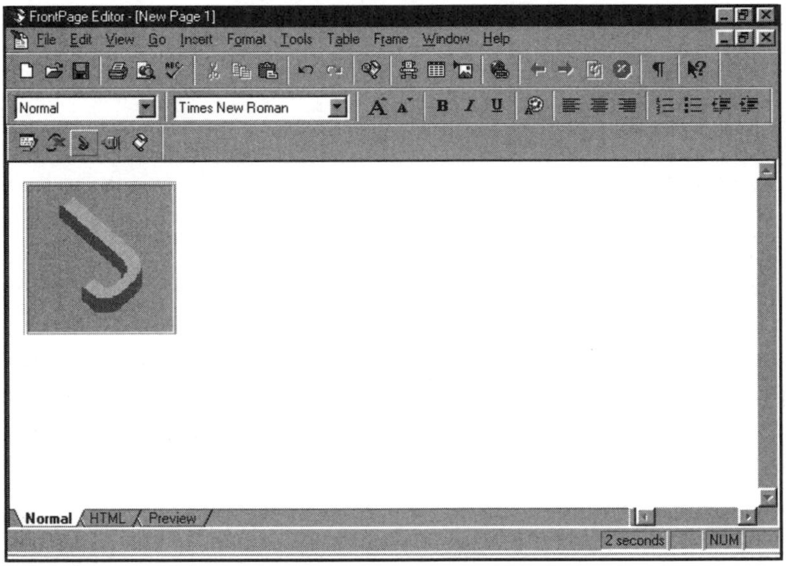

Figure 10-8

Inserting a Plug-In

Plug-ins were originally created for Netscape users, although they are now supported by Microsoft Internet Explorer users. Clicking the Insert Plug-In button, the fifth button on the Advanced toolbar, displays the Plug-In Properties dialog box, as seen in Figure 10-9.

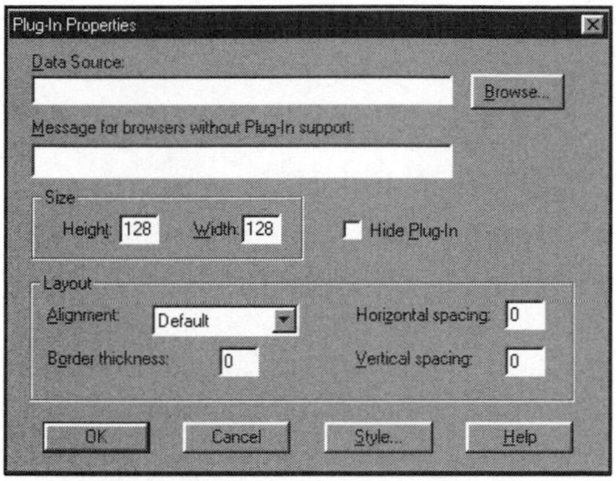

Figure 10-9

Data Source. In this text box, specify the file location or URL of the plug-in, or click the Browse button to select the plug-in.

Message for browsers without plug-in support. For browsers that do not support plug-ins, use this text box to enter HTML that determines what those browsers will display in place of the plug-in. For example, typing *Dino* will cause that word to appear in the browser in place of the plug-in. You can also type HTML to add font, size, and other attributes to the text. You can also enter HTML in this text box to show an image in place of the plug-in, such as *<img src="images/Dino.gif">*. In this case, *Dino.gif* is in the Images folder of the Web site the page belongs to.

Size. In this section, you can adjust the size of the plug-in by entering the height and width in pixels.

> **TIP** You can adjust the size of a plug-in on a page by selecting it and then dragging its border controls with the mouse.

Hide Plug-In. Select this check box if you don't want the plug-in to appear on the page.

Layout. In the Layout section, you specify the position of the plug-in on the page.

- **Alignment.** Specifies a type of alignment between the plug-in and the text around it.
- **Border Thickness.** Sets a black border around the plug-in. The width of the border is measured in pixels.
- **Horizontal Spacing.** Sets a specified horizontal spacing (in pixels) from the plug-in to the nearest object or text on the current line, on both sides of the plug-in.
- **Vertical Spacing.** Sets a specified vertical spacing (in pixels) from the plug-in to the nearest object or text on the line above and/or below the plug-in.

Inserting VBScript or JavaScript

Using a scripting language, such as VBScript or JavaScript, in a Web page gives you a lot more capabilities. With the support of a script-enabled browser, you can use VBScript or JavaScript to read and modify form elements, perform event handling, interact with the browser, and manipulate objects. Writing VBScript or JavaScript is beyond the scope of this book, but this section will give you an introduction.

VBScript is a scripting language developed by Microsoft and is based on Visual Basic for Applications. JavaScript is a scripting language developed by Netscape and is based on the C programming language. Scripts are included in the HTML and can be understood by a browser that supports that particular scripting language.

You can insert scripts, such as VBScript or JavaScript, by using the Insert Script button, the rightmost button on the Advanced toolbar. Clicking the Insert Script button displays the Script dialog box, as seen in Figure 10-10.

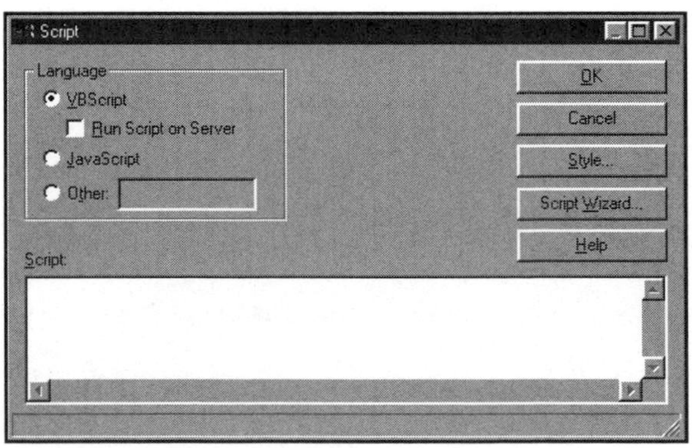

Figure 10-10

The language section allows you to specify the scripting language. Selecting the RunScript On Server check box causes the VBScript to run on the server and not the client. The Script scrolling text box allows you to actually insert a script. You can access the Script Wizard by clicking the Script Wizard button. The Script Wizard is a tool that helps you generate scripts. It contains a code view option that allows you to see the code that is being generated. Figure 10-11 shows a sample from the Script Wizard.

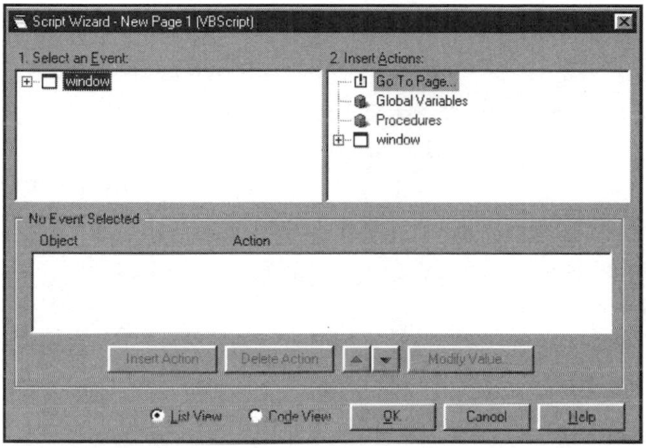

Figure 10-11

The basic methodology behind the wizard is that you select an object and an associated event, and then select an action to take place when the event is triggered. Once you are finished with the wizard, the VBScript or JavaScript code is inserted and an icon representing the script is placed onto the page.

Cascading Stylesheets (CSS)

One of the hardest things about working in HTML has been the inability to be able to customize the text. In the past, if you wanted to make text in a certain *point size* (the term used to define the size of a letter), or adjust the *leading* (the space between lines) of a paragraph, you were plain out of luck. With the advent of cascading stylesheets (CSS), you now have that power.

You can define attributes of a *style*, its font, color, size, leading, indents, and so on, and you can combine many different styles into a *sheet*, creating a *stylesheet*. The term *cascading* means that you can use multiple styles to control different elements on a single page, and the browser will apply styles in a cascading order to resolve conflicts, and to define which styles take precedence. Cascading stylesheets work in three different ways:

- **External Stylesheet.** This is probably the most powerful CSS option. You create one stylesheet and link as many pages to it as you like. If you need to make a change, you need to do it in only one place. An external, or linked, stylesheet is a separate file and has a .css extension.
- **Embedded Styles Sheet.** With this method, you place the stylesheet in the HTML of the page, but the styles only apply to that page.
- **Inline Styles.** You can apply the properties of a *style* to an individual element on a page by writing the style definition around the HTML tag for that element.

If a page in your site is linked to an external stylesheet and you create an embedded, or inline, stylesheet, those styles will add to or override the attributes defined in the external stylesheet.

We'll walk through these stylesheet methods, one at a time.

External Stylesheets

When you create a linked stylesheet in the FrontPage Explorer, it can be used on any of the pages in the current Web. As I mentioned earlier, this is one of the more powerful CSS options, but it comes with a small price: You need to know how to write the stylesheet yourself. You can easily find information on the correct stylesheet syntax, by doing a search on the Web.

NOTE Writing stylesheets is beyond the scope of this book, but this is the basic methodology. Style definitions can be any HTML tag, like *h2*, and they're followed by a list of properties which are contained within curly braces, with each property separated by a semicolon. A basic example would look like this: h2 {font-size: 14 pt; line-height: 16 pt; font-style: italic; font-family: arial; color: blue; text-align: center}. In this example, anytime you would use the heading 2 style in FrontPage, on a page using this stylesheet, the text would be blue Arial italic centered and be 14 pts in size with 16 pts of leading.

1. Open the site you want to create the stylesheet for in the Explorer and select the Folders icon on the Views bar.
2. In Folder view, select the topmost folder in the left pane. This is the folder that begins with *http://*.
3. Create a new page by selecting the New Page button, or by right-clicking in the right pane and selecting New Page from the pop-up menu.
4. Rename the new page so that it has a .css extension. It's wise to use an easily recognizable name, like *styles.css*.
5. The file is no longer an HTML file, and it can't contain any HTML tags. Double-click the page to open it in Notepad, and delete all of the HTML tags.
6. Type in the rules that will define your stylesheet. It should look something like the example shown in Figure 10-12 below.

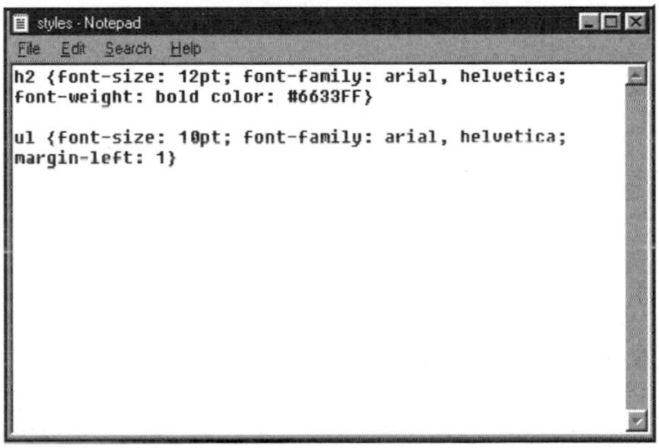

Figure 10-12

In this Figure, any text styled h2 will display in 12pt Arial Bold, and be in blue. If a user doesn't have Arial, like a Mac user, the font will move to the next one in line, Helvetica. The second style uses the ul tag. Any text that uses that tag will display in 10pt Arial and be indented 1 inch from the left.

7. Exit Notepad when you've finished defining the styles.

You can easily edit this stylesheet by repeating the steps outlined here and making any changes you like.

Linking to an External Stylesheet

Once you've created your stylesheet, you need to link it to the pages on your site. In order to link to the stylesheet, you need to create a link tag that points to it in the HTML of the page. The process goes like this:

1. In the Editor, open the page that you want to add the stylesheet link to.
2. Select the HTML View tab at the bottom of the Editor window.
3. Type a *link* tag, with an *href* pointing to the stylesheet, and place it between the *head* tags. Figure 10-13 shows how it should look in the Editor.

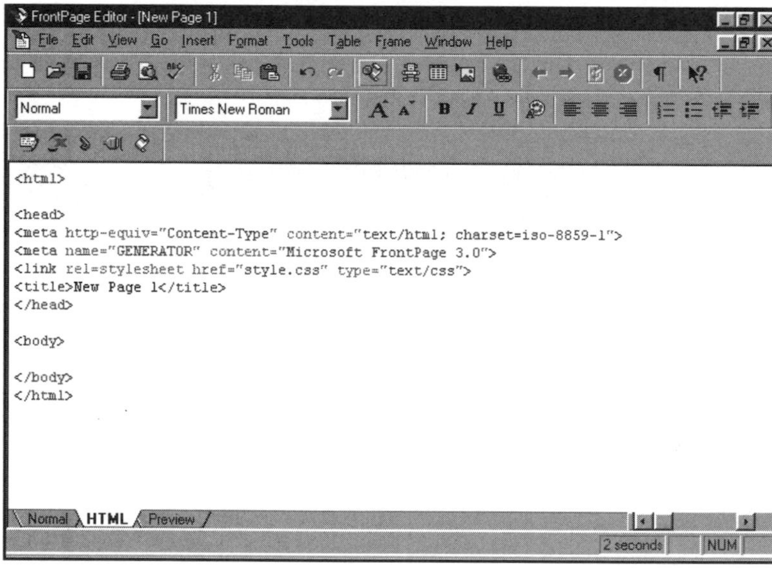

Figure 10-13

You must place this link on each page individually. Remember that you can always go back into the stylesheet file in the Explorer and modify the stylesheet, and there's no need to make any further changes to the individual pages. That's all there is to it.

Embedded Stylesheets

If you have a page in your site that you want to control individually, then an embedded stylesheet may be just the ticket. You can have an external stylesheet set up for many of your pages, and use the embedded stylesheet for certain pages where you might want to override the linked stylesheet. If you use an embedded stylesheet on a page that already contains a external stylesheet link, the embedded styles will either add to or override the external stylesheet.

To add an embedded stylesheet to a page, do the following:

1. Open the page in the Editor.
2. Select Stylesheet from the Format menu. This brings up the Format Stylesheet dialog box, as seen in Figure 10-14.

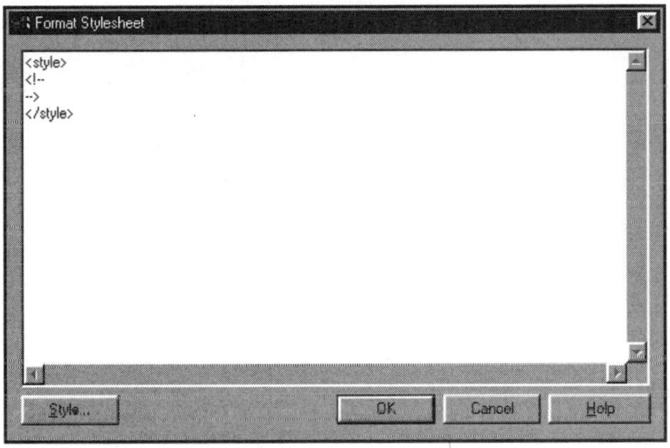

Figure 10-14

Notice the comment tags, <!-- and -->, most browsers will ignore tags they don't recognize, such as <style>, but they will display the text you type between the tags. In order to ensure that your stylesheet doesn't display as regular text in browsers that don't support stylesheets, you need to create your embedded stylesheet between the comment tags.

3. In between the comment tags, type the name of HTML tag you wish to apply the stylesheet to, like h1 for example, and then enter a space. Then define the stylesheet by typing the style attributes for the element.
4. When you're finished, click OK, and the embedded stylesheet is saved back to the page.

To edit an embedded stylesheet, follow steps 1 and 2 above, and then make any changes you like.

If you're adding an embedded stylesheet to a page that will also contain a link to an external stylesheet, you need to do a little extra step. Before you add your embedded styles, and in between the comment tags, type *@import URL (/style.css)*, where *style.css* is the name of the linked stylesheet, this is shown in Figure 10-15 below. You still need to include the link in the HTML, as described above in the section, "External Stylesheets."

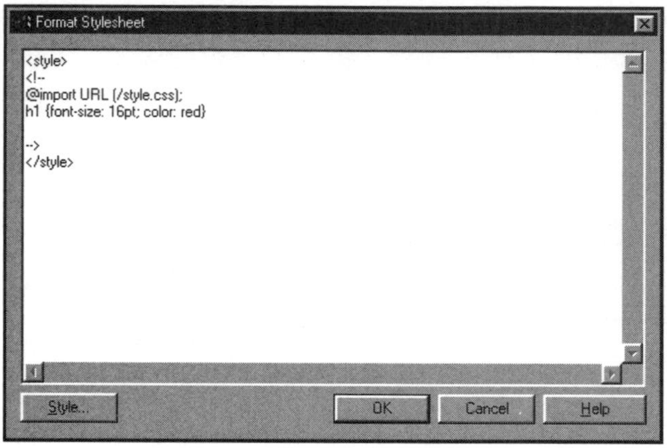

Figure 10-15

Inline Stylesheets

With Inline styles, you can quickly and easily change the appearance of a tag, or a group of tags on the page. If you want to define unique properties to a word in a paragraph, the entire paragraph itself, or almost any other element on the page, you can use the Inline style procedure, described here.

First, select the element or elements in the Editor's Normal View that you want to apply the style to, then follow these steps:

1. Right-click the selection and choose its properties dialog box from the pop-up menu. For example, if you selected only a few words, you'd select the Font Properties dialog box, but if you selected the entire paragraph, you'd select Paragraph Properties.
2. Click the Style button in the properties dialog box, bringing up the Style dialog box. If the Style button is not on the Properties dialog box for the selected element, you can't apply an inline style to that element.
3. In the Style dialog box, define the properties of the selected element. When you're finished, click OK. The inline style is applied to the element and the result is displayed in the Editor.

If you use an Inline stylesheet on a page that already contains an external stylesheet link, the Inline styles will either add to or override the external stylesheet.

The Style Button

You've seen this button all over that place, right? And you've probably been wondering, "When am I going to find out what that thing does?" Well this is it—I hope it was worth the wait.

If you're having trouble with the stylesheet syntax, or if you have absolutely no desire to even try it, you can still use stylesheets, effectively, on your pages. This procedure outlines the creation of an embedded stylesheet on the page, but selecting the Style button on any properties dialog box that has one will apply styles to that element. Here's how to use the Style button to create an embedded stylesheet:

1. In the Editor, open the page that you want to include the stylesheet.
2. Select Stylesheet from the Format menu to bring up the Format Stylesheet dialog box, as seen in Figure 10-16.

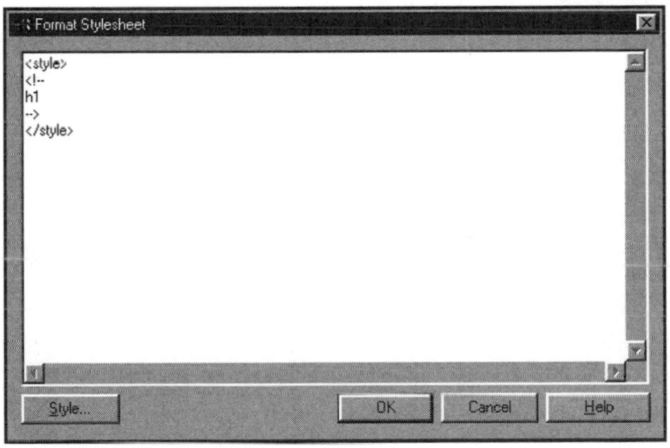

Figure 10-16

The Format Stylesheet dialog box with the h1 tag entered, before using the Style button.

3. In between the comment tags, type the name of the HTML tag you wish to apply the stylesheet to, and then enter a space.
4. Select the Style button. This brings up the Style dialog box (see Figure 10-17), from which you can define every attribute you can think of to your text.

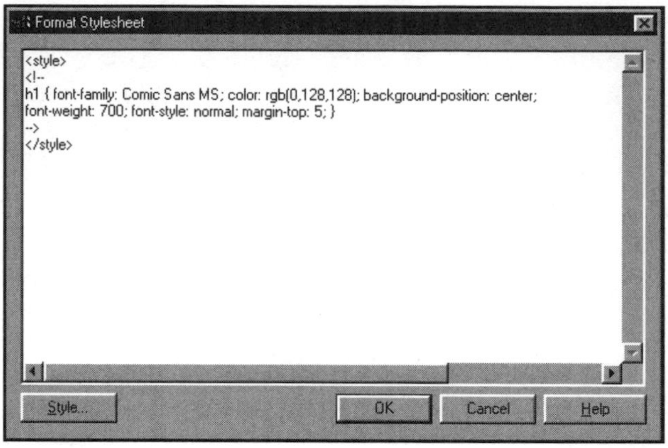

Figure 10-17

The Format Stylesheet dialog box, after using the Style button. The style definitions have been added automatically. Note that the style will display in one long line; it was wrapped purposely here so that the entire style could be displayed.

TIP You can edit any embedded stylesheet using the Style dialog box, even a stylesheet that you wrote yourself. On any page that has an embedded stylesheet, select Stylesheet from the Format menu. In the Format Stylesheet dialog box, click anywhere between the curly brackets of the style you want to edit. This brings up the Style dialog box which details the properties currently assigned to the style. You can modify the style in any way you like from here.

Making Classes

Let's say that your pal John is making a site for his son's daycare, and he wants all of the heading 1's in the site to be in a different color. He already knows that he wants to use an embedded stylesheet, but how? All John has to do is add what is known as a *class* to any style and he could potentially have any number of versions of the style. A class is defined by typing a period and a name after the HTML tag. For example, to achieve the multi-colored heading 1's for the daycare site, John could have styles, *h1.green*, *h1.red*, and *h1.blue*, and so on, each one exactly the same as the other except for the font color.

Follow these steps to add classes to a stylesheet:

1. Select Stylesheet from the Format menu to bring up the Format Stylesheet dialog box.
2. Type in your first class name, *h1.green*. Remember to put it between the comment tags.
3. Click the Style button and apply the common attributes that you want all of the h1's to have, like size, margins, or indent. Remember to make the font color green for this one (see Figure 10-18).

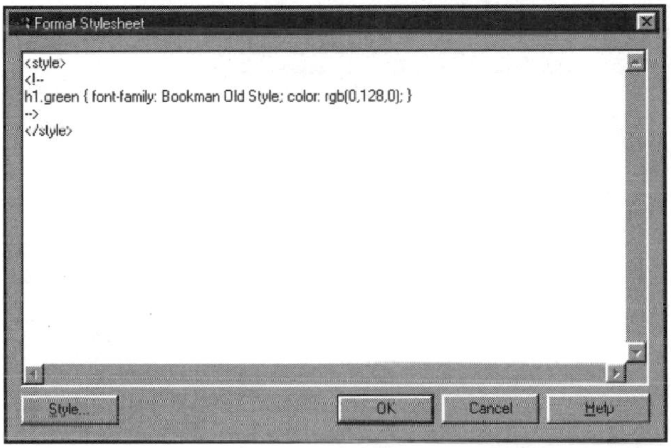

Figure 10-18

The first class h1.green and its attributes.

4. Copy the entire line of the style and paste it below *h1.green*.
5. Change the name of the class to *h1.red*.
6. Place your cursor anywhere within the curly brackets of *h1.red* (see Figure 10-19), and then click the Style button.
7. In the Style dialog box, seen in Figure 10-20, change the color of the text to Red, and then click OK.
8. Repeat this process for each style class you wish to define. When you're finished, click OK to close the Format Stylesheet dialog box.

Each new class will now be listed in the Style drop-down menu in the Editor for that page.

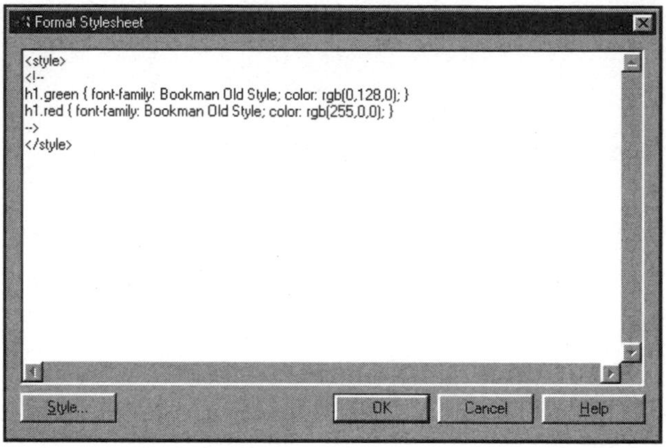

Figure 10-19

This screen shows the new class, h1.red, below the first class.

You can also create classes by selecting the properties dialog box for a given element, and then click the Style button. Figure 10-20 shows the Style dialog box, with the Class tab selected.

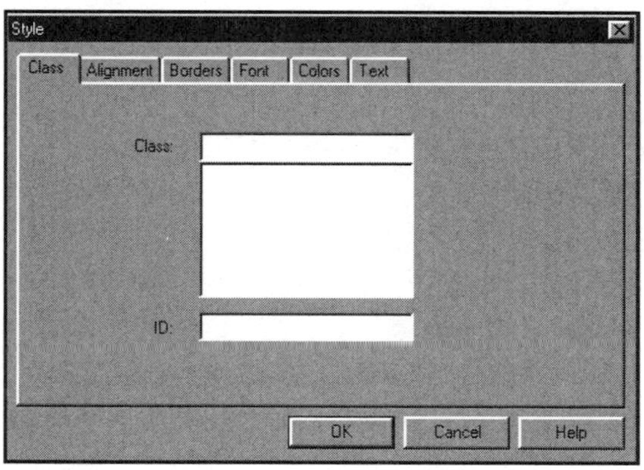

Figure 10-20

Type the class name you wish to use or select one from the list. Then apply the attributes to the class using the remaining tabs on the dialog box. You can apply class styles to various elements, like images via the Image Properties dialog box, paragraphs via the Paragraph Properties dialog box, or tables via the Table Properties dialog box.

Applying a Style to Text

Now that you know how to create different types of stylesheets and get them linked or embedded on your page, you need to apply the style to some text on the page. You can do this in two different ways:

- Highlight the text in the Editor and select the appropriate style from the Style drop-down menu. This option will work only for embedded stylesheets.
- In HTML view in the Editor, add the tag yourself.

If you're using an external stylesheet, it's a good idea to print out the .css file; that way, you have all of the names and definitions as a handy reference.

Dynamic HTML—What the Heck Is It?

So, do you want to add a little action to your page, well, do ya? If you're using a browser that supports dynamic HTML, then you're ready to power up, leave the kiddies behind, and join the big boys. Dynamic HTML harnesses the power of the latest and most powerful browsers. You can make text fly right off of your page, or apply cool transition effects between pages—the power is in your hands, so grab hold, and take advantage; step into the world of dynamic HTML.

WARNING Be aware that these features will only work in a browser that supports Dynamic HTML, like Internet Explorer 4.0.

Animations

If you want to make words and letters dance on the page, apply one of the many animation options built into the FrontPage Editor.

Select the text that you want to animate, and choose Animation from the format menu, then select any one of the many effects listed. When the user enters a pages that contains an animation effect, the animation will play and the text will end up where you entered it on the page in the Editor. FrontPage comes with 14 different animation effects choices, as follows:

Fly From Bottom
Fly From Left
Fly From Right
Fly From Top
Fly From Bottom-left
Fly From Bottom-Right
Fly From Top-left
Fly From Top-Right
Fly Top Right By Word
Fly Bottom Right By Word
Drop In By Word
Spiral
Zoom In
Zoom Out

Each of these effects are played when the user firsts visits the page. These advanced controls will play only in browsers that support dynamic HTML; all older browsers will just ignore the effects and display the elements as if dynamic HTML didn't exist.

Page Transitions

You can add a little magic to your page, and you don't even need a top hat or a fuzzy rabbit. If you want to add that something extra to set a page apart from the rest, try one of the transition effects included with FrontPage. For example, you can have the page fade through as the user visits or exits a page, or you can have the page dissolve away. A transition effect is seen either when a user first enters or exits a page in the site, or the site itself.

You implement transition effects via the Page Transitions dialog box, shown in Figure 10-21. To view the dialog box, select Page Transition from the format menu.

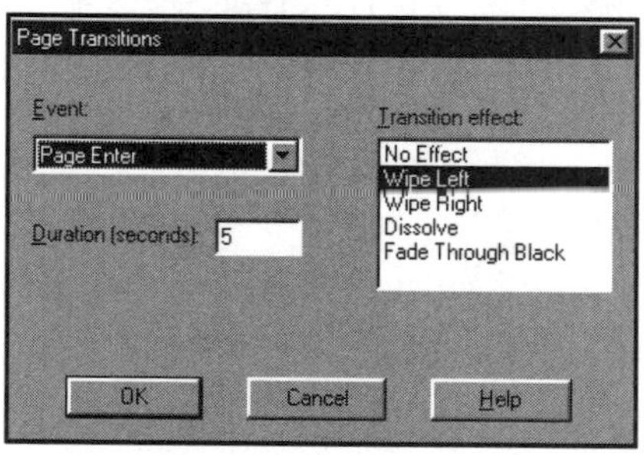

Figure 10-21

To set a Page Transition, first you pick an event, then select an effect, and finally, choose the duration, in seconds, that the effect will take to complete. It's a good idea to keep the duration time low—you don't want the transition to get in the way of a enjoyable user experience.

Collapsible Outlines

If you have information styled in a list, you can add a little action to show and hide the contents of the list. When the user comes to the page, they'll see the first item in the list; as they mouseover the list item, the next item in the list appears, and so on, throughout the list.

Select the Collapsible Outlines check box on the List Properties dialog box to add the Collapsible Outline feature to the selected list on the current page.

Form Field Extensions

If you've created a form, FrontPage automatically sets a certain tab order for each field in the form, based on when it was placed on the page. If you want to define your own custom tab order, enter a number between 1 and 999 in the Tab Order field of the Form Field Properties dialog box.

When a user is viewing your form, they can tab through the fields in the order you define; number 1 first, number 2 second, and so on. This is a great help for users who have disabilities and anyone who has trouble using a mouse. If your site is being viewed in a browser that doesn't support tab order, then the default order will be available.

Database Integration

If you want to be able to access data in a database and display results on a Web page, this section will help you get started. With the Database Region Wizard, you can send Structured Query Language (SQL) queries to an Open Data Base Connectivity (ODBC) database that's available from the Web server. When someone visits your page and enters a query, it's run based on the SQL parameter field values. The results of the query are used with a custom form handler—in this case an Active Server Page (ASP)—to generate the information for display in a browser.

Active Server Pages

An *ASP* is basically the same as any other HTML page, except that it contains server-side scripting, embedded within the HTML. Any Web servers that are compatible with ASP can read and then execute the server-side scripts in the HTML.

Database Region Wizard

To start the wizard, choose Database from the Insert menu and select Database Region Wizard from the pop-up. Figure 10-22 shows the first screen of the wizard.

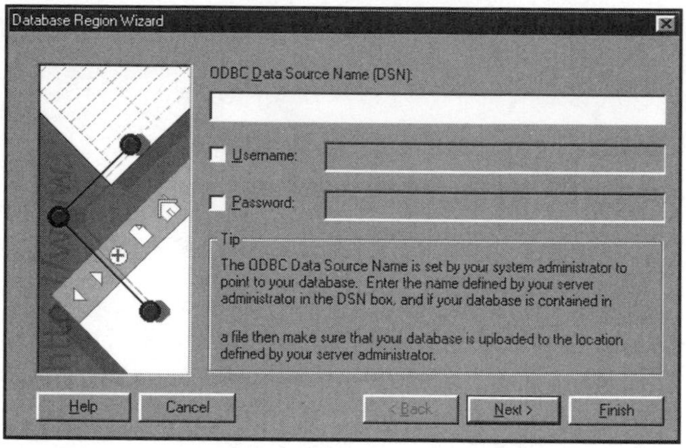

Figure 10-22

The first screen of the Database Region configures connection to the ODBC database.

Database Connection

In this section, you specify the ODBC data source name, the user name, and the password.

- **ODBC Data Source Name (DSN).** Enter the ODBC data source you want to connect to. This data source is defined using the ODBC Administrator and must be configured as a system data source. You must fill in this text box.

  If the Web server runs on Windows 95 or Windows NT Server 4.0, and the database resides on the same server, you can create the named ODBC data source using the "32bit ODBC" or "ODBC" entry in the Windows Control Panel. For other ODBC configurations, consult the documentation for your database.

- **Username.** If the database system you're connecting to requires a user name, select the Username check box and enter the user name in the corresponding text box.

- **Password.** If the database system you're connecting to requires a password, select the Password check box and enter the password in the corresponding text box.

Click the Next button to move to the next screen of Database Region Wizard, seen in Figure 10-23. Remember that you can always use the Back button to move backward through the wizard.

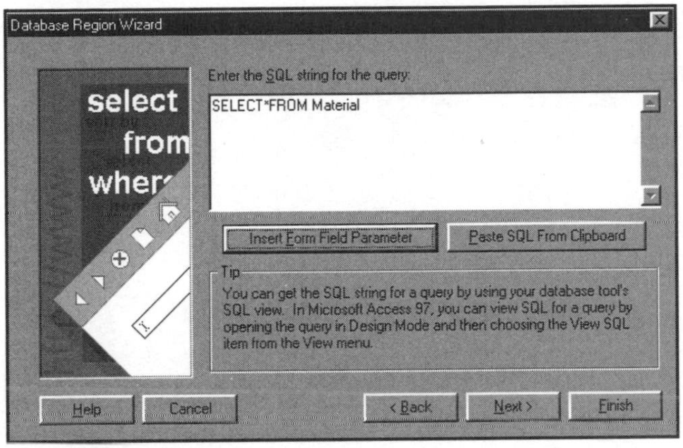

Figure 10-23

In the second screen of the Database Region Wizard, you define SQL queries for the ODBC database on your server.

This screen allows you to enter one or more SQL queries, by typing them in directly or pasting them in from the clipboard. To paste a SQL query from the clipboard do the following: Create a query in Access, select the SQL view in Access, and then copy the SQL query and paste it into the Database Region Wizard by selecting the Paste SQL From Clipboard button.

Insert Form Field Parameter

Clicking this button brings up the Insert Form Field Parameter dialog box, where you can insert an IDC parameter value for the SQL query.

Click the Next button to move to the next screen of the wizard, shown in Figure 10-24.

Add the names of the query fields in your database by selecting the Add Field button and entering the field name in the Add Field dialog box. If you would like the database to be displayed in a table on the page, enable the Show The Query In Table check box.

When you finish entering information in the Database Region Wizard, click the Finish button. FrontPage will write the appropriate client-side code to the page, and place a database information component on your page. If you've added the database component to an existing page, when you save the page, FrontPage will warn you that it must be renamed with .asp extension in order for the database to become active. If you're saving the page for the first time, FrontPage automatically recognizes the database and inserts the .asp extension for you.

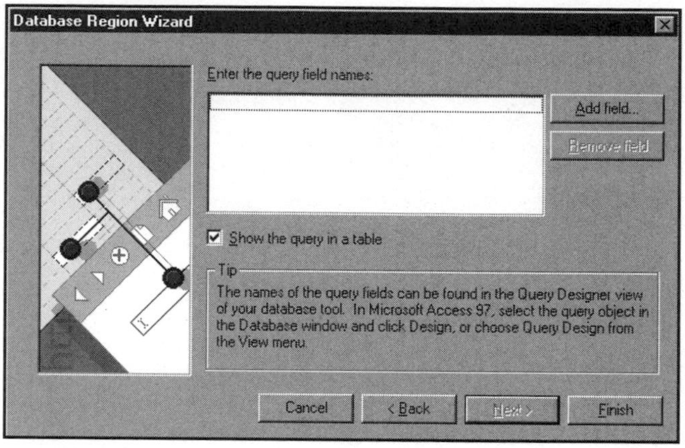

Figure 10-24

In the third screen of the Database Region Wizard, you query field names.

Modify the Database

You can open the Database Region Wizard to modify the settings you've already entered, by right-clicking the Database Region Wizard component and choosing Database Region Properties from the pop-up menu. If you want to quickly enter a new query field name or choose from an existing one, right-click the Database Region Wizard element and select Database Column Value Properties from the pop-up menu.

The ability to access information in a database from a Web page is a powerful feature. This section has given you a brief introduction to the feature, which you can explore further.

Give Me a PUSH

If you've been paying attention to the Internet lately, you've undoubtedly heard the term *push technology* used a lot. Push is one of the latest technologies on the scene and promises to change the way we use the Internet. The basic idea behind it is that you can get custom information delivered to your computer and view it when you want to—even offline.

FrontPage uses what's known as a *channel*, which allows users to receive notification when pages in your site are modified, or to browse your site offline by subscribing to your site. A channel can also display as a screen saver or as a desktop component in browsers that support this technology. In FrontPage, you can define a channel for the current Web or selected pages in the Web, and then you can create a button that allows users to subscribe to your channel, and finally, you publish the Web as a channel to the server. You begin by using the Channel Definition Wizard.

Channel Definition Wizard

The Channel Definition Wizard runs you through the steps needed to create a channel, and creates a Channel Definition Format (CDF) file. This CDF file lets users see your site as a channel by providing an index of information available in the channel and the means by which the user can update that information. By taking the choices you make in the wizard, the CDF file can let users subscribe to your Web as a channel or see it as a screen saver or a desktop component, and even receive e-mail when the channel is modified.

Before You Use the Wizard

Here are a few things to think about before running the Channel Definition Wizard:

- If you want some branding on your channel, like logos and icons, prepare these ahead of time so they'll be available when you use the wizard. A logo should be an 80x32 pixel GIF, and it's used to identify your channel in the browser. To identify the pages in your channel, use an icon image (this should be a 16x16 pixel GIF).
- If you don't want all of the pages in your Web to be available in the channel, organize the channel pages in their own folder or various subfolders. You can create and modify a folder structure in the Explorer's Folder view; for more information, see Chapter 3.

Using the Channel Definition Wizard

Choose Define Channel from the Tools menu in the FrontPage Explorer. This starts the Channel Definition Wizard. Each step of the wizard contains descriptions of the information required. Fill out the information needed, and select the Next button after each step.

When you get to step 7, the final step, there are two Advanced Options that require a little explanation.

If you would like the wizard to place a Subscribe button on the page for you, and you're using shared borders and Navigation buttons, enable the first check box. If you want to test your Channel locally, clear the Prepare for Publishing button. If you want to publish the Web right now, enter a URL in the Prepare for Publishing text field.

When you've finished making your selections, click the Save button. FrontPage will create the CDF file in the Explorer. You can rerun the wizard at any time by double-clicking the CDF file in Navigation, All Files, or Folders views.

Create a Subscribe Button Yourself

If your Web doesn't use navigation bars, or you choose not to have the wizard create the Subscribe button for you, you can add one to a page yourself by creating a link from the page in the Editor to the CDF file in the Web. The following steps describe this procedure:

1. In the Editor, open the page that you want to create the button on. The most common location is on the home page of your site.
2. Choose the display method of the button, either an image or text, and select it.
3. If your button is text, click the Create Or Edit Hyperlink button, or choose Hyperlink from the Edit menu. If you want your button to be an image, draw a hotspot over the image with the Rectangular Hotspot tool (on the Image toolbar). This brings up the Create Or Edit Hyperlink dialog box.
4. In the Create Or Edit Hyperlink dialog box, select the CDF file in the current Web as the target of the Hyperlink, and then click OK.

That's all there is to it.

Publishing a Channel

When you want to publish or republish your channel to a remote server on the World Wide Web, rerun the Channel Definition Wizard, and then click the Next button until you reach step 7. In the Advanced Options area of the dialog box, enable the Prepare for Publishing check box, and then enter the URL that you want to publish to. Click OK when you've finished.

In the Explorer, click the Publish button on the menu bar. If you're re-publishing to the same location, FrontPage will publish the channel. If you're publishing to a location for the first time, enter the URL that you want to publish to.

Once you've published a channel, the CDF file will only allow users to subscribe from that location. If they had previously subscribed to the channel in a different location, they'll have to subscribe again in the new location. Every time you change locations, users will have to subscribe again in order to see the channel.

Accessibility

When you create this great site, you want it to be available to the most people possible, no matter how they use the Web. Sometimes as we're clicking away on this button and that one, enjoying all of the cool colors and graphics, the fancy layouts, and the sophisticated interactive elements popular today, we tend to forget about the person that can't see or the person who has trouble using the mouse or keyboard, not to mention the person who has a slow connection.

There are a few things you can do to improve the accessibility of your site, without giving up the flash. These are not so much advanced features of FrontPage, as they are advanced ways to *think* about the creation of your site.

- Always use the Alternative Text option on the Image Properties dialog box, and make the text short and functional. Do this for *every* graphic on your site, whether it's navigational or decorative.
- If you're using thumbnail images and linking to a larger version of the picture, add descriptive text to the page along with the larger graphic. That way, a person using a reader device can get a complete description of the image when they follow the thumbnail link.
- If you use image maps as the only way to navigate through your site, the person who can't see or has graphics turned off can't navigate the site, even if you use alternative text. You can easily place a text-only version of your navigation at the bottom of every page, so your site's navigable by everyone.
- If it's at all possible, create a separate text-only version of your site and give users a choice. If that's impossible, then consider making text-only versions of selected pages in your site and placing a text-only link from the graphic page to the text-only page. For instance, if you have an online catalog, you can easily generate a text-only descriptive page for your products.

There are many more ways to make your site accessible to everyone. You can find more information by doing a search on the Web.

Other Advanced Features

FrontPage includes other advanced features that you should know about but that are too technical to discuss at length in this book. For more information on these features, see the FrontPage Web site at www.microsoft.com/frontpage/.

The following are two examples of the many FrontPage-related topics on the FrontPage Web site:

- The FrontPage Software Developer's Kit (SDK), which can be downloaded from the Microsoft Web site, allows you to create custom wizards and custom FrontPage components, add custom menu commands, and create custom "Designer HTML" fragments that can be added to pages in the Editor using drag and drop.
- FrontPage supports integration with Microsoft Visual SourceSafe (VSS), in order to provide multi-user revision control on changes made to the Web site.

Coming Up

Next, we'll round out our tour of FrontPage by looking at FrontPage's server-related offerings, including the Microsoft Personal Web Server, the FrontPage Personal Web Server, and the FrontPage Server Extensions.

CHAPTER 11

Web Servers

FrontPage Knows Servers

All the wonderful Web sites you'll design and create with FrontPage will more than likely be stored on a Web server. A Web server is software or a computer that stores Web sites, scripts, databases, and other related files, and makes Web pages accessible from a browser. Since the term can refer to either software or a computer, you must look at the context to determine which it is referring to. The Web server market is becoming large and competitive, with versions of Web servers that meet various needs and run on different platforms.

This chapter discusses how FrontPage interacts with the numerous Web servers; it does not discuss the pros and cons of the servers themselves. For information on the advantages and disadvantages of major Web servers, look in Internet-related periodicals and on the server manufacturers' World Wide Web sites.

Once you make a choice of a Web server to use with FrontPage (perhaps you already have a server up and running), chances are that FrontPage will interact with it smoothly. FrontPage supports the most popular shareware and commercial Web servers in use today, via software programs and scripts known as the *FrontPage Server Extensions*, which are discussed later in this chapter. (You'll also find a list of the Web servers that FrontPage supports later in the chapter.) The Server Extensions are the go-between from the FrontPage client to the Web server, helping both parties communicate behind the scenes.

If you're lucky, you might not need to buy a Web server at all; the FrontPage Bonus Pack includes the Microsoft Personal Web Server for Windows 95, and the FrontPage installation includes the FrontPage Personal Web Server.

It's Server Time

The Microsoft Personal Web Server and the FrontPage Personal Web Server are ideal for working directly with FrontPage-created Web sites. They are best used for testing sites and for acting as the main server for a low-volume intranet at a small company or organization.

Many FrontPage Web site developers create their sites locally, on a network or even on a single computer, and test them with the Personal Web Servers before moving the site to a higher-volume server within their company. The Personal Web Servers can help you test all aspects of a FrontPage site, including links to the Internet and the World Wide Web, the use of *FrontPage components*, the *Database Region Wizard*, forms, and any other content that requires communication between the client and the server.

TIP The Microsoft Personal Web Server supports ISAPI DLLs in addition to CGI scripts.

The servers fully support the Hypertext Transfer Protocol (HTTP) and Common Gateway Interface (CGI) standards. They are compatible with existing CGI scripts, so you don't need to be concerned with writing new scripts if you decide to use one of the Personal Web Servers.

The Personal Web Servers usually don't need to be configured; they're configured automatically when you install them. The Microsoft Personal Web Server can be installed from the Bonus Pack and the FrontPage Personal Web Server can be installed during the FrontPage installation. You can run the servers on a local computer or on a computer connected to a network. If you create and edit sites using the Personal Web Servers over a network, you can often expect the communication between the FrontPage client and the Personal Web Servers (for example, when opening or saving a Web site) to be slower.

The Microsoft Personal Web Server is the preferred Web server for use with FrontPage. In fact, the FrontPage Setup program encourages you to install the Microsoft Personal Web Server rather than the FrontPage Personal Web Server. For more information on the Microsoft Personal Web Server, see the section "Microsoft Personal Web Server," later in this chapter.

Although the Personal Web Servers are excellent for testing and for use as low-volume Web servers, you might need a server that can handle higher traffic. For example, if you use the Microsoft Personal Web Server with Windows NT Workstation, the license permits only 10 simultaneous

Web connections. If you need to support higher traffic, you can use Windows NT Server and Internet Information Server (IIS), or a UNIX Web server that can support FrontPage.

The FrontPage Server Extensions

Suppose for a second that you're stranded in the Ukraine, but you speak only a wee bit of Ukrainian. Can you survive? Probably. Can you communicate? Sure, maybe a smidge. But can you communicate *well?* Probably not. You need a translator, or one of those English-to-Ukrainian pocket dictionaries, to make sure you come across the way you want to.

The FrontPage Server Extensions perform this kind of translation duty between your FrontPage site and a Web server. Each set of Server Extensions is software that lives on the Web server and gets involved whenever communication takes place between your site and the server. Since these extensions are available for a variety of Web servers, FrontPage can communicate with many different Web servers.

TIP For the Microsoft Personal Web Server, Peer Web Services, and IIS, the many Server Extension components are implemented as ISAPI DLLs; for all other Web servers, they're implemented as CGI scripts.

The FrontPage Server Extensions are a good bargain for a number of reasons:

- They're free.
- They make uploading a site to a Web server fast and easy with FrontPage.
- They allow you to set author and end-user permissions for your Web sites.
- They ensure that FrontPage components work the way they're intended to. For example, if you use a Search Component in your FrontPage site, the Server Extensions ensure that the component performs as it's supposed to. Without the Server Extensions installed, the FrontPage component won't work.

Web Servers and Platforms

As of this writing, FrontPage Server Extensions are available for the following Web servers.

Commercial Web servers:

- Microsoft Internet Information Server (for Windows NT Server 3.51 and 4.0)
- Microsoft Peer Web Services (for Windows NT Workstation 4.0)
- Microsoft Personal Web Server (for Windows 95; included with the FrontPage 98 Bonus Pack)
- FrontPage Personal Web Server (for Windows 95; included with FrontPage 98)
- Netscape Enterprise Server (for Windows NT and UNIX)
- Netscape FastTrack Server (for Windows 95, Windows NT, and UNIX)
- Netscape Commerce Server (for Windows NT and UNIX)
- Netscape Communications Server (for Windows NT and UNIX)
- O'Reilly WebSite and WebSite Professional (for Windows 95 and Windows NT)

Noncommercial Web servers:

- NCSA (for UNIX)
- Apache (for UNIX)
- CERN (for UNIX)

Platforms:

- Microsoft Windows 95
- Microsoft Windows NT Workstation and Windows NT Server
- UNIX (Solaris, SunOS, HP/UX, IRIX, BSDi, Linux, and Digital UNIX)

Where to get 'em. The FrontPage Server Extensions for all Windows 95-based and Windows NT-based Web servers (including those from Microsoft, Netscape, and O'Reilly) are included with FrontPage 98 and are installed automatically when you install FrontPage. You can download the FrontPage Server Extensions for UNIX–based Web servers from the FrontPage Web site at www.microsoft.com/frontpage/..

Extracting the Server Extensions. Server Extensions are typically in the form of a self-extracting file or EXE file. Follow the specific instructions accompanying the Server Extensions to extract them on your Web server. Normally, you just double-click on the EXE file to begin the process.

The normal FrontPage Server Extensions setup process emphasizes ease of installation and is oriented toward a low-security intranet environment. However, Internet Service Providers that want to host the FrontPage Server Extensions, or customers who want a higher-security installation, should visit the Web Presence Providers section of the FrontPage Web site at www.microsoft.com/frontpage/. Here you can download the documentation and software provided for Web Presence Providers.

Server Administration

You can perform most everyday server management tasks in the FrontPage Explorer. For example, you can specify users; specify access rights for users; specify settings to work with a *proxy server;* and, based on the Web server, administer passwords via commands on the Explorer's menus. Most of these commands are related to site-specific tasks and are discussed in Chapters 3 and 5.

The Server Administrator

The FrontPage Server Administrator is a program that helps you carry out numerous tasks related to installing and uninstalling Server Extensions and configuring various elements of the Web servers you use with FrontPage.

SHORTCUT You'll find a shortcut labeled *FrontPage Server Administrator* in the C:\Program Files\ Microsoft FrontPage folder, or whatever folder you installed FrontPage in. You can launch the Windows version of the Server Administrator by double-clicking that shortcut in the Windows Explorer.

FrontPage comes with two flavors of the Server Administrator: a Windows version, as seen in Figure 11-1 on the next page, and a command-line version. Both are typically found in the Program Files\Microsoft FrontPage\bin folder on the drive or server that FrontPage is installed on. The Windows version is FPSRVWIN.EXE, and the command-line version is FPSRVADM.EXE. You can launch either application by double-clicking it in the Windows Explorer.

Below are step-by-step procedures for tasks you can perform with the Windows version of the FrontPage Server Administrator. Explicit directions for using the command-line version can be found in FrontPage's online help under the topic "FrontPage Server Administrator—Command Line Version."

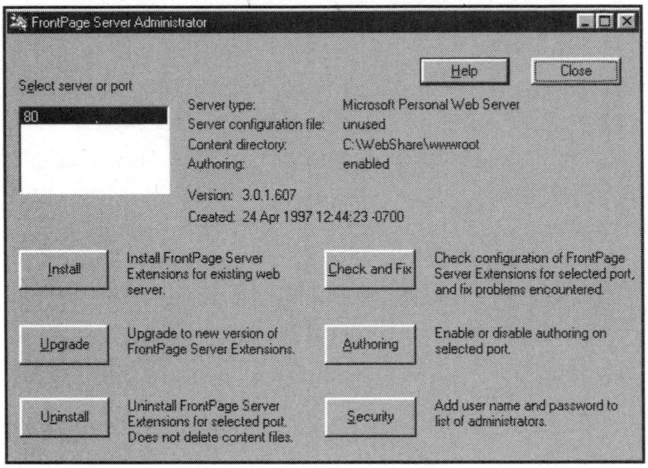

Figure 11-1

The Windows version of the FrontPage Server Administrator.

TIP

FrontPage supports multi-homing for all Web servers that offer this feature. Multi-homing is the ability of a single Web server to host sites for multiple domain names; for example, the domains *www.bill.com* and *www.vivian.com,* might actually reside on a single server. This option might be available to you during your Server Extensions configuration.

Installing the FrontPage Server Extensions

To install a set of FrontPage Server Extensions for an existing Web server, you must first install the Web server software—and it's a good idea to test it using a browser to ensure that it works properly. Also, the files required to install the Server Extensions on your Web server need to be copied to the server and extracted if necessary.

To install the Server Extensions, follow these steps:

1. Launch the FrontPage Server Administrator.
2. Click the Install button. In the Configure Server Type dialog box, from the Server Type drop-down list, select your Web server type, and then click OK.

   A dialog box or multiple dialog boxes will appear, depending on the server you're installing the Server Extensions for.
3. Follow the instructions, and enter the appropriate information when prompted.

4. When you return to the FrontPage Server Administrator dialog box, click Close.

Uninstalling the FrontPage Server Extensions

To uninstall Server Extensions for a particular port, do the following:

1. Shut down the server.
2. Launch the FrontPage Server Administrator.
3. From the Select Port Number list, select the port for the Server Extensions you want to uninstall.
4. Click Uninstall. A Server Administrator dialog box appears, asking you to confirm the uninstall operation.
5. Click OK.
6. A message box is displayed indicating a successful uninstall; click OK.
7. In the FrontPage Server Administrator dialog box, click Close.

Uninstalling Server Extensions does not remove content files such as HTML files or image files.

Changing a Server's Port Number

To change a server's port number, you must first uninstall the Server Extensions on that port, change the port number, and then reinstall the Server Extensions.

To change the port number of a Web server that already has the Server Extensions running, do the following:

1. Shut down the server.
2. Launch the FrontPage Server Administrator.
3. From the Select Port Number list, select the port number you want to change.
4. Click Uninstall to remove the Server Extensions from the port. Click OK in the Server Administrator dialog box to accept your action, and when a dialog box appears indicating a succsssful uninstall, click OK.
5. Change the server's port number according to the directions supplied with the Web server. For example, for the FrontPage Personal Web Server, you would change the port number in the server configuration file (*httpd.cnf*).
6. Click Install in the FrontPage Server Administrator to reinstall the Server Extensions for the new port. Select the server type in the Configure Server Type dialog box and click OK. Follow the instructions, and enter the appropriate information when prompted.

7. If asked whether you want to restart the server, click Yes.
8. When you return to the FrontPage Server Administrator dialog box, click Close.

Adding an Administrator Name and Password

As described in Chapters 3 and 5, you can administer user names and possibly passwords in the Explorer using the Permissions command and the Change Password command. Depending on your Web server, you might also be able to add administrator names and passwords using the FrontPage Server Administrator. The advantage of using the FrontPage Server Administrator to add administrator names is that you don't have to have a site open in the Explorer, and in fact you can add administrator names and passwords for any site on any Web server you have access to. Simply follow these steps:

1. Launch the FrontPage Server Administrator.
2. Click the Security button. You'll see the Administrator Name And Password dialog box. (If you are using a Microsoft Web server, the Password section of the dialog may not be there, because passwords are handled at the system level. See the section "Passwords" in Chapter 5, for more information.)
3. Enter the name of the site in the Web Name text box, and the name of the administrator in the Name box.
4. If the password section is available, enter a password, and then confirm it in the Confirm Password text box. If the name is already registered, the password will be changed to the password you enter.
5. Click OK to close the Administrator Name And Password dialog box.
6. In the FrontPage Server Administrator dialog box, click Close.

TIP If you are using the Microsoft Personal Web Server, the Password text box, and the Confirm Password text box will not be displayed in the Administrator Name And Password dialog box. Passwords for the Microsoft Personal Web Server are handled by a Web-based Internet Services Administrator. See the section "Microsoft Personal Web Server" later in this chapter for more information.

Enabling or Disabling Authoring on a Selected Port

Disabling authoring on a port means the Explorer and the Editor will not be able to access any sites on that port. So, if you want all your FrontPage sites on a particular port to be uneditable with FrontPage, you can do the following:

1. Launch the FrontPage Server Administrator.
2. From the Select Port Number list, select the port on which you want to enable or disable authoring.
3. Click the Authoring button. The Enable/Disable Authoring dialog box appears, indicating whether authoring is currently enabled or disabled on the port.
4. Make your selection to enable or disable authoring for the port.
5. If you want Secure Sockets Layer (SSL) authoring, select the Require SSL For Authoring check box. This ensures that all authoring operations on the port are performed with SSL security.
6. After you make your selections, click OK.
7. In the FrontPage Server Administrator dialog box, click Close.

Upgrading Older FrontPage Sites When You Install a New Version of the FrontPage Server Extensions

When you install a new version of the FrontPage Server Extensions, you must upgrade sites created in the older version. This copies the necessary software to the content folders in the sites associated with the selected port. Content files or image files in the sites will not be changed.

Here's how to upgrade those old sites:

1. Launch the FrontPage Server Administrator.
2. Click the Upgrade button.
3. You'll see a Server Administrator dialog box telling you of the impending operation. Click OK. The Server Administrator upgrades the sites associated with the selected port. When the upgrade is finished, a dialog box is displayed confirming the operation. Click OK, and you are returned to the FrontPage Server Administrator dialog box.
4. Click Close to close the dialog box.

For more information on server administration and Server Extensions, you can consult FrontPage online help and visit the FrontPage Web site at www.microsoft.com/frontpage/.

Microsoft Personal Web Server

The Microsoft Personal Web Server provides capabilities for administration and configuration. When you first install the Personal Web Server, it is automatically configured to run. You should see a new icon in the lower right of your taskbar, indicating this.

If you double-click this icon, you see the Personal Web Server Properties dialog box, which has four tabs. You can also display this dialog box by clicking the Start button, choosing Control Panel from the Settings menu, and then double-clicking the Personal Web Server icon.

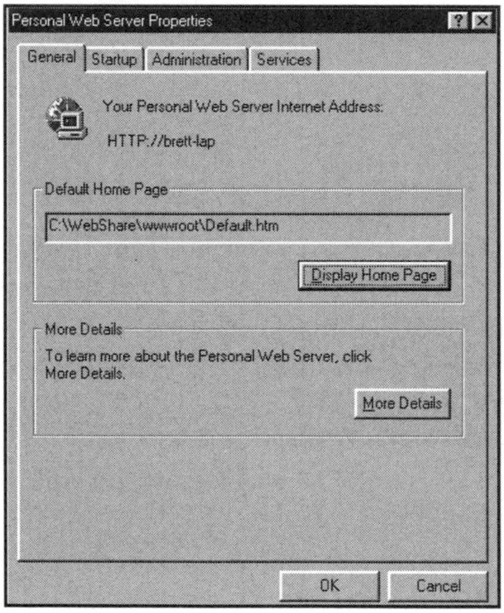

Figure 11-2

The General tab of the Personal Web Server Properties dialog box (shown in Figure 11-2 above) contains the server's Internet address, the home-page address, and a Display Home Page button. It also contains a More Details button, which when clicked displays information in your browser about the Personal Web Server such as getting started with the Personal Web Server, Personal Web Server Administration, and FTP Server Administration.

The Startup tab (as shown in Figure 11-3) contains information about the Web server state and enables you to start or stop the server. The Options section allows you to specify whether the Web server should start every time you start up your computer, and whether to display the Web server icon on the taskbar.

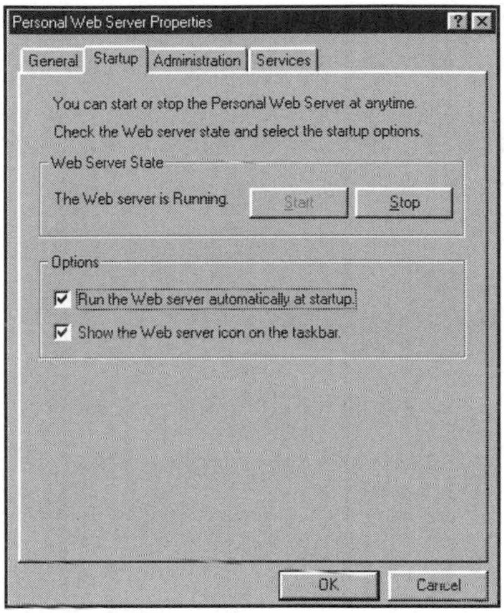

Figure 11-3

The Administration tab (shown in Figure 11-4) allows you to start the Web-based Personal Web Server administration tool. This lets you perform remote administration using a Web browser.

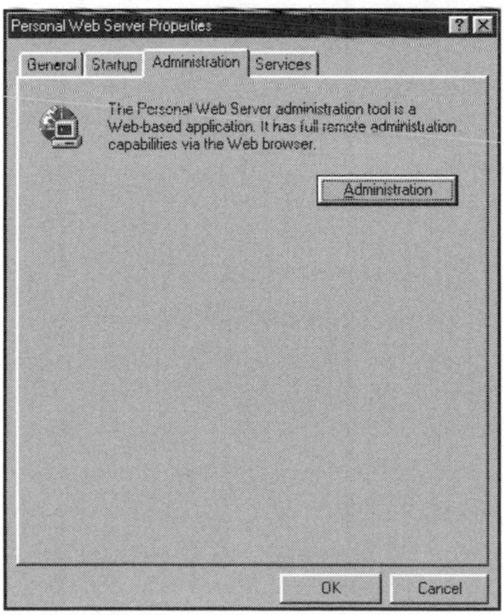

Figure 11-4

When you click the Administration button, the Internet Services Administrator page is displayed in your Web browser, as shown in Figure 11-5.

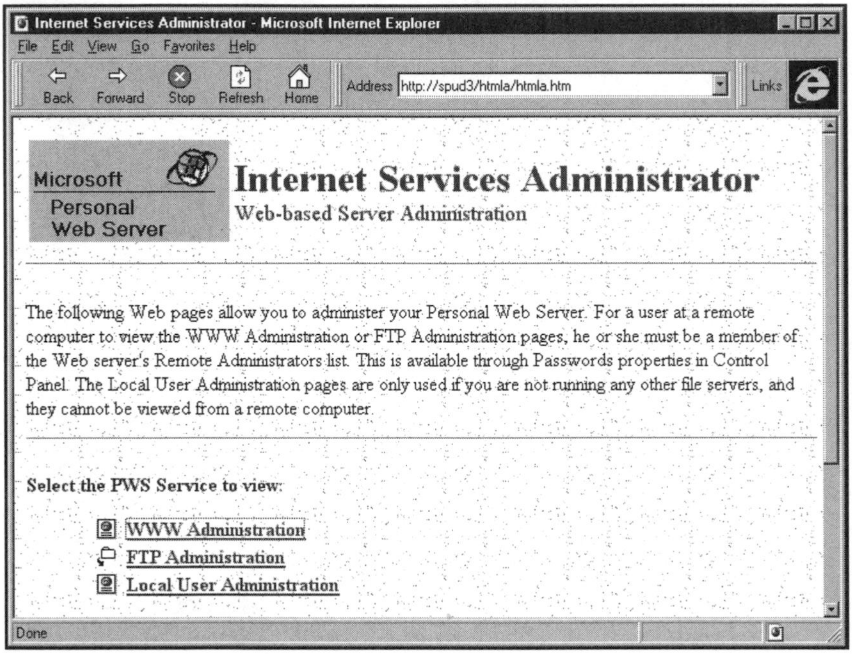

Figure 11-5

From here you can click links for WWW, FTP, and Local User Administration. If you click the WWW Administration link, the Internet Services Administrator - WWW page is displayed (as shown in Figure 11-6). From here, you can click the Service tab, which allows you to adjust password and other settings.

On the Directories tab, you can edit, add, or delete folders in your Web sites. The Logging tab allows you to configure your Web server log file, which by default is named *InetServer_Event.log* and is stored in the Windows folder.

If you click the Local User Administration link on the Internet Services Administrator page, the Internet Local User Administrator page is displayed. From here you can administer users and groups. These users and groups can then be added to sites using the Permissions command in the Explorer.

The final tab of the Personal Web Server Properties dialog box (in Figure 11-7), Services, allows you to change the properties as well as start or stop the FTP or HTTP services. When you select a service and click the

Properties button, the service's Properties dialog box is displayed. In this dialog box, you can set startup options and adjust home settings.

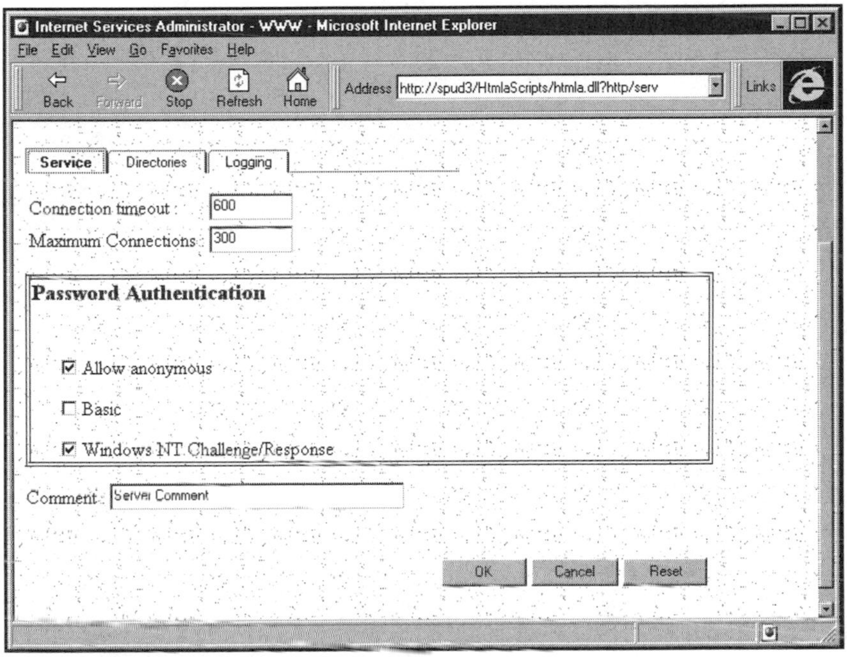

Figure 11-6

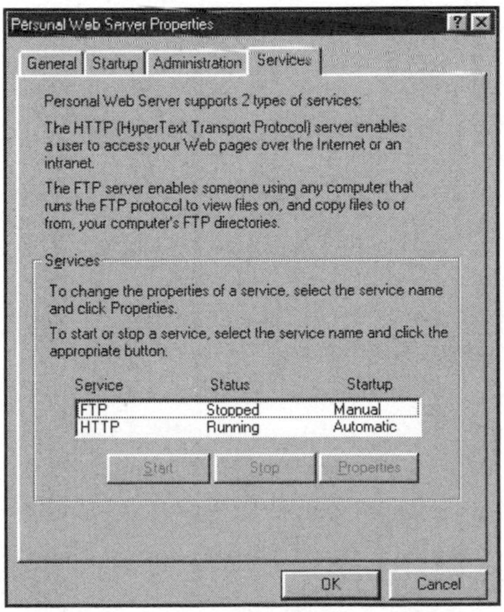

Figure 11-7

For more information on the Microsoft Personal Web Server, consult the documentation by clicking the More Details button on the General tab of the Personal Web Server Properties dialog box, or consult the FrontPage Web site, which is located at www.microsoft.com/frontpage/.

Internet Service Providers

You can always forgo the potential headaches of running your own Web server and let someone else take the aspirin for a change. Internet Service Providers (ISPs), also called Web hosts, are companies that house your site on their server and provide you with a variety of services—often for a very low fee when compared with the cost of hospitalizing those who suffer nervous breakdowns when their Web servers go on the fritz three times in the same week.

Most ISPs charge periodic fees (often monthly, biannually, or annually) to house your site; theses fees generally include a maximum megabyte allotment on the server, as well as at least one e-mail account. Most ISP's also offer some help in getting set up, and usually have CGI scripts and other goodies available to subscribers.

The advantages of using the services of an ISP include not having to worry about maintaining a Web server in-house, and faster user access to your site. ISPs often have the fastest connections available on the Internet. In addition, you avoid the expense and hassle of having to install a *firewall server* to protect your company's computing resources if your site is on the World Wide Web.

The disadvantages are relatively few; among them is the fact that you're not the one in control. Nearly all business owners dream of having business go so well that their sites must expand to meet the growing consumer need for information; if these dreams come true for you, it might be easier (and ultimately less expensive) to manage a large site in-house instead of over a distance.

There are hundreds of ISPs nationwide that have the FrontPage Server Extensions installed and are specifically set up to host FrontPage sites. You can find a complete list at www.microsoft.com/frontpage/.

If your Web site is already hosted by an ISP that does not support FrontPage, and you'd like to turn the site into a FrontPage site, refer the ISP to the FrontPage Web Presence Providers (WPP) information in the FrontPage Web site. In the meantime, you can still post your FrontPage site to your ISP as long as the ISP provides you with FTP access for posting your Web content. Whether or not your ISP supports FrontPage, you can use the Publish FrontPage Web command in the FrontPage Explorer to easily post your Web content. When you use this command, if FrontPage doesn't detect the FrontPage Server Extensions on your ISP's Web server, it will automatically launch the Web Publishing Wizard, if it is installed. The wizard allows you to post your site to Web servers that do not have the FrontPage Server Extensions installed. (The wizard can be installed from the FrontPage Bonus Pack.)

For more information on the Web Publishing Wizard, see its online help. For more information on the Publish FrontPage Web command, see Chapter 3. For more information on FrontPage and ISPs, see the FrontPage Web site.

APPENDIX A

Installing FrontPage

So you're ready to take the big step and install Microsoft FrontPage 98 with Bonus Pack. It's not such a big step, really; compared with installing some other applications, it's very easy. This appendix will step you through your installation of FrontPage 98, whether you're installing it for the first time or installing it over a previous version.

Before you install FrontPage, however, you should read the file README.TXT, which is on the FrontPage CD-ROM. It contains specific information on known problems with FrontPage, additional tips on running and troubleshooting FrontPage, technical support information and contacts, and more.

System Requirements

To use Microsoft FrontPage 98 with Bonus Pack, you need:

- Personal or multimedia computer with 486 or higher processor
- Microsoft Windows 95 operating system or Windows NT Workstation version 3.51 Service Pack 5 or later
- 8 MB of memory for use on Windows 95, or 16 MB of memory for use on Windows NT Workstation; 16 MB recommended for Microsoft Personal Web Server
- 30 MB of available hard-disk space
- CD-ROM drive
- VGA or higher-resolution video adapter (Super VGA, 256-color recommended)
- Microsoft Mouse, Microsoft IntelliMouse, or compatible pointing device

The Internet features of FrontPage 98 require you to have Internet access; Internet and other online access might require payment of a separate fee to a Internet service provider.

Other Bonus Pack components have separate hard-disk space requirements as follows:

- 11 MB for Microsoft Internet Explorer
- 1 MB for Microsoft Personal Web Server
- 1 MB for Microsoft Web Publishing Wizard
- 2 MB for Internet Mail and News Reader
- To use Microsoft Image Composer, you need:
- 16 MB of memory (32 MB recommended)
- Hard disk space required: 15 MB (compact); 30 MB (typical); or 300 MB (complete)
- VGA, 256-color (Super VGA TrueColor with 2 MB of video memory recommended)

Installing FrontPage 98

Below are instructions for installing FrontPage 98. If you already have a previous version installed, consult the section titled "Upgrading to FrontPage 98 from FrontPage 1.1" later in this appendix before you install FrontPage 98.

1. Exit all Windows applications on your computer.
2. Insert the FrontPage 98 with Bonus Pack CD-ROM in your computer's CD-ROM drive.
3. After a moment, you should see the opening FrontPage 98 With Bonus Pack screen, as shown in Figure A-1 below.

   If you don't see this screen, launch SETUP.EXE from the CD-ROM. In Windows 95 or Windows NT version 4.0, select the CD-ROM drive in the Windows Explorer and double-click SETUP.EXE. In Windows NT version 3.51, you can do this by opening a window to your CD-ROM drive in File Manager and double-clicking SETUP.EXE.
4. Click on Install FrontPage 98.

Figure A-1

NOTE If you do not have a Personal Web server installed, you'll see a dialog box asking whether you want to install that component first. If you want to use the Microsoft Personal Web Server, you should install it at this stage. You can easily remove the server from your system later, so unless you know for certain you don't want to use the server, click Yes.

If you click No, you'll move to the Welcome screen of the Setup Wizard, described in step 3. If you click Yes, a License Agreement dialog box will be displayed for the Microsoft Personal Web Server. If, after reading the license agreement, you click the I Agree button, the Microsoft Personal Web Server will be installed on your computer. You'll then see a Personal Web Server dialog box asking whether you want to restart your computer.

Click Yes, and this will restart your computer. Once your computer has restarted, return to the original FrontPage 98 installation screen as described earlier. Click on Install FrontPage 98 to continue with the installation.

5. If a Web server is running on your computer, a Question dialog box will appear, asking if you want to temporarily stop the server to continue the installation. Click Yes to continue. You will not see this screen if you're running IIS or the Personal Web Server.

6. In the Welcome screen of the Setup Wizard, you're asked to exit all Windows programs before proceeding with the installation. Do so, and then click Next.
7. In the FrontPage Registration screen, type your name and your company name in the appropriate text boxes, and then click Next.
8. FrontPage asks you to confirm that your name and company information is correct. Click Yes if it's correct, or click No to return to the previous screen to change the information.
9. A license agreement dialog box appears. Read through the agreement, and click Yes to accept the terms and move on to the next step of the installation

TIP If you want to quit Setup before it installs FrontPage, click Cancel in any screen that is displayed. No files will be copied to your hard drive.

10. In the Setup Type screen, you're asked to select either the Typical or the Custom installation. The differences are as follows.

    Typical installation. Setup installs the FrontPage client software, the FrontPage Personal Web Server (if one is not already installed), and the FrontPage Server Extensions.

    Custom installation. You can select any available combination of the FrontPage client software, the FrontPage Personal Web Server, and/or the Server Extensions. In a network setting, you can select a Custom setup if you only want to install the FrontPage client software on a local computer.

TIP Web sites created in FrontPage 97 are fully compatible with FrontPage 98. See page 364 for more information.

Select either the Typical or Custom option, and then click Next. If you select Typical, skip to step 16. If you select Custom, proceed to step 11.

In the Destination Directory section of the Setup Type dialog box, Setup tells you where it will install FrontPage. The Windows 95 default folder is C:\Program Files\Microsoft FrontPage, and the Windows NT default folder is C:\Microsoft FrontPage.

If you want to install FrontPage in a different folder, click the Browse button to locate and select the folder, and then click OK to return to the Destination Path screen. Click Next to continue.

11. If you selected a Custom installation, the Select Components screen appears and allows you to select which portions of FrontPage to install.

Select any available combination of the Client Software, FrontPage Personal Web Server, and Server Extensions check boxes. The Browse button allows you to specify a folder in which to install FrontPage. Based on your selections, the Space Required and Space Available values are updated. The Disk Space button allows you to see the space available on other drives. After you finish making your selections, click Next.

12. If you are installing on a computer running Windows NT 3.51, the next screen is the Select Program Folder screen. Here you can select a program folder, which is by default Microsoft FrontPage, or enter a new one. After you select a program folder, click Next to continue.

13. Now you're just about done—you'll see the Start Copying Files screen, where you can confirm the information you entered in the wizard. Verify everything in the Current Settings list box.

If you want to change any information that you've entered in the wizard, click the Back button until you reach the appropriate screen(s). Make the necessary changes, and then click Next until you once again reach the Start Copying Files screen. Click Next to have Setup begin copying files to your hard disk.

14. You might encounter some Server Administrator dialog boxes as the setup process nears completion.

Enter the appropriate information in these dialog boxes, write down any necessary information, and then click OK to continue with the installation. If you see a dialog box asking you whether to restart the server to complete installation of the WWW Service of the Microsoft Personal Web Server, click Yes. You might also encounter a dialog box recommending that you restart Windows to complete the installation.

15. If you don't need to restart, you'll typically see the Setup Complete screen, which is the final wizard screen. You can start using FrontPage immediately by selecting the Start The FrontPage Explorer Now check box. Click Finish to complete your FrontPage installation.

Upgrading to FrontPage 98 from FrontPage 97

This section describes some issues to consider when upgrading to FrontPage 98 from FrontPage 97.

Installing FrontPage 98 over FrontPage 97

If you install FrontPage 98 in the same folder as FrontPage 97, it will be upgraded to FrontPage 98. If you do not want to overwrite FrontPage 97, you must install FrontPage 98 in a different folder.

Upgrading the FrontPage Personal Web Server to the Microsoft Personal Web Server

If you have the FrontPage Personal Web Server installed on the default port (80) and you try to install the Microsoft Personal Web Server, a setup dialog box will appear, asking if you want instructions for switching to the Microsoft Personal Web Server.

If you click Yes and you have a browser installed, an HTML file opens in your browser. (If you do not have a browser installed, you can install Microsoft Internet Explorer 3.0 from the Bonus Pack.) This HTML file (*upgrade.htm*), which is on the FrontPage 98 CD-ROM, has information on the following topics:

- Upgrading your FrontPage 97 Personal Web Server and content to the new Microsoft Personal Web Server
- Using both the FrontPage Personal Web Server and the Microsoft Personal Web Server on the same machine
- Migrating existing content

Importing Preexisting FrontPage 97 Sites into FrontPage 98

To import any preexisting FrontPage 97 sites, select Import from within the Explorer and select the From Web button, or choose Import an Existing Web from the New FrontPage Web dialog box. In each case, the Import Web Wizard will launch and then ask you a series of questions.

For more information on the Import Web Wizard, see Chapter 4. For another method of importing your existing FrontPage 1.1 Web sites—using the Publish FrontPage Webs command—see the HTML file named *upgrade.htm* on the FrontPage 97 CD_ROM (described earlier).

Uninstalling FrontPage 98

If by some freak of nature you lose control of your mind by drinking seven triple grande almond mochas in the space of an hour and decide you want to uninstall FrontPage 98, here's all you have to do:

In Windows 95 or Windows NT 4.0. In the Windows Control Panel, double-click the Add/Remove Programs icon, select Microsoft FrontPage 98 from the list box on the Install/Uninstall tab, and click Add/Remove. A dialog box will appear, asking you to confirm the removal. Click Yes to begin the uninstall process. The UnInstallShield program will display a screen with the status of the uninstall. Address any dialog boxes that might appear. When the UnInstallShield program is done, read any messages that it displays and click the OK button to complete the process.

In Windows NT 3.51. The procedure is the same as with Windows 95 or Windows NT 4.0, but instead of using Add/Remove Programs, you double-click the Uninstall FrontPage icon in the Microsoft FrontPage program group.

Uninstalling the Microsoft Personal Web Server

In Windows 95. In the Windows Control Panel, double-click the Add/Remove Programs icon, select Personal Web Server from the list box on the Install/Uninstall tab, and click Add/Remove. A dialog box will appear, asking you to confirm the removal. Click Yes to begin the uninstall process. When it's done, a message box will be displayed indicating that you must restart your computer to complete the removal. Click OK.

Index

A

access, 20, 96, 105–109, 339
active graphics, 54, 200–210
ActiveX control, 207, 208, 313–316
ad banners, 202–204
adding, 18–19
  an existing Web site, 30
  cells in a table, 155–156
  comments, 265–266
  confirmation of, 271–272
  new pages, 44
  tasks, 57
administrative processes, 18–19, 20, 95–96, 347–357. *See also* Explorer; management
advanced features, 311–340
alignment
  between ActiveX control and text around it, 315
  of cells, 148
  of images, 243–244
  of Java applet, 318
  of paragraphs, 179
  of plug-in, 320
  of text on marquees, 205
anchors (bookmarks), 185–189
animation, 54, 207–208, 331–332
applets, 316–318
ASCII character set, 177–178
authors, 115–116, 351
Auto Thumbnail, 184–185, 195–196

B

background color, 149, 206, 211–212
background images, 54, 152, 212, 234–235, 255
background sounds, 198–199
banners, 202–204
bookmarks, 185–189
borders, 163, 196–198, 244, 315
brightness, 254
Browser, 112–113, 191, 217–218. *See also* Web browsers
browsers. *See* Browser; Web browsers
buttons for exploring the site. *See* navigation

C

cells, 148, 150, 153–159
CGI Script, 258, 296, 306, 344
channel, 336–338
check boxes, 89, 90, 285–286
client software. *See* Editor; Explorer
clip art, 152, 237–238
collapsible outlines, 333
colors
  of background, 149, 206–208
  bit depth and number of, 231
  button, 201
  changing to black and white, 252
  classes of, 328–330
  effect & effect, 201

in HTML, 233–234
hyperlink, 213
management of, 231–235
in tables, 152–153
of text, 174, 213
in Themes view, 54
columns
adding, 145–147, 156
changing width of, 38, 56, 59
deleting, 156
erasing, 147–148
moving, 157
selecting, 155
command buttons (pushbuttons), 51, 56, 63, 273, 286–289, 338
commands, 217–227
comments, insertion of, 265–266
Common Gateway Interface Script, 258, 296, 306, 344
components, 257–273, 292–294, 302–305, 359–360
configuration, 66–67, 69–71, 260–261, 272–273, 302–306
confirmation pages, 291–294, 298–301
content, 15, 20–21, 114–115, 269–270
contrast, 254
cutting, copying and pasting, 127–128

D

database integration, 333–336
data-collection forms, 274–289
Default Web Language, 68–69
definitions, as type of list, 134
deleting
cells, 148
columns, 147–148
files, 63
frames, 166
horizontal lines, 184
line breaks, 182
navigation bars, 195
rows and columns in a table, 156
sites, 62
tasks, 57
text, 127
development process, 13–21, 113–114
directories, 68, 95, 133
discussion groups, 95–96, 296
dithering, 251
downloading, speed of, 14, 209
dragging and dropping, 39, 129–130, 190–191
drop-down list, 278–281, 290–291, 313

E

editing, 95–96, 190, 248, 328
Editor, 8, 9, 122–125
adjusting settings, 124–125
beginning construction, 125–134
customization of Web templates, 74
HTML and the, 121–122
image manipulation in, 251–255
as a mini-browser, 219
stopping an action, 227
tables and, 143
testing the site on, 112
using page templates, 75
view tabs, 214–217
editors, configuration of, 69–71
effect & effect color, 201
e-mail, 48, 90, 189, 298–299
Explorer, 8–9, 25–71
access to page templates, 75
access to Web templates, 74
dragging links from, 190–191
getting started, 26–27
links to site in, 188
point of view, 32–60
saving images in, 237
export, of files from a site, 65–66

F

fading pages, 332
FastTrack server, 104
feedback form page, 275–276
Feedback page, 42, 84, 87–88
field extensions, 333
files
Channel Definition, 337, 338
copying, during installation, 363
creating links to, 188
cutting, copying and pasting, 127–130
deleting, 63
drag and drop with, 39

files, *continued*
exporting, 65–66
importing into a site, 63–64
opening, 59
opening page from, 136–137
renaming, 38
sending form results to, 297–298
sorting, 34
sound, 198
video, 209–210
viewing properties, 59–60
find and replace, 222–226
firewalls, 103, 110–111, 356
flipping of images, 253
folders, 30, 33–38, 68, 96, 362–363
fonts, 173–178
footers, 90, 141
formatting marks, 125
form fields, 273, 289–291
forms, 273–306
applications with results, 169, 295–301
confirmation, 291–292
creating and using, 273–306
data-collection, 274–289
field extensions, 333
search, 206
specifying settings, 294–295
validation rules, 271
frames, 77–79, 160–170
framesets, 161, 165–167
"friendly name" of page, 41
FrontPage 97–98
installing, 360–365
with Microsoft Office, 9–11, 35, 127–130, 237–238
uninstalling, 364–365
FrontPage Software Developer's Kit, 80, 101, 340
FTP protocol, 62, 354, 356

G

GIF, 231, 240, 248–251, 337
graphics, 229–255. *See also* color; images
active, 54, 207–208, 331–332
clip art, 152, 237–238
formats, 230–231
Graphics Exchange Format (GIF), 231, 240, 248–251, 337
growth of a site, 18–19

H

handlers, 274, 294, 295–301, 306
header cells, 154–155
headers, 90, 141
headings, 130–132
hierarchy. *See* levels
hit counter, 207
homepage
definition, 6
format, 84–85
icon, 48
return to, 16, 45
title of, 41
horizontal lines, 183–184
horizontal spacing, 244, 315, 318, 320
hotspots, 241–242, 247–248, 250
hover button, 200–202
HTML, 121–122
colors in, 233–234
default to, 68–69
designer, 340
dynamic, 331–333
editors, 7
Encoding Section, 214
files, icon for, 35
file when upgrading, 364
form results and, 297–298
frames view tab, 170
inserting, 312
marquees and, 204
stylesheets and, 322–323
hyperlinks. *See* links
Hypertext Transfer Protocol (HTTP), 344, 354

I

icons, 35, 48, 91, 113, 311
image maps, 68, 246–247, 339
images. *See also* graphics
on ad banners, 203–204
adding to cells, 159
alignment of, 243–244

Auto Thumbnail of, 184–185
background. *See* background images
changing properties of, 239–245
classes of, 330
cropping, 252
custom, 202
insertion into pages, 235–238
manipulation of, 238–255
movement of, 54, 207–208, 331–333
placeholders for, 87
quality selection, 240
saving, 236–237
size of, 184–185, 202, 232, 244–245
testing, 112
timing of, 268–269
vs. content, aesthetics of, 229
imports, 29
of file into a site, 63–64
from Microsoft Word, 36
of preexisting FrontPage 97 sites into FrontPage 98, 364
of Web site into FrontPage Web site, 96–100
information flow, planning, 13–17
inserting
files, 127–128
horizontal lines, 183
HTML, 312
Java Applet, 316–318
plug-in, 318–320
tables, 149–151
tables within tables, 159–160
installation, 360–365
interlaced presentation of image, 240
Internet, 3–7, 21
Internet Information Servicer (IIS), 8
Internet Protocol (IP), 5, 9
Internet Service Providers (ISP), 356–357
Internet Services Administrator page, 354
intranets, 7, 8, 17–21
IP address, 108–109, 139
ISAPI Script, 296, 306, 345

J

Java Applet, inserting, 316–318
JavaScript, 68, 290, 320–321
Joint Photographic Experts Group (JPEG), 230–232, 250, 251

K

keyboard style, 176–177

L

Language tab, 68–69
levels, 15–16, 20, 41–42. *See also* structure
links
to ad banners, 203
to an external stylesheet, 324
broken, 48
color of, 213
from Confirmation Form to Feedback Form, 294
creating, 190, 191
dragging from the Explorer, 190–191
editing, 190
errors in, 48
following, 219
hotspots for, 241–242, 250
to hover button, 201
icons for, 48
to pages or bookmarks, 187–189
removing, 189
secure, 104
selecting, 189
verification of, 49–52, 112
lists, 132–134
drop-down, 278–281, 290–291, 313
paragraph style options, 179–181
types of, 133
logo, 90, 160
loops, for playing of video, 242–243

M

maintenance of Web site. *See* management
management, 103–116. *See also* administrative processes
of color, 231–235
of page files, 134–142
responsibility for, 18
in Tasks view, 58
updating and, 114–116
margins, 165, 182, 213
marking, tasks, 57
marquees, 204–206
menu list, 133

meta tags, 214
Microsoft Office, 9–11, 35, 127–130, 187
Microsoft Personal Web Server, 8–9, 29, 258, 305, 344–345, 352–356
  installation of FrontPage 98 and, 361
  security and, 104, 108
  uninstalling, 365

N

names
  of pages, 41, 211
  of sites, 29, 67
  of tasks, 56–57
navigation, 16–17, 39–47, 191–195, 201
Netscape, 104, 191, 318
networks, 4, 315–316
Normal Page, 75, 79
Normal View, 214–215
NSAPI Script, 296, 306
numbered list, 133

O

Open Data Base Connectivity (ODBC), 333–335
opening
  files, 59
  frame pages, 167
  page files, 135–139
  sites, 27, 31–32
outlines, collapsible, 333

P

pages
  Active Server, 333
  adding to a site, 63, 100–101
  applying a theme to, 184
  closing, 139
  confirmation, 291–294, 299–301
  creating links to, 187–189
  creation of, 121–170
  custom templates for, 79–80
  deleting from structure, 45
  displaying, in a frame, 167–169
  exclusion from search, 259
  expansion of view, 44–45
  fine-tuning, 173–227
  frames, 162–163
  insertion of images into, 235–238
  integration of Microsoft Office files, 127–130
  Internet Services Administrator, 354
  links to new, 189
  moving among currently open, 227
  opening, 135–139
  presention of one on another, 266–267
  printing, 140–142
  properties of, 210–214
  saving, 139–140
  splitting, in a frameset, 167
  templates for, 75–77
  title of, 41, 211
  transitions from, 332
paragraphs
  aligning, 179
  changing styles, 178–179
  classes of, 330
  creation of new, 178
  formatting, 178–184
  horizontal lines, 183–184
  indenting, 179
  line breaks, 181–182
  list properties of, 179–181
passwords, 69, 109–110, 334, 350
paths, 49
permissions, 105–109
Photoshop, 232–233
platforms, extensions for, 346
plug-in, inserting, 318–320
ports, 349–350, 351
previewing, 46, 112–113, 142, 151, 217–218
printing, 46, 140–142
protocols. *See* FTP protocol; HTML; Hypertext Transfer Protocol; Internet Protocol; SSL; Transmission Control Protocol
proxy servers, 103, 110–111, 347
publishing a channel, 338
pushbuttons, 273, 286–288
push technology, 336

R

radio buttons, 273
Redo, 218–219
Refresh, 46, 60, 227
registration form handler, 296–297

registration of users. *See* permissions; security
remote activities, updating site content, 115
renaming a file, 38
replace, 222–226
resample, of a resized image, 254
reset, of image manipulation, 253
resolution, 218, 240–241
reversal of images, 253
rotation, 45, 202, 253
rows, 145–147, 153, 155, 156, 157

S

scrolling text box, 283–285
searching, 84, 206, 222–226
Secure Sockets Layer (SSL), 27, 30, 61, 104–105
security, 19–20, 69, 104–111
Server Administrator, 347–357
Server Extensions, 9, 62, 68, 343, 345–349, 351
servers. *See* Web servers
size
  of ActiveX control, 315
  to fit, 45
  of frames page, 164–165
  of images, 184–185, 202, 232, 244–245, 254
  of Java applet, 317
  of marquees, 206
  of plug-in, 319
  of site, control of, 18–19
  of text, 174
  of a View, changing, 60
  of windows, changing, 124
sorting, 34, 56
sounds, 198–199, 202
special characters, 177–178
speed, 14, 78, 209
spell check, 11, 26, 220–222
SQL queries, 333, 335
SSL (Secure Sockets Layer), 27, 30, 61, 104–105
status, 49–52, 68, 125
structure
  changing, 43–45
  deletion of page from, 45
  overview, 41–43
  refreshing, 46
  updating, conservation in, 114
Structured Query Language, 333, 335
style button, 327–328
stylesheets, 151, 321–331
subscript, 177
superscript, 177
symbols, 177–178
system requirements, 359–360

T

Table of Contents page, 77–78, 84, 89
tables, 143–160
  adding a blank paragraph after, 156
  changing properties of, 151–153
  classes of, 330
  inserting, within tables, 159–160
  inserting into a site, 149–151
target frames, default, 169–170
Tasks view, 18, 37–38, 54–58, 94, 219–220
templates, 29, 73–80
testing, 17, 49–52, 112–113
text
  adding to a page
  adding to a table, 151
  applying style to, 331
  color, 174, 213
  comments, 265–266
  cutting, copying and pasting, 127
  deleting, 127
  find and replace for, 223–226
  form results as, 299
  on a GIF, 248–250
  one-line text box, 281–283
  as replacement for image, 16, 241, 339
  scrolling text box, 283–285
  size, 174
  turning into a list, 179–180
  user-submitted, confirmation of, 270–272
themes, 52–54, 92–93, 184
thesaurus, 11, 226–227
timing of appearance on screen, 268–270
title of page, 41, 211
toolbars
  advanced, 312
  Image, 245–246, 252–255
  Show/Hide Paragraph, 125, 150
  Tables, 144–149
  Undo/Redo, 127
  working with, 124

Transmission Control Protocol (TCP), 5, 9
transparent presentation of image, 240

U

undoing, 218–219
uninstalling, 364–365
updating sites, 89, 114–116. *See also* management
  content, 115–116
  by multiple authors, 115–116
  remote, 115
  responsibility for, 18
  search limitations due to, 261
  timestamp of last, 262–263
  for traffic, 116
upgrading, 351, 364
URL, 65, 138, 300, 315
user-entered information, 270–272, 274–289, 295–301
usernames, 292, 334, 350
utilities and useful commands, 217–227

V

validation, of form fields, 289–291
Validation Scripts, 68, 290
VBScript, 68, 320–321
vertical spacing, 244, 315, 318, 320
video, 209–210, 242–243

W

washout, 252
watermark, 212
Web. *See* Web sites; World Wide Web
Web browsers, 5, 17, 112. *See also* Browser
Web servers, 343–357. *See also* Microsoft Personal Web Server
  administration, 347–357
  changing, 60–62, 116
  changing port number, 349–350
  checking for support of SSL, 104
  commercial, extensions for, 346
  communication with user. *See* handlers
  definition, 8
  for intranet sites, 19
  noncommercial, extensions for, 346
  permissions for, 108–109
  proxy, 103, 110–111, 347
Web sites
  adding Navigation view to old, 46–47
  adding new page to, 63
  changing servers for, 60–62
  changing settings, 66–69
  closing, 62
  custom templates, 80
  deleting, 62
  development process, 13–21, 113–114
  going live with, 113–114
  icon for unfinished portions of, 91
  management of, 103–116
  Microsoft, 6
  opening pages from, 136–138
  permissions for specific, 107–108
  saving, 94
  summary of, 266
  testing of, 112–113
  updating, 114–116
  upgrading with installation of new version of FrontPage Server Extensions, 351
Web templates, 74–75
windows, changing size of, 124
wizards, 29, 63, 73, 81–101, 302, 333–338, 357
World Wide Web, 3–7, 9, 188

W. Brett Polonsky has more than 10 years of experience in award-winning graphic design and art direction. Self-taught in computers, he learned on early Macintosh computers and PageMaker 1.0, and has climbed the ladder to high-end Web development, incorporating site planning, structure, UI, and design. He has consulted as a Web producer at Microsoft, helping to create one of their largest Intranet sites. He lives in Kirkland, Washington, with his wife, Janell, and his two children, Gage, 5, and Emma, 2.

Brett's other business interests include Polonsky Design, a firm that he runs with his wife Janell, specializing in graphic design for print and online. He is also the co-founder and president of Skywards Consulting, Inc., a Web presence development company dedicated to designing and implementing Web solutions for corporate clients. Visit the Skywards site at www.skywards.com, or email brett@skywards.com.

Kerry A. Lehto wonders how many more career interests he'll pursue and is elated he never settled on just one. His work history intertwines news and sports journalism, archaeology, and computing. He also has taught college-level English grammar, "crunched" conference evaluations for various high-tech firms, and worked "Grasshopper Patrol" for the USDA in Wyoming. He has a BA in Journalism from the University of Wyoming (go Pokes) and an MA in Journalism from the University of Oregon (go Ducks). His spare time is filled building his Peanuts collection, desperately seeking Snoopy and Woodstock at thrift stores and antique stores in the Puget Sound area. He currently manages an internal web site at Microsoft and crafts other projects via his Kirkland, Washington-based business, KL Communications. To reach Kerry, e-mail him at tigerpaw@accessone.com.

The manuscript for this book was prepared and submitted to Microsoft Press in electronic form. Text files were prepared using Microsoft Word 7.0 for Windows. Pages were composed using Adobe PageMaker 6.01 for Macintosh, with text in Garamond Light and display type in Frutiger Bold. Composed pages were delivered to the printer as electronic prepress files.

Cover Graphic Designer
Greg Erickson

Interior Graphic Designer
Kim Eggleston

Indexer
Nanette Cardon

Learn to build great Web pages— At a Glance!

U.S.A. **$16.99**
U.K. £15.49
Canada $23.99
ISBN 1-57231-637-3

For fast answers, a picture is worth a thousand words. Here's the visual way to quickly get to work using the powerful features of Microsoft® FrontPage 98. MICROSOFT FRONTPAGE 98 AT A GLANCE lets you focus on a particular task and shows you, with clear, numbered steps, the easiest way to get it done.

Microsoft Press® products are available worldwide wherever quality computer books are sold. For more information, contact your book or computer retailer, software reseller, or local Microsoft Sales Office, or visit our Web site at mspress.microsoft.com. To locate your nearest source for Microsoft Press products, or to order directly, call 1-800-MSPRESS in the U.S. (in Canada, call 1-800-268-2222).

Prices and availability dates are subject to change.

Microsoft® Press

Register Today!

Return this
Official Microsoft® FrontPage® 98 Book
registration card for
a Microsoft Press® catalog

U.S. and Canada addresses only. Fill in information below and mail postage-free. Please mail only the bottom half of this page.

1-57231-629-2A | ***OFFICIAL MICROSOFT® FRONTPAGE® 98 BOOK*** | ***Owner Registration Card***

NAME

INSTITUTION OR COMPANY NAME

ADDRESS

CITY STATE ZIP

NO POSTAGE
NECESSARY
IF MAILED
IN THE
UNITED STATES

BUSINESS REPLY MAIL
FIRST-CLASS MAIL PERMIT NO. 53 BOTHELL, WA

POSTAGE WILL BE PAID BY ADDRESSEE

MICROSOFT PRESS REGISTRATION
OFFICIAL MICROSOFT®
FRONTPAGE® 98 BOOK
PO BOX 3019
BOTHELL WA 98041-9946